BIG IDEAS MATH®

Modeling Real Life

Grade K

Common Core Edition

Volume 2

Ron Larson
Laurie Boswell

Erie, Pennsylvania
BigIdeasLearning.com

Big Ideas Learning, LLC
1762 Norcross Road
Erie, PA 16510-3838
USA

For product information and customer support, contact Big Ideas Learning
at 1-877-552-7766 or visit us at BigIdeasLearning.com.

Cover Image
Paul Lampard /123RF.com, enmyo/Shutterstock.com

Printed in the U.S.A.

ISBN 13: 978-1-64208-316-3

3 4 5 6 7 8 9 10—23 22 21 20

About the Authors

Ron Larson

Ron Larson, Ph.D., is well known as the lead author of a comprehensive program for mathematics that spans school mathematics and college courses. He holds the distinction of Professor Emeritus from Penn State Erie, The Behrend College, where he taught for nearly 40 years. He received his Ph.D. in mathematics from the University of Colorado. Dr. Larson's numerous professional activities keep him actively involved in the mathematics education community and allow him to fully understand the needs of students, teachers, supervisors, and administrators.

Laurie Boswell

Laurie Boswell, Ed.D., is the former Head of School at Riverside School in Lyndonville, Vermont. In addition to textbook authoring, she provides mathematics consulting and embedded coaching sessions. Dr. Boswell received her Ed.D. from the University of Vermont in 2010. She is a recipient of the Presidential Award for Excellence in Mathematics Teaching and is a Tandy Technology Scholar. Laurie has taught math to students at all levels, elementary through college. In addition, Laurie has served on the NCTM Board of Directors and as a Regional Director for NCSM. Along with Ron, Laurie has co-authored numerous math programs and has become a popular national speaker.

Dr. Ron Larson and Dr. Laurie Boswell began writing together in 1992. Since that time, they have authored over four dozen textbooks. This successful collaboration allows for one voice from Kindergarten through Algebra 2.

Contributors, Reviewers, and Research

Big Ideas Learning would like to express our gratitude to the mathematics education and instruction experts who served as our advisory panel, contributing specialists, and reviewers during the writing of *Big Ideas Math: Modeling Real Life*. Their input was an invaluable asset during the development of this program.

Contributing Specialists and Reviewers

- **Sophie Murphy**, Ph.D. Candidate, Melbourne School of Education, Melbourne, Australia
  Learning Targets and Success Criteria Specialist and Visible Learning Reviewer
- **Linda Hall**, Mathematics Educational Consultant, Edmond, OK
  Advisory Panel
- **Michael McDowell**, Ed.D., Superintendent, Ross, CA
  Project-Based Learning Specialist
- **Kelly Byrne**, Math Supervisor and Coordinator of Data Analysis, Downingtown, PA
  Advisory Panel
- **Jean Carwin**, Math Specialist/TOSA, Snohomish, WA
  Advisory Panel
- **Nancy Siddens**, Independent Language Teaching Consultant, Las Cruces, NM
  English Language Learner Specialist
- **Kristen Karbon**, Curriculum and Assessment Coordinator, Troy, MI
  Advisory Panel
- **Kery Obradovich**, K–8 Math/Science Coordinator, Northbrook, IL
  Advisory Panel
- **Jennifer Rollins**, Math Curriculum Content Specialist, Golden, CO
  Advisory Panel
- **Becky Walker**, Ph.D., School Improvement Services Director, Green Bay, WI
  Advisory Panel and Content Reviewer
- **Deborah Donovan**, Mathematics Consultant, Lexington, SC
  Content Reviewer
- **Tom Muchlinski**, Ph.D., Mathematics Consultant, Plymouth, MN
  Content Reviewer and Teaching Edition Contributor
- **Mary Goetz**, Elementary School Teacher, Troy, MI
  Content Reviewer
- **Nanci N. Smith**, Ph.D., International Curriculum and Instruction Consultant, Peoria, AZ
  Teaching Edition Contributor
- **Robyn Seifert-Decker**, Mathematics Consultant, Grand Haven, MI
  Teaching Edition Contributor
- **Bonnie Spence**, Mathematics Education Specialist, Missoula, MT
  Teaching Edition Contributor
- **Suzy Gagnon**, Adjunct Instructor, University of New Hampshire, Portsmouth, NH
  Teaching Edition Contributor
- **Art Johnson**, Ed.D., Professor of Mathematics Education, Warwick, RI
  Teaching Edition Contributor
- **Anthony Smith**, Ph.D., Associate Professor, Associate Dean, University of Washington Bothell, Seattle, WA
  Reading and Writing Reviewer
- **Brianna Raygor**, Music Teacher, Fridley, MN
  Music Reviewer
- **Nicole Dimich Vagle**, Educator, Author, and Consultant, Hopkins, MN
  Assessment Reviewer
- **Janet Graham**, District Math Specialist, Manassas, VA
  Response to Intervention and Differentiated Instruction Reviewer
- **Sharon Huber**, Director of Elementary Mathematics, Chesapeake, VA
  Universal Design for Learning Reviewer

Student Reviewers

- T.J. Morin
- Alayna Morin
- Ethan Bauer
- Emery Bauer
- Emma Gaeta
- Ryan Gaeta
- Benjamin SanFrotello
- Bailey SanFrotello
- Samantha Grygier
- Robert Grygier IV
- Jacob Grygier
- Jessica Urso
- Ike Patton
- Jake Lobaugh
- Adam Fried
- Caroline Naser
- Charlotte Naser

Research

Ron Larson and Laurie Boswell used the latest in educational research, along with the body of knowledge collected from expert mathematics instructors, to develop the *Modeling Real Life* series. The pedagogical approach used in this program follows the best practices outlined in the most prominent and widely accepted educational research, including:

- *Visible Learning*
  John Hattie © 2009
- *Visible Learning for Teachers*
  John Hattie © 2012
- *Visible Learning for Mathematics*
  John Hattie © 2017
- *Principles to Actions: Ensuring Mathematical Success for All*
  NCTM © 2014
- *Adding It Up: Helping Children Learn Mathematics*
  National Research Council © 2001
- *Mathematical Mindsets: Unleashing Students' Potential through Creative Math, Inspiring Messages and Innovative Teaching*
  Jo Boaler © 2015
- *What Works in Schools: Translating Research into Action*
  Robert Marzano © 2003
- *Classroom Instruction That Works: Research-Based Strategies for Increasing Student Achievement*
  Marzano, Pickering, and Pollock © 2001
- *Principles and Standards for School Mathematics*
  NCTM © 2000
- *Rigorous PBL by Design: Three Shifts for Developing Confident and Competent Learners*
  Michael McDowell © 2017
- Common Core State Standards for Mathematics
  National Governors Association Center for Best Practices and Council of Chief State School Officers © 2010
- *Universal Design for Learning Guidelines*
  CAST © 2011
- Rigor/Relevance Framework®
  International Center for Leadership in Education
- *Understanding by Design*
  Grant Wiggins and Jay McTighe © 2005
- Achieve, ACT, and The College Board
- *Elementary and Middle School Mathematics: Teaching Developmentally*
  John A. Van de Walle and Karen S. Karp © 2015
- *Evaluating the Quality of Learning: The SOLO Taxonomy*
  John B. Biggs & Kevin F. Collis © 1982
- *Unlocking Formative Assessment: Practical Strategies for Enhancing Students' Learning in the Primary and Intermediate Classroom*
  Shirley Clarke, Helen Timperley, and John Hattie © 2004
- *Formative Assessment in the Secondary Classroom*
  Shirley Clarke © 2005
- *Improving Student Achievement: A Practical Guide to Assessment for Learning*
  Toni Glasson © 2009

Standards for Mathematical Practice

Make sense of problems and persevere in solving them.

- Multiple representations are presented to help students move from concrete to representative and into abstract thinking.
- *Think and Grow: Modeling Real Life* examples use problem-solving strategies, such as drawing a picture, circling knowns, and underlining unknowns.

Reason abstractly and quantitatively.

- Visual problem solving models help students create a coherent representation of the problem.
- *Explore and Grows* allow students to investigate math to understand the reasoning behind the rules.

Construct viable arguments and critique the reasoning of others.

- *Explore and Grows* help students make conjectures and build a logical progression of statements to explore their conjecture.
- Collaborative activities and discussions provide students the opportunity to critique the reasoning of others.

Model with mathematics.

- Real-life situations are translated into pictures, diagrams, tables, equations, or graphs to help students analyze relations and to draw conclusions.
- Real-life problems are provided to help students learn to apply the mathematics that they are learning to everyday life.
- Real-life problems incorporate other disciplines to help students see that math is used across content areas.

Use appropriate tools strategically.

- Students can use a variety of hands-on manipulatives to solve problems throughout the program.
- A variety of tool papers, such as number bonds and ten frames, are available as students consider how to approach a problem.

Attend to precision.

- Exercises encourage students to formulate consistent and appropriate reasoning.
- Cooperative learning opportunities support precise communication.

Look for and make use of structure.

- *Learning Targets* and *Success Criteria* at the start of each chapter and lesson help students understand what they are going to learn.
- *Explore and Grows* provide students the opportunity to see patterns and structure in mathematics.
- Real-life problems help students use the structure of mathematics to break down and solve more difficult problems.

Look for and express regularity in repeated reasoning.

- Opportunities are provided to help students make generalizations.
- Students are continually encouraged to check for reasonableness in their solutions.

Achieve the Core

Meeting Proficiency

As standards shift to prepare students for college and careers, the importance of focus, coherence, and rigor continues to grow.

FOCUS *Big Ideas Math: Modeling Real Life* emphasizes a narrower and deeper curriculum, ensuring students spend their time on the major topics of each grade.

COHERENCE The program was developed around coherent progressions from Kindergarten through eighth grade, guaranteeing students develop and progress their foundational skills through the grades while maintaining a strong focus on the major topics.

RIGOR *Big Ideas Math: Modeling Real Life* uses a balance of procedural fluency, conceptual understanding, and real-life applications. Students develop conceptual understanding in every *Explore and Grow*, continue that development through the lesson while gaining procedural fluency during the *Think and Grow*, and then tie it all together with *Think and Grow: Modeling Real Life*. Every set of practice problems reflects this balance, giving students the rigorous practice they need to be college- and career-ready.

Major Topics in Kindergarten

Counting and Cardinality

- Know number names and the count sequence.
- Count to tell the number of objects.
- Compare numbers.

Operations and Algebraic Thinking

- Understand addition as putting together and adding to, and understand subtraction as taking apart and taking from.

Number and Operations in Base Ten

- Work with numbers 11–19 to gain foundations for place value.

Use the color-coded Table of Contents to determine where the major topics, supporting topics, and additional topics occur throughout the curriculum.

- Major Topic
- Supporting Topic
- Additional Topic

1 Count and Write Numbers 0 to 5

2 Compare Numbers 0 to 5

■ Major Topic
■ Supporting Topic
■ Additional Topic

3 Count and Write Numbers 6 to 10

Compare Numbers to 10

Compose and Decompose Numbers to 10

- Major Topic
- Supporting Topic
- Additional Topic

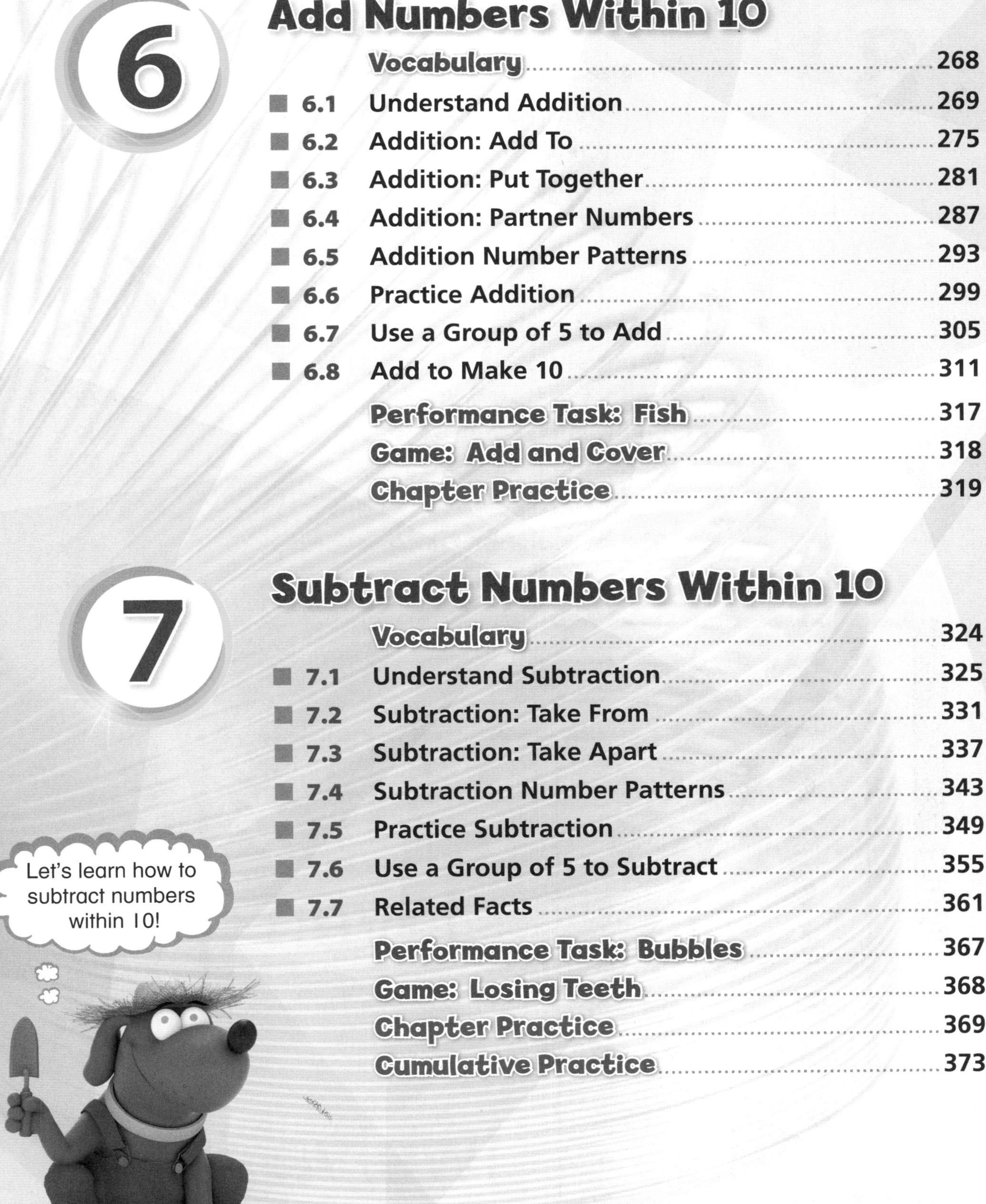
Let's learn how to subtract numbers within 10!

6 Add Numbers Within 10

7 Subtract Numbers Within 10

8 Represent Numbers 11 to 19

9 Count and Compare Numbers to 20

10 Count to 100

11 Identify Two-Dimensional Shapes

12 Identify Three-Dimensional Shapes and Positions

■ Major Topic
■ Supporting Topic
■ Additional Topic

13 Measure and Compare Objects

8 Represent Numbers 11 to 19

- What kinds of objects can you see in the night sky?
- How many bright stars are in each group shown? How many are there in all?

Chapter Learning Target:
Understand numbers.

Chapter Success Criteria:
- I can identify a group of objects.
- I can describe numbers as a group.
- I can write numbers.
- I can count objects.

Name ___________________________

8 Vocabulary

Review Words
five
addition sentence

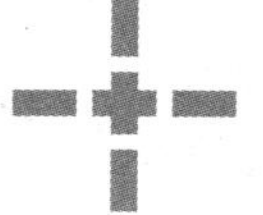

Directions: Count the shooting stars in the sky. Write the number. You see 2 more shooting stars in the sky. Draw the shooting stars. Then write an addition sentence to tell how many shooting stars there are in all.

Chapter 8 Vocabulary Cards

eighteen

eleven

fifteen

fourteen

nineteen

seventeen

sixteen

thirteen

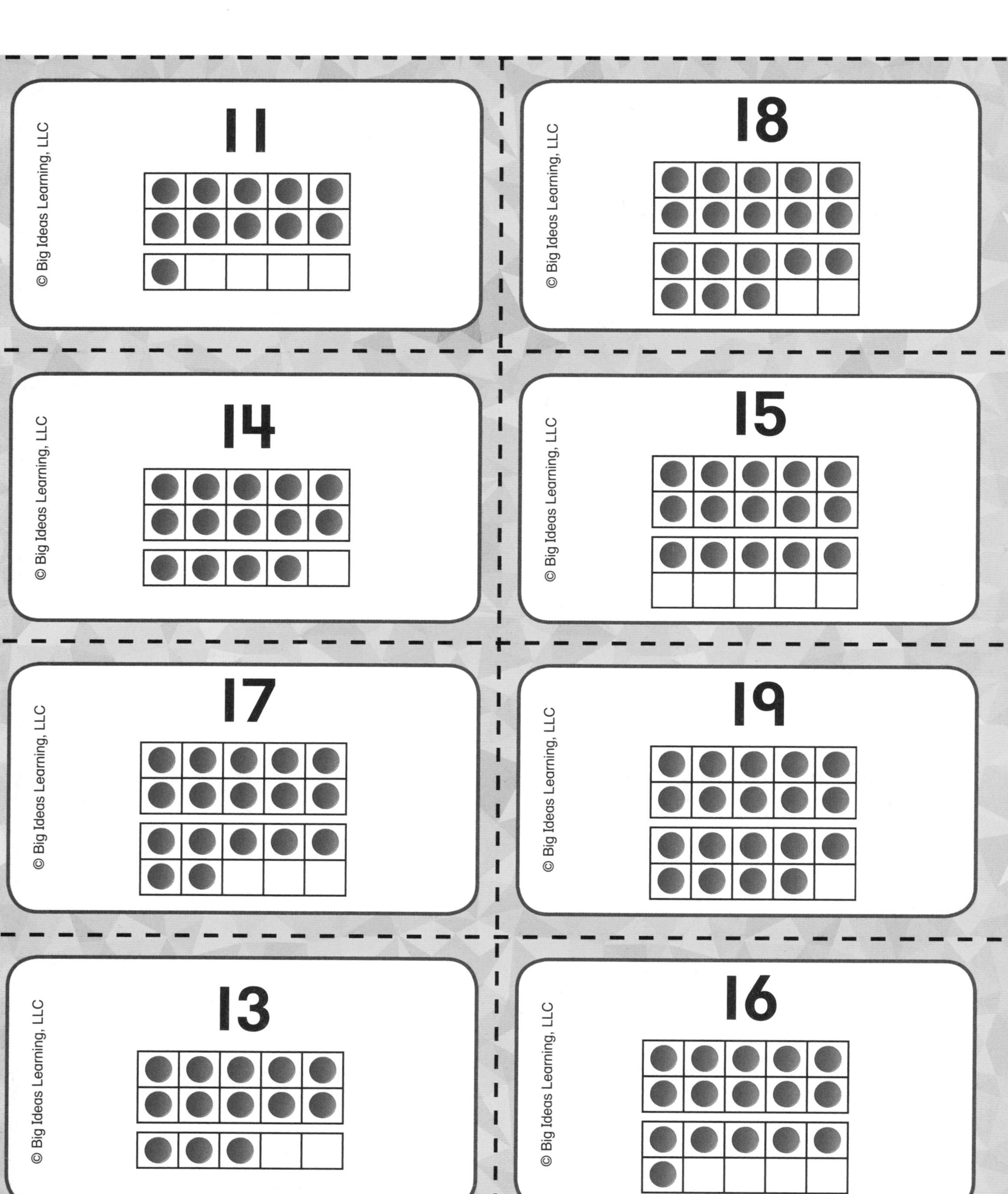
11
© Big Ideas Learning, LLC
18
© Big Ideas Learning, LLC
14
© Big Ideas Learning, LLC
15
© Big Ideas Learning, LLC
17
© Big Ideas Learning, LLC
19
© Big Ideas Learning, LLC
13
© Big Ideas Learning, LLC
16
© Big Ideas Learning, LLC

Chapter 8 Vocabulary Cards

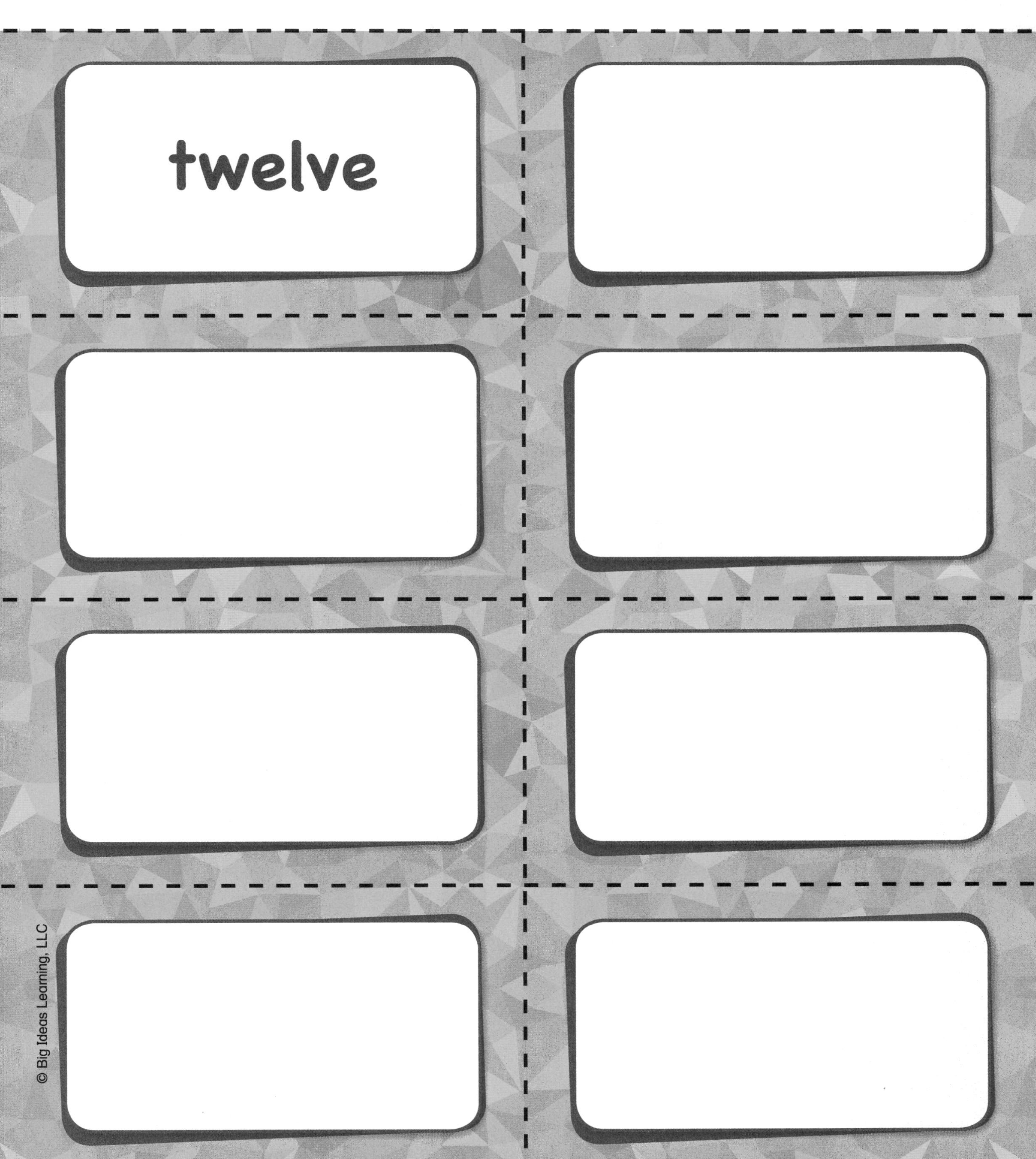

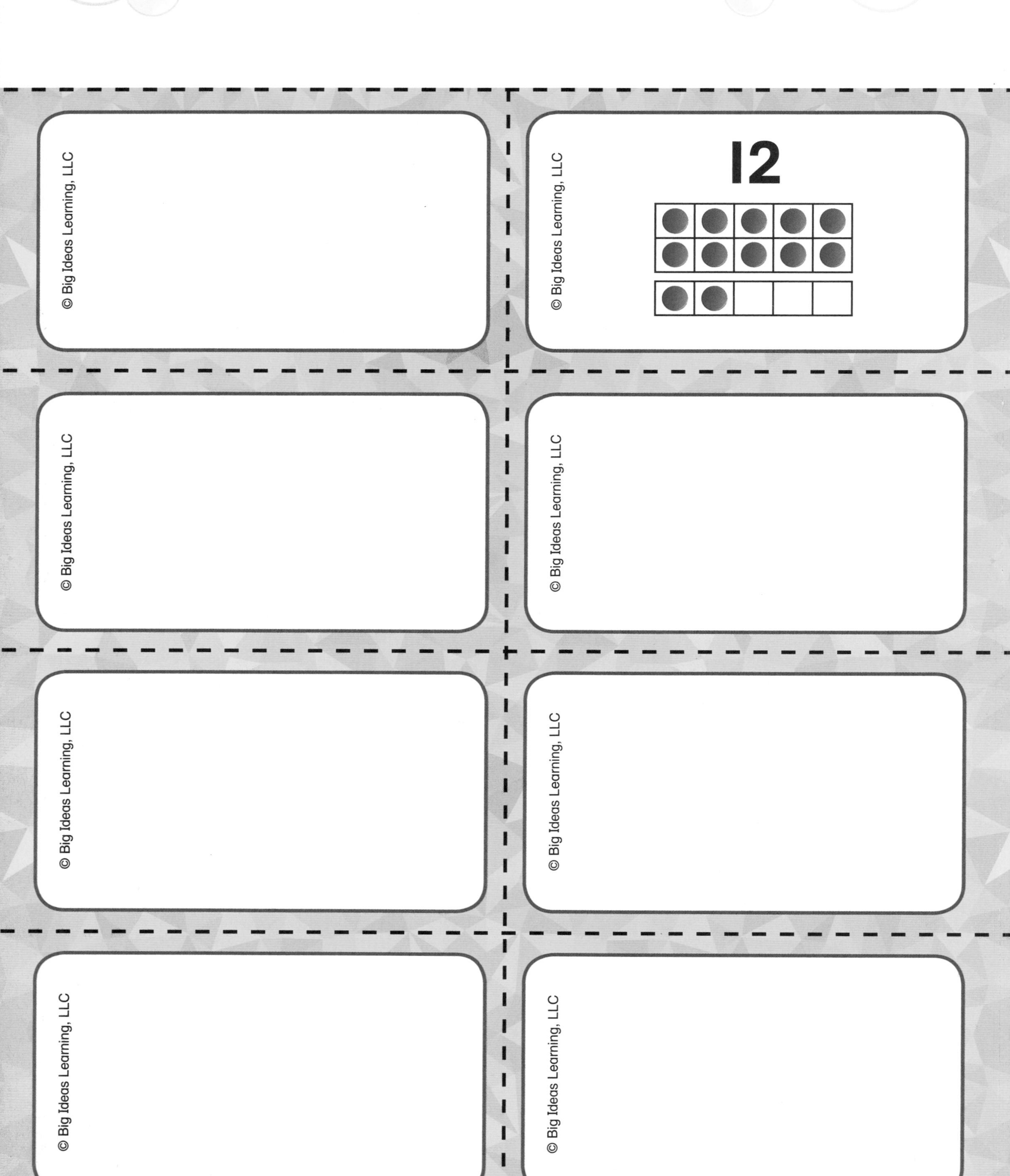
12

Name ______________________________

Identify Groups of 10 8.1

Learning Target: Find a group of 10 objects and tell how many more objects there are.

Explore and Grow

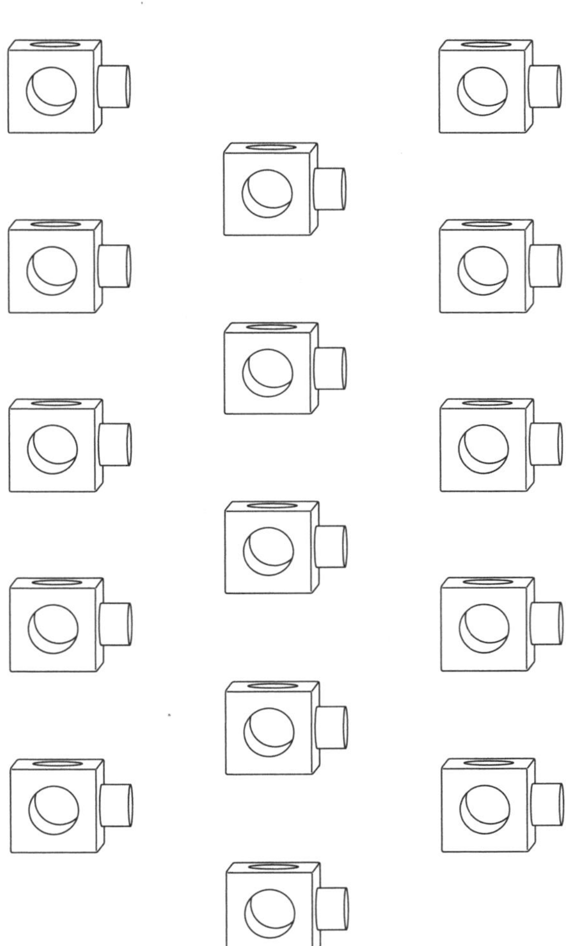

Directions: Count and circle 10 linking cubes. Color the extra linking cubes.

Think and Grow

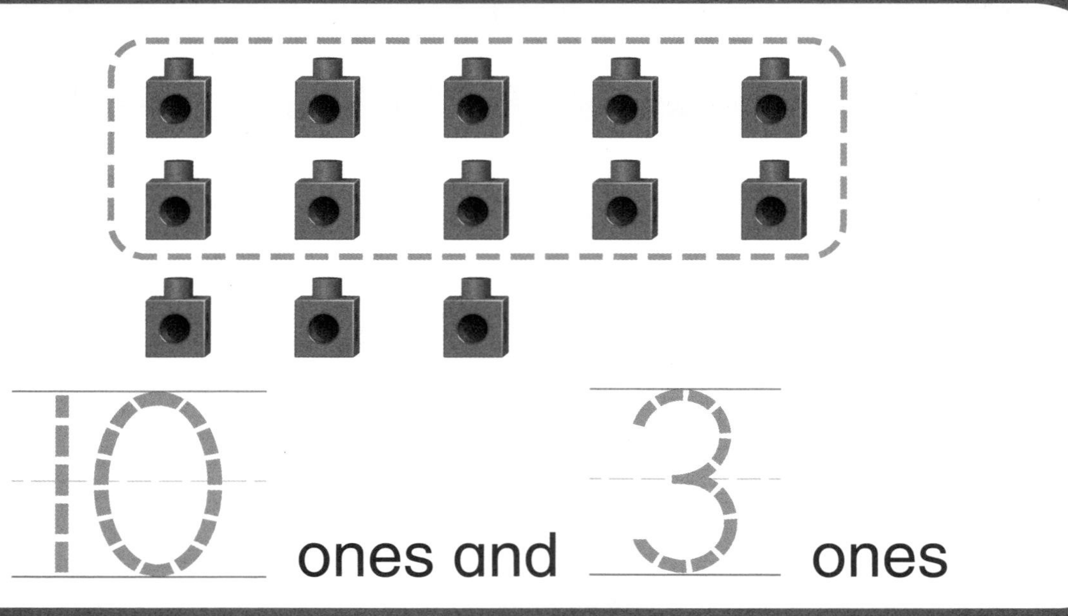

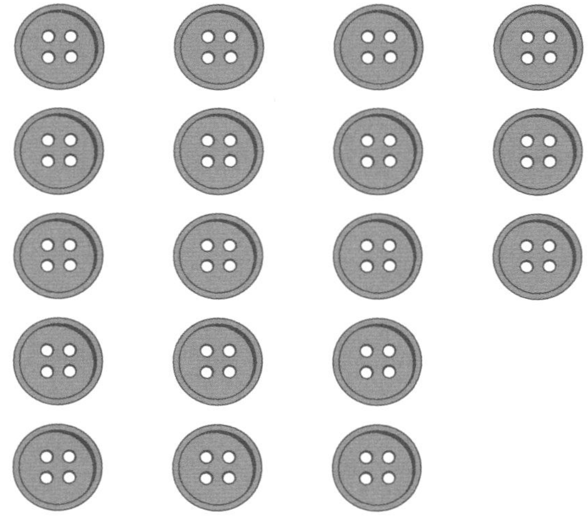

Directions: Circle 10 objects. Tell how many more objects there are. Then write the numbers.

Name

Apply and Grow: Practice

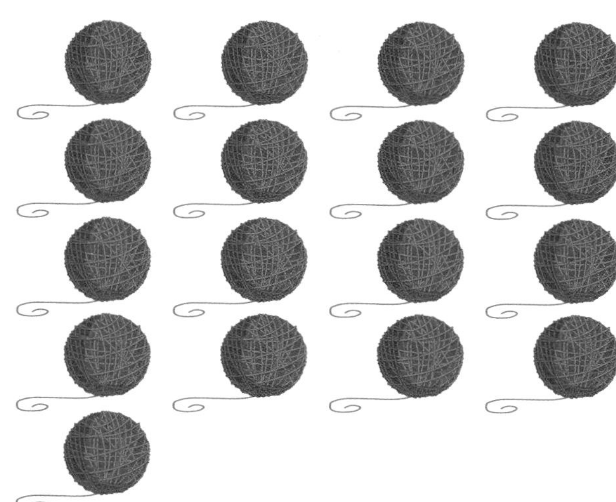

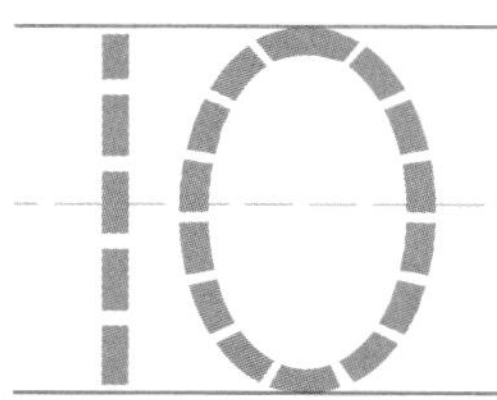

10 ones and ______ ones

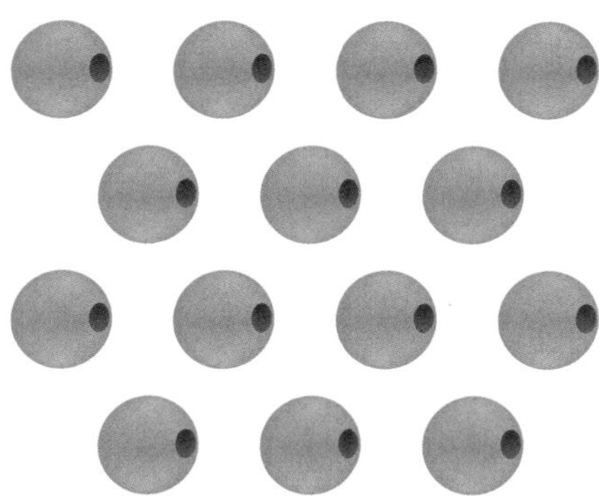

______ ones and ______ ones

Directions: 1 and 2 Circle 10 objects. Tell how many more objects there are. Then write the numbers.

Think and Grow: Modeling Real Life

10 ones and 1 one

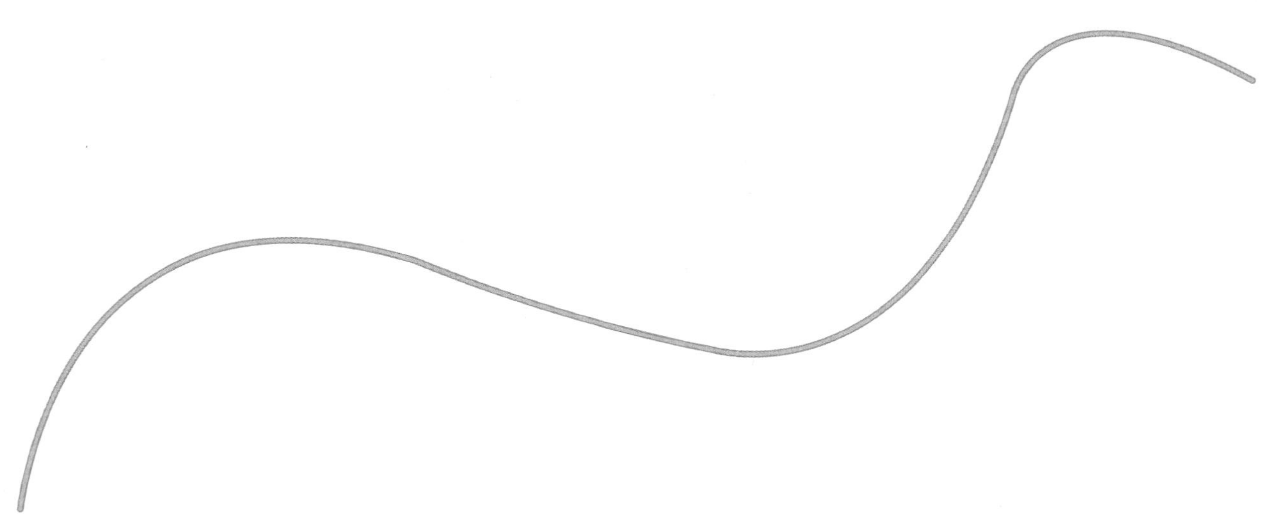

10 ones and 6 ones

Directions: Draw beads on the string to show how many beads there are in all. Circle 10 beads.

Name ______________________

Practice **8.1**

Learning Target: Find a group of 10 objects and tell how many more objects there are.

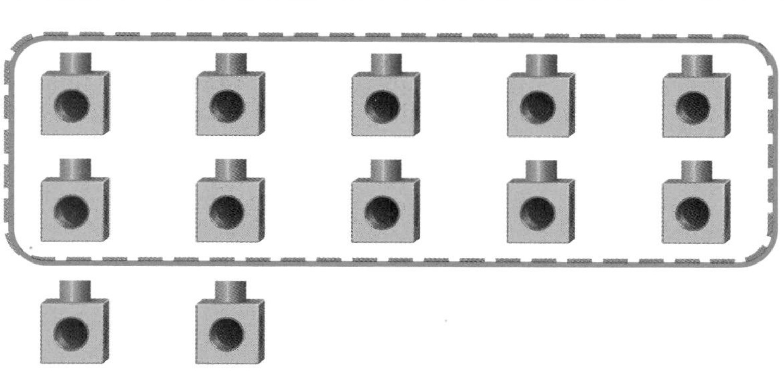

10 ones and 2 ones

Directions: Circle 10 linking cubes. Tell how many more linking cubes there are. Then write the numbers.

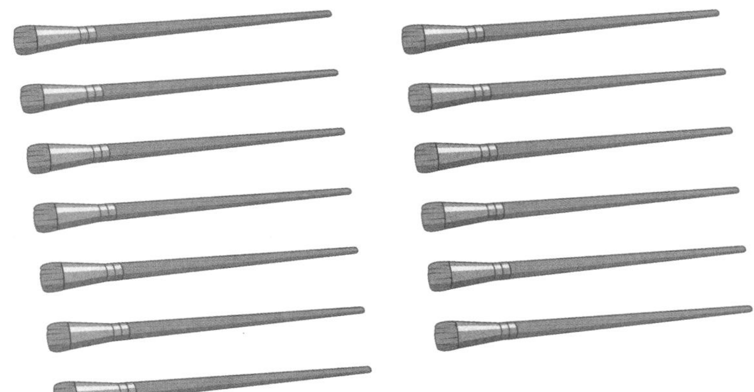

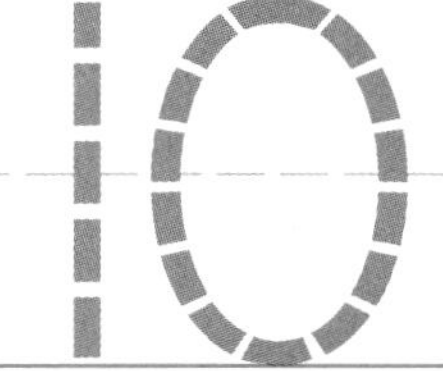

ones and ______ ones

Directions: 1 Circle 10 paintbrushes. Tell how many more paintbrushes there are. Then write the numbers.

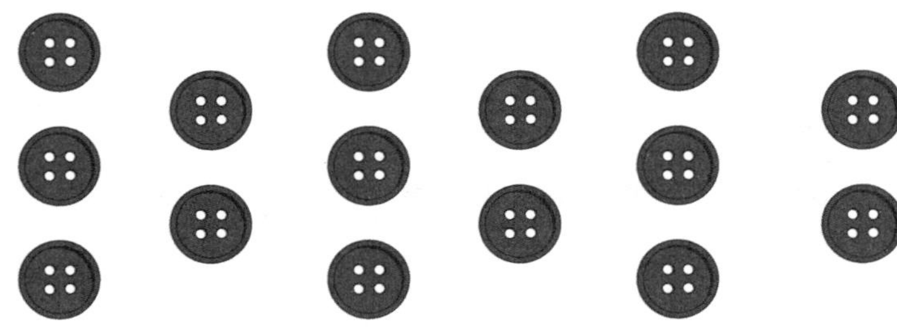

ones and ones

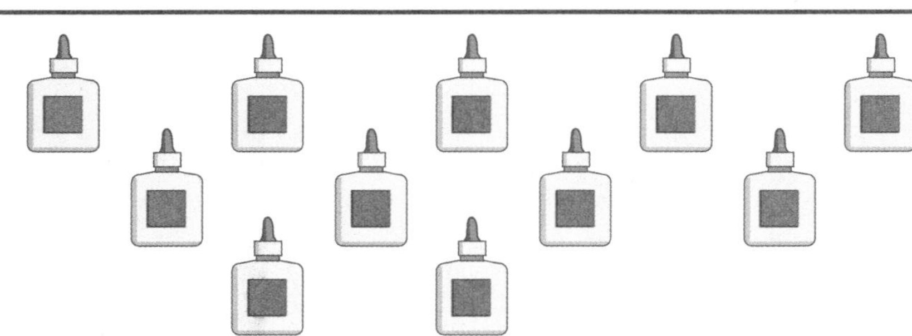

ones and ones

10 ones and 7 ones

Directions: 2 and 3 Circle 10 objects. Tell how many more objects there are. Then write the numbers. 4 Draw beads on the string to show how many beads there are in all. Circle 10 beads.

Name ____________________

Count and Write 11 and 12

8.2

Learning Target: Count and write the numbers 11 and 12.

Explore and Grow

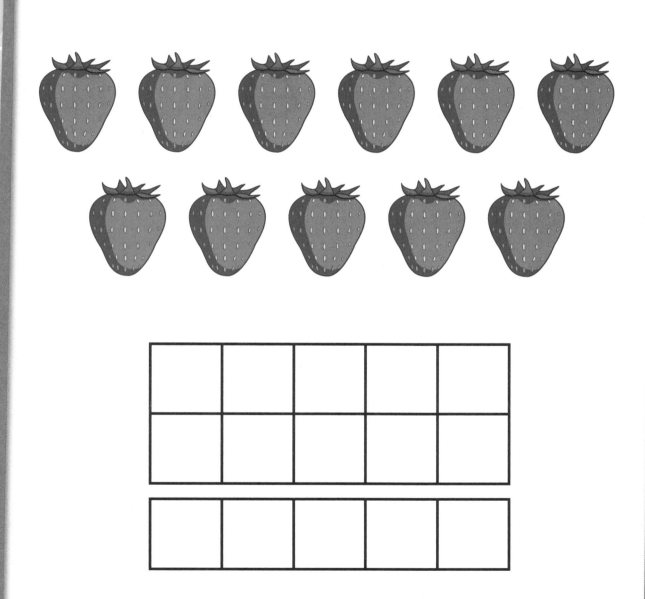

Directions: Place a linking cube on each strawberry. Slide cubes to fill the ten frame. Slide the extra cubes to the five frame.

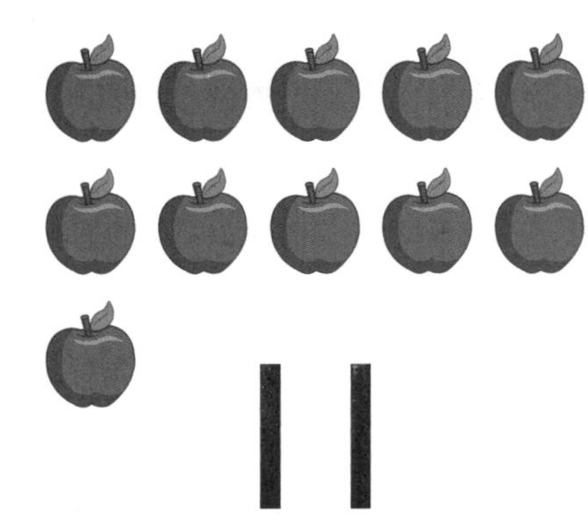

11

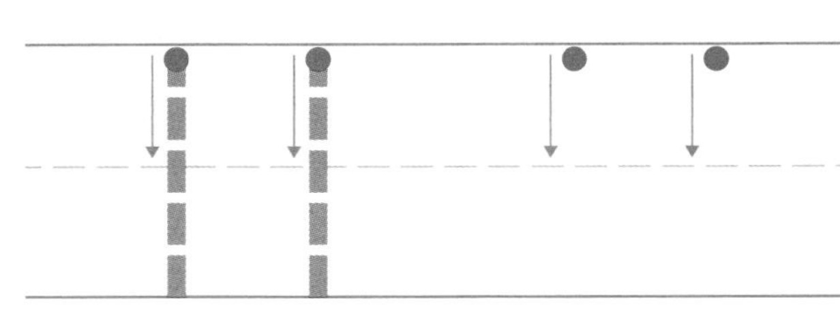

eleven

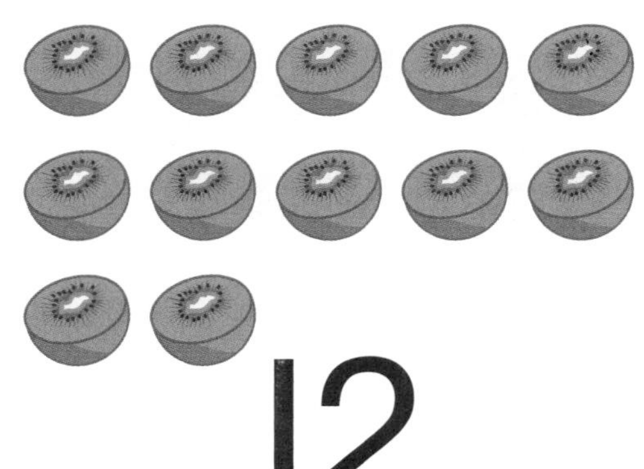

12

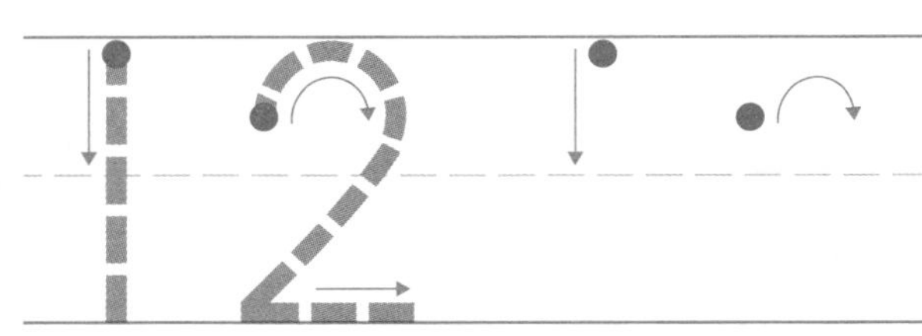

twelve

Directions:

- Count the fruit. Say the number. Trace and write the number.
- Count the fruit. Say the number. Write the number.

Name ____________________

Apply and Grow: Practice

____

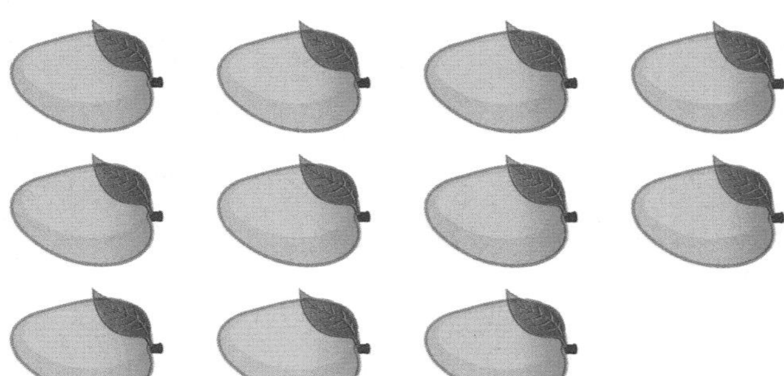

____

____

____

Directions:  Count the objects. Say the number. Write the number.

Think and Grow: Modeling Real Life

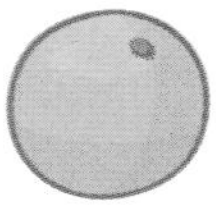

Directions: You have 12 oranges in your cart. There are 11 apples in the bin. Draw the oranges in the cart and the apples in the bin. Then write the numbers.

Name ______________________

Practice 8.2

Learning Target: Count and write the numbers 11 and 12.

eleven

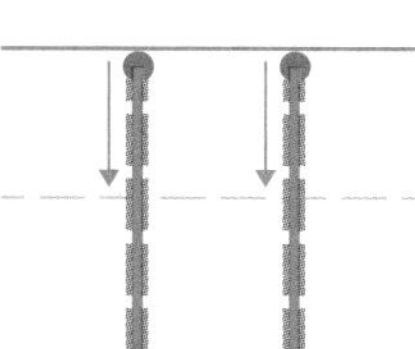

twelve

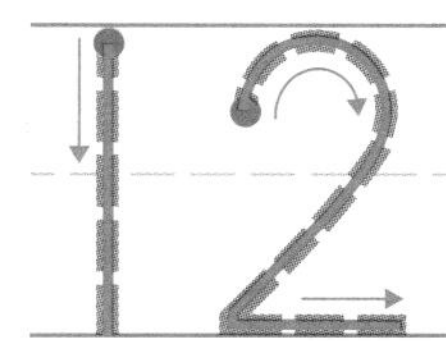

Directions: Count the linking cubes. Say the number. Write the number.

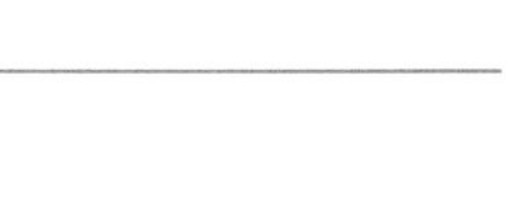

Directions: 1 and 2 Count the objects. Say the number. Write the number.

3

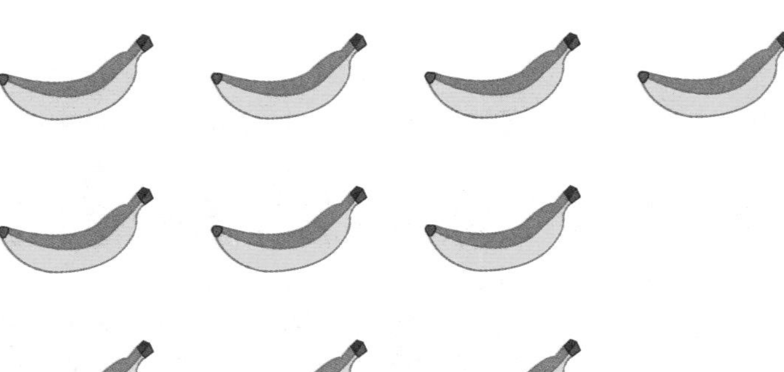

4

5

Directions: 3 and 4 Count the fruit. Say the number. Write the number.
5 Draw 12 cherries on the tree. Write the number.

Name ___________________________

Understand 11 and 12

8.3

Learning Target: Understand the numbers 11 and 12.

Explore and Grow

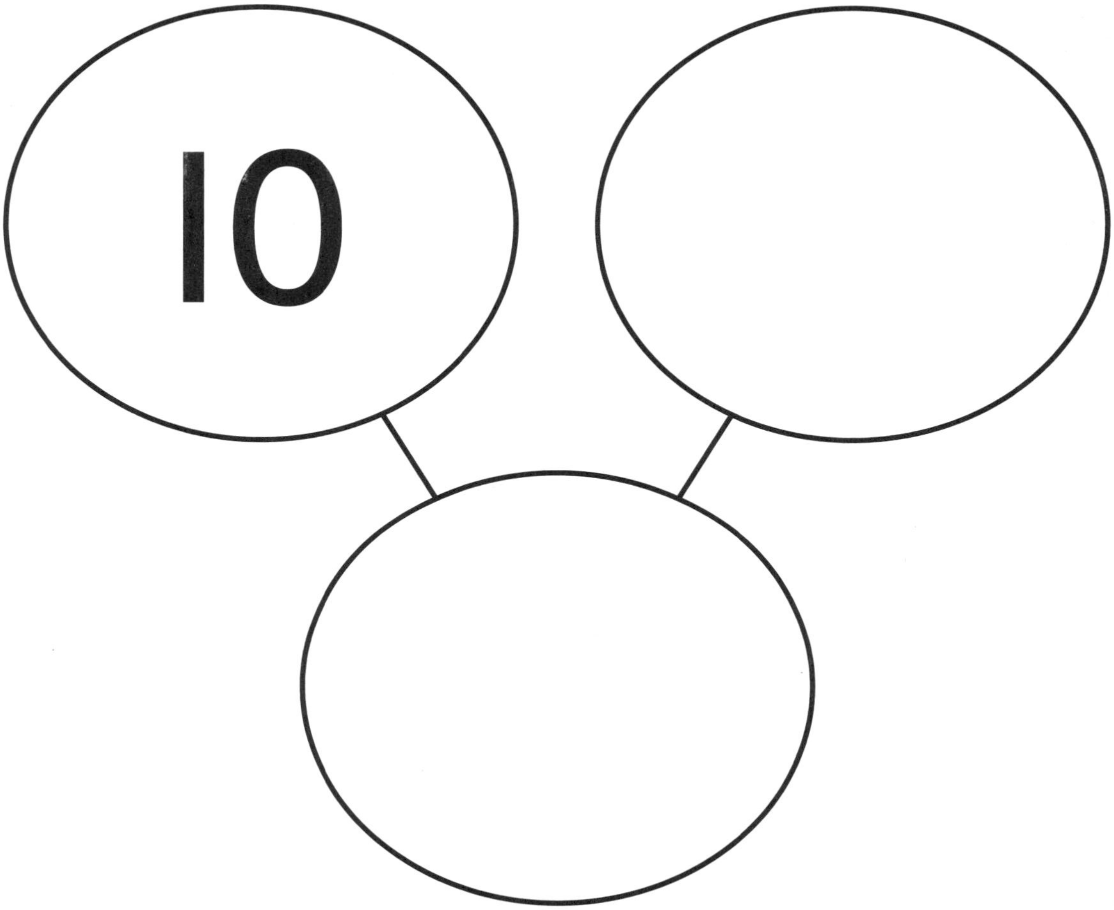

10

10 and _______ is _______.

Directions: Place the 10 and 1 cards as the parts on the number bond. Slide the cards and hide the zero with the 1 card to make the whole. Write the parts and the whole.

Think and Grow

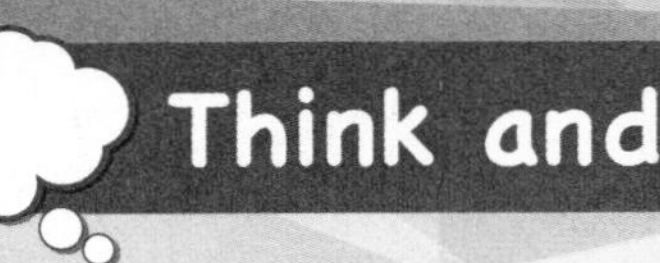

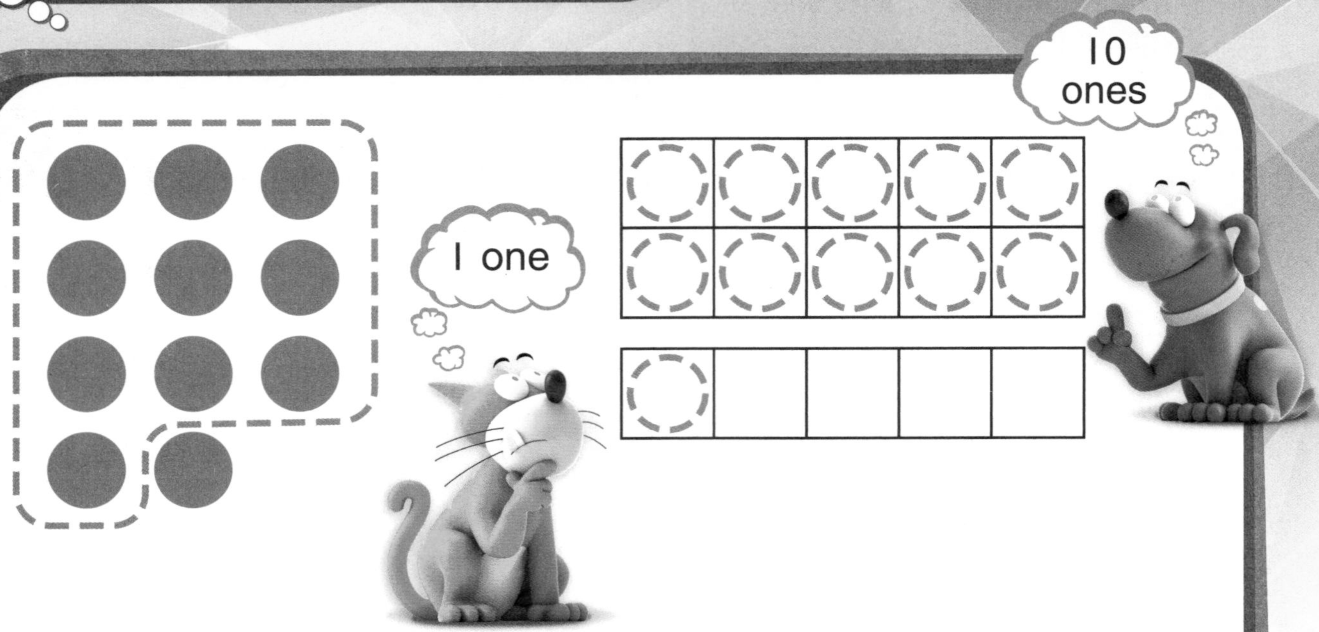

$11 = 10 + 1$

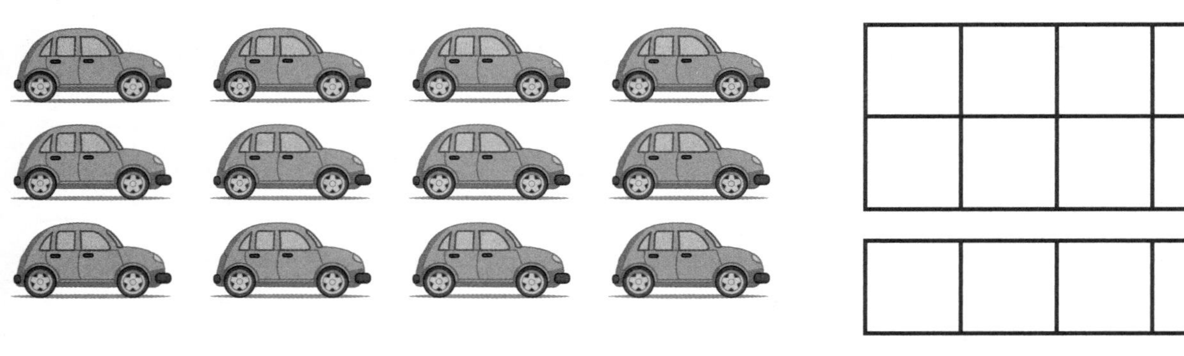

$___ = 10 + ___$

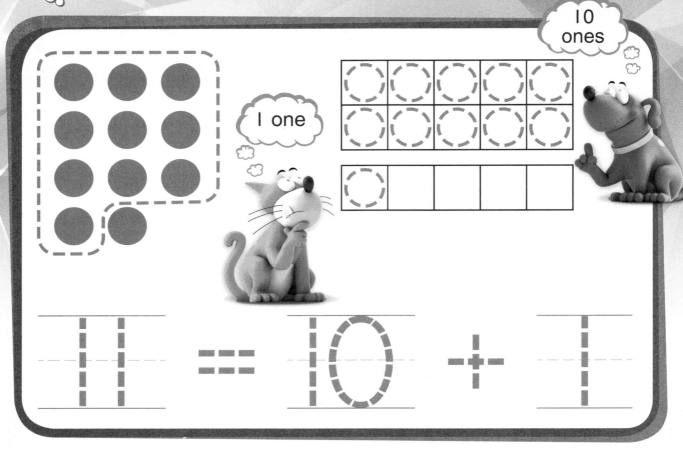

Directions: Circle 10 objects. Draw dots in the ten frame to show how many objects are circled. Draw dots in the five frame to show how many more objects there are. Use the frames to write an addition sentence.

Name ____________________

Apply and Grow: Practice

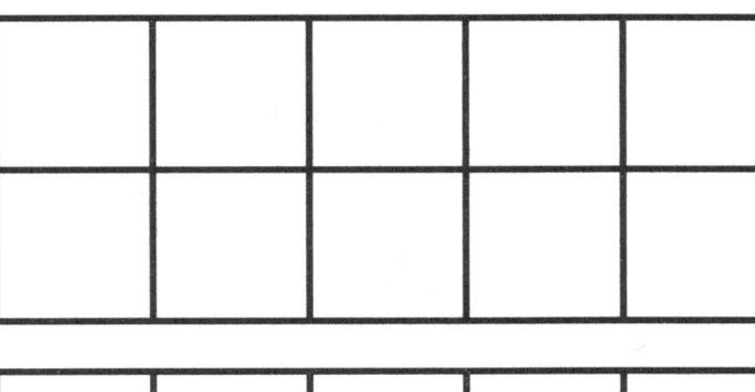

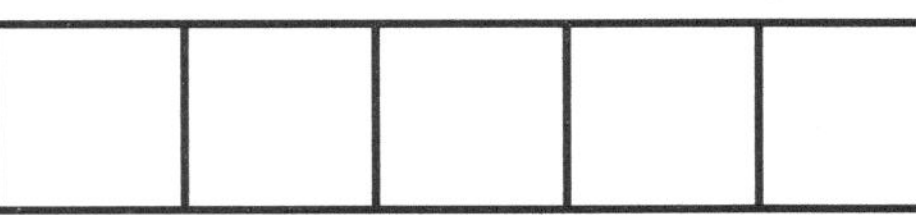

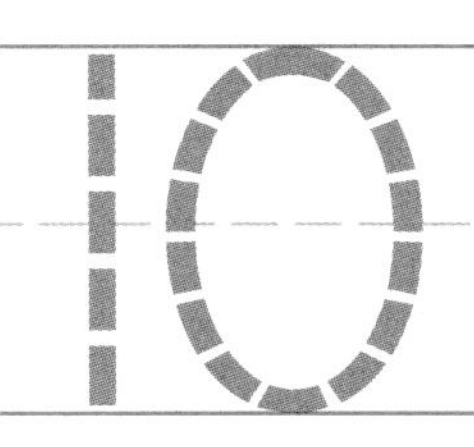

____ = 10 + ____

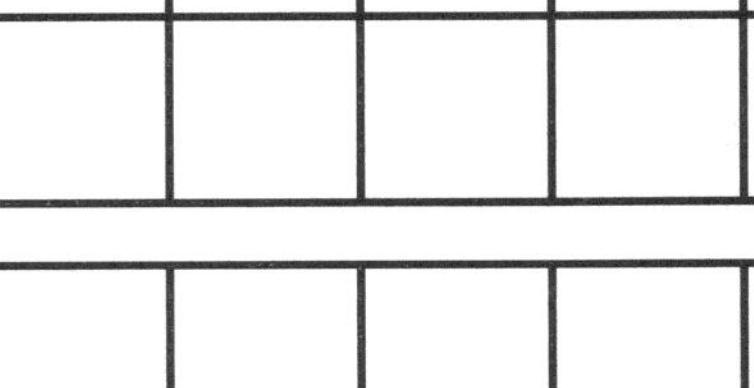

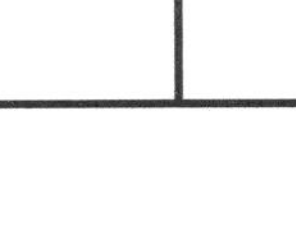

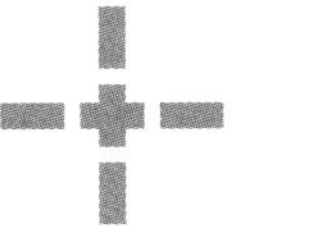

____ = ____ + ____

Directions: 1 and 2 Circle 10 vehicles. Draw dots in the ten frame to show how many vehicles are circled. Draw dots in the five frame to show how many more vehicles there are. Use the frames to write an addition sentence.

Think and Grow: Modeling Real Life

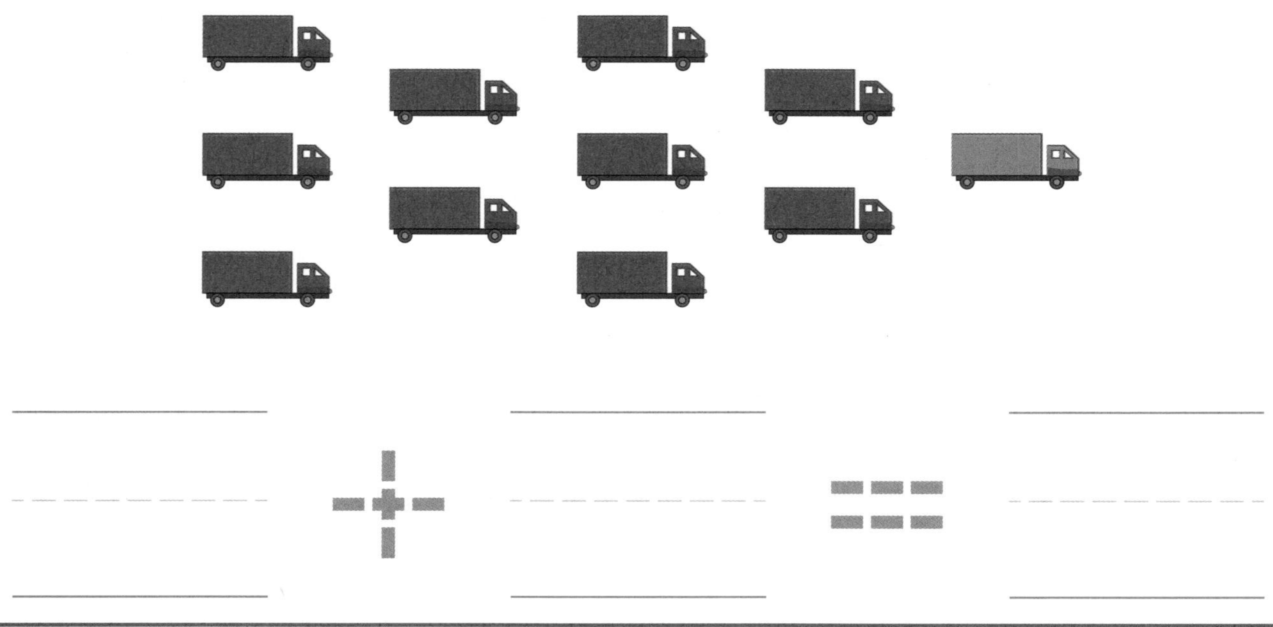

Directions:

- You have blue trucks. Your friend has red trucks. Circle your trucks. Write an addition sentence to match the picture. How many trucks do you have? Circle the number.
- You have yellow trains. Your friend has green trains. Circle your trains. Write an addition sentence to match the picture. How many trains does your friend have? Circle the number.

Name ____________________

Practice 8.3

Learning Target: Understand the numbers 11 and 12.

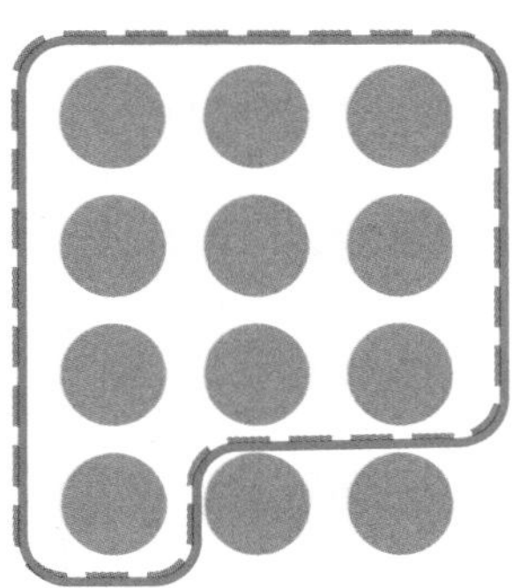

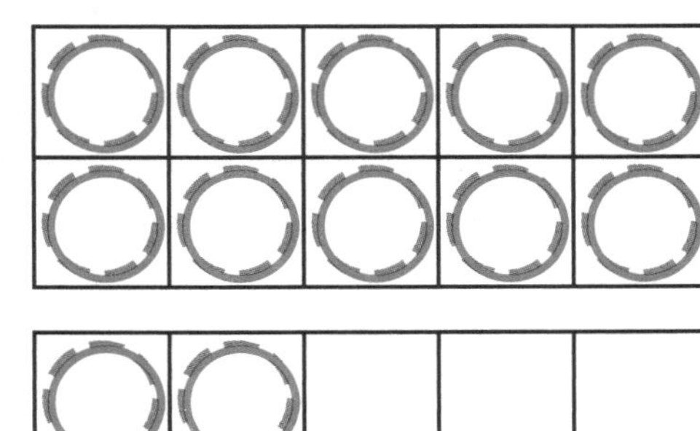

12 = 10 + 2

Directions: Circle 10 objects. Draw dots in the ten frame to show how many objects are circled. Draw dots in the five frame to show how many more objects there are. Use the frames to complete the addition sentence.

1

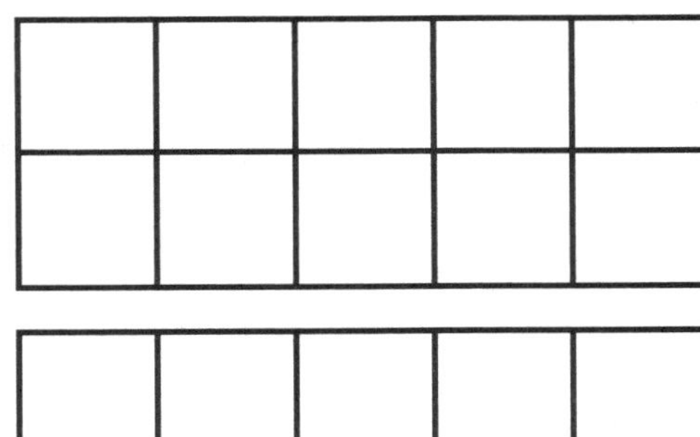

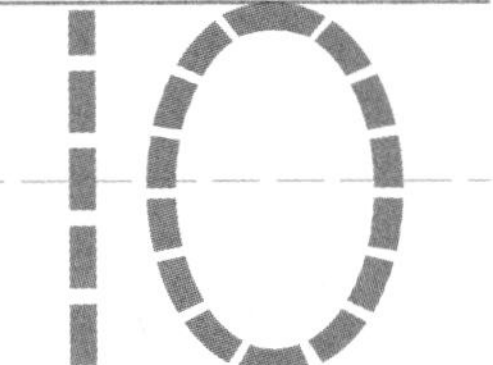

____ = 10 + ____

Directions: 1 Circle 10 trucks. Draw dots in the ten frame to show how many trucks are circled. Draw dots in the five frame to show how many more trucks there are. Use the frames to write an addition sentence.

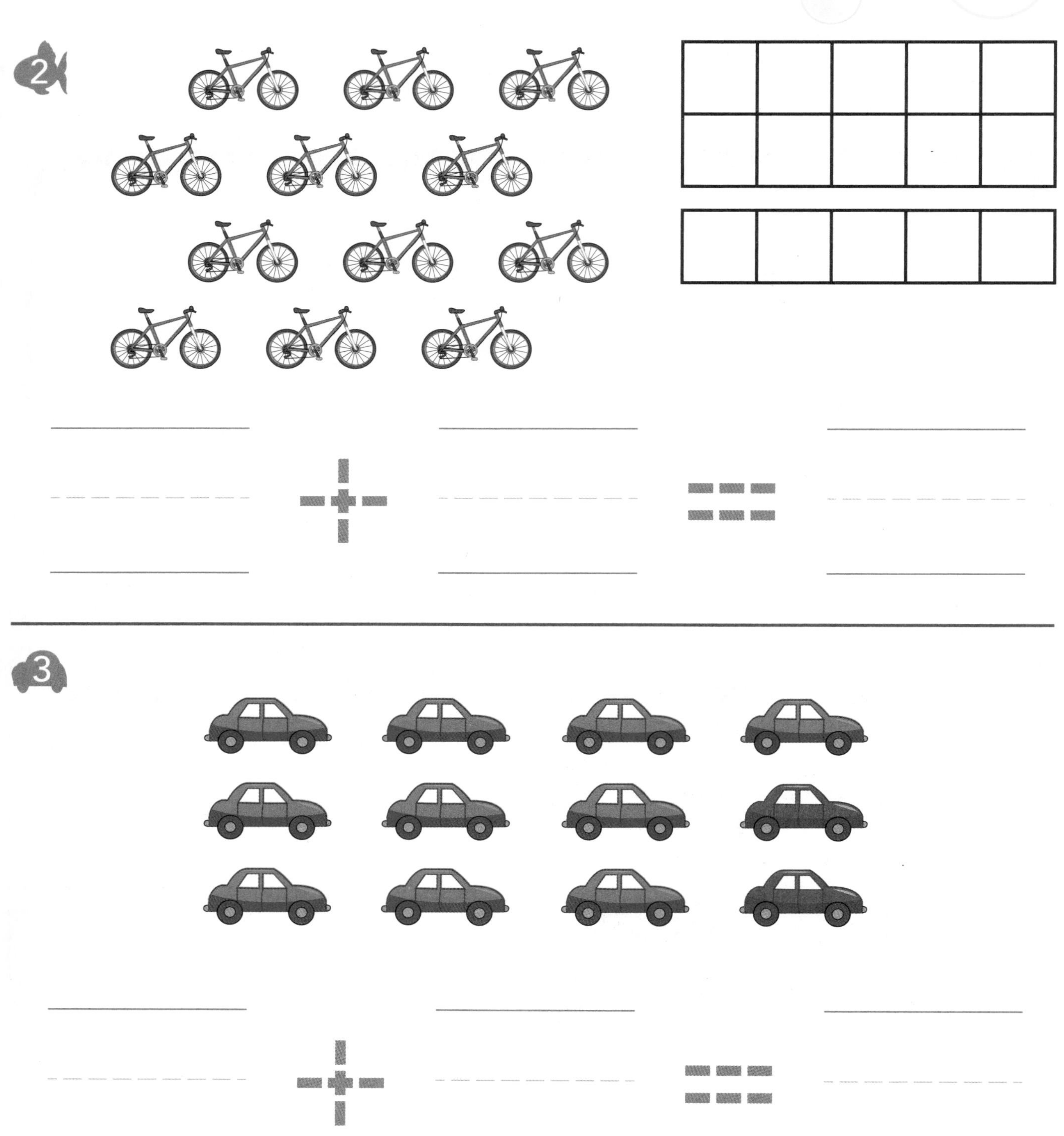

Directions: 2 Circle 10 bicycles. Draw dots in the ten frame to show how many bicycles are circled. Draw dots in the five frame to show how many more bicycles there are. Use the frames to write an addition sentence. 3 You have red cars. Your friend has blue cars. Circle your cars. Write an addition sentence to match your picture. How many cars does your friend have? Circle the number.

Name ______________________

Count and Write 13 and 14

8.4

Learning Target: Count and write the numbers 13 and 14.

Explore and Grow

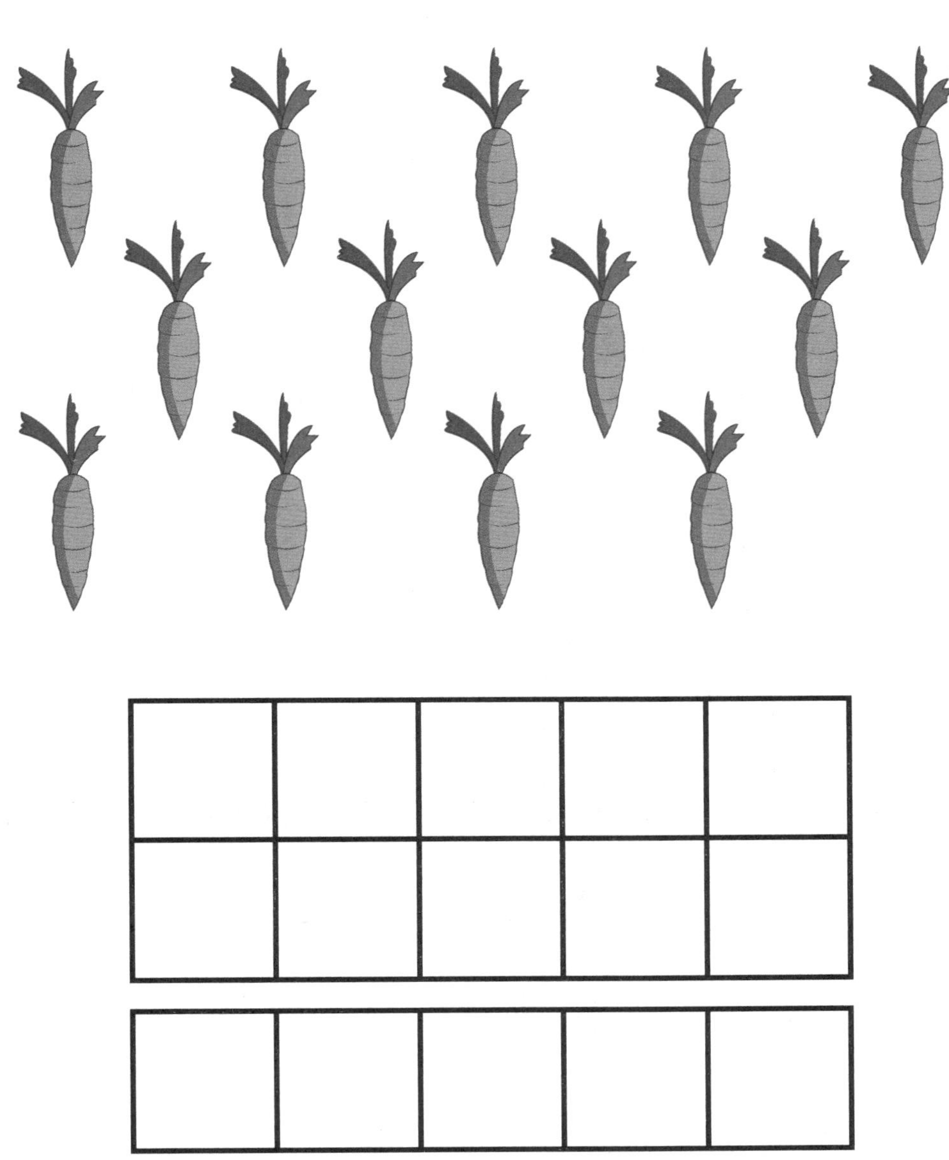

Directions: Place a linking cube on each carrot. Slide cubes to fill the ten frame. Slide the extra cubes to the five frame.

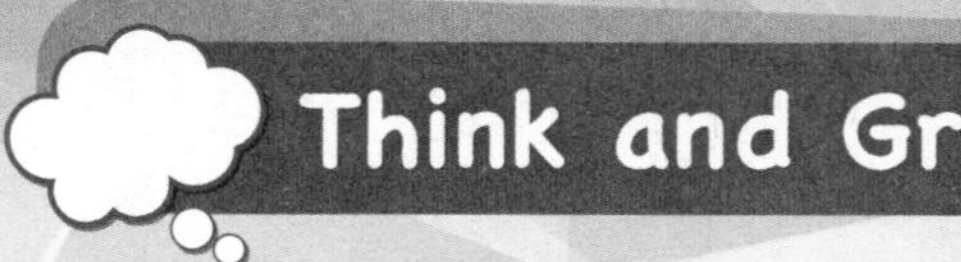

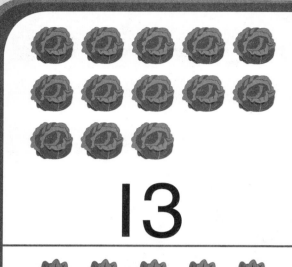

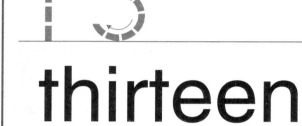

Think and Grow

13

13

thirteen

14

14

fourteen

______

______

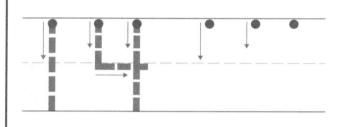

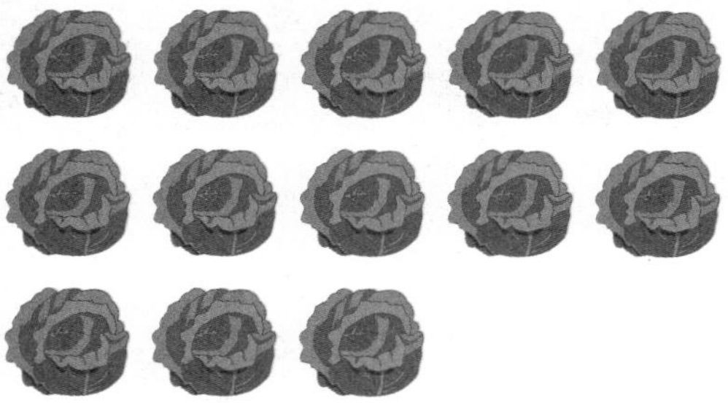

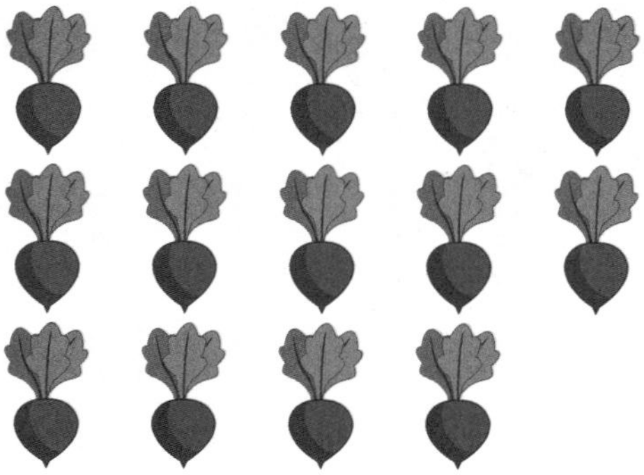

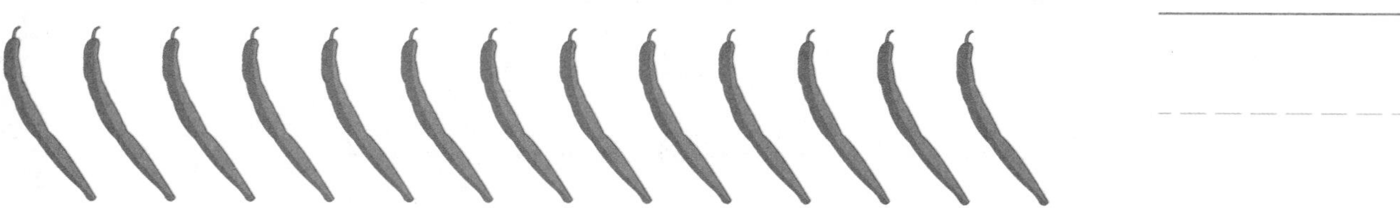

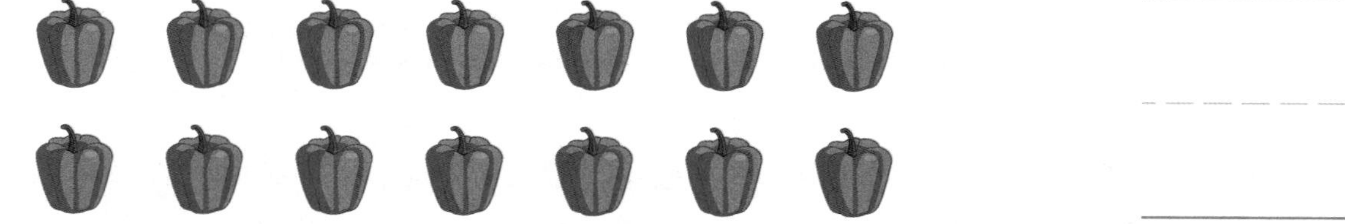

Directions:

- Count the vegetables. Say the number. Trace and write the number.
- Count the vegetables. Say the number. Write the number.

Name ________________

Apply and Grow: Practice

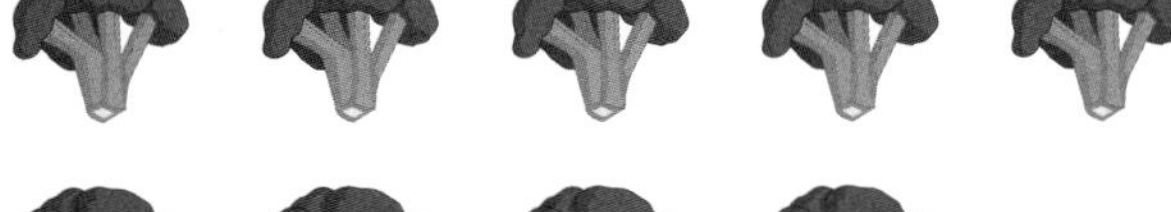

Directions: 1 – 4 Count the objects. Say the number. Write the number.

Think and Grow: Modeling Real Life

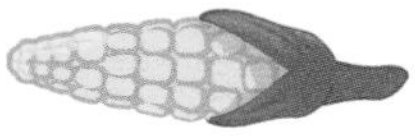

Directions: A store has 14 cucumbers and 13 ears of corn in the bins. Draw the cucumbers and the ears of corn. Then write the numbers.

Name ______________________

Practice 

Learning Target: Count and write the numbers 13 and 14.

thirteen

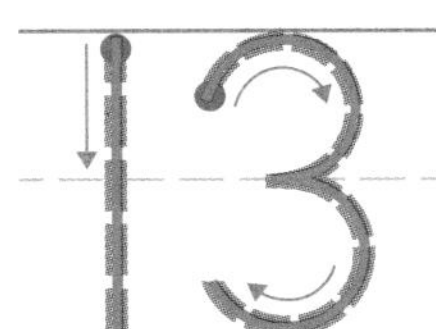

fourteen

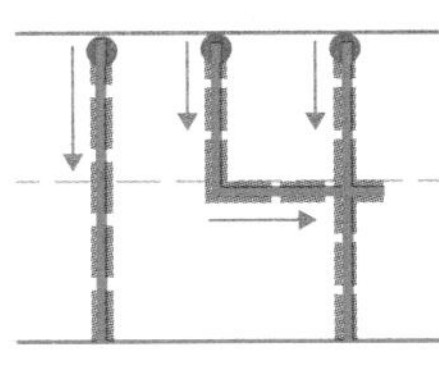

Directions: Count the linking cubes. Say the number. Write the number.

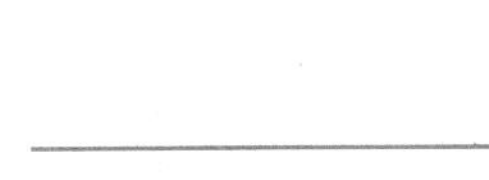

Directions: 1 and 2 Count the objects. Say the number. Write the number.

3

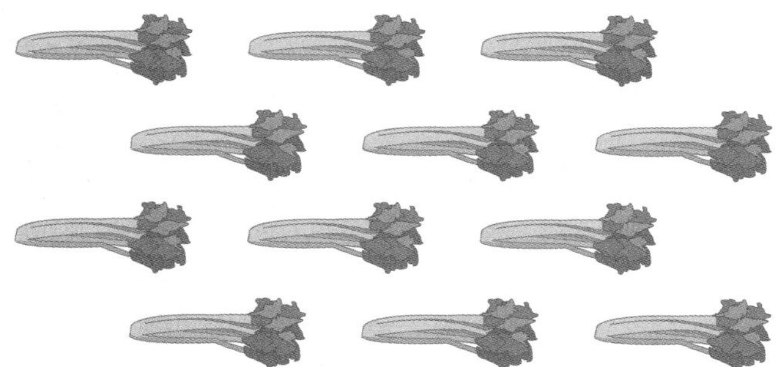

4

5

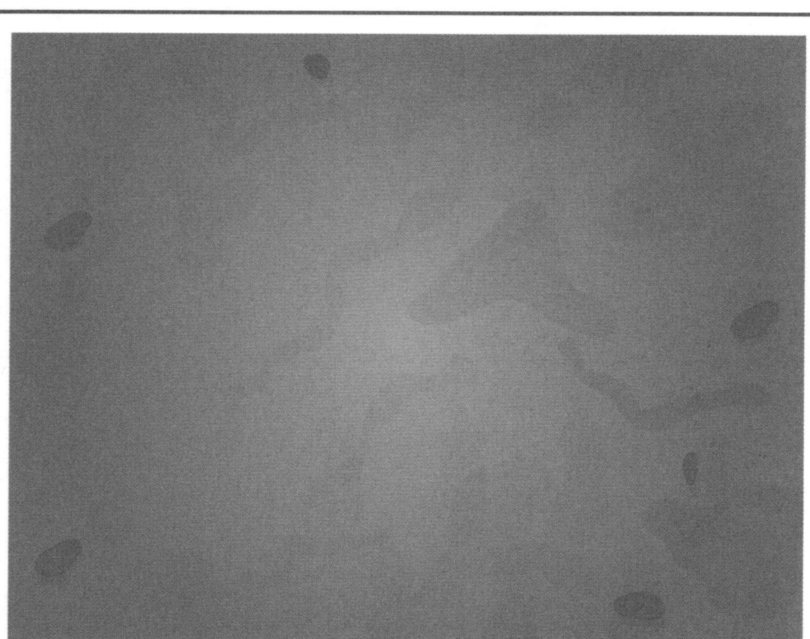

Directions: 3 and 4 Count the vegetables. Say the number. Write the number.
5 Draw 14 heads of lettuce in the dirt. Write the number.

Name ______________________

Learning Target: Understand the numbers 13 and 14.

Explore and Grow

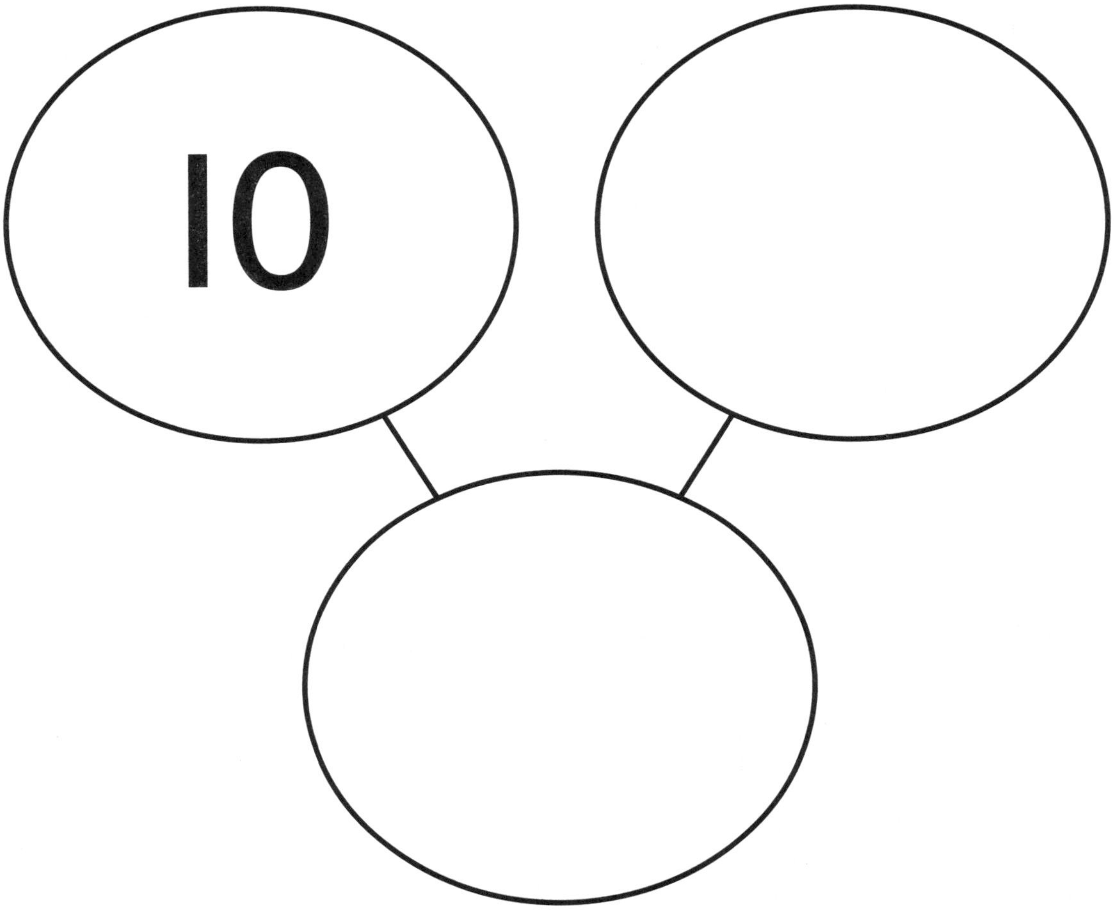

10

10 and ______ is ______.

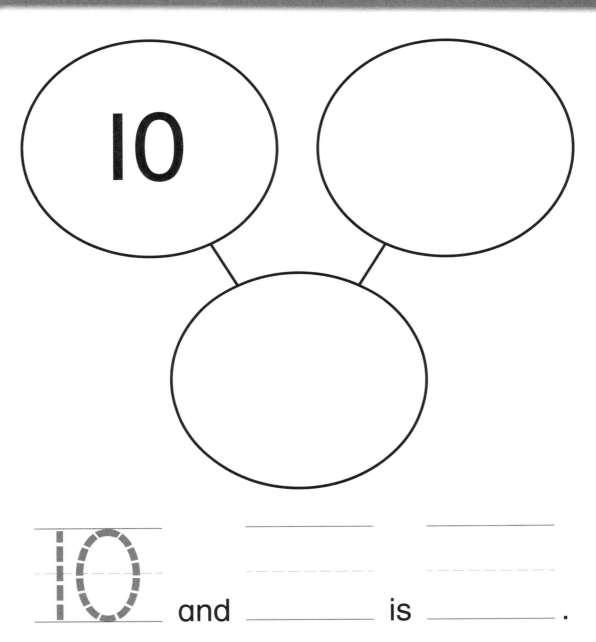

Directions: Place the 10 and 3 cards as the parts on the number bond. Slide the cards and hide the zero with the 3 card to make the whole. Write the parts and the whole.

Think and Grow

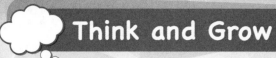

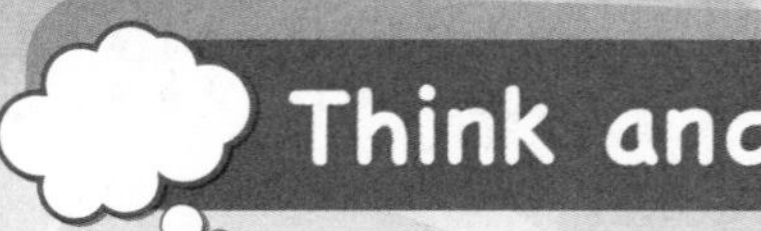

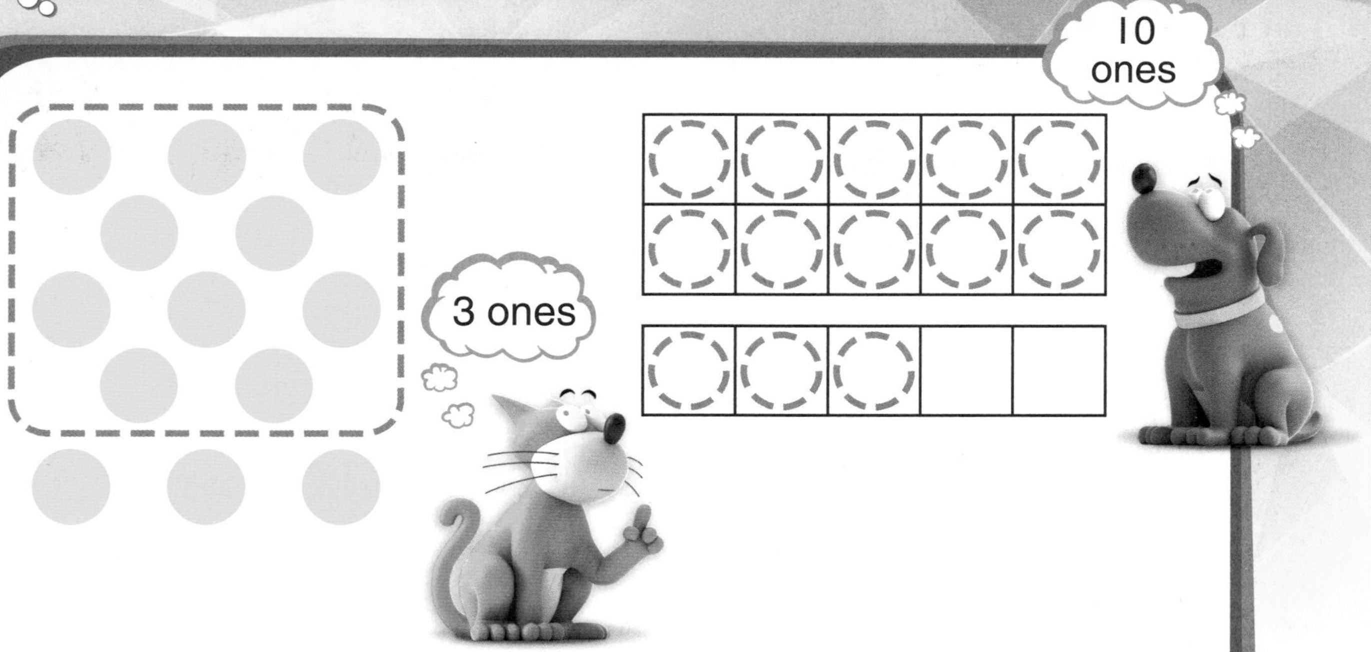

13 = 10 + 3

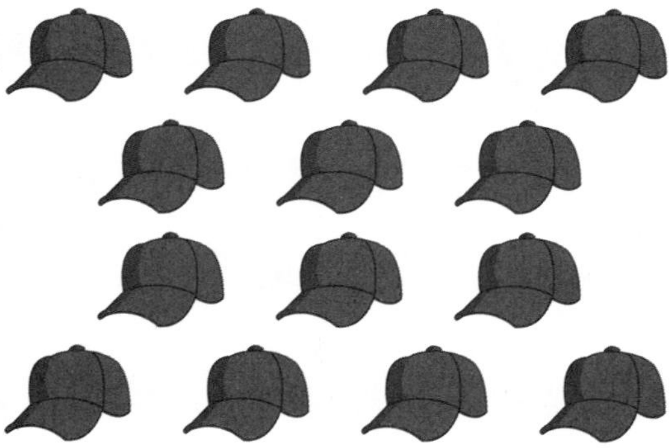

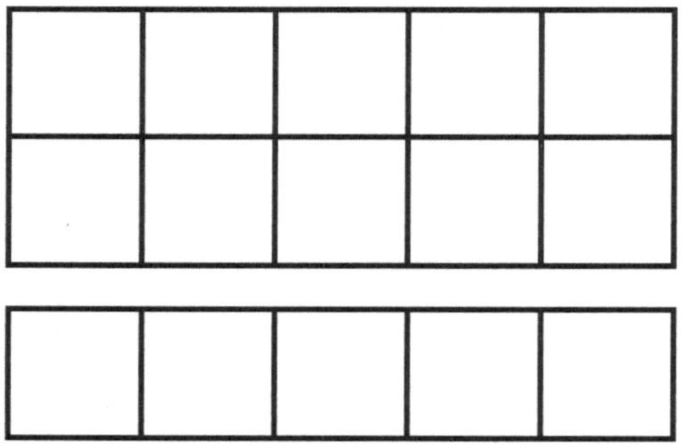

___ = 10 + ___

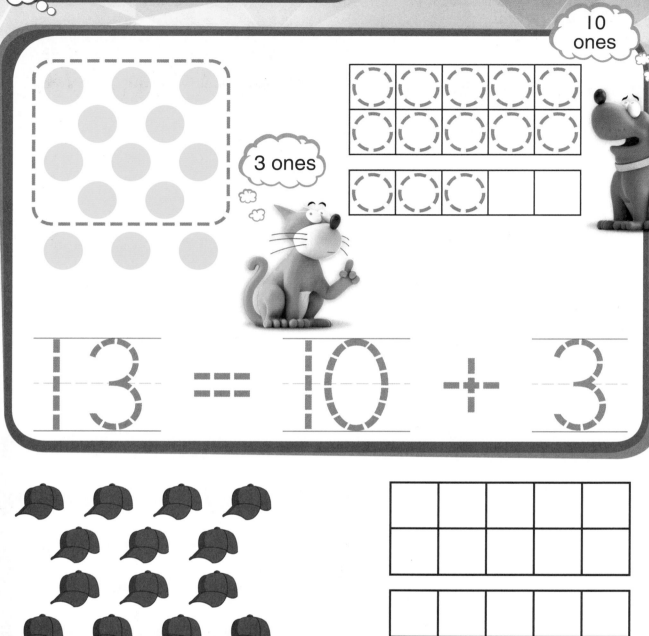

Directions: Circle 10 objects. Draw dots in the ten frame to show how many objects are circled. Draw dots in the five frame to show how many more objects there are. Use the frames to write an addition sentence.

Name ______________________________

Apply and Grow: Practice

1

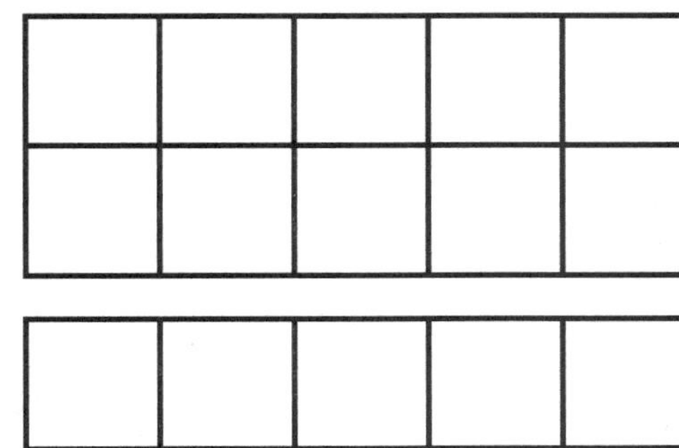

_______  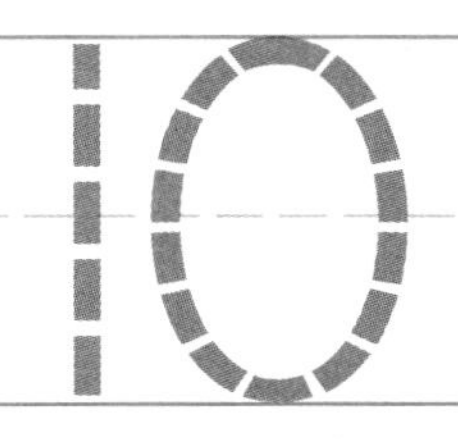  _______

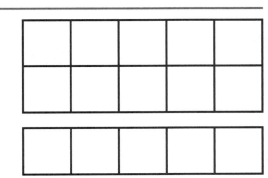

_______  _______  _______

Directions: 1 and 2 Circle 10 hats. Draw dots in the ten frame to show how many hats are circled. Draw dots in the five frame to show how many more hats there are. Use the frames to write an addition sentence.

Think and Grow: Modeling Real Life

______ + ______ = ______

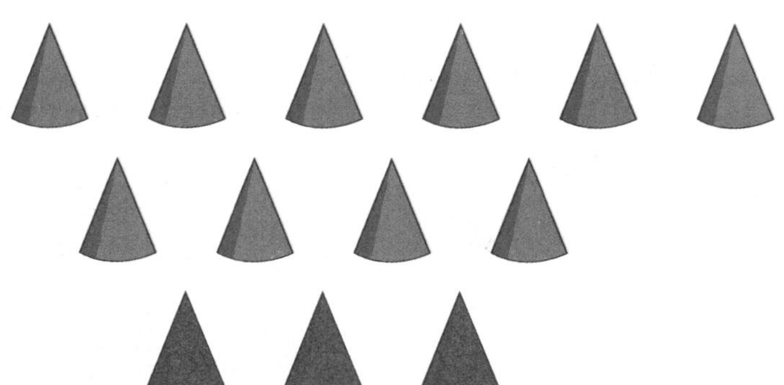

______ + ______ = ______

Directions:

- You have striped party hats. Your friend has polka-dot party hats. Circle your hats. Write an addition sentence to match the picture. How many hats do you and your friend have in all? Circle the number.
- You have red party hats. Your friend has blue party hats. Circle your hats. Write an addition sentence to match the picture. How many hats do you have? Circle the number.

Name ______________________

Practice 8.5

Learning Target: Understand the numbers 13 and 14.

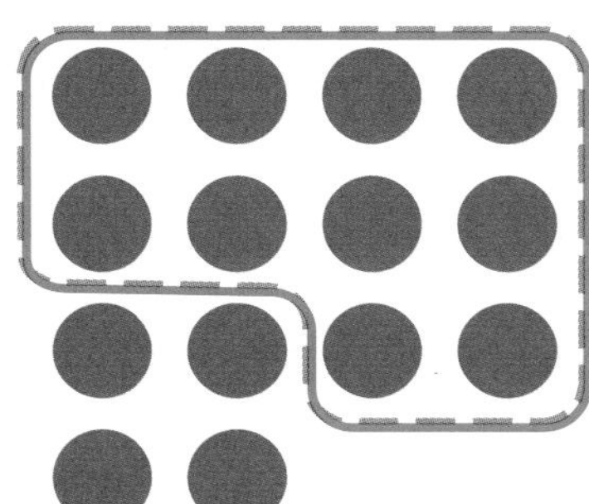

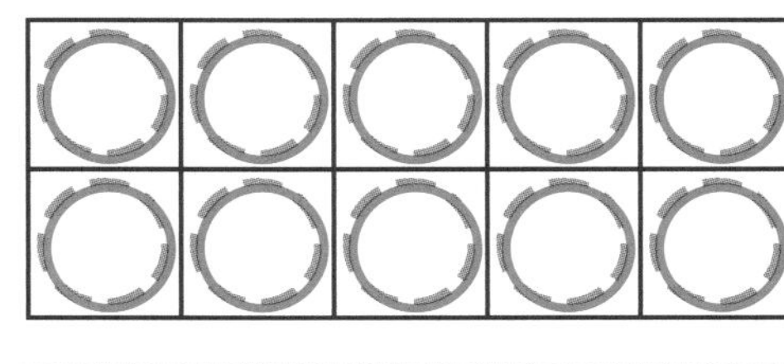

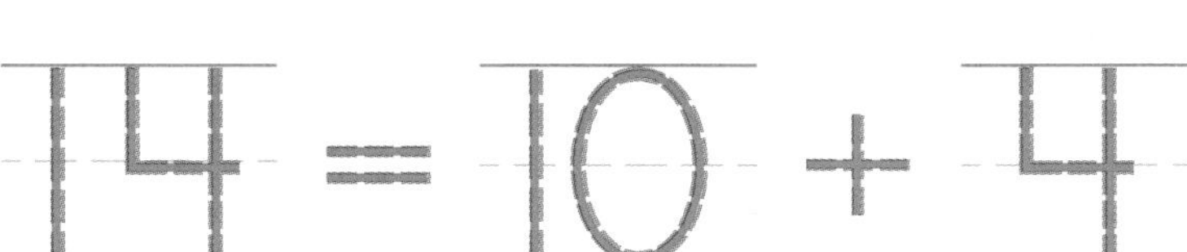

Directions: Circle 10 objects. Draw dots in the ten frame to show how many objects are circled. Draw dots in the five frame to show how many more objects there are. Use the frames to complete the addition sentence.

1

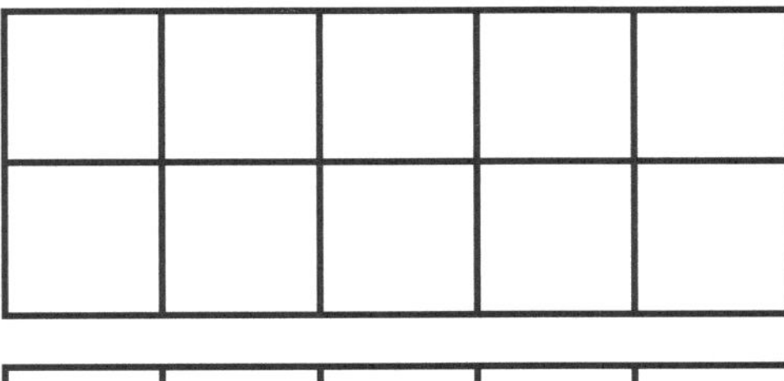

______ = ______  ______

Directions: 1 Circle 10 hats. Draw dots in the ten frame to show how many hats are circled. Draw dots in the five frame to show how many more hats there are. Use the frames to write an addition sentence.

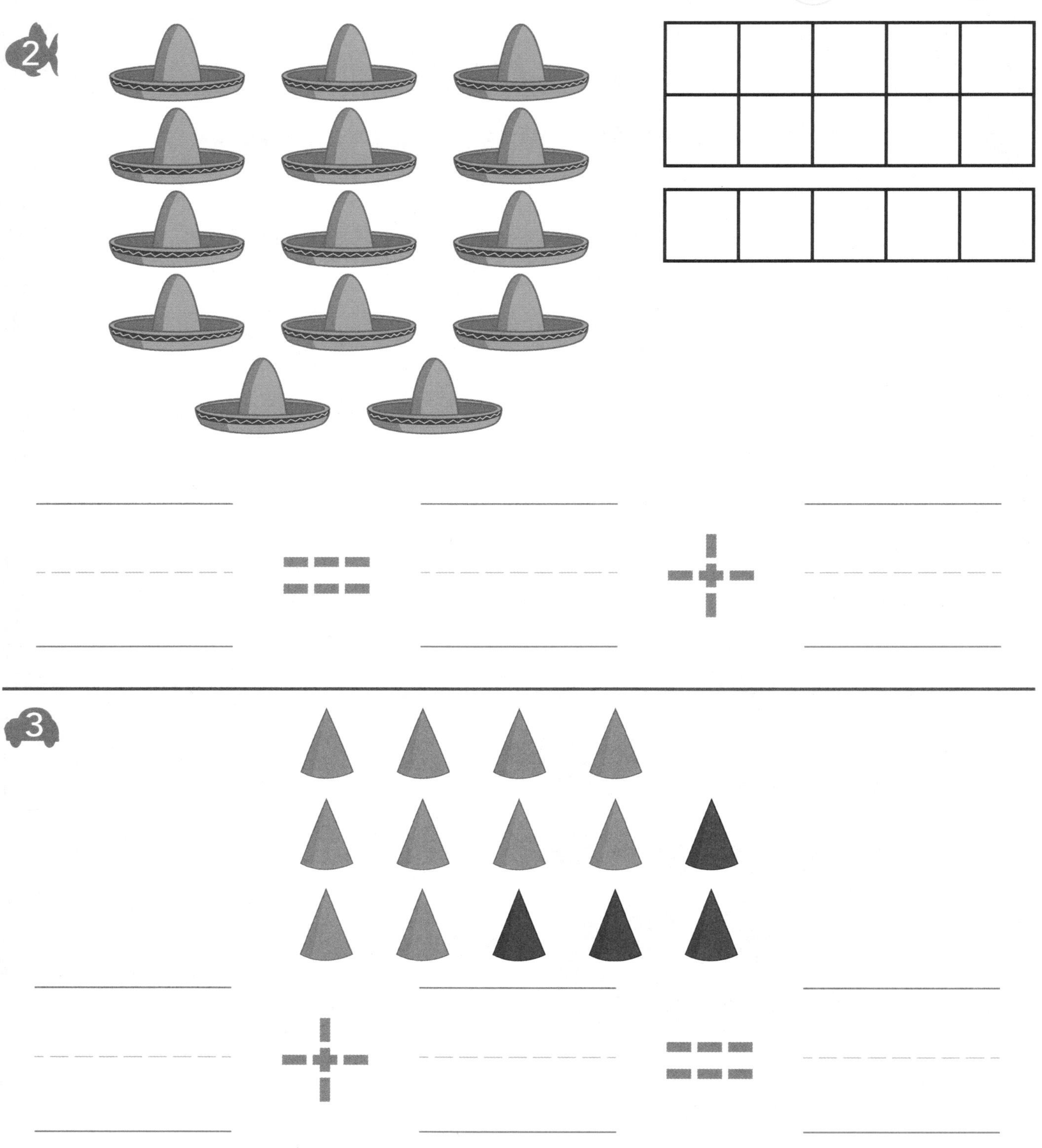

Directions: 2 Circle 10 hats. Draw dots in the ten frame to show how many hats are circled. Draw dots in the five frame to show how many more hats there are. Use the frames to write an addition sentence. 3 You have green party hats. Your friend has purple party hats. Circle your hats. Write an addition sentence to match the picture. How many hats do you have? Circle the number.

Name ______________________________

Count and Write 15

8.6

Learning Target: Count and write the number 15.

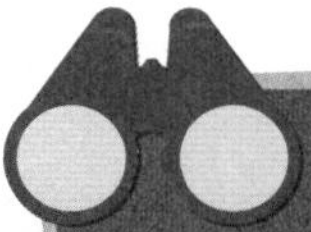

Explore and Grow

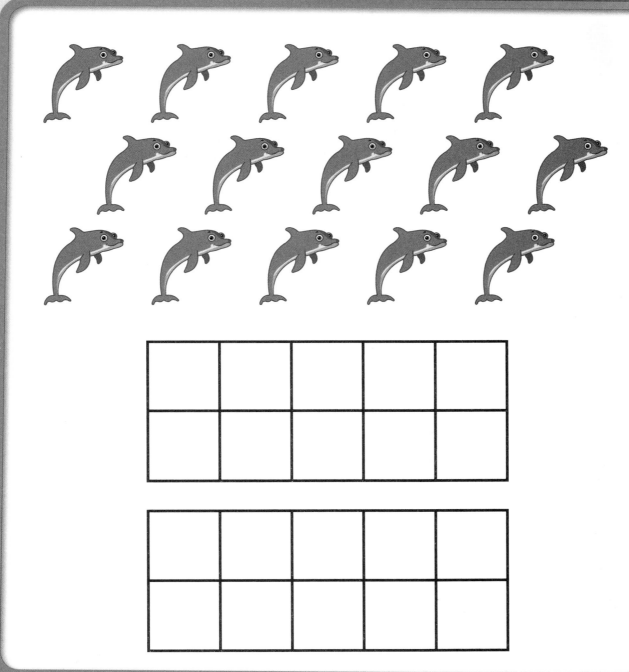

Directions: Place a linking cube on each dolphin. Slide cubes to fill the top ten frame. Slide the extra cubes to the bottom ten frame.

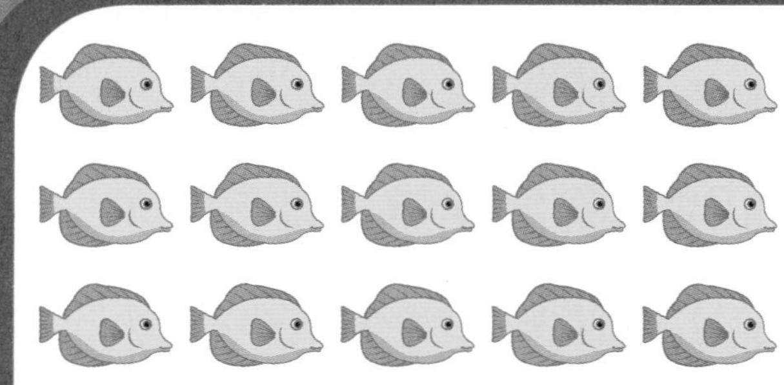

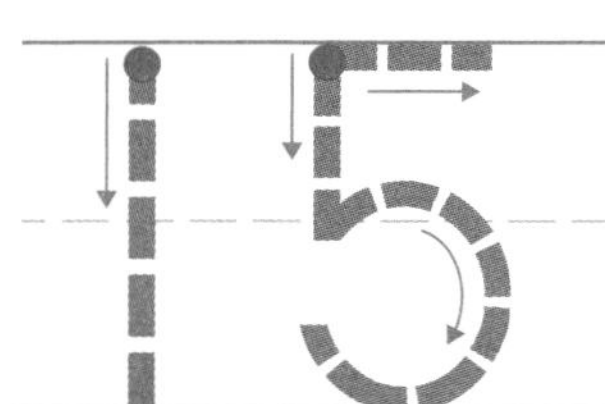

15

fifteen

Directions:

- Count the fish. Say the number. Trace and write the number.
- Count the fish. Say the number. Write the number.

Name ____________

Apply and Grow: Practice

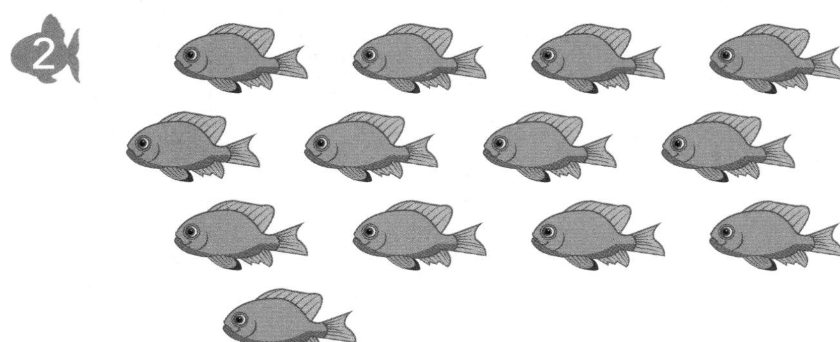

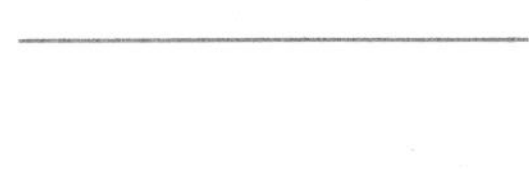

Directions: 1–4 Count the objects. Say the number. Write the number.

Think and Grow: Modeling Real Life

Directions: 11 blue fish swim near the top of the water. 15 red fish swim near the shipwreck. Draw the fish. Then write the numbers.

Name ____________________

Practice 8.6

Learning Target: Count and write the number 15.

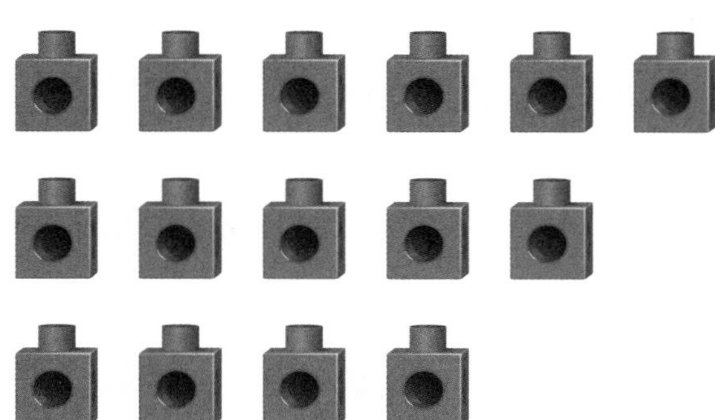

fifteen

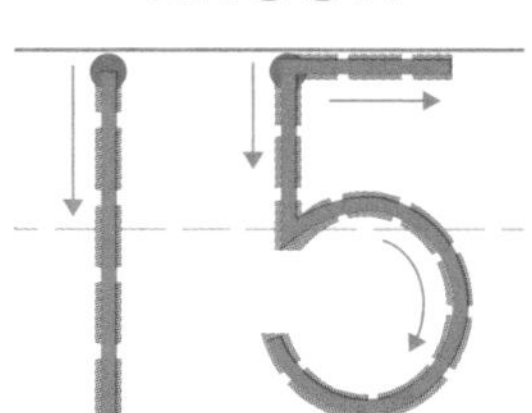

Directions: Count the linking cubes. Say the number. Write the number.

____

____

Directions: 1 and 2 Count the objects. Say the number. Write the number.

3

4

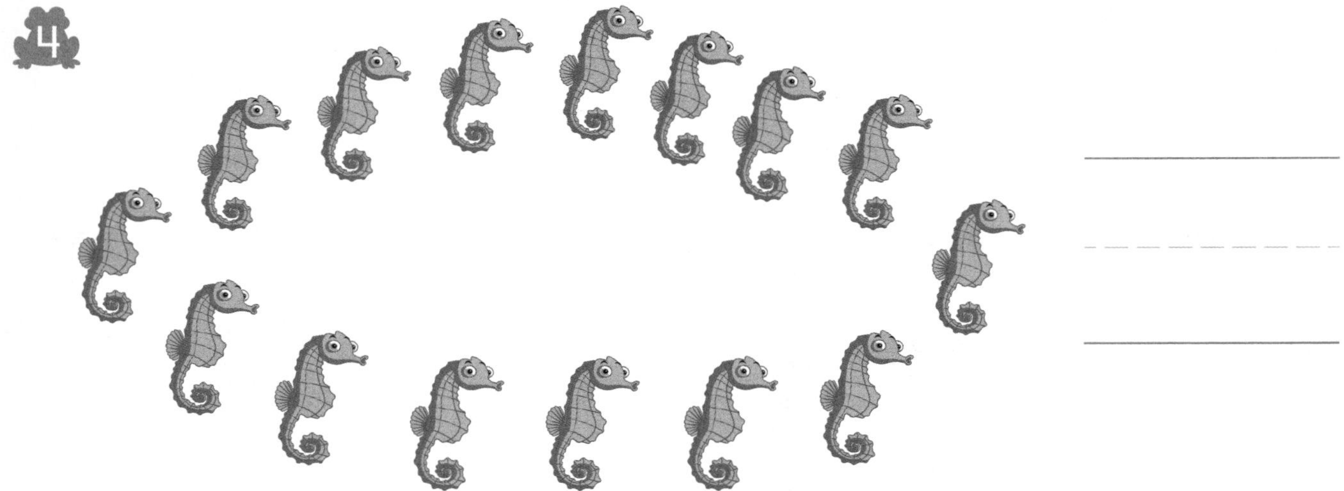

Directions: 3 and 4 Count the sea creatures. Say the number. Write the number. 5 Draw 15 bubbles in the water. Write the number.

Name ________________

Understand 15 **8.7**

Learning Target: Understand the number 15.

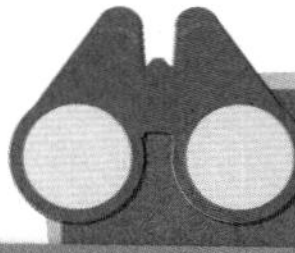

Explore and Grow

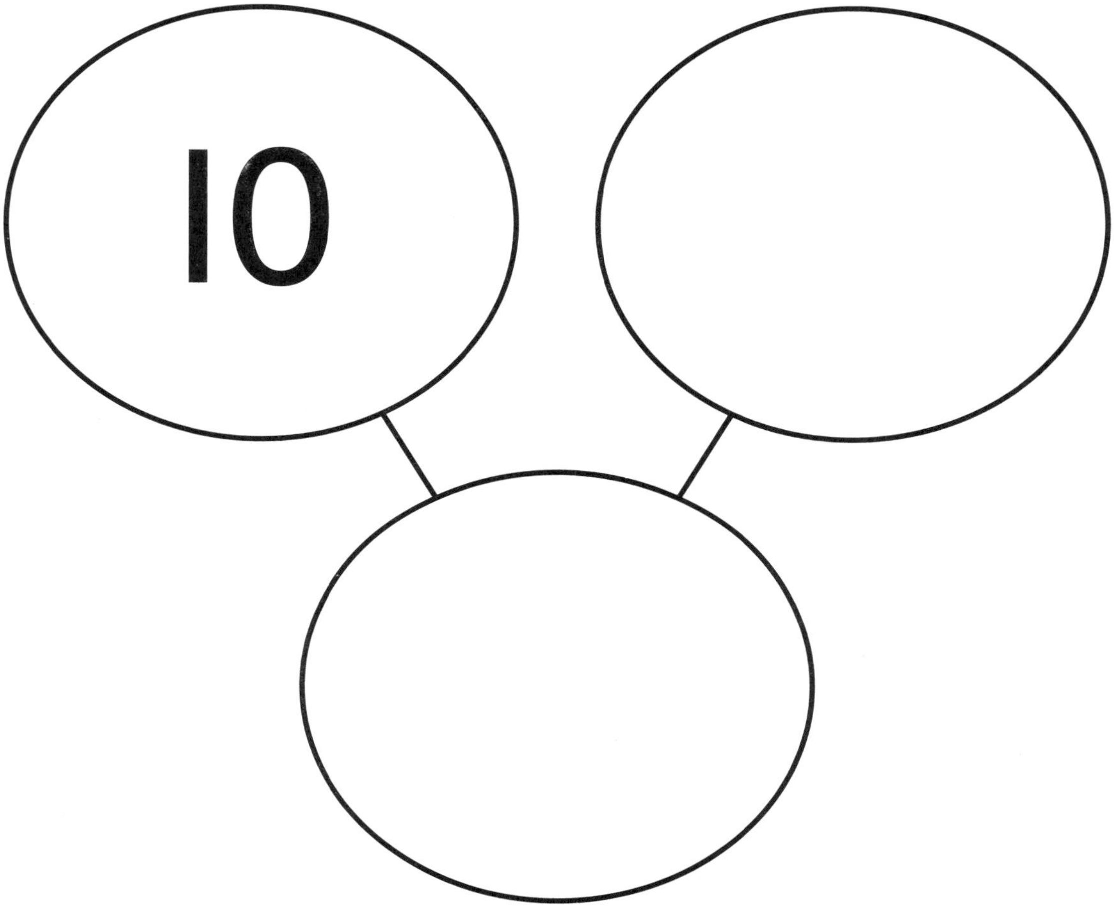

10

10 and ______ is ______.

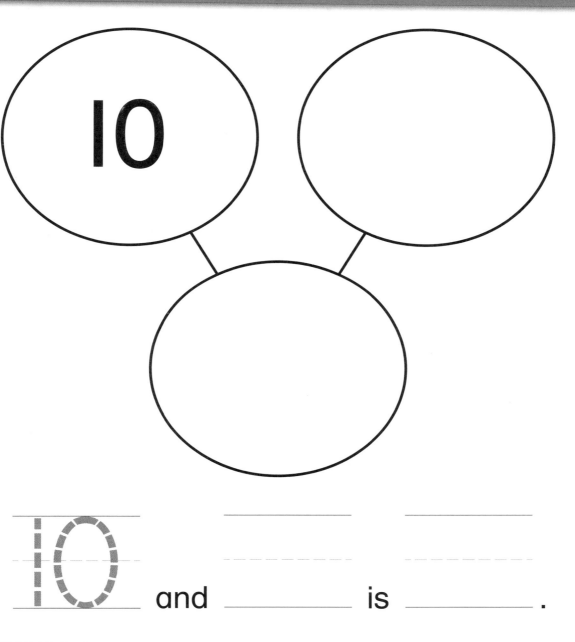

Directions: Place the 10 and 5 cards as the parts on the number bond. Slide the cards and hide the zero with the 5 card to make the whole. Write the parts and the whole.

Think and Grow

5 ones

10 ones

15 = 10 + 5

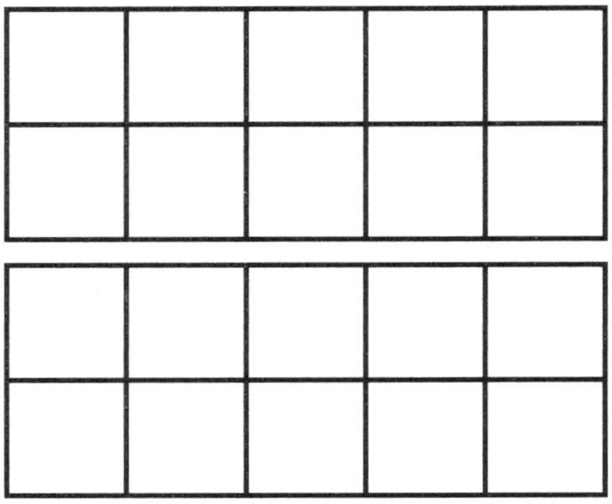

___ = 10 + ___

Directions: Circle 10 objects. Draw dots in the top ten frame to show how many objects are circled. Draw dots in the bottom ten frame to show how many more objects there are. Use the ten frames to write an addition sentence.

Name ____________________

Apply and Grow: Practice

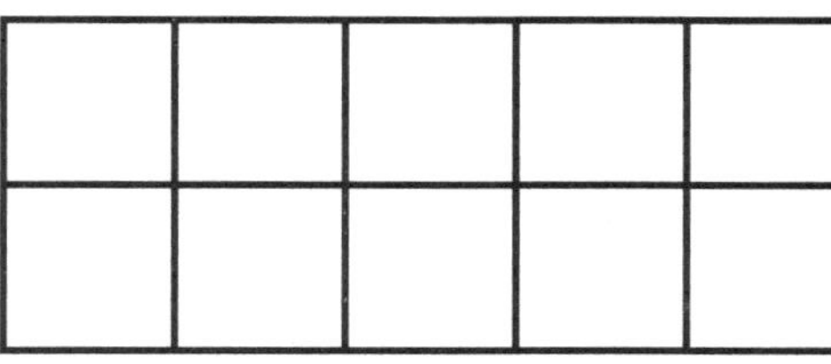

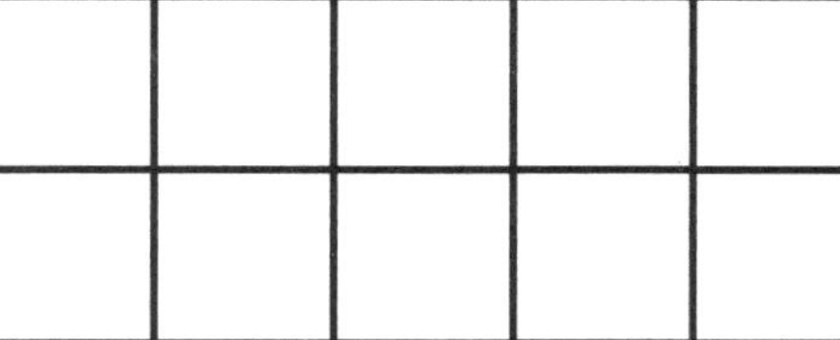

____ = 10 + ____

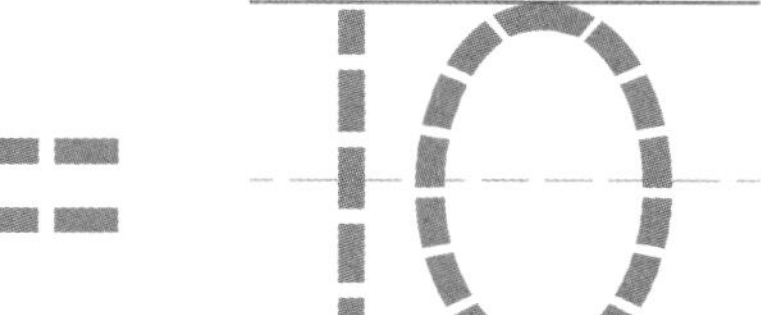

2

____ = ____ + ____

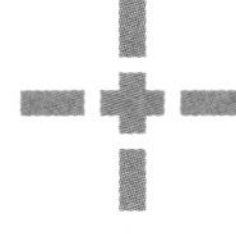

Directions: 1 and 2 Circle 10 flowers. Draw dots in the top ten frame to show how many flowers are circled. Draw dots in the bottom ten frame to show how many more flowers there are. Use the ten frames to write an addition sentence.

Think and Grow: Modeling Real Life

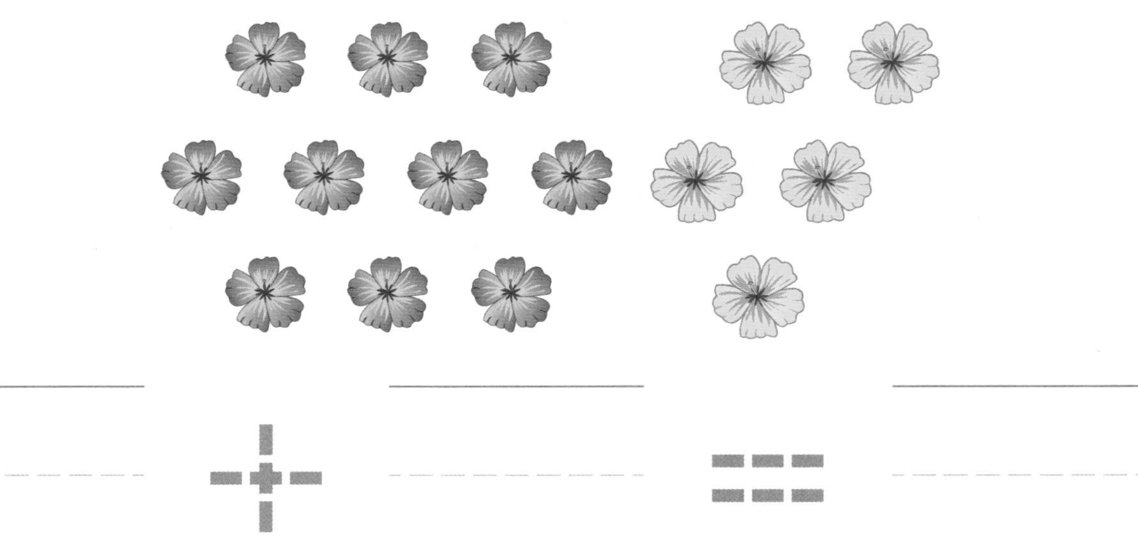

____ + ____ = ____

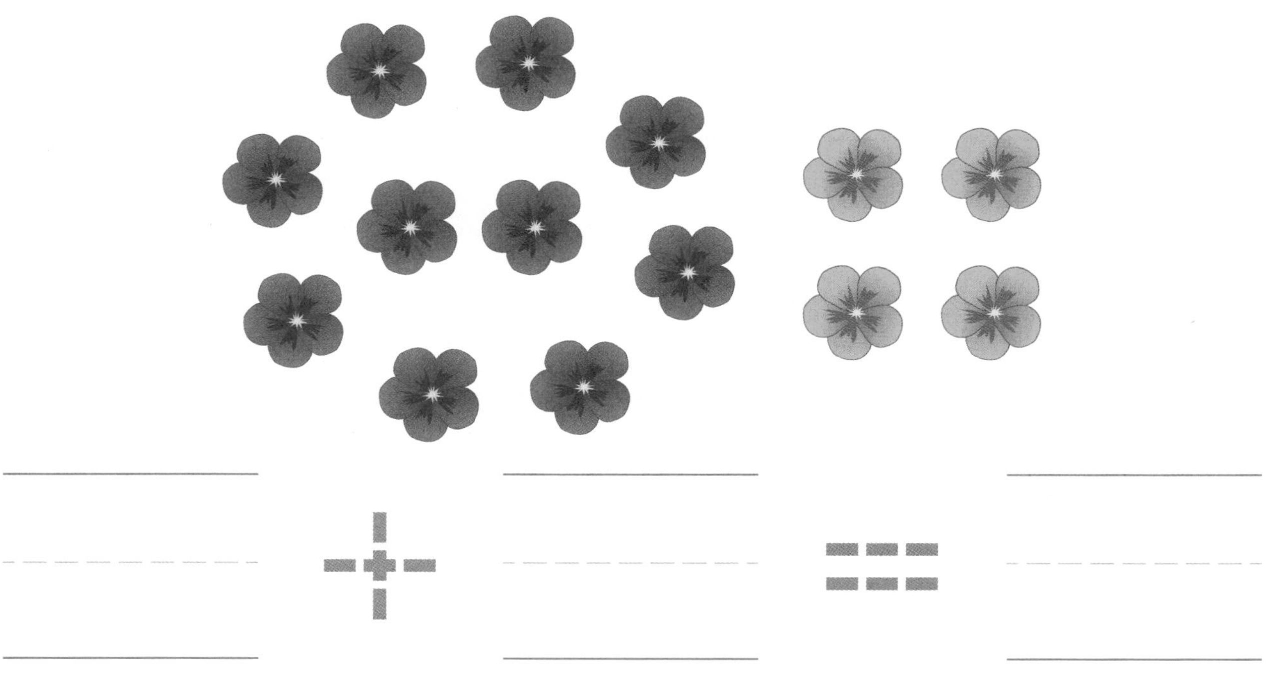

____ + ____ = ____

Directions:

- You have pink flowers. Your friend has yellow flowers. Circle your flowers. Write an addition sentence to match the picture. How many flowers does your friend have? Circle the number.
- You have blue flowers. Your friend has orange flowers. Circle your flowers. Write an addition sentence to match the picture. How many flowers do you and your friend have in all? Circle the number.

Name ___________________________

Practice **8.7**

Learning Target: Understand the number 15.

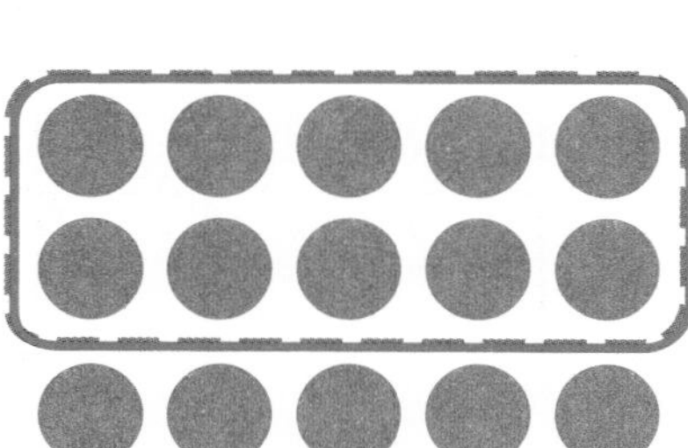

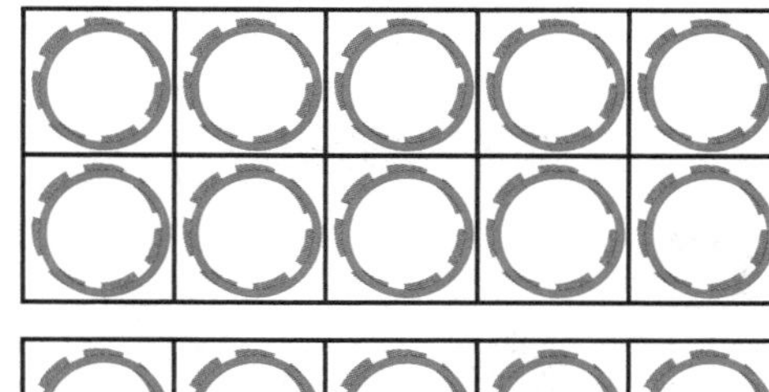

15 = 10 + 5

Directions: Circle 10 objects. Draw dots in the top ten frame to show how many objects are circled. Draw dots in the bottom ten frame to show how many objects are not circled. Use the ten frames to complete the addition sentence.

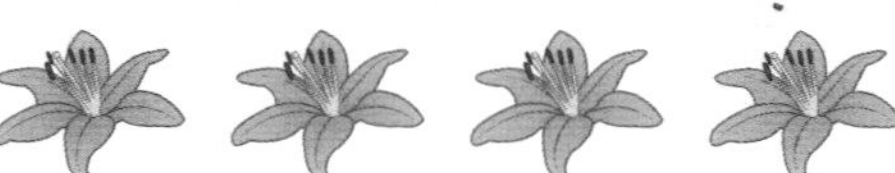

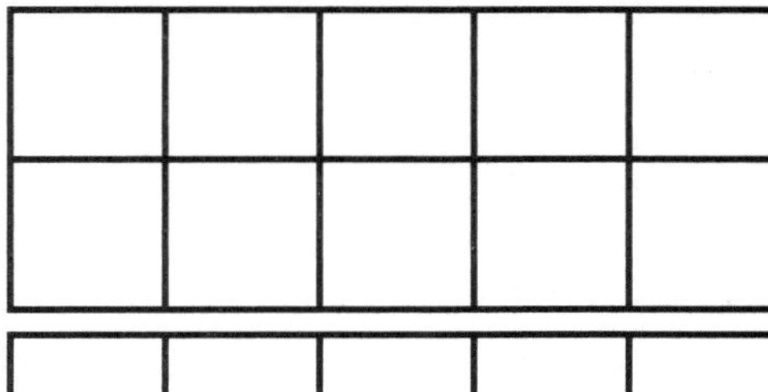

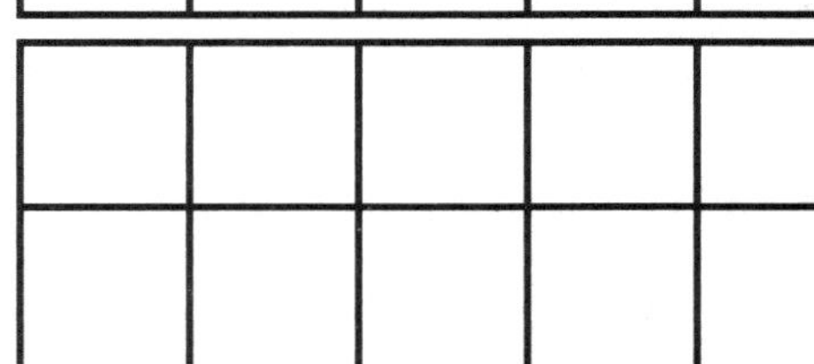

_____ 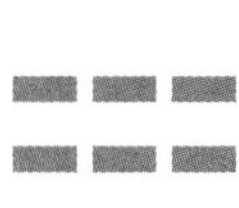 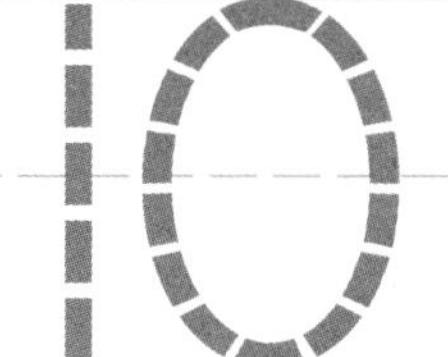  _____

Directions: 1 Circle 10 flowers. Draw dots in the top ten frame to show how many flowers are circled. Draw dots in the bottom ten frame to show how many more flowers there are. Use the ten frames to write an addition sentence.

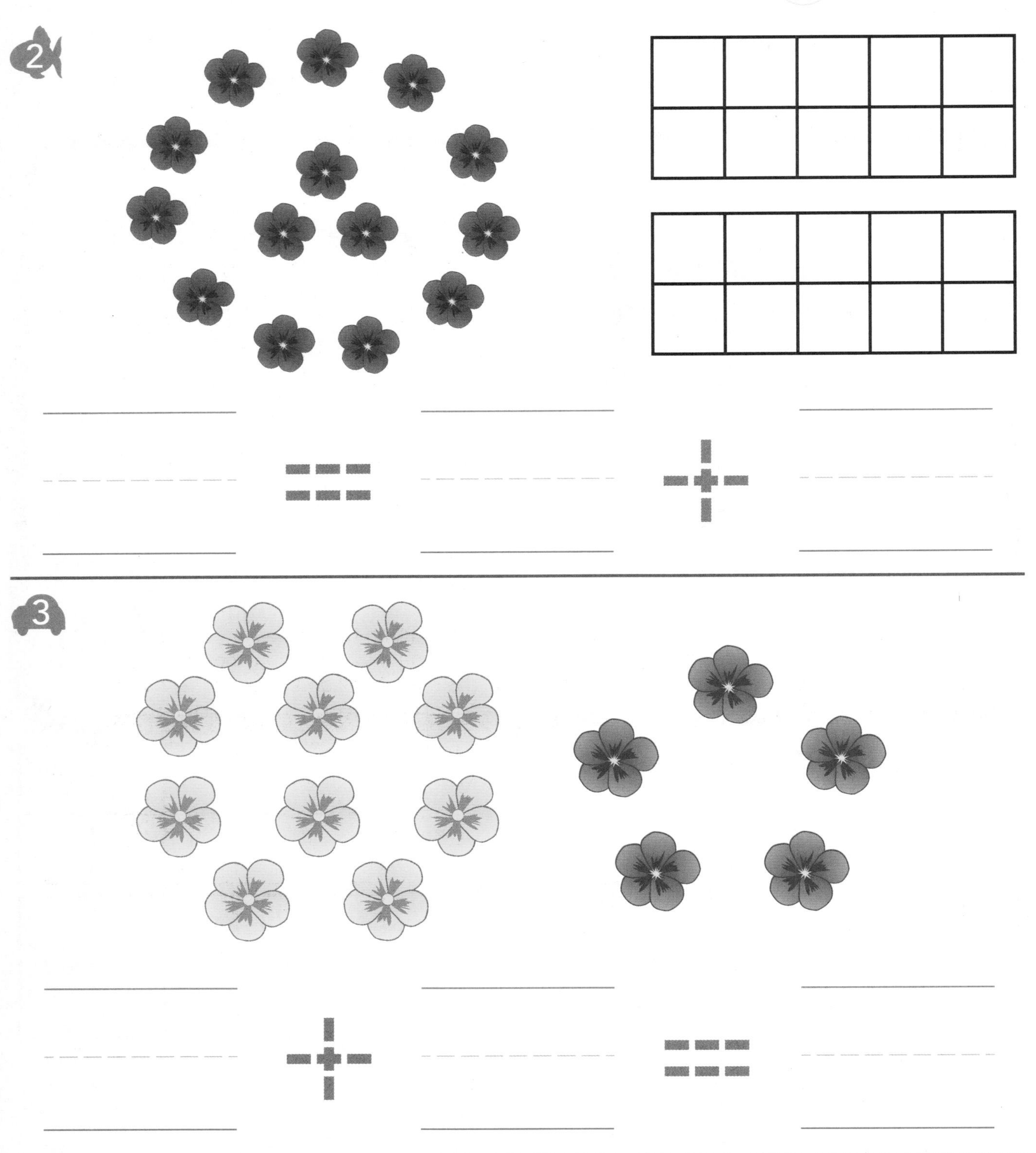

Directions: 2 Circle 10 flowers. Draw dots in the top ten frame to show how many flowers are circled. Draw dots in the bottom ten frame to show how many more flowers there are. Use the ten frames to write an addition sentence. 3 You have yellow flowers. Your friend has red flowers. Circle your flowers. Write an addition sentence to match the picture. How many flowers do you and your friend have in all? Circle the number.

Name ______________________________

Count and Write 16 and 17

8.8

Learning Target: Count and write the numbers 16 and 17.

Explore and Grow

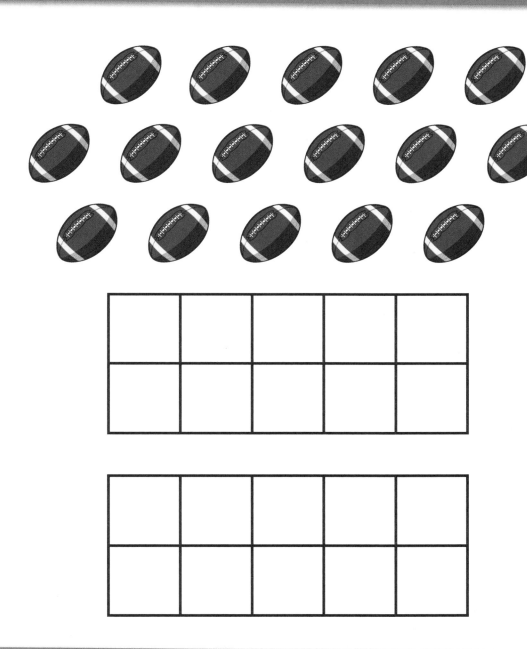

Directions: Place a linking cube on each football. Slide cubes to fill the top ten frame. Slide the extra cubes to the bottom ten frame.

Think and Grow

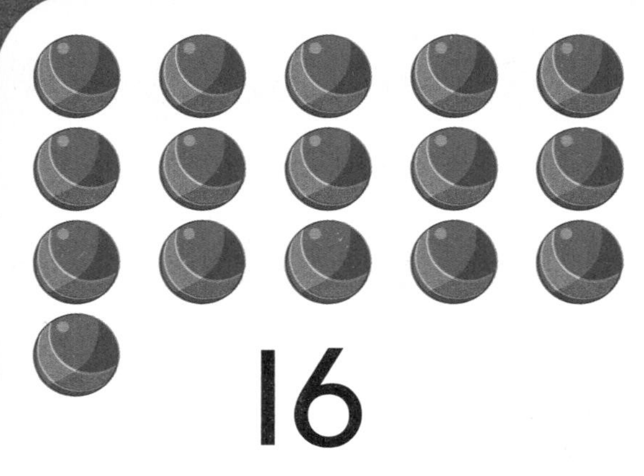

16

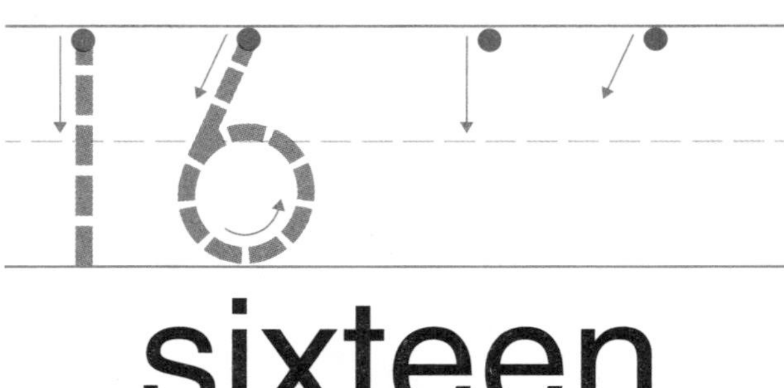

sixteen

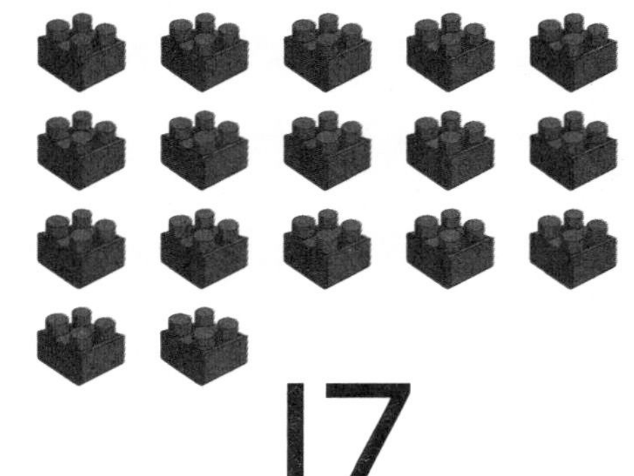

17

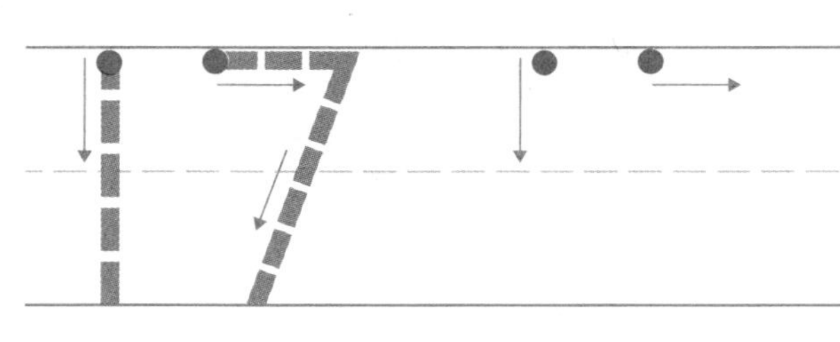

seventeen

Directions:

- Count the objects. Say the number. Trace and write the number.
- Count the objects. Say the number. Write the number.

Name ____________________

Apply and Grow: Practice

Directions:  Count the objects. Say the number. Write the number.

Think and Grow: Modeling Real Life

Directions: There are 17 blocks on the floor and 16 books on the shelves. Draw the blocks and the books. Then write the numbers.

Name ______________________

Learning Target: Count and write the numbers 16 and 17.

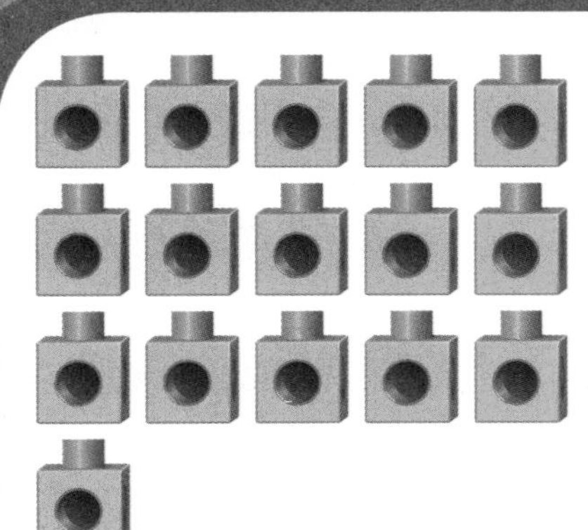

sixteen

16

seventeen

17

Directions: Count the linking cubes. Say the number. Write the number.

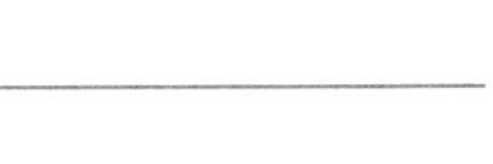

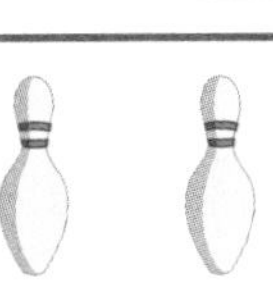

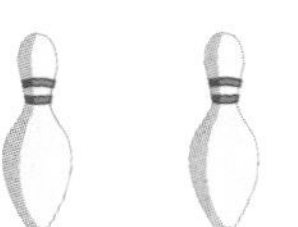

Directions: 1 and 2 Count the objects. Say the number. Write the number.

3

4

5

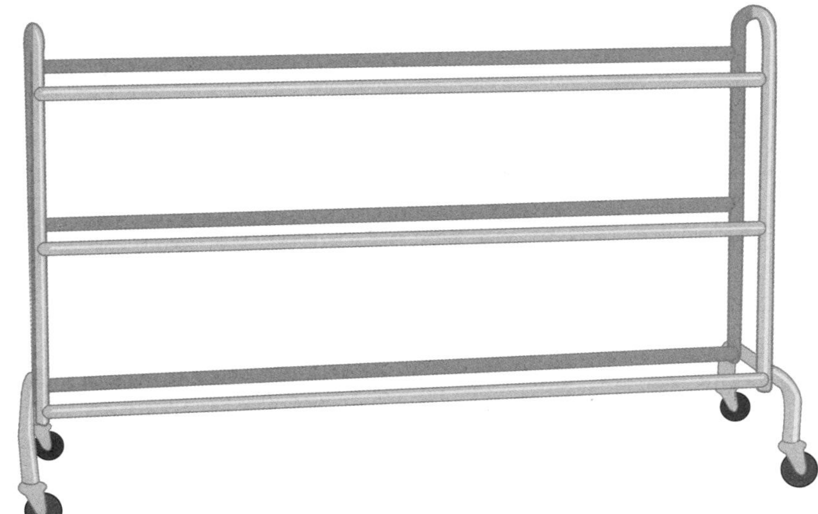

Directions: 3 and 4 Count the objects. Say the number. Write the number.
5 Draw 17 balls on the ball rack. Write the number.

Name ______________________

Learning Target: Understand the numbers 16 and 17.

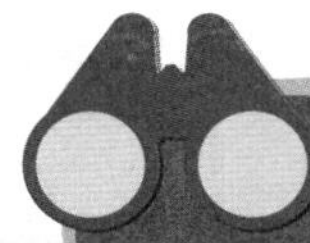

Explore and Grow

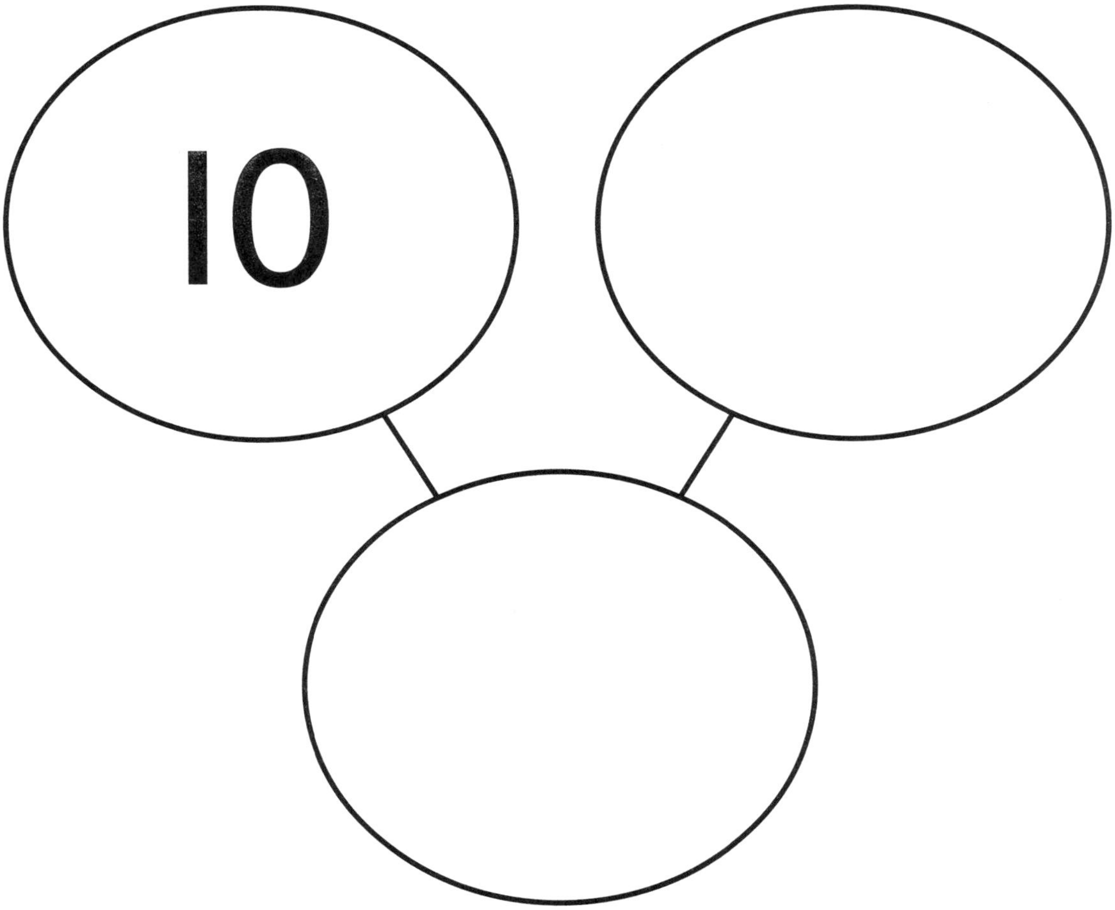

10

10 and ______ is ______.

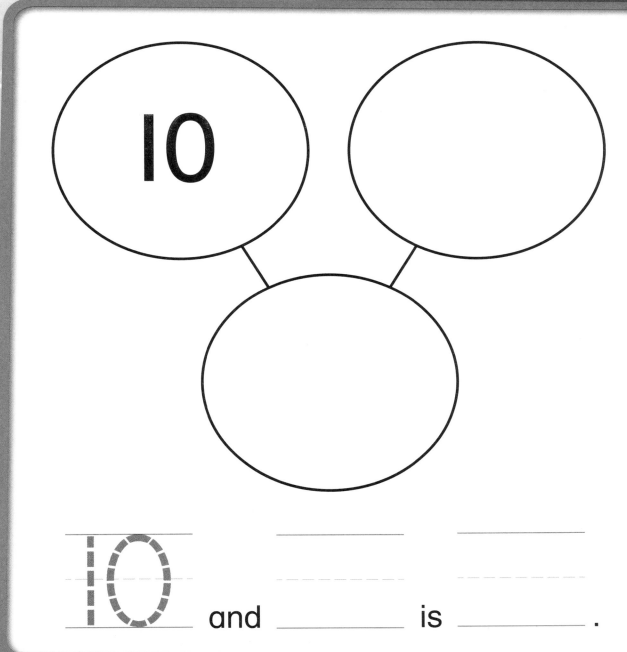

Directions: Place the 10 and 6 cards as the parts on the number bond. Slide the cards and hide the zero with the 6 card to make the whole. Write the parts and the whole.

10 ones

6 ones

16 = 10 + 6

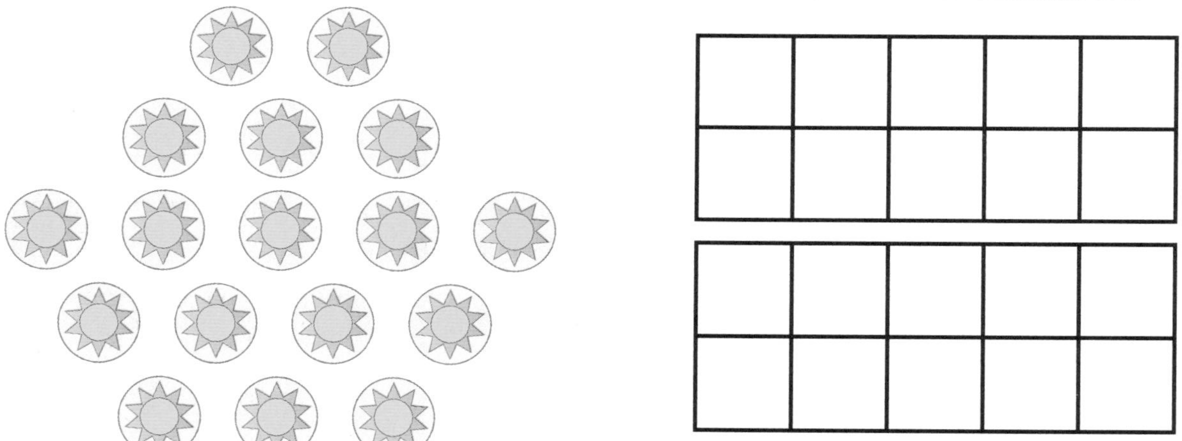

___ = 10 + ___

Directions: Circle 10 objects. Draw dots in the top ten frame to show how many objects are circled. Draw dots in the bottom ten frame to show how many more objects there are. Use the ten frames to write an addition sentence.

Name ______________________________

Apply and Grow: Practice

1

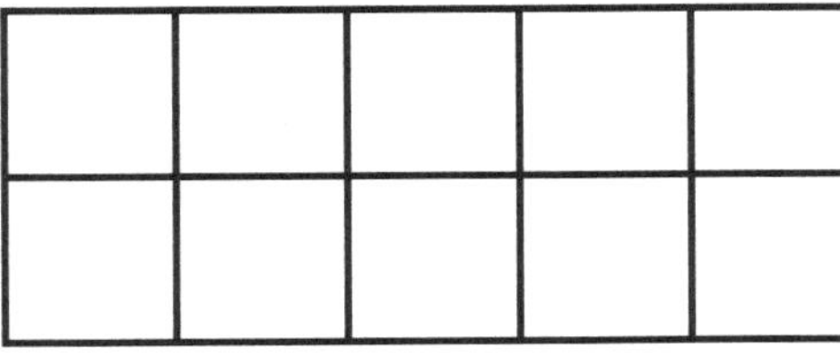

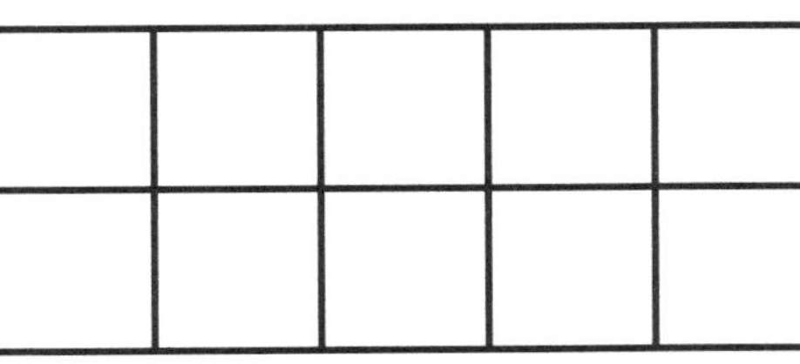

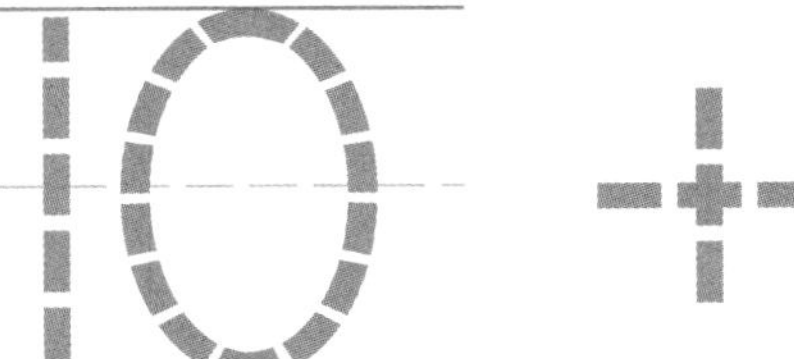

2

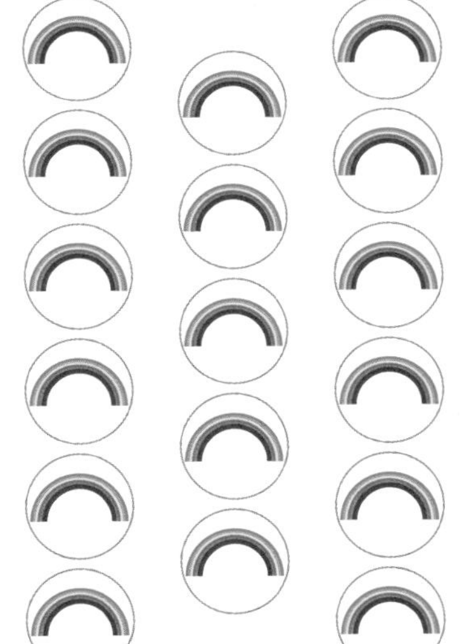

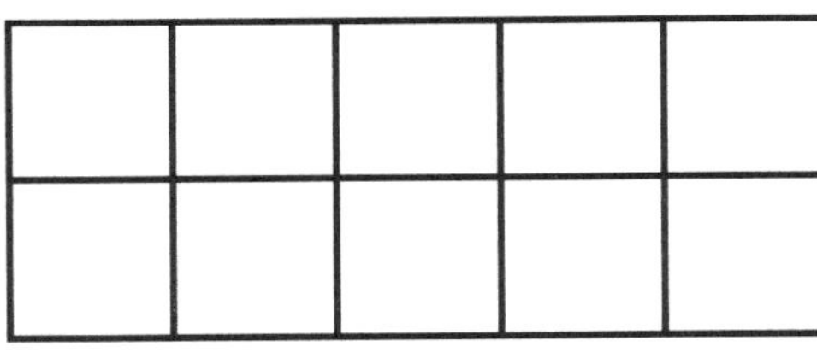

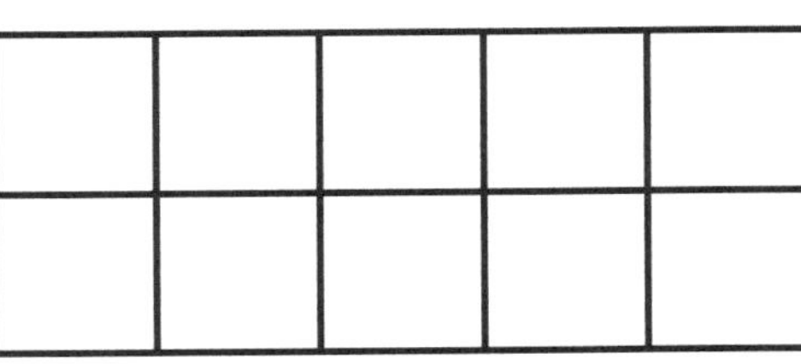

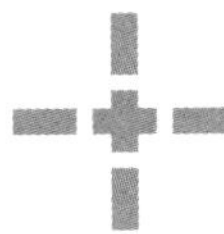

Directions: 1 and 2 Circle 10 objects. Draw dots in the top ten frame to show how many objects are circled. Draw dots in the bottom ten frame to show how many more objects there are. Use the ten frames to write an addition sentence.

Think and Grow: Modeling Real Life

Directions:

- You put yellow stickers on a page. Your friend puts red stickers on the same page. Circle your stickers. Write an addition sentence to match the picture. How many stickers does your friend put on the page? Circle the number.
- You put blue stickers on a page. Your friend puts green stickers on the same page. Circle your stickers. Write an addition sentence to match the picture. How many stickers does your friend put on the page? Circle the number.

Name ______________________________

Practice 8.9

Learning Target: Understand the numbers 16 and 17.

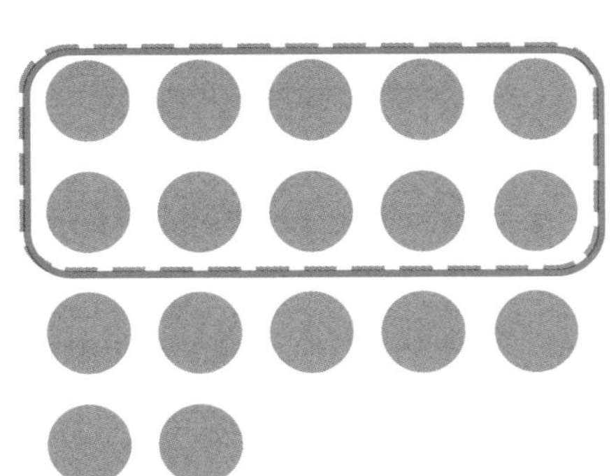

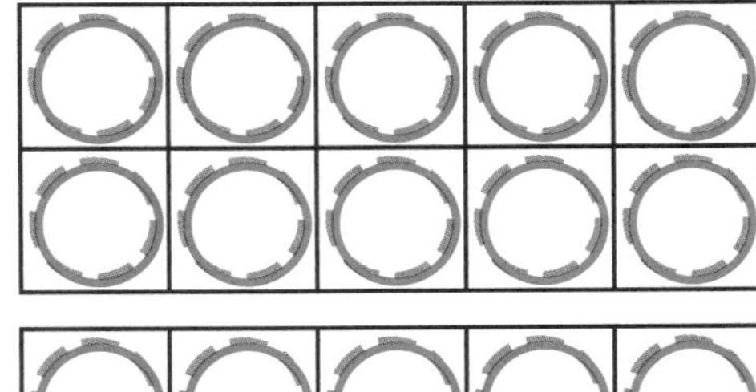

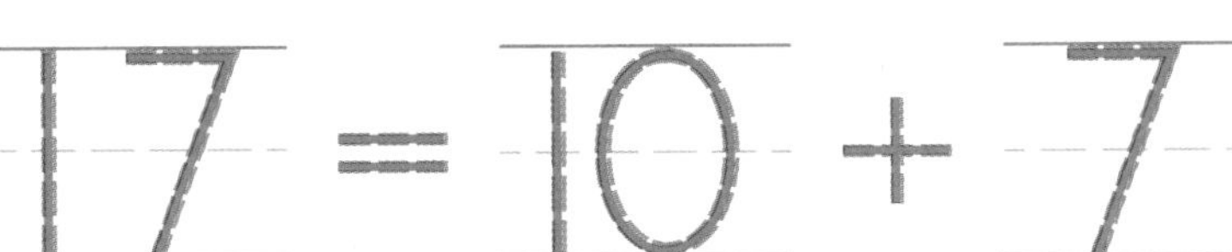

17 = 10 + 7

Directions: Circle 10 objects. Draw dots in the top ten frame to show how many objects are circled. Draw dots in the bottom ten frame to show how many objects are not circled. Use the ten frames to complete the addition sentence.

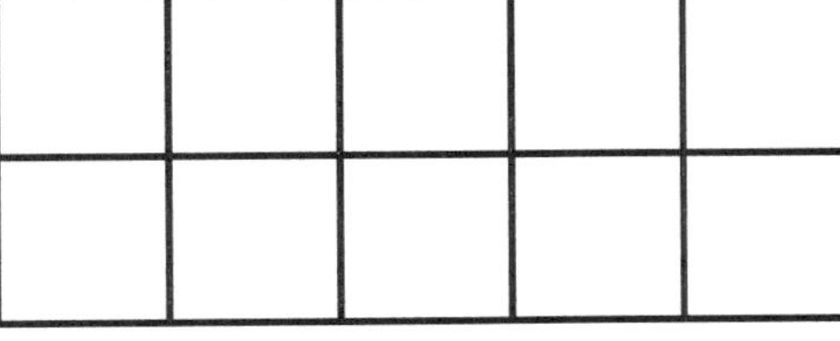

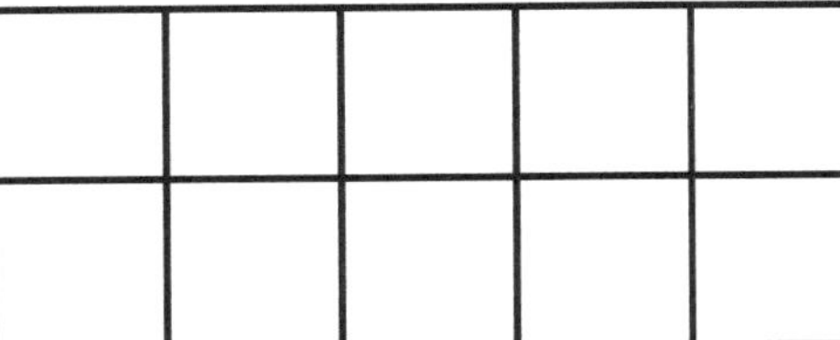

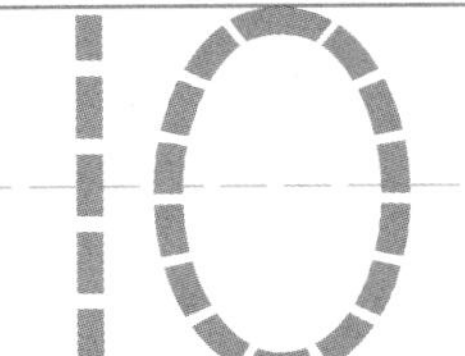

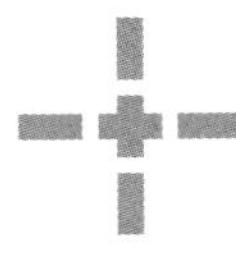

____ = 10 + ____

Directions: 1 Circle 10 stars. Draw dots in the top ten frame to show how many stars are circled. Draw dots in the bottom ten frame to show how many more stars there are. Use the ten frames to write an addition sentence.

2

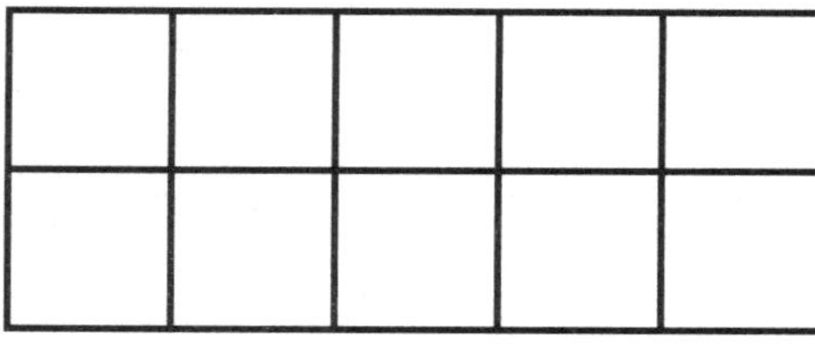

3

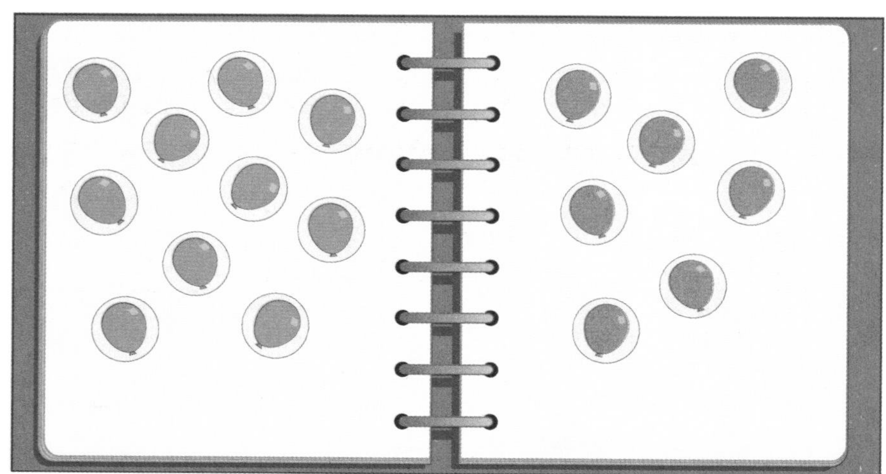

Directions: 2 Circle 10 butterflies. Draw dots in the top ten frame to show how many butterflies are circled. Draw dots in the bottom ten frame to show how many more butterflies there are. Use the ten frames to write an addition sentence. 3 You put orange stickers on a page. Your friend puts blue stickers on the next page. Circle your stickers. Write an addition sentence to match the picture. How many stickers does your friend put on the next page? Circle the number.

Name ______________________

Count and Write 18 and 19

8.10

Learning Target: Count and write the numbers 18 and 19.

Explore and Grow

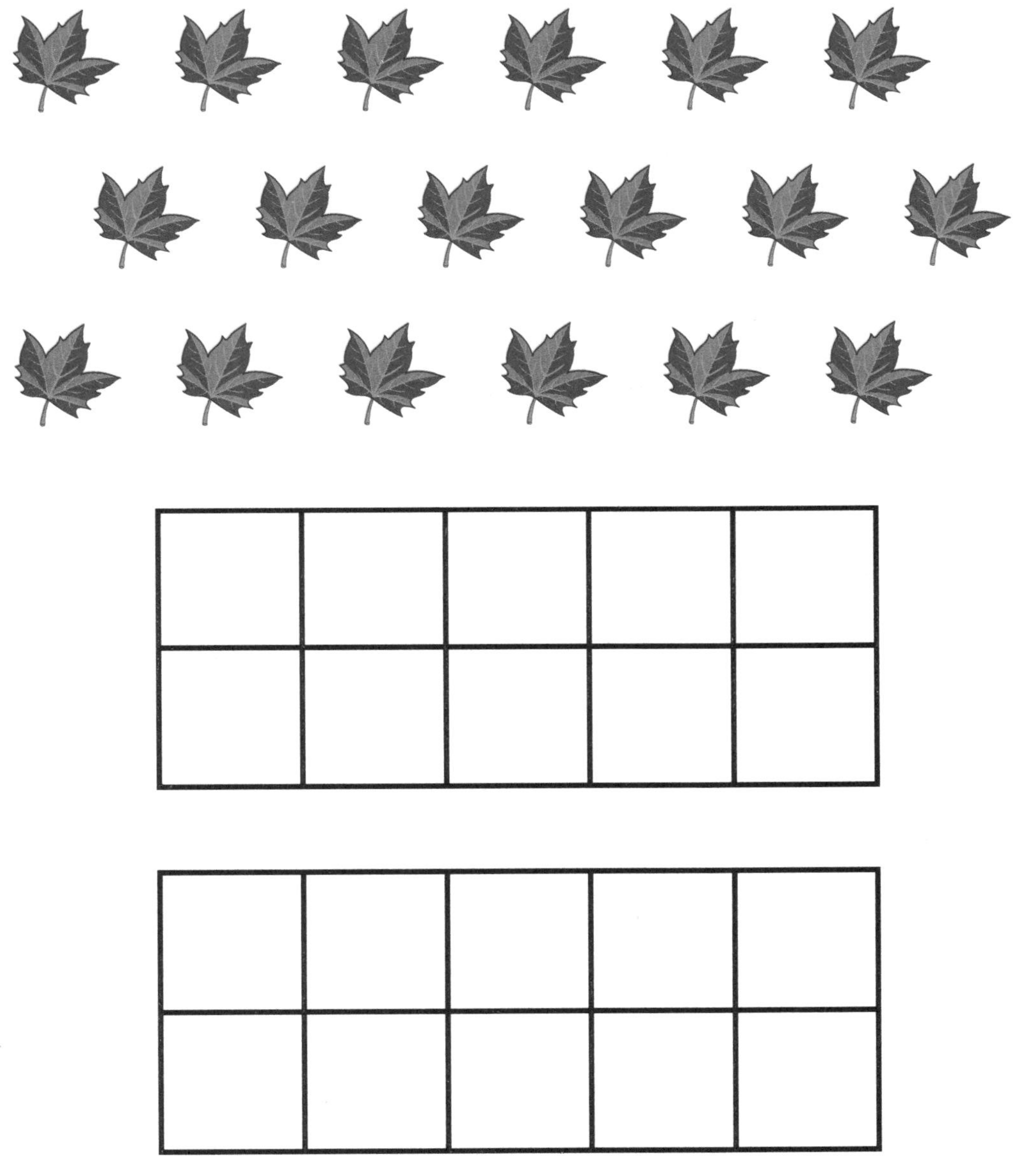

Directions: Place a linking cube on each leaf. Slide cubes to fill the top ten frame. Slide the extra cubes to the bottom ten frame.

Think and Grow

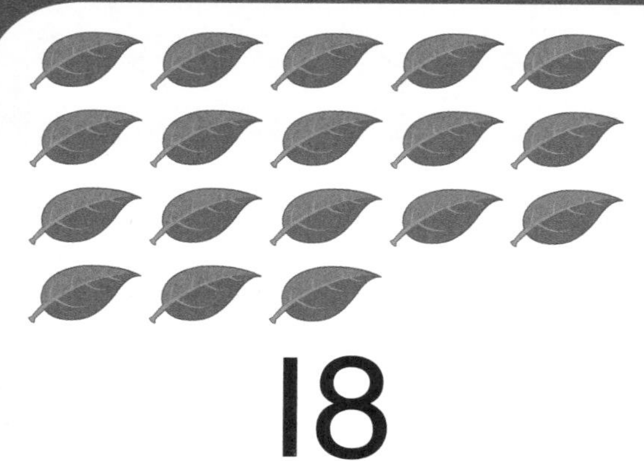

18

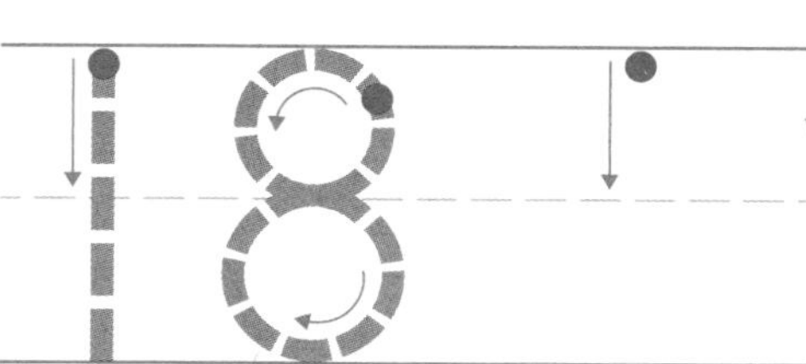

eighteen

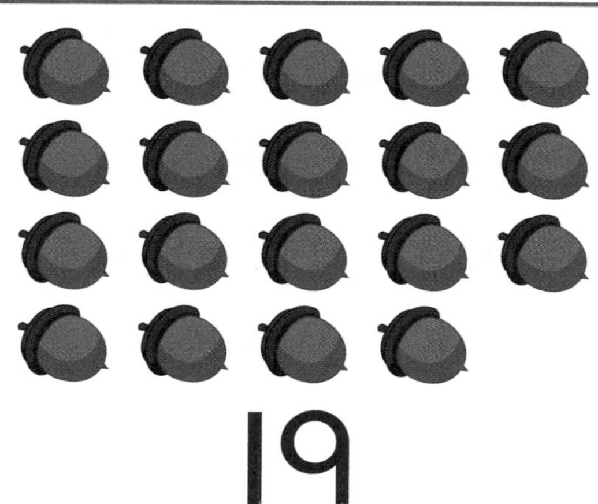

19

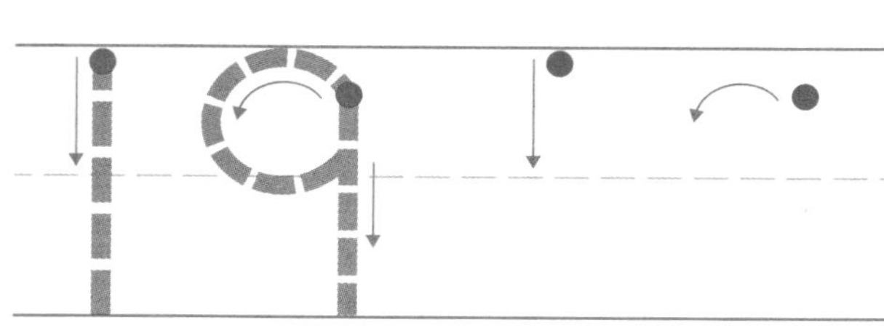

nineteen

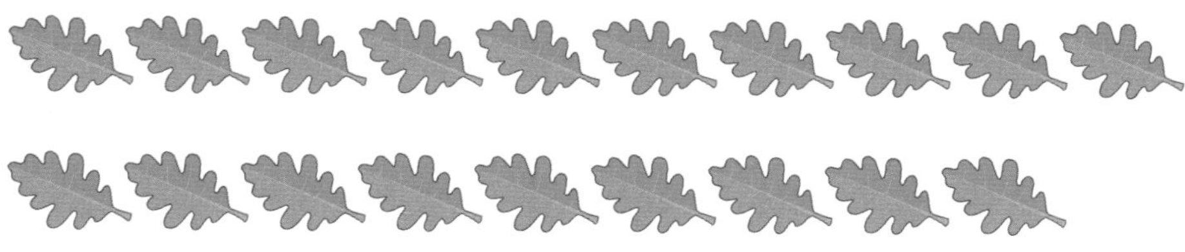

Directions:

- Count the objects. Say the number. Trace and write the number.
- Count the objects. Say the number. Write the number.

Name ______________________________

Apply and Grow: Practice

1

2

3

4

Directions: 1–4 Count the objects. Say the number. Write the number.

Think and Grow: Modeling Real Life

Directions: There are 19 red leaves on the ground. There are 18 orange leaves left on the tree. Draw the leaves on the ground and the leaves on the tree. Write the numbers.

Name ___________________________

Practice 8.10

Learning Target: Count and write the numbers 18 and 19.

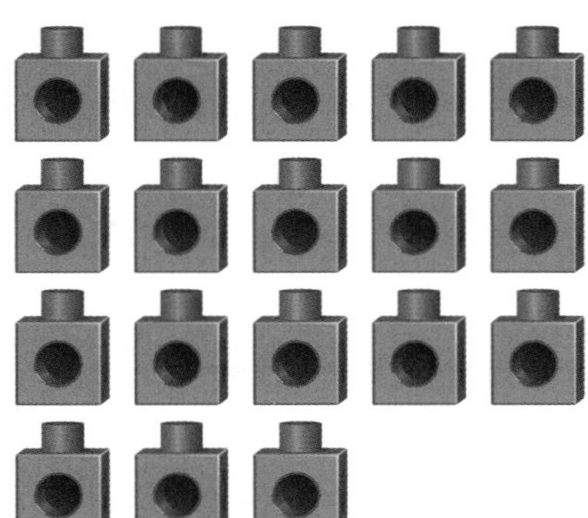

eighteen

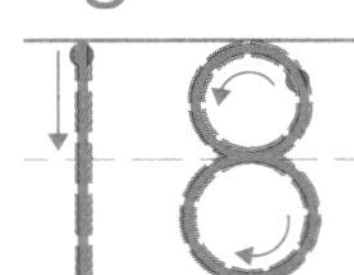

nineteen

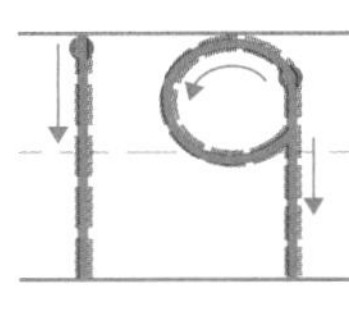

Directions: Count the objects. Say the number. Write the number.

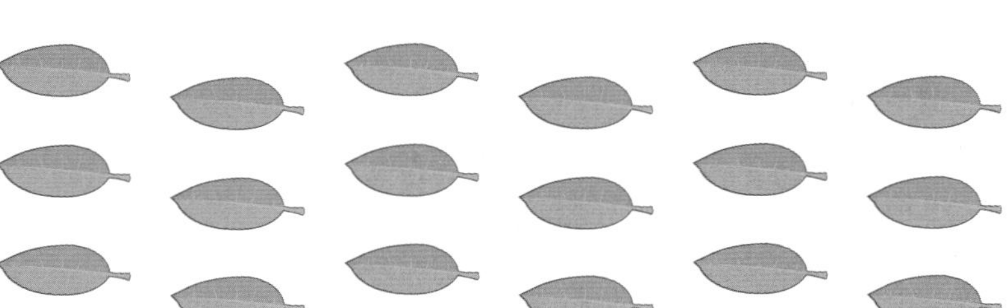

Directions: 1 and 2 Count the objects. Say the number. Write the number.

3

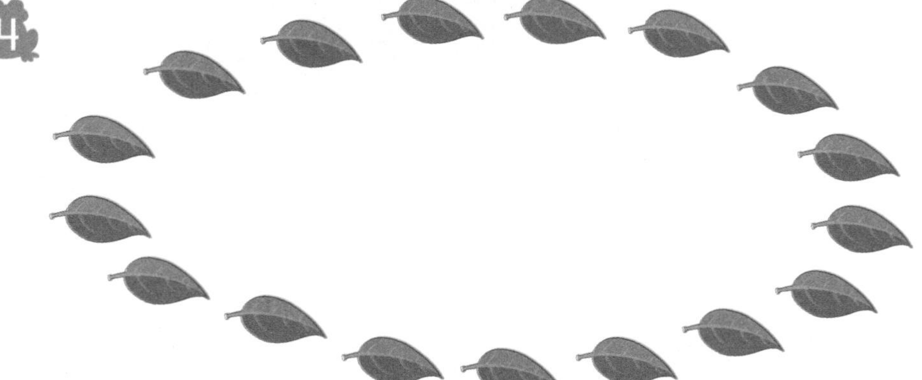

5

Directions: 3 and 4 Count the objects. Say the number. Write the number.
5 Draw 18 acorns on the ground. Write the number.

Name ______________________

Learning Target: Understand the numbers 18 and 19.

Explore and Grow

10

10 and ______ is ______ .

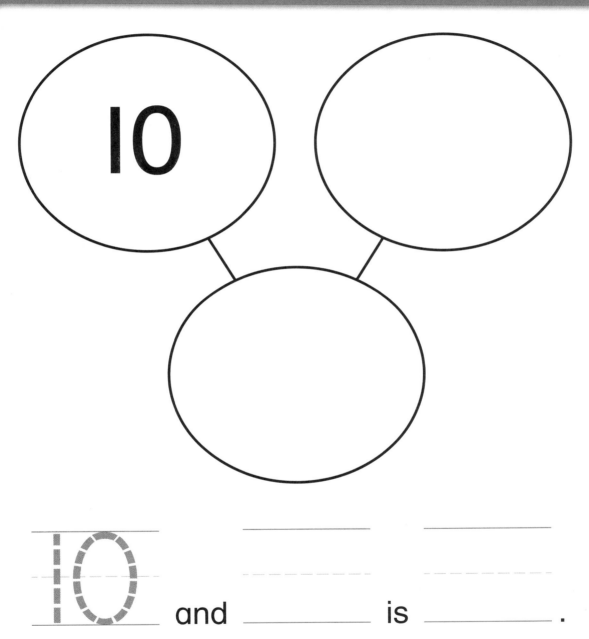

Directions: Place the 10 and 8 cards as the parts on the number bond. Slide the cards and hide the zero with the 8 card to make the whole. Write the parts and the whole.

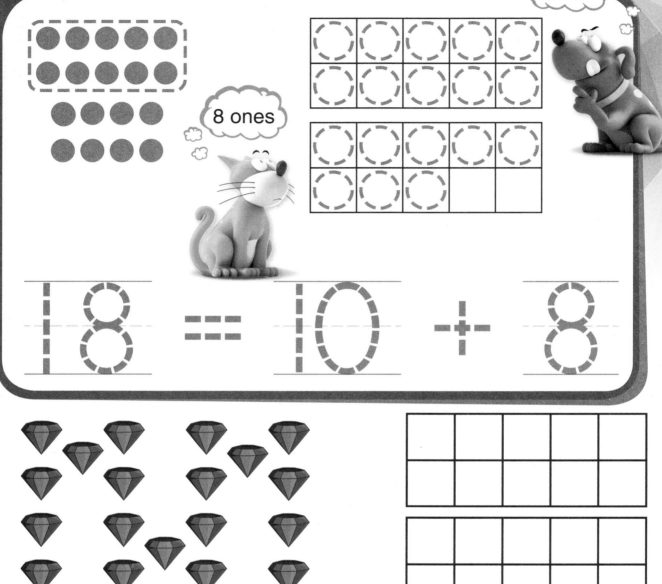

Think and Grow

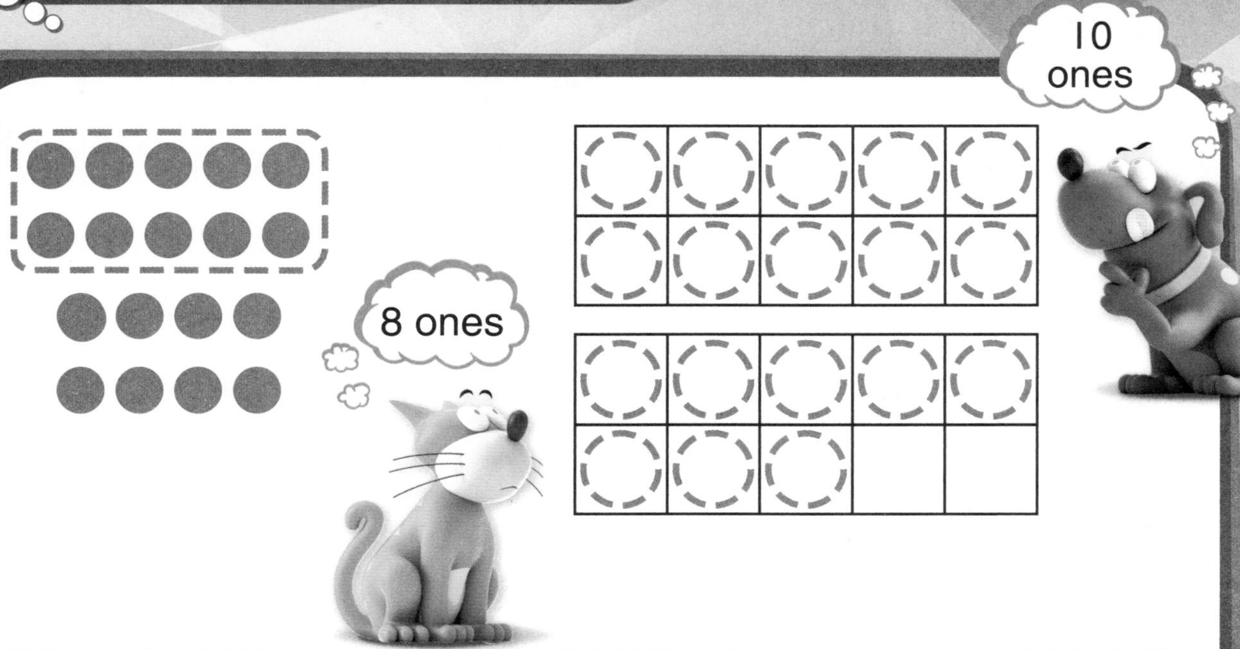

18 = 10 + 8

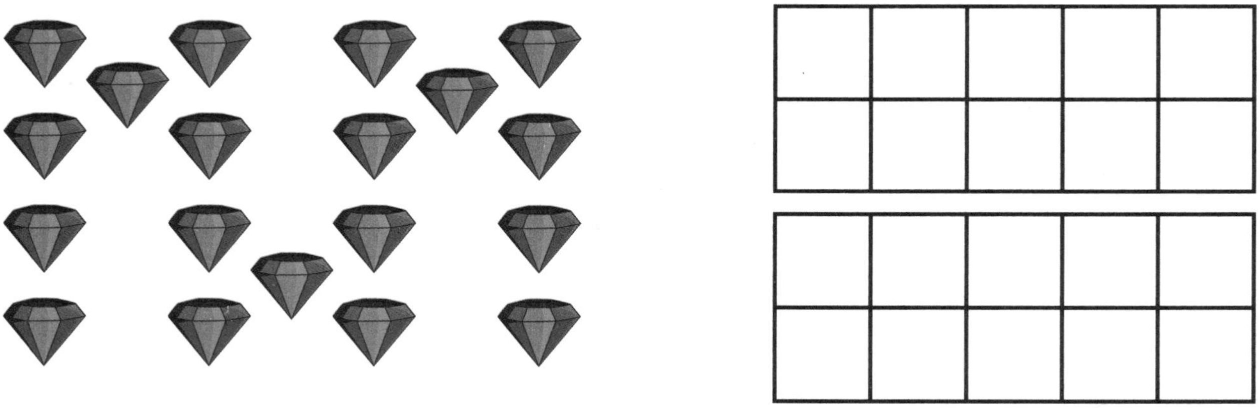

___ = 10 + ___

Directions: Circle 10 objects. Draw dots in the top ten frame to show how many objects are circled. Draw dots in the bottom ten frame to show how many more objects there are. Use the ten frames to write an addition sentence.

Name ______________________________

Apply and Grow: Practice

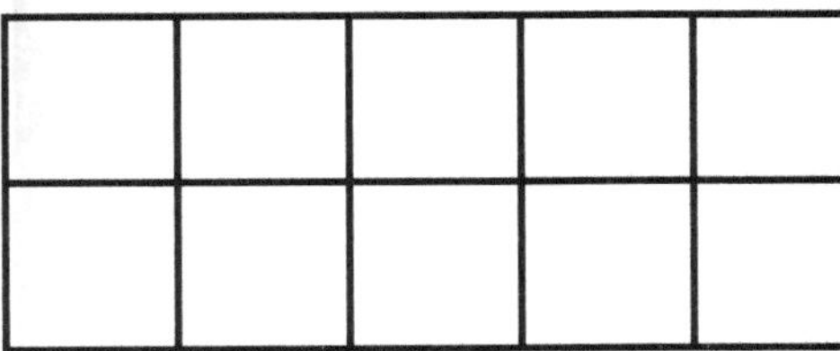

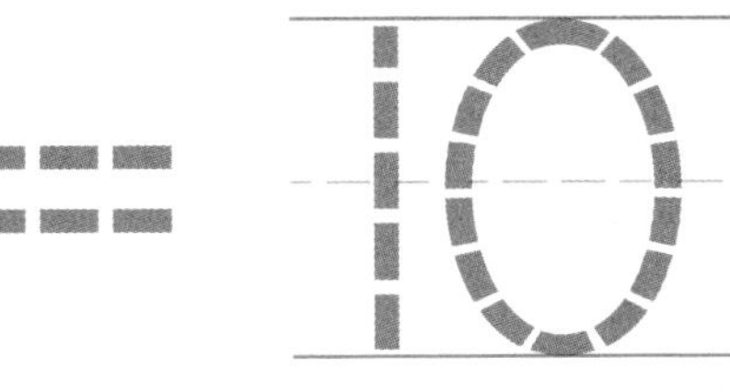

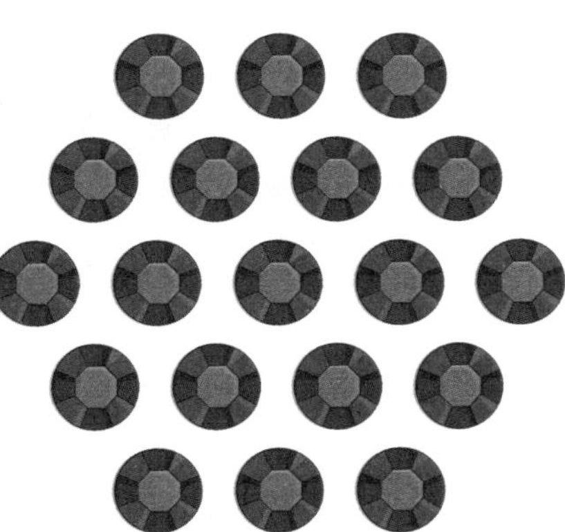

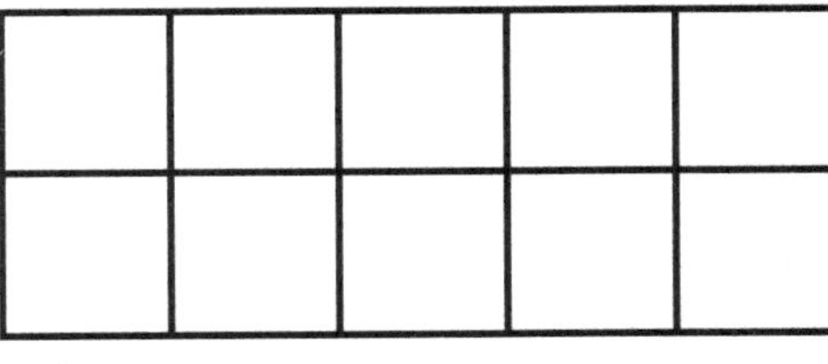

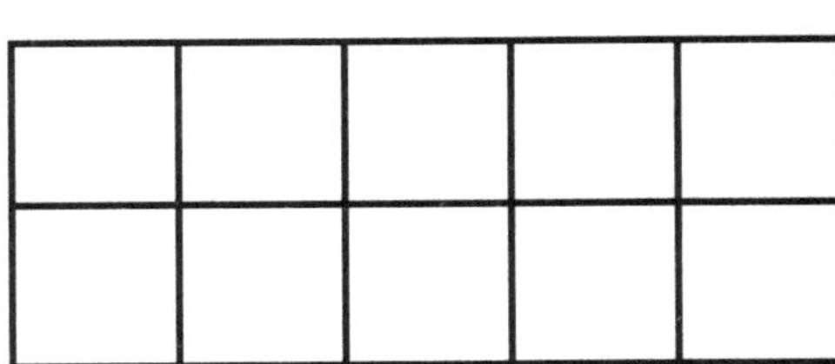

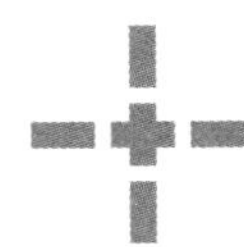

Directions: 1 and 2 Circle 10 gemstones. Draw dots in the top ten frame to show how many gemstones are circled. Draw dots in the bottom ten frame to show how many more gemstones there are. Use the ten frames to write an addition sentence.

Think and Grow: Modeling Real Life

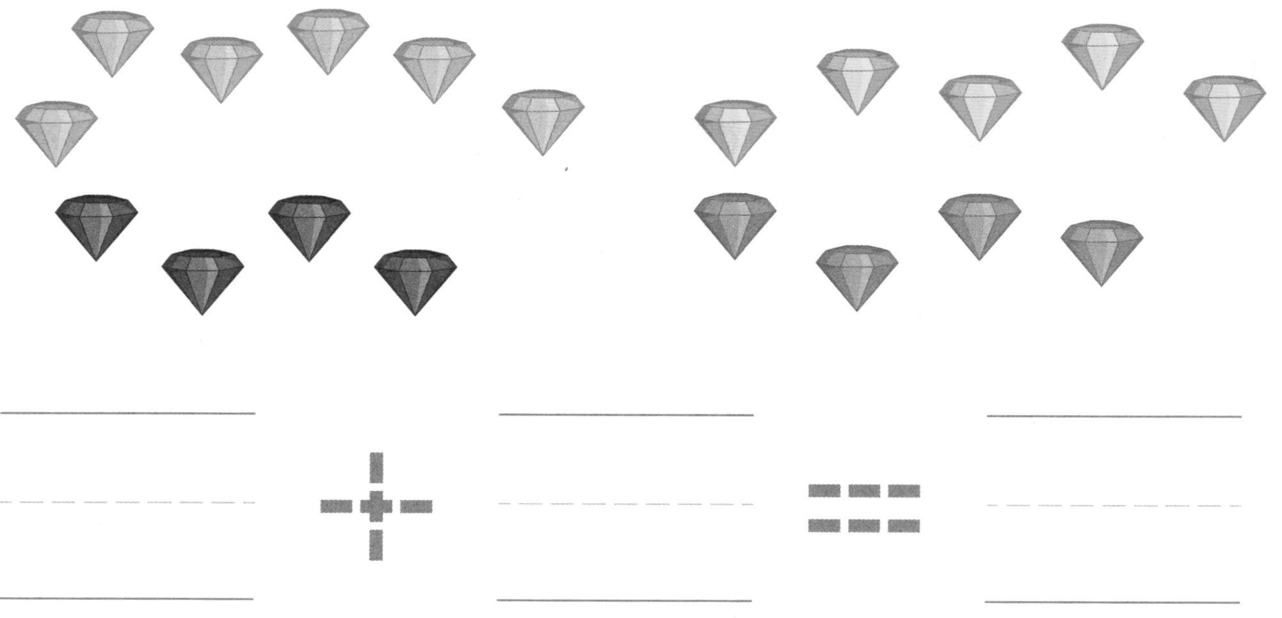

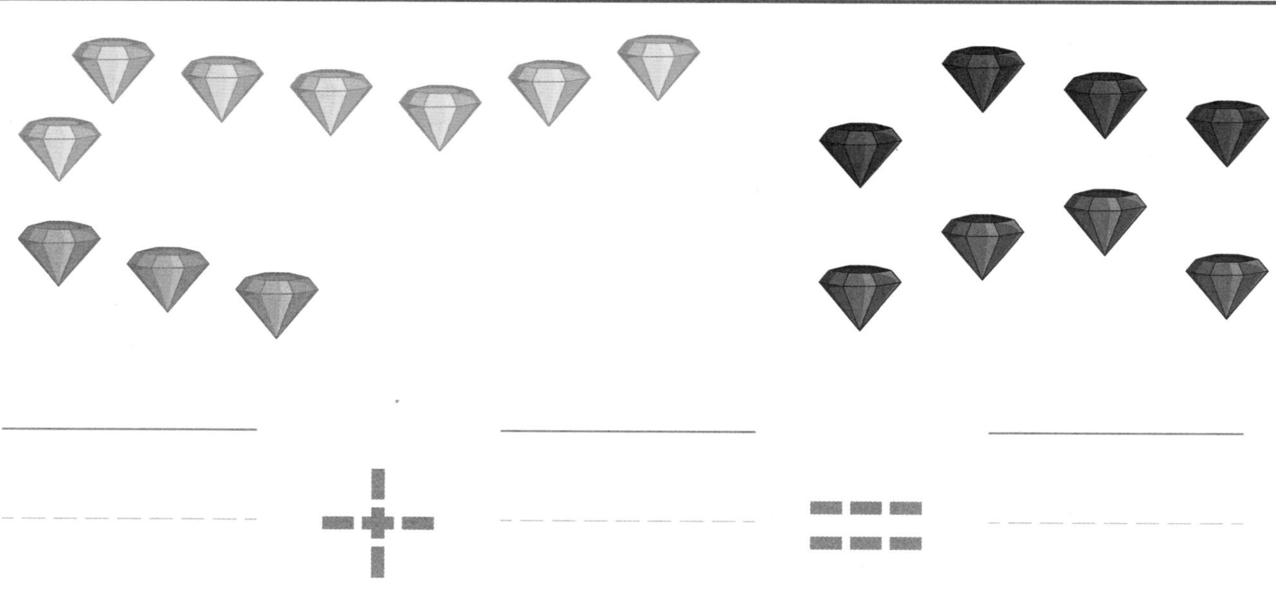

Directions:

- You have pink gemstones and blue gemstones. Your friend has silver gemstones and gold gemstones. Circle your gemstones. Write an addition sentence to match the picture. How many gemstones do you have? Circle the number.
- You have gold gemstones and silver gemstones. Your friend has purple gemstones and green gemstones. Circle your gemstones. Write an addition sentence to match the picture. How many gemstones does your friend have? Circle the number.

Name ______________________

Learning Target: Understand the numbers 18 and 19.

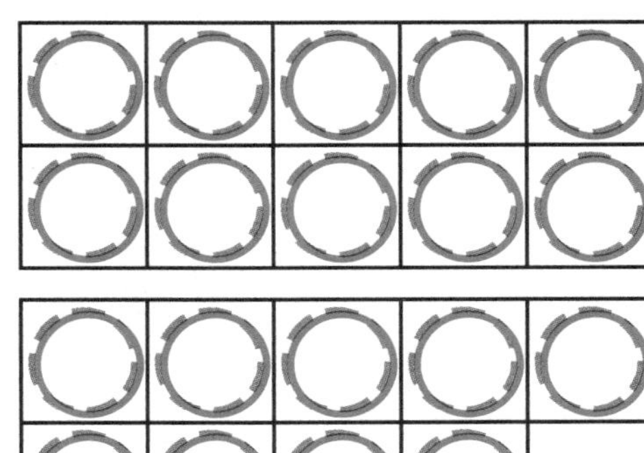

19 = 10 + 9

Directions: Circle 10 objects. Draw dots in the top ten frame to show how many objects are circled. Draw dots in the bottom ten frame to show how many more objects there are. Use the ten frames to complete the addition sentence.

1

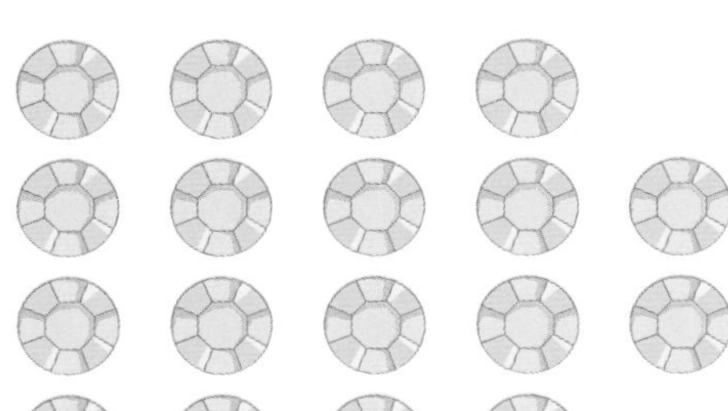

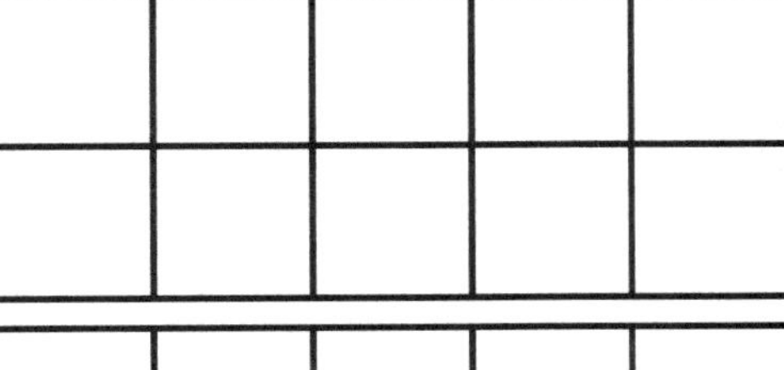

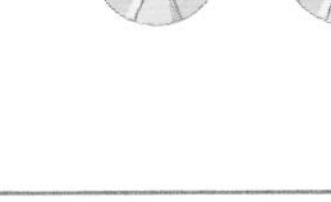

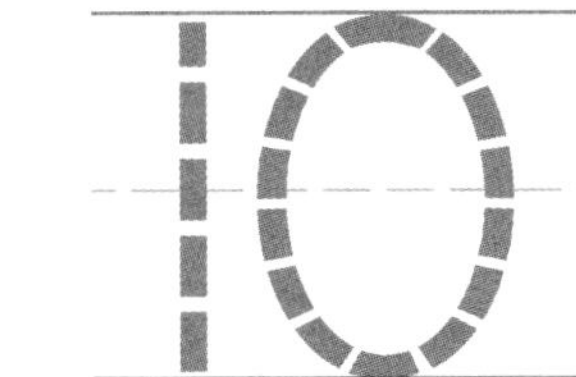

_____ = 10 + _____

Directions: 1 Circle 10 gemstones. Draw dots in the ten frame to show how many gemstones are circled. Draw dots in the bottom ten frame to show how many more gemstones there are. Use the ten frames to write an addition sentence.

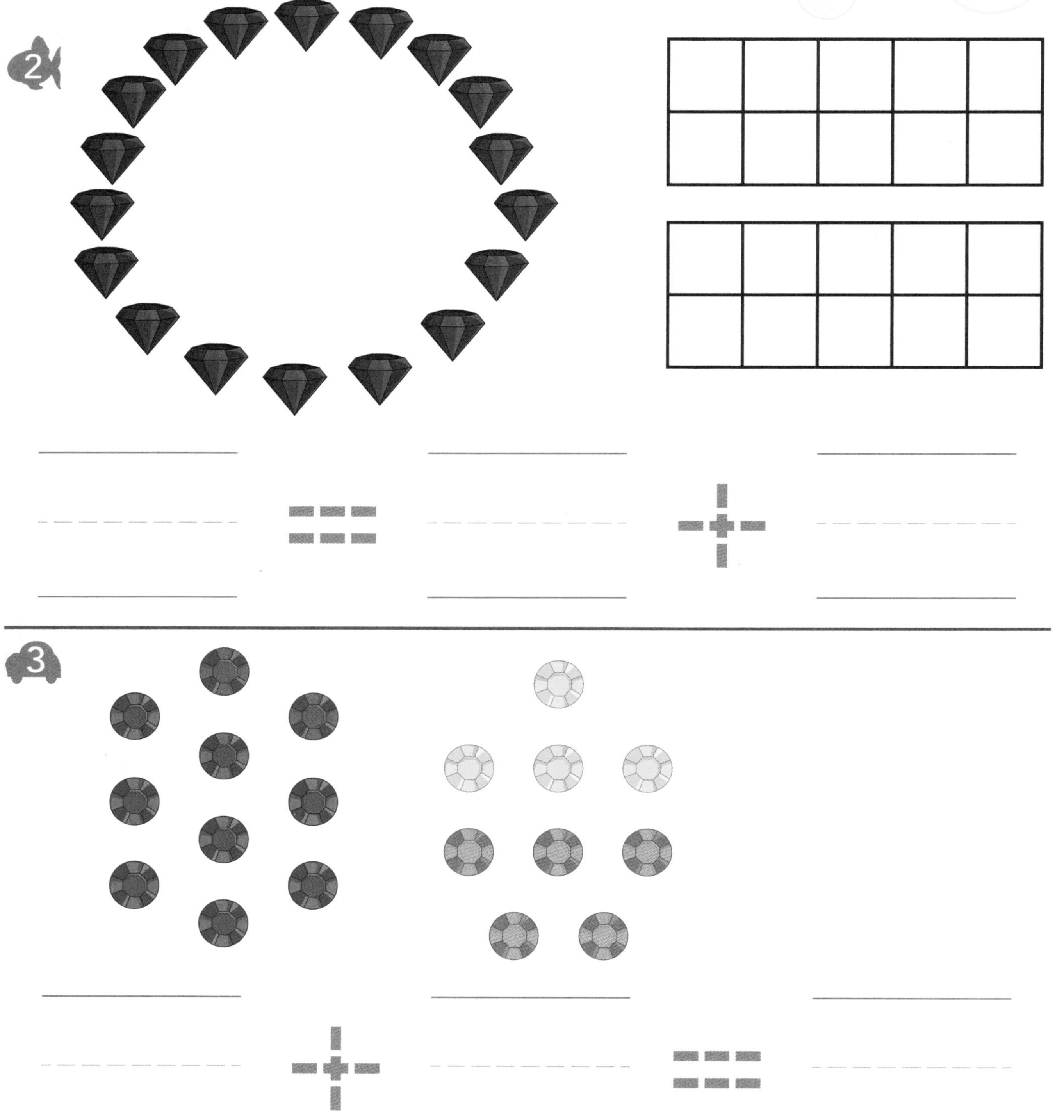

Directions: 2 Circle 10 gemstones. Draw dots in the top ten frame to show how many gemstones are circled. Draw dots in the bottom ten frame to show how many more gemstones there are. Use the ten frames to write an addition sentence.
3 You have red gemstones and blue gemstones. Your friend has yellow gemstones and silver gemstones. Circle your gemstones. Write an addition sentence to match the picture. How many gemstones does your friend have? Circle the number.

Name ______________________

Performance Task 8

1

______ + ______ = ______

2

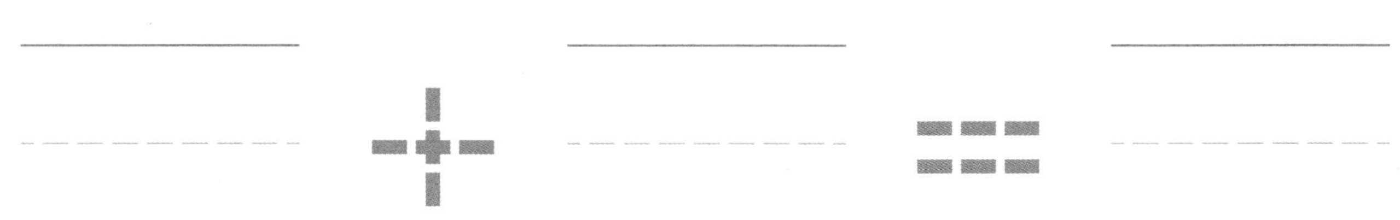

______ + ______ = ______

Directions: 1 Classify the stars into 2 categories. Circle to show each group. Then write an addition sentence to tell how many stars there are in all. 2 There are red stars and blue stars in the sky. The number of red stars is 1 more than 9. The number of blue stars is greater than 5, but less than the number of red stars. Draw and color the stars. Then write an addition sentence to tell how many stars there are in all.

Number Flip and Find

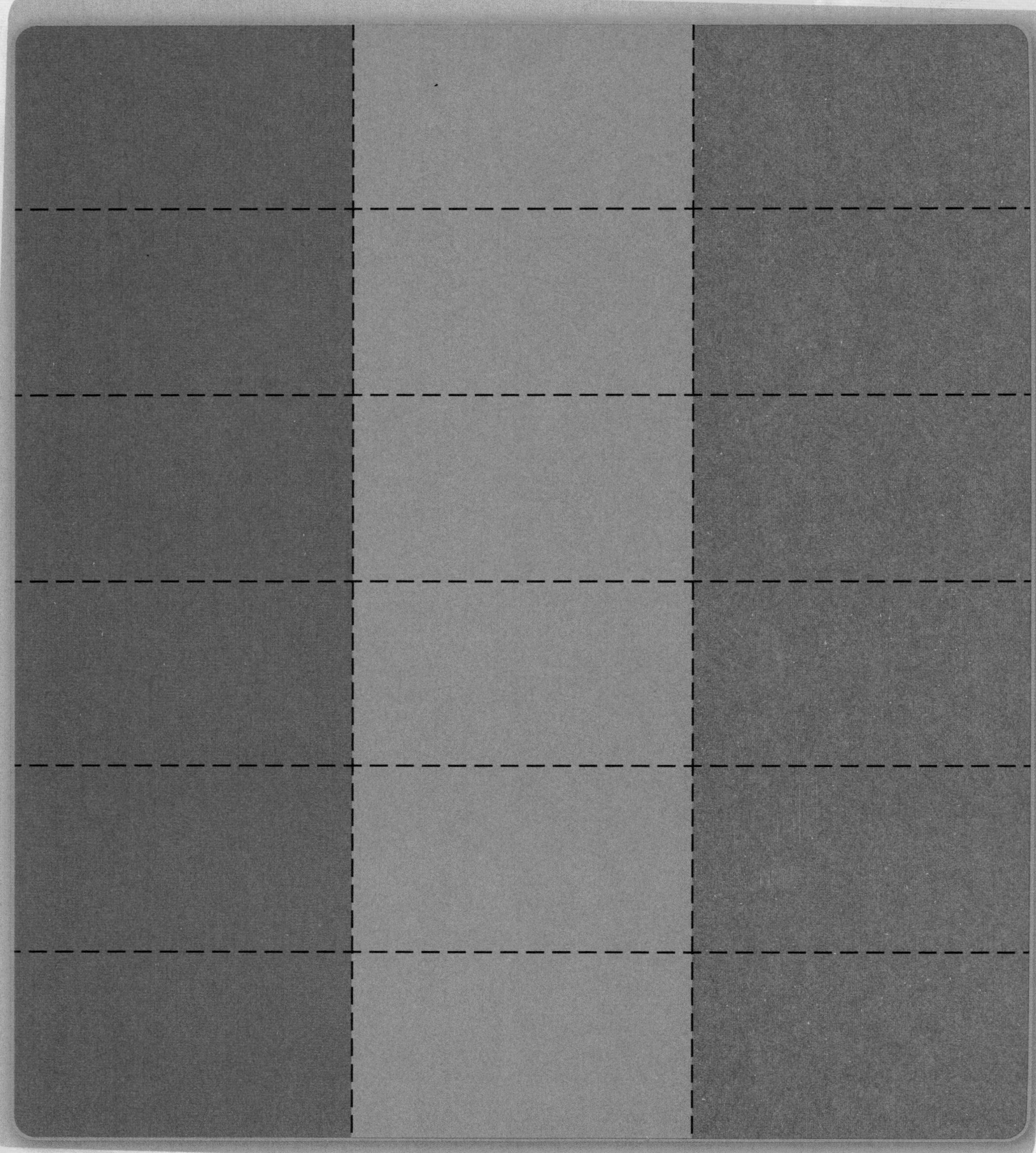

Directions: Place the Number Flip and Find Cards facedown in the boxes. Take turns flipping 2 cards. If your cards show the same number, keep the cards. If your cards show different numbers, flip the cards back over. Repeat this until all cards are gone.

Name ______________________

Chapter Practice 8

8.1 Identify Groups of 10

1

10 ones and ______ ones

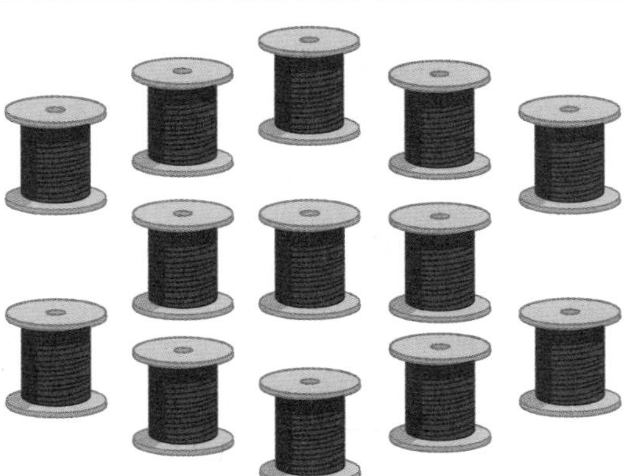

______ ones and ______ ones

Directions: 1 and 2 Circle 10 objects. Tell how many more objects there are. Then write the numbers.

8.2 Count and Write 11 and 12

8.3 Understand 11 and 12

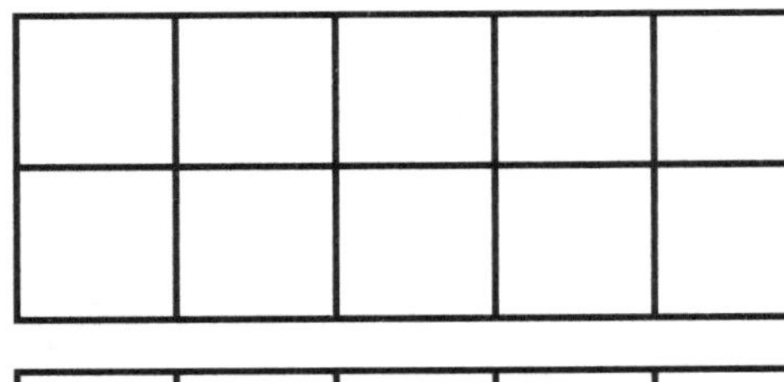

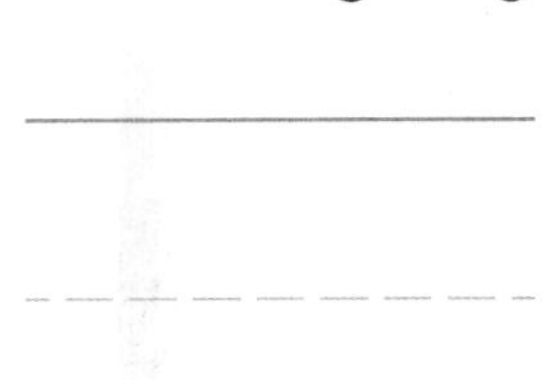

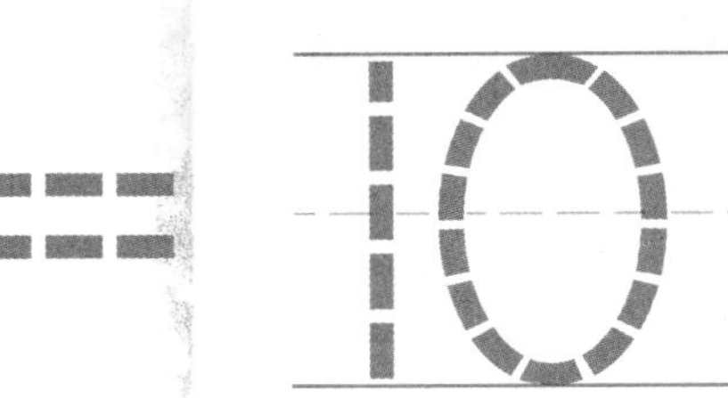

Directions: 3 and 4 Count the fruit. Say the number. Write the number. 5 Circle 10 buses. Draw dots in the ten frame to show how many buses are circled. Draw dots in the five frame to show how many more buses there are. Use the frames to write an addition sentence.

8.4 Count and Write 13 and 14

6

7

8.5 Understand 13 and 14

8

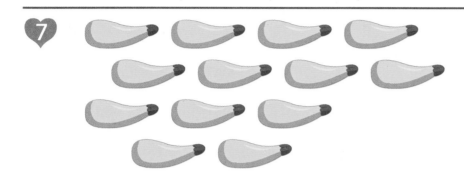

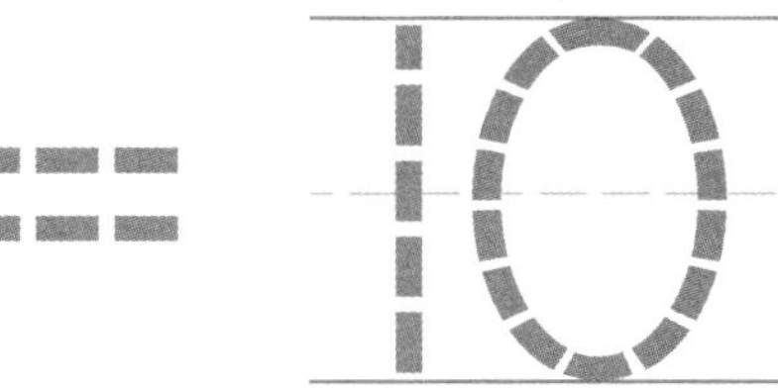

Directions: 6 and 7 Count the vegetables. Say the number. Write the number. 8 Circle 10 hats. Draw dots in the ten frame to show how many hats are circled. Draw dots in the five frame to show how many more hats there are. Use the frames to write an addition sentence.

8.6 Count and Write 15

8.7 Understand 15

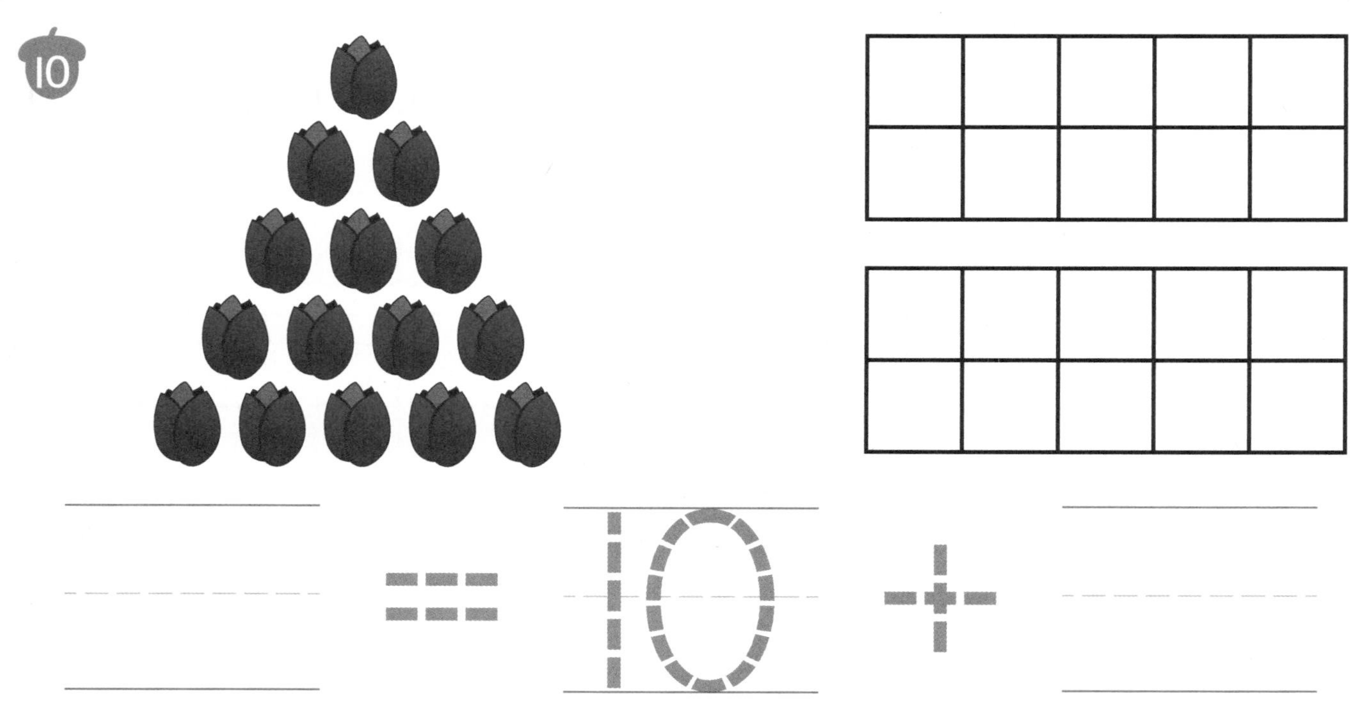

Directions: Count the fish. Say the number. Write the number. Circle 10 flowers. Draw dots in the top ten frame to show how many flowers are circled. Draw dots in the bottom ten frame to show how many more flowers there are. Use the ten frames to write an addition sentence.

8.8 Count and Write 16 and 17

11

8.9 Understand 16 and 17

12

Directions: 11 Count the yo-yos. Say the number. Write the number. 12 Circle 10 stickers. Draw dots in the top ten frame to show how many stickers are circled. Draw dots in the bottom ten frame to show how many more stickers there are. Use the ten frames to write an addition sentence.

 8.10 Count and Write 18 and 19

8.11 Understand 18 and 19

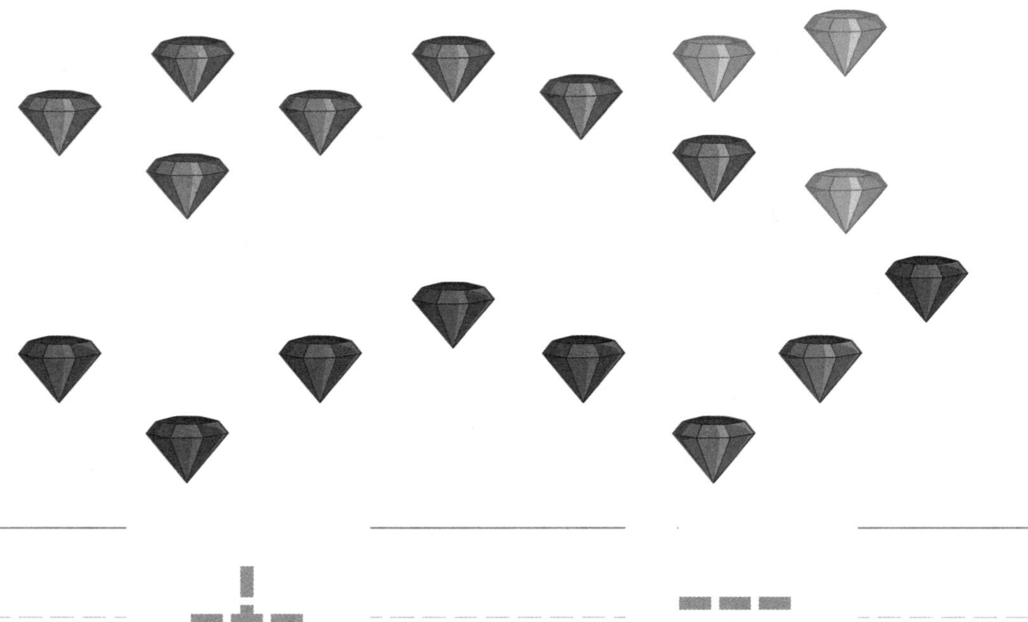

+ =

Directions: 13 Count the leaves. Say the number. Write the number. 14 You have blue gemstones and orange gemstones. Your friend has purple gemstones and green gemstones. Circle your gemstones. Write an addition sentence to match the picture. How many gemstones do you and your friend have in all? Circle the number.

9 Count and Compare Numbers to 20

Chapter Learning Target:
Understand counting.

Chapter Success Criteria:
- I can identify numbers.
- I can name numbers.
- I can show numbers with objects.
- I can order numbers.

- What is your favorite kind of fruit?
- How many apples are in the picture? Are there more red apples or green apples here?

Name ______________________

9 Vocabulary

Review Words
equal
greater than

Directions: Count the fruit in each group. Write each number. Is the number of apples equal to the number of bananas? Circle the thumbs up for *yes* or the thumbs down for *no*. Circle the number that is greater than the other number.

Chapter 9 Vocabulary Cards

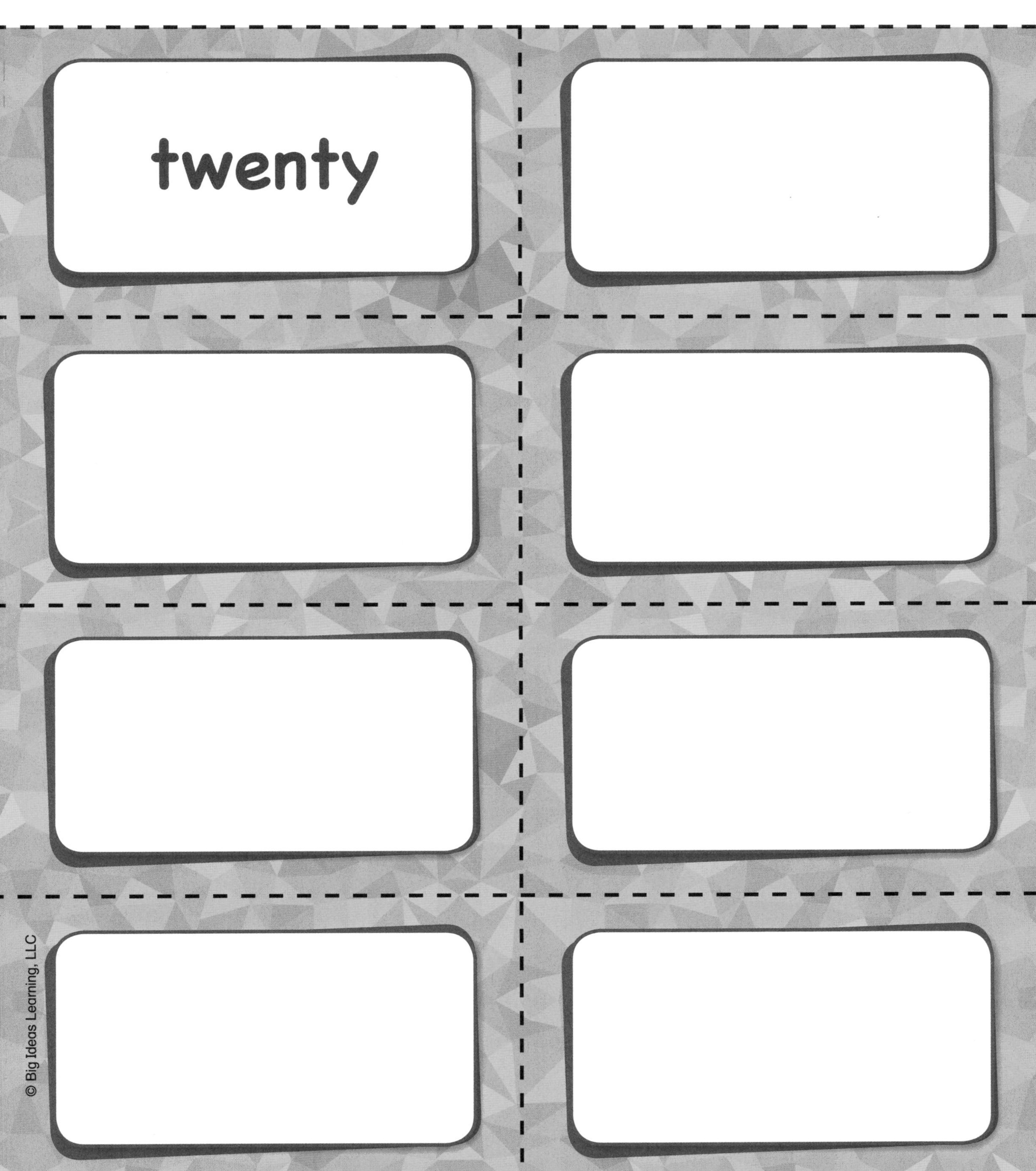

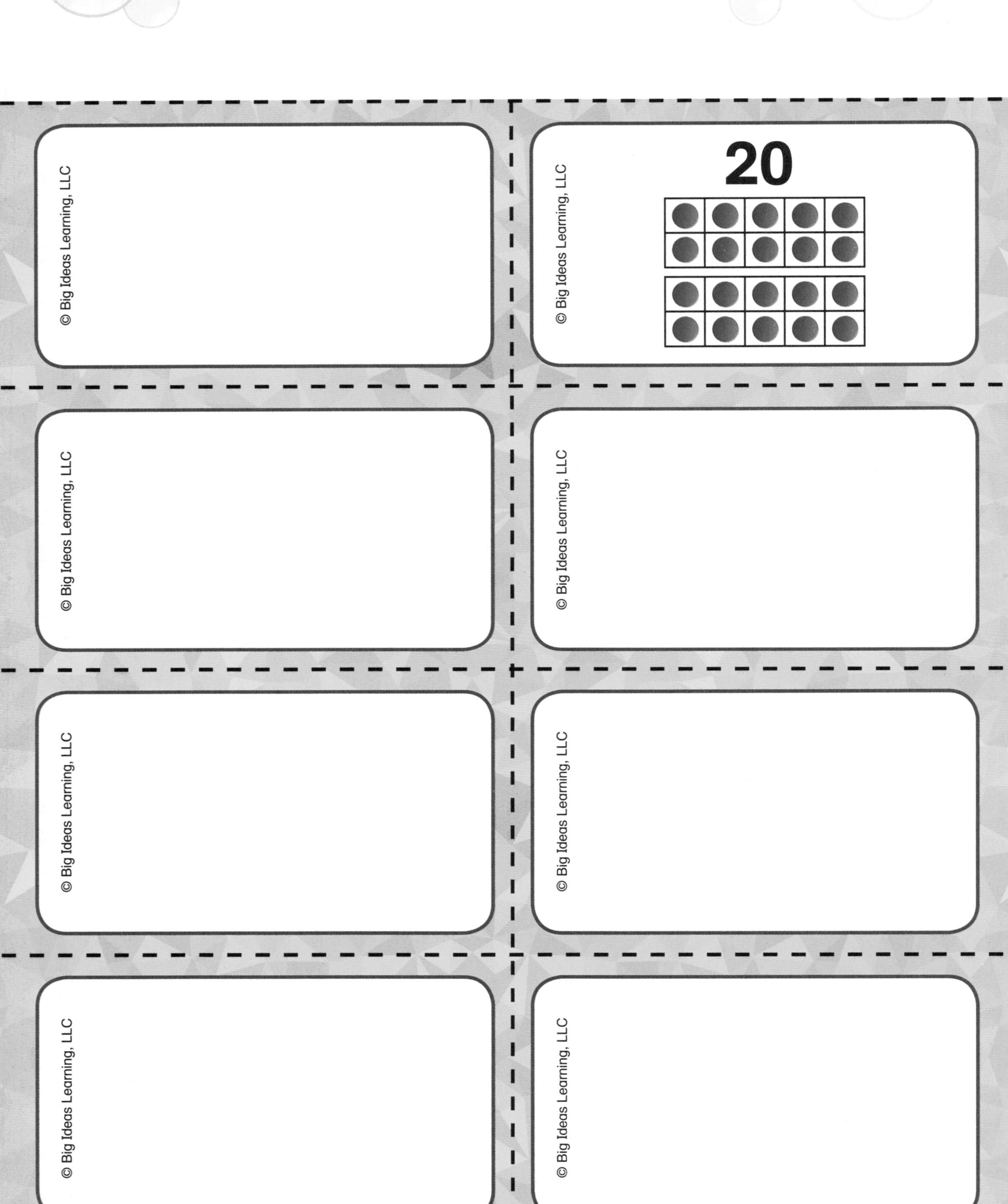
© Big Ideas Learning, LLC
20
© Big Ideas Learning, LLC
© Big Ideas Learning, LLC
© Big Ideas Learning, LLC
© Big Ideas Learning, LLC
© Big Ideas Learning, LLC
© Big Ideas Learning, LLC
© Big Ideas Learning, LLC

Name ______________________

Model and Count 20 9.1

Learning Target: Show and count the number 20.

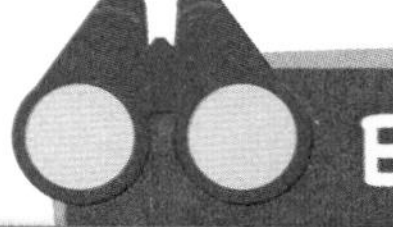

Explore and Grow

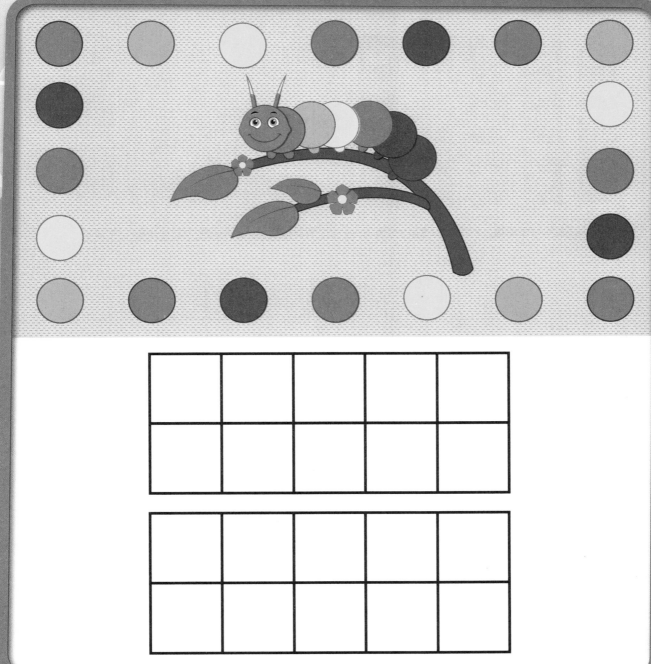

Directions: Place 20 linking cubes on the carpet. Slide the cubes to the ten frames.

Think and Grow

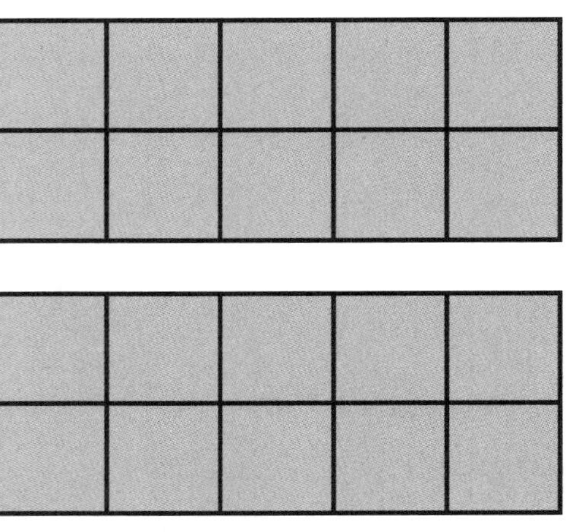

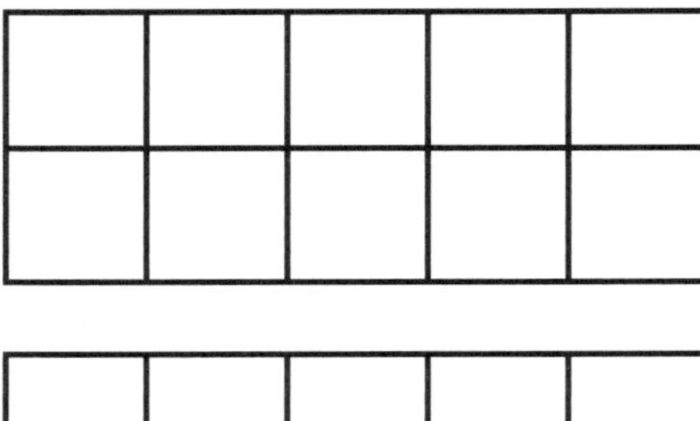

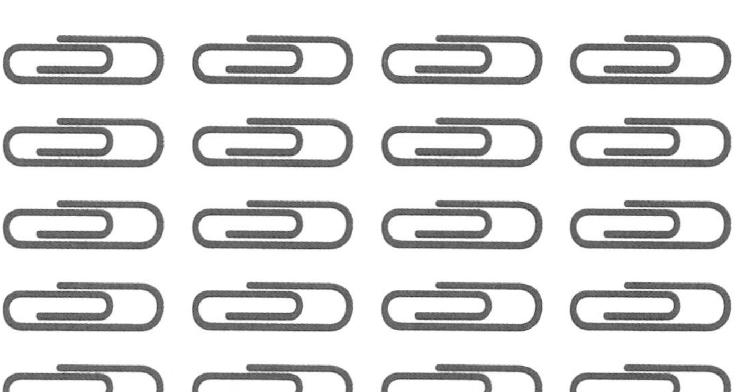

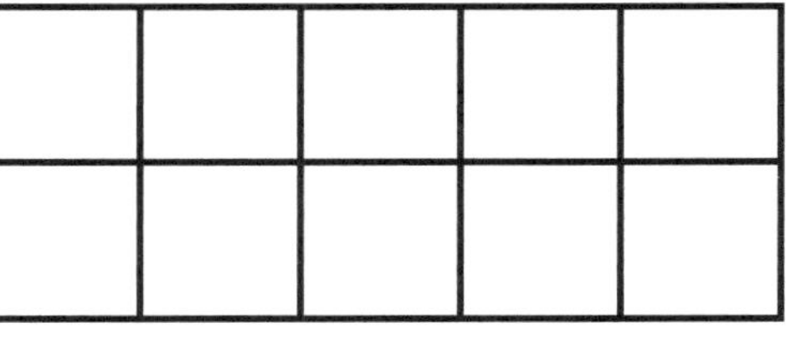

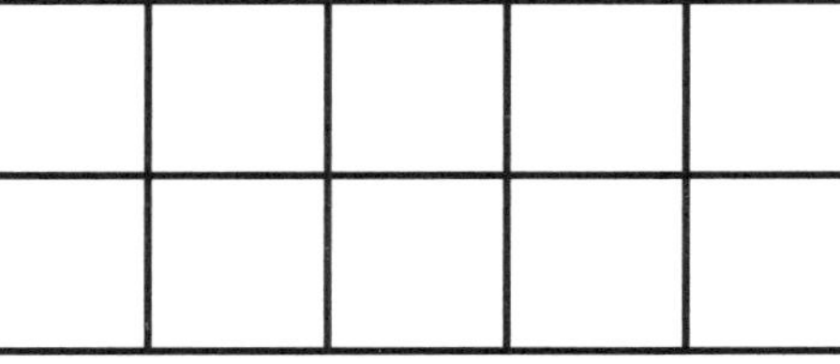

Directions: Count the objects. Color the boxes to show how many.

Name ________________________________

Apply and Grow: Practice

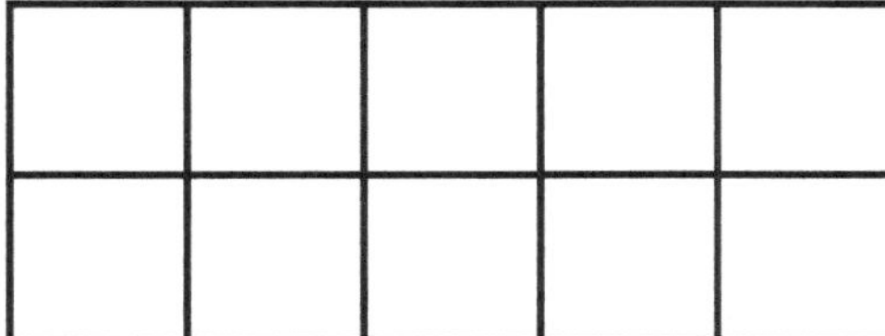

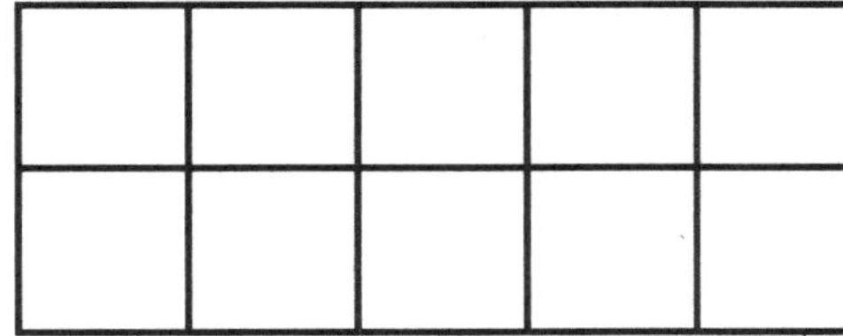

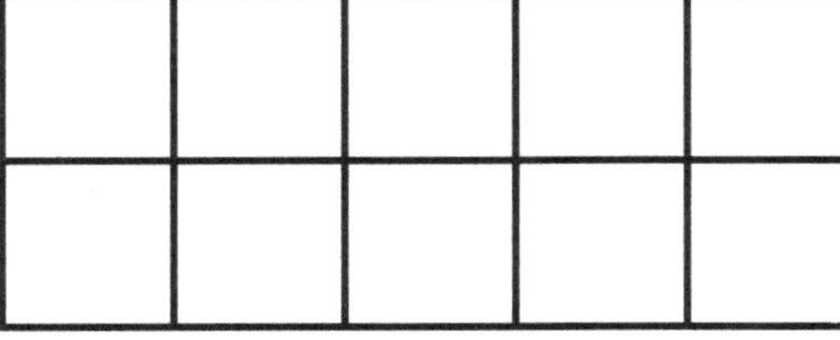

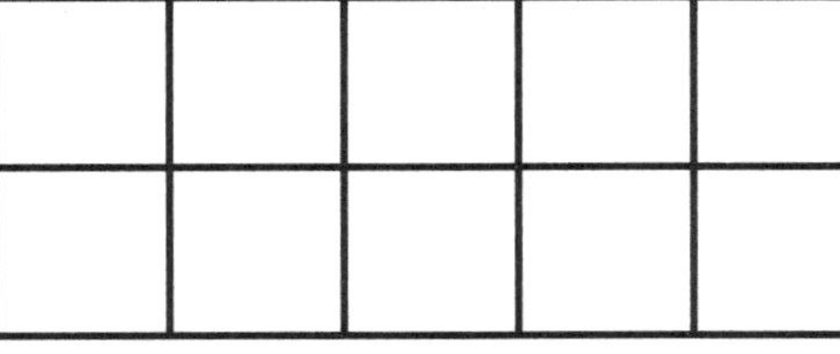

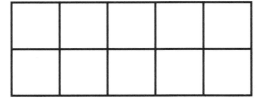

Directions: 1–3 Count the objects. Color the boxes to show how many.

Think and Grow: Modeling Real Life

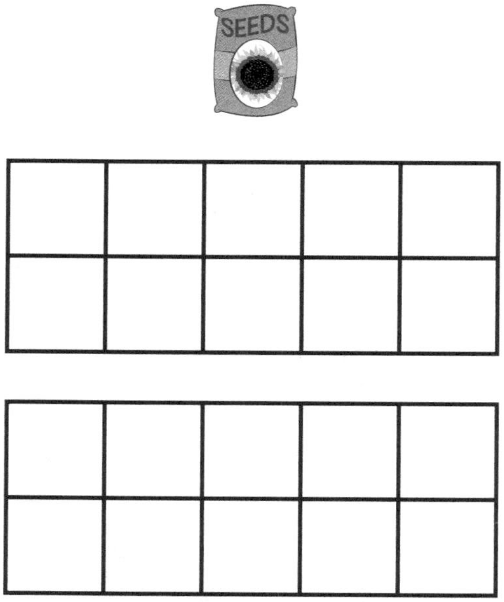

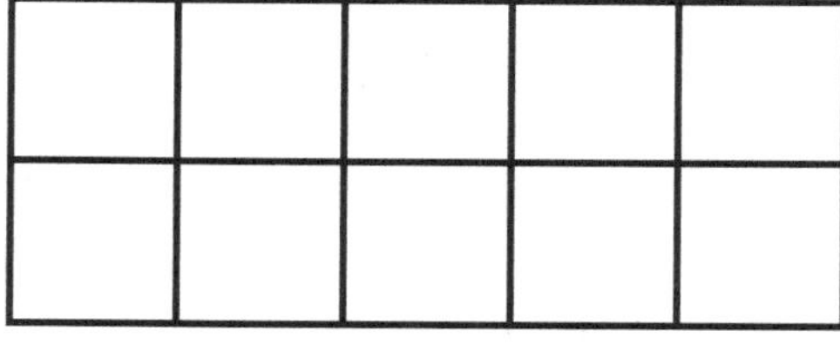

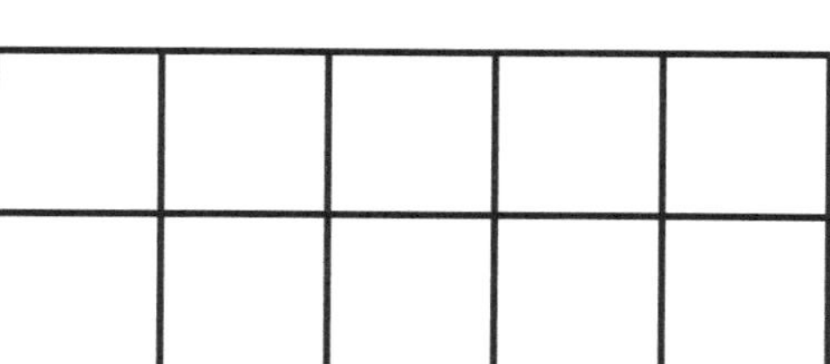

Directions: Count the objects in the picture. Color the boxes to show how many.

Name ______________________

Practice 9.1

Learning Target: Show and count the number 20.

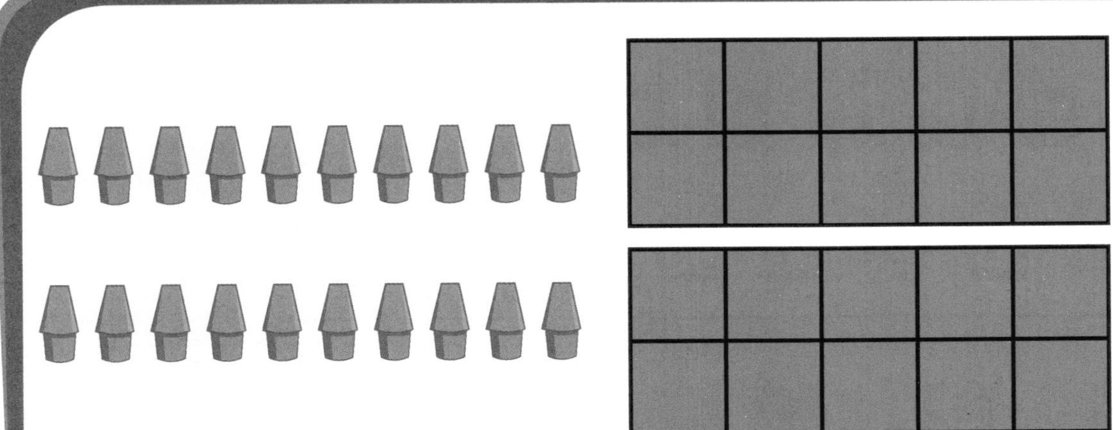

Directions: Count the erasers. Color the boxes to show how many.

1

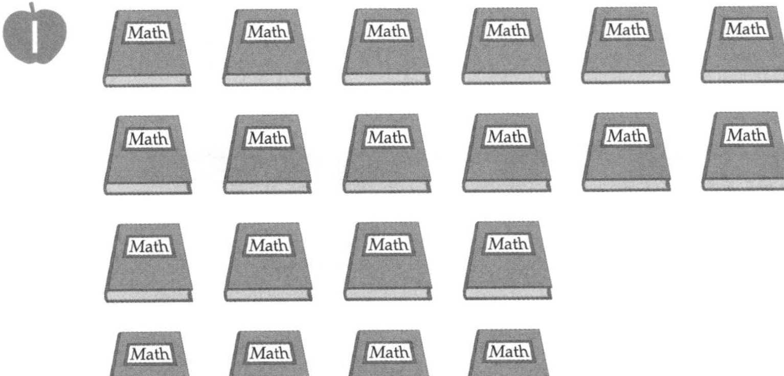

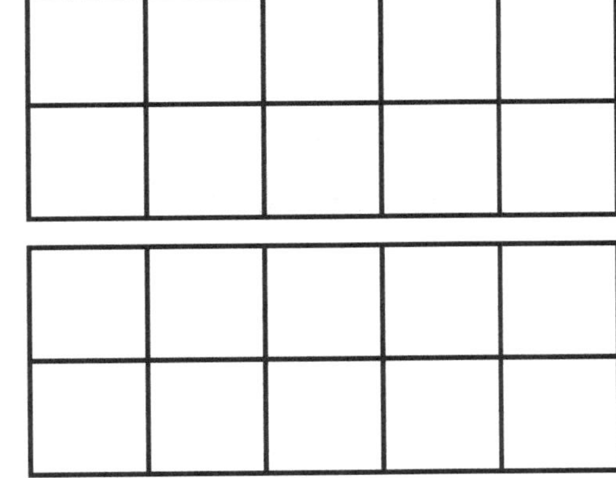

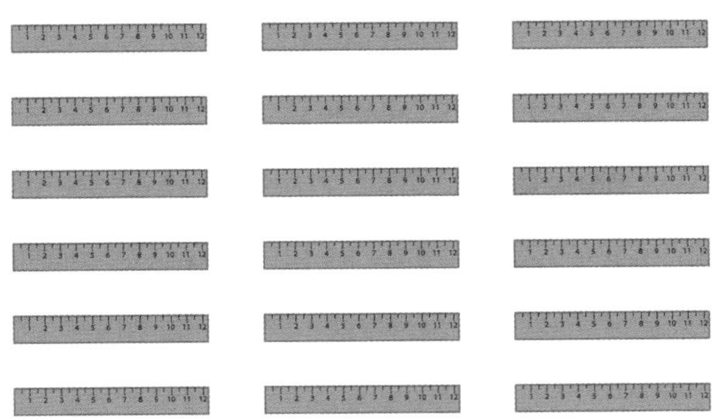

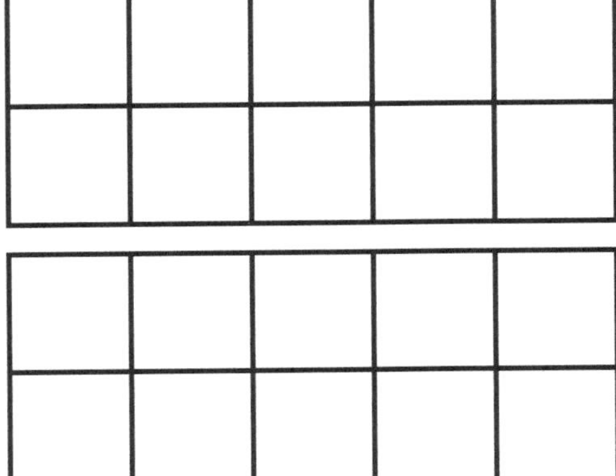

Directions: 1 and 2 Count the objects. Color the boxes to show how many.

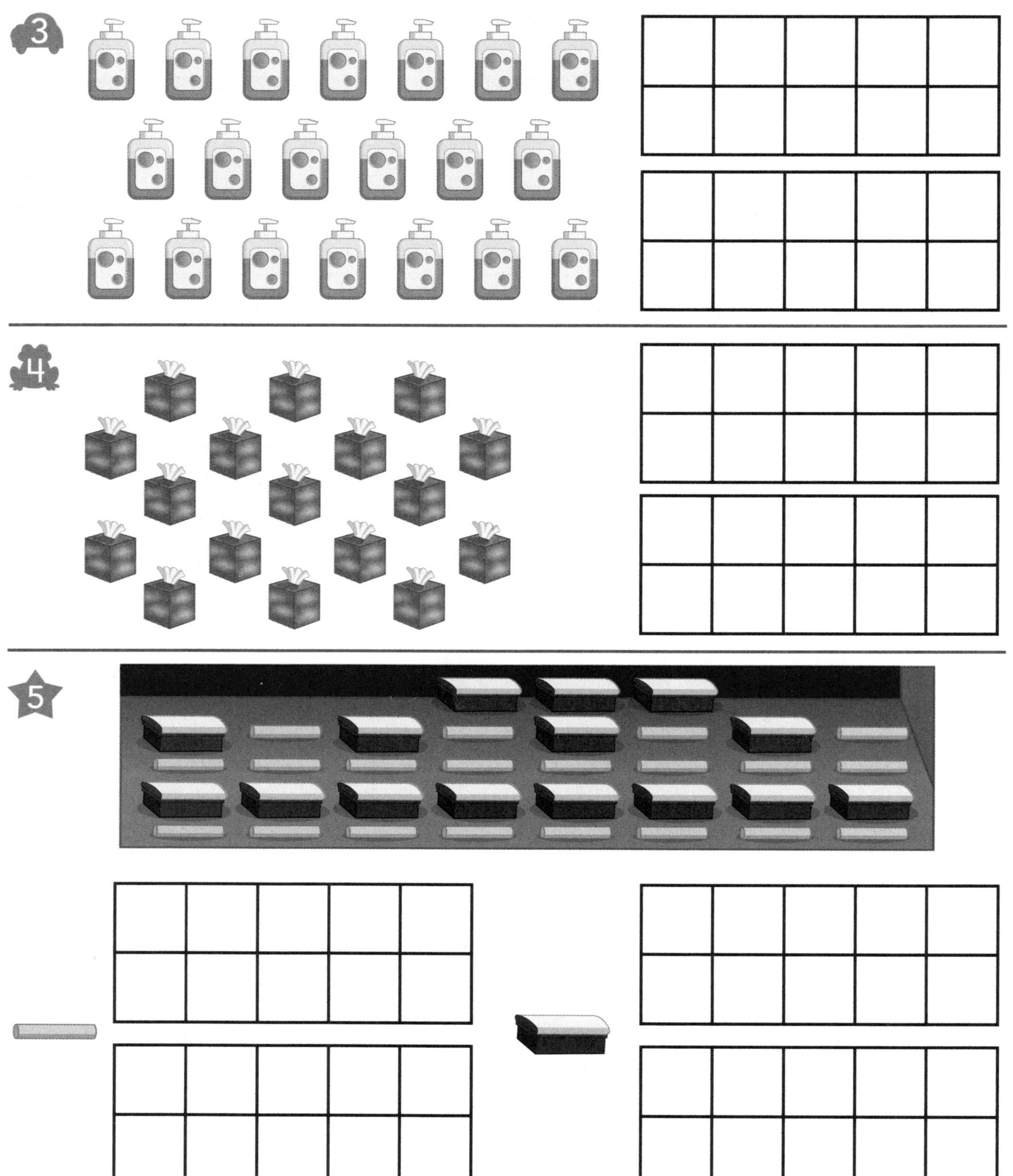

Directions: 3 and 4 Count the objects. Color the boxes to show how many.
5 Count the objects in the picture. Color the boxes to show how many.

Name ___________________________

Count and Write 20

9.2

Learning Target: Count and write the number 20.

Explore and Grow

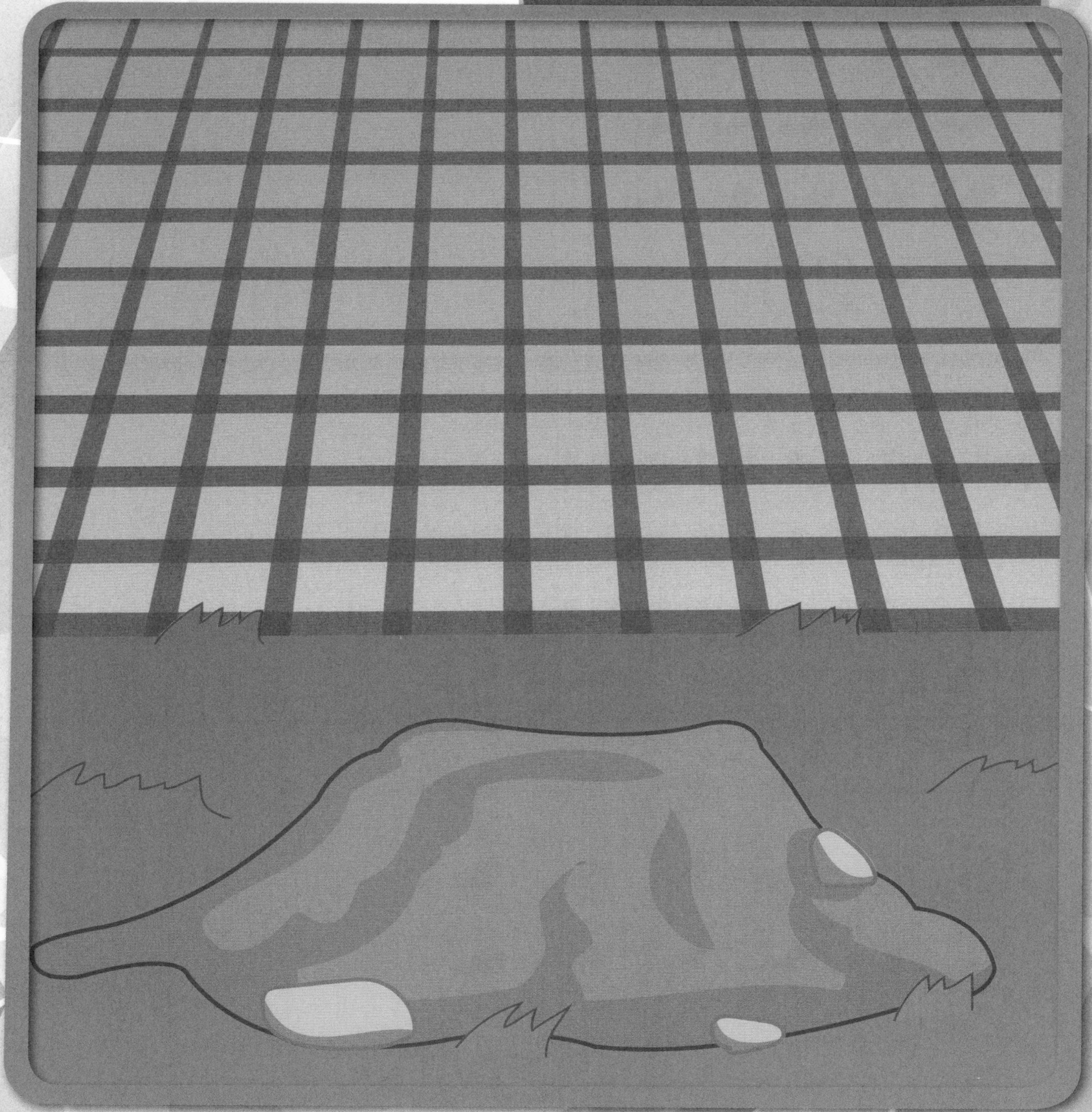

Directions: Use linking cubes to show how many ants are in the story *Ants at the Picnic*. Write how many ants are in the story.

Think and Grow

20

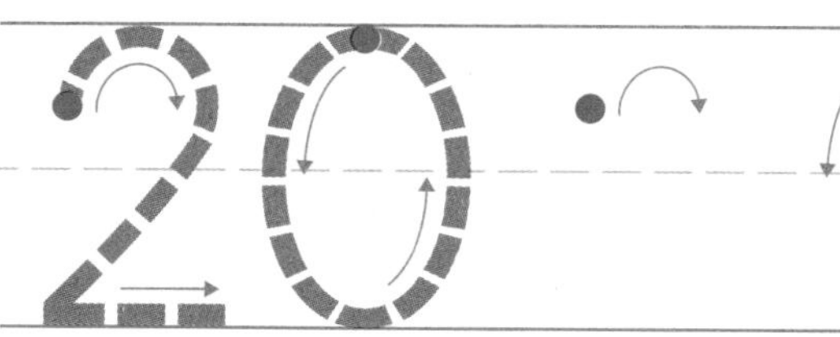

twenty

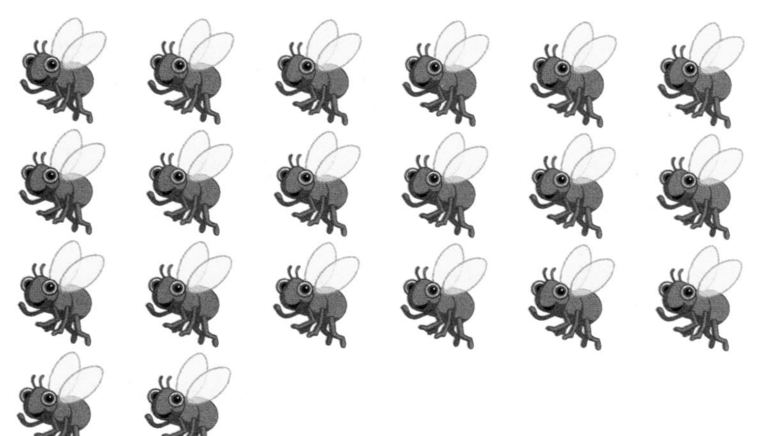

Directions:

- Count the grasshoppers. Say the number. Trace and write the number.
- Count the insects. Say the number. Write the number.

Name ___

Apply and Grow: Practice

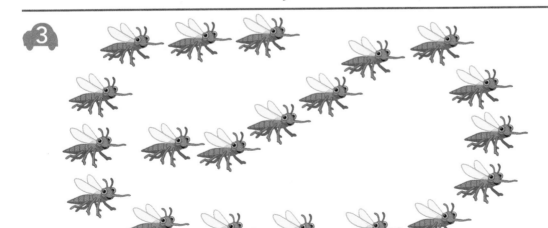

Directions: 1–3 Count the insects. Say the number. Write the number.

Think and Grow: Modeling Real Life

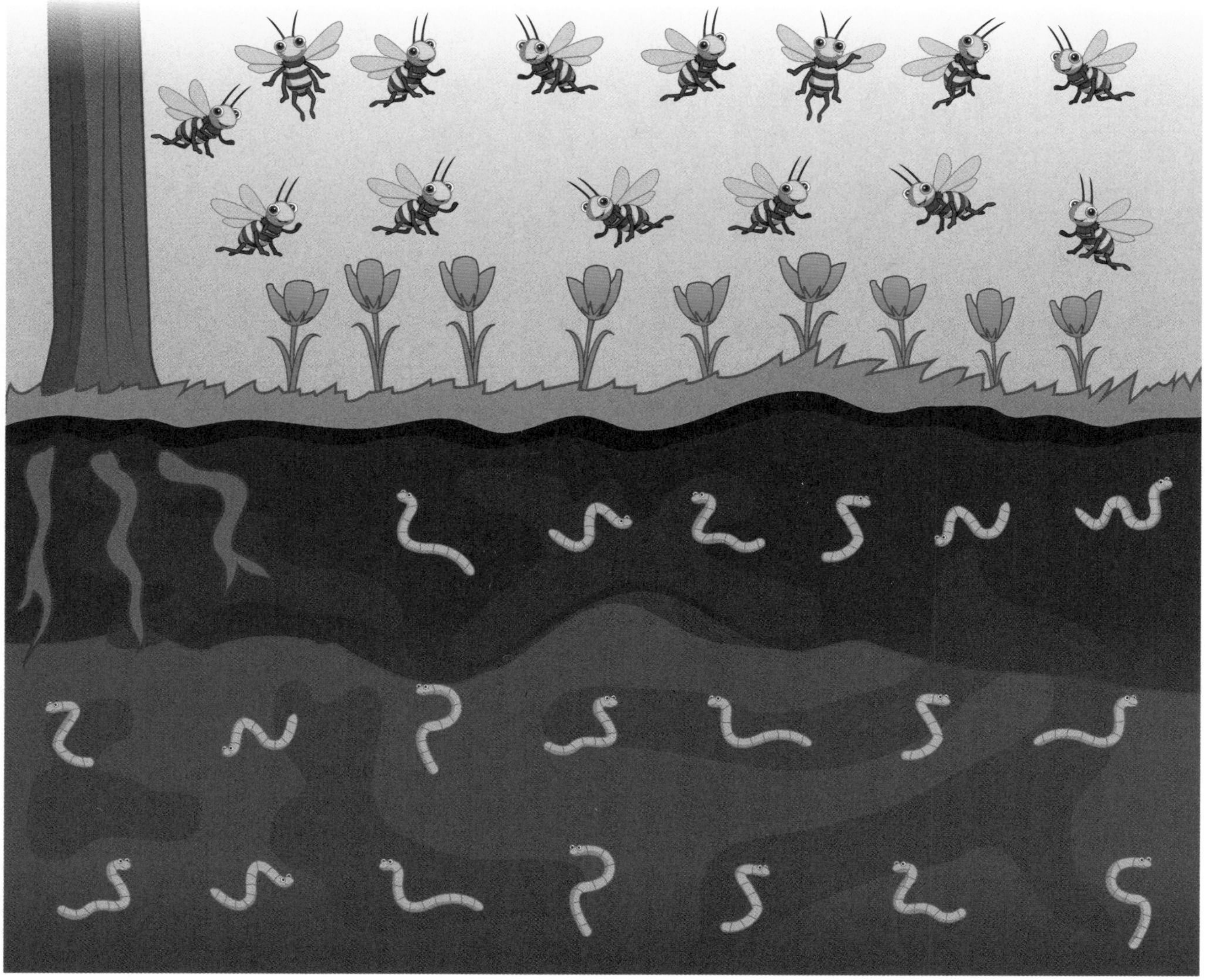

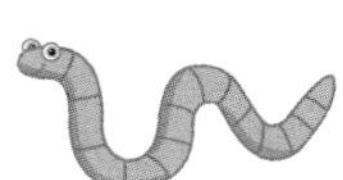

Directions: Count the animals in the picture. Say the number. Write the number.

Name ______________________

Learning Target: Count and write the number 20.

twenty

20

Directions: Count the insects. Say the number. Write the number.

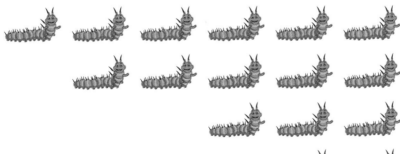

1

______

2

______

Directions: 1 and 2 Count the insects. Say the number. Write the number.

3

5

Directions: 3 and 4 Count the insects. Say the number. Write the number.
5 Count the insects in the picture. Say the number. Write the number.

Name ______________________

Count to Find How Many

9.3

Learning Target: When told a number, count that many objects.

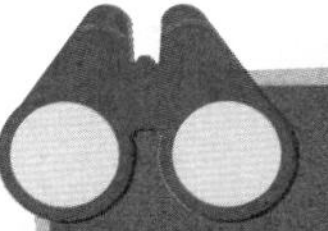

Explore and Grow

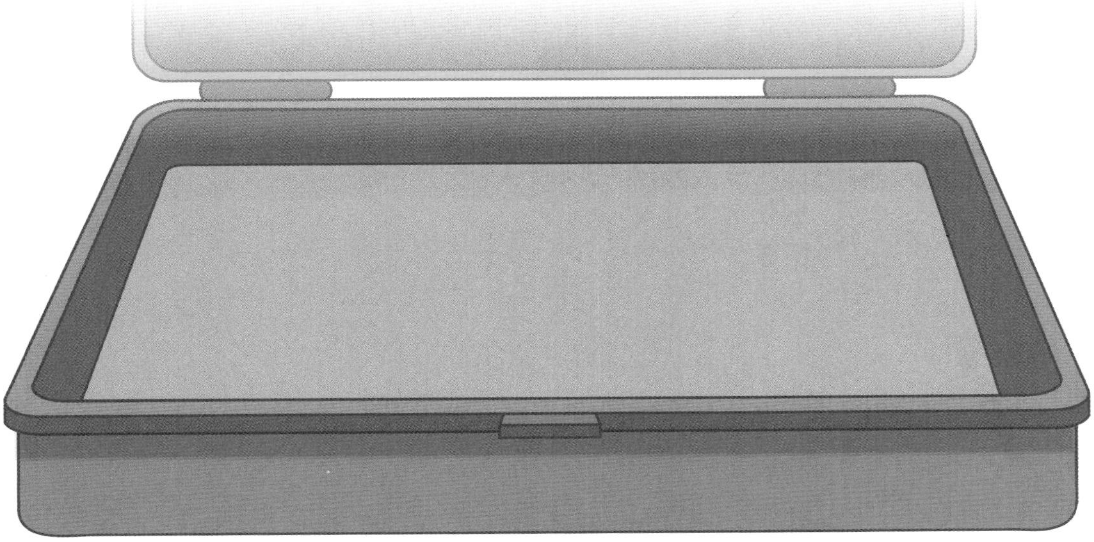

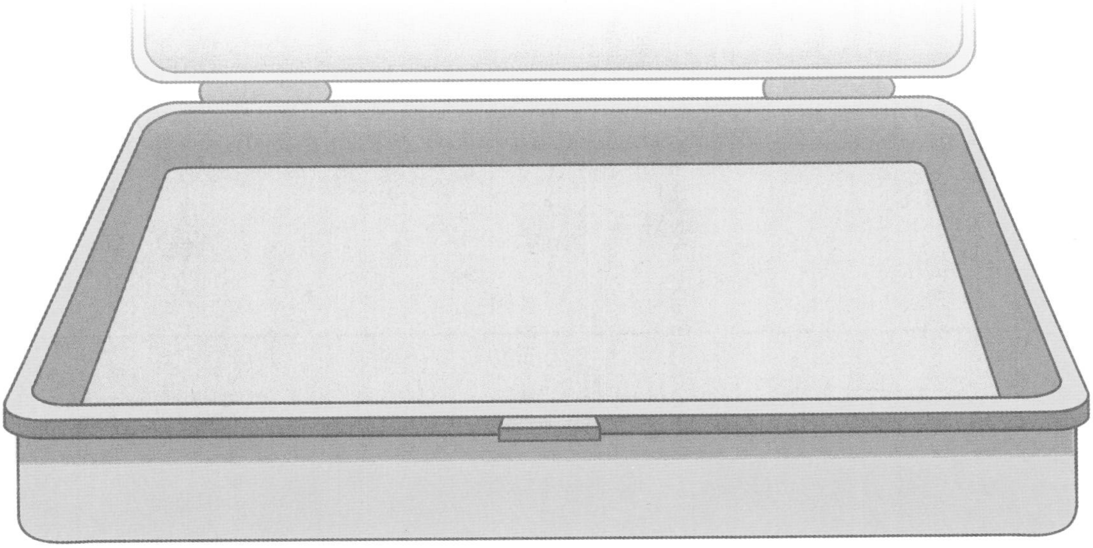

Directions: You have 14 crayons in your box. Your friend has 11 crayons in his box. Use linking cubes to show the crayons in each box.

Think and Grow

2

17

5

12

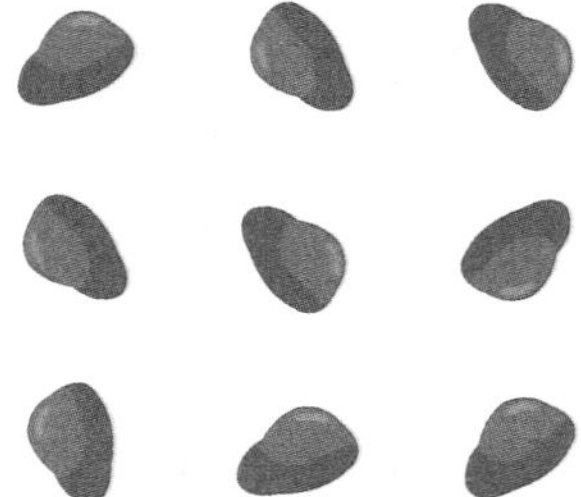

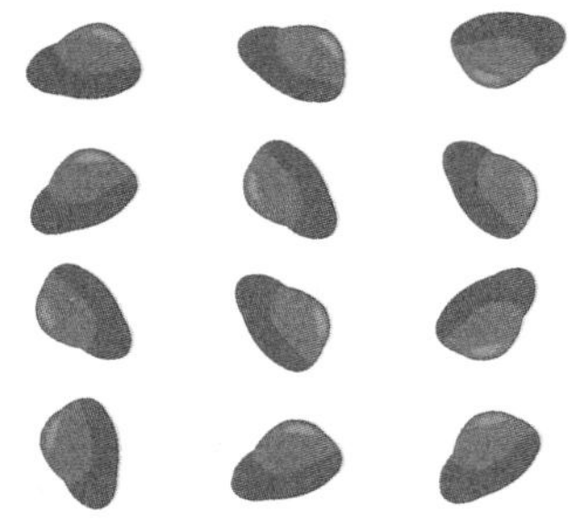

Directions: Circle the group that has the given number of objects.

Name ________________

Apply and Grow: Practice

10

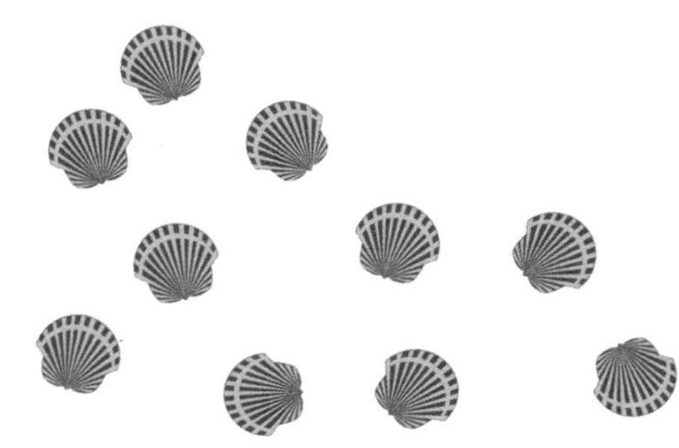

15

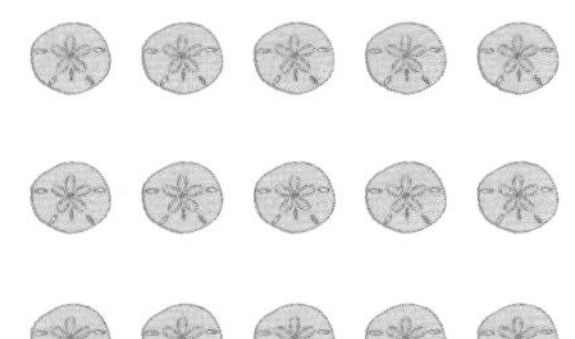

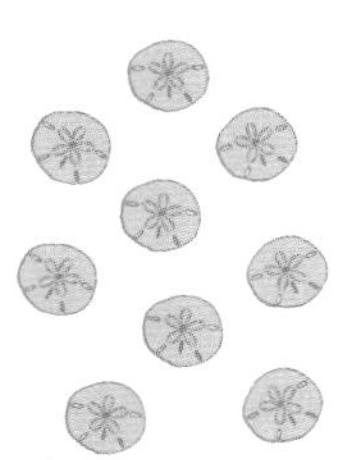

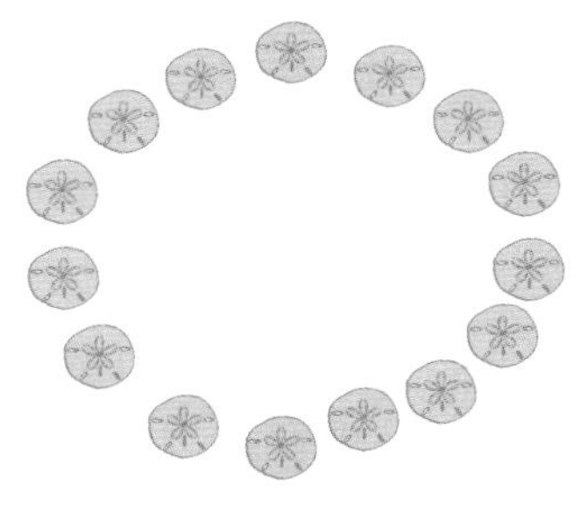

3

19

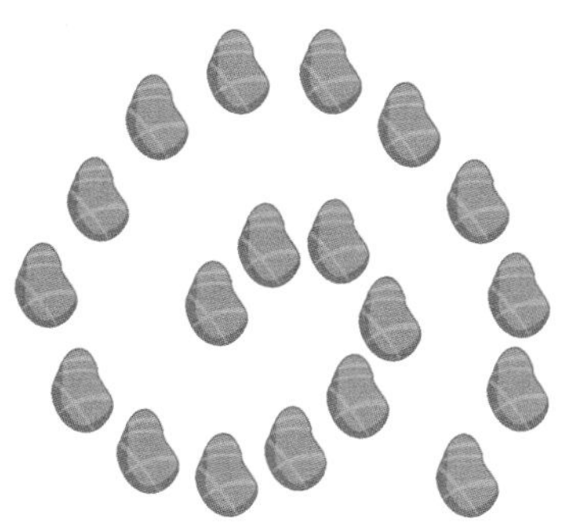

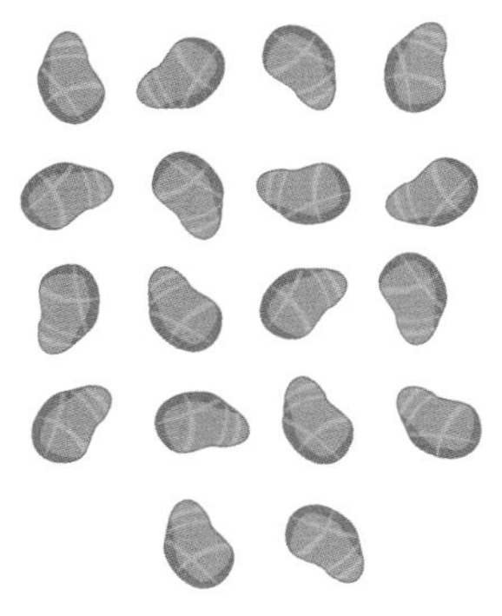

Directions: 1 – 3 Circle any group that has the given number of objects.

Think and Grow: Modeling Real Life

Directions: You have 20 coins in your piggy bank. You drop and break your piggy bank. Did you find all of your coins? Circle the thumbs up for *yes* or the thumbs down for *no*.

Name ______________________

Practice 9.3

Learning Target: When told a number, count that many objects.

1

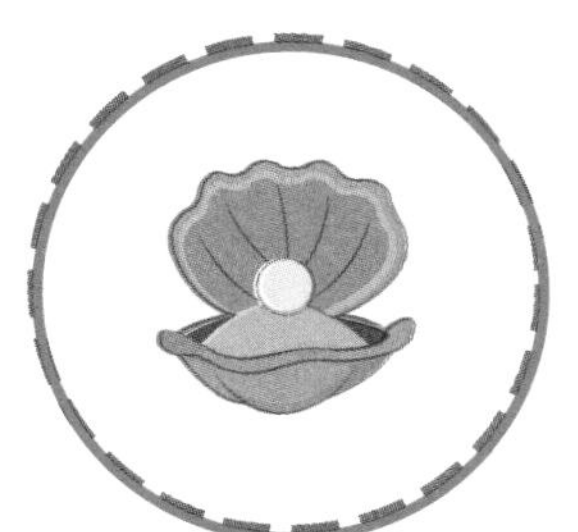

Directions: Circle the group that has the given number of objects.

4

7

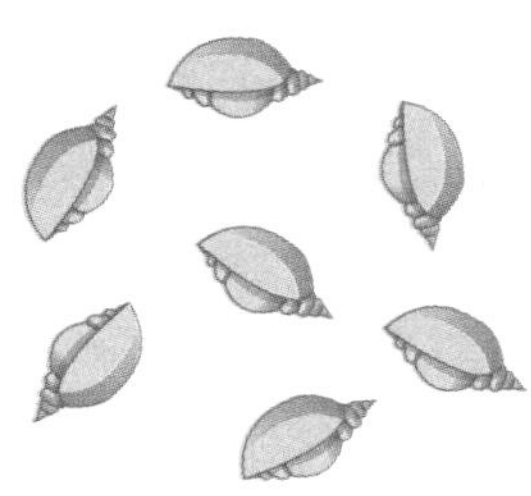

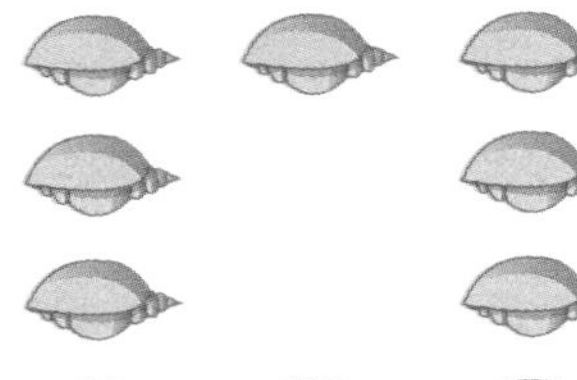

Directions: 1 and 2 Circle the group that has the given number of objects.

3

13

4

18

5

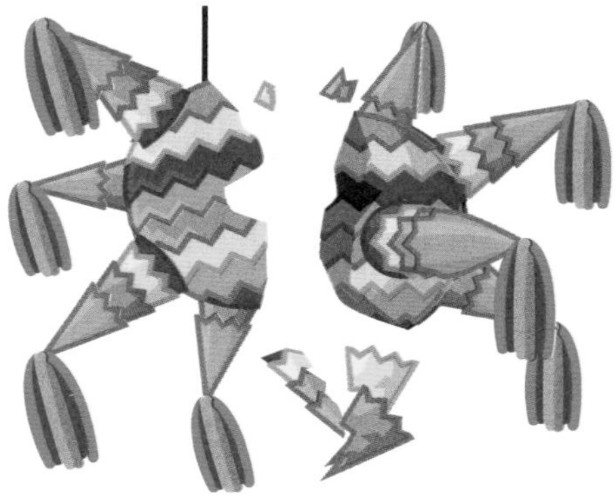

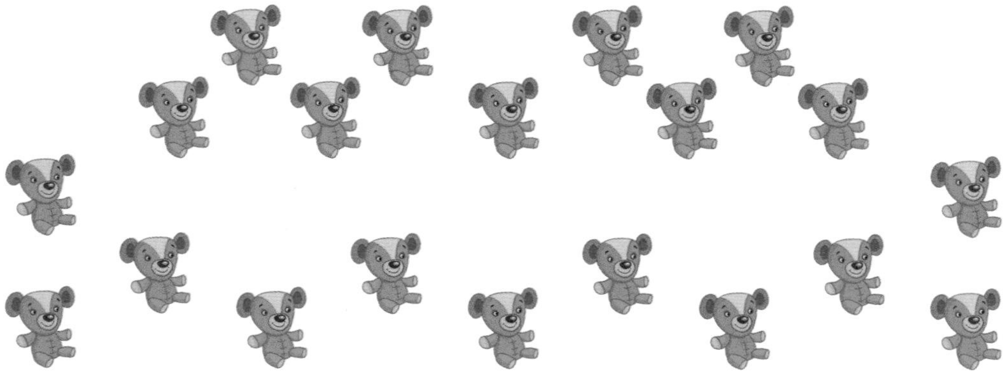

Directions: 3 and 4 Circle any group that has the given number of objects.
5 You have 20 toys in your piñata. You break your piñata. Did you find all of your toys? Circle the thumbs up for *yes* or the thumbs down for *no*.

Name

Learning Target: Count forward from any number.

Count Forward from Any Number to 20

Explore and Grow

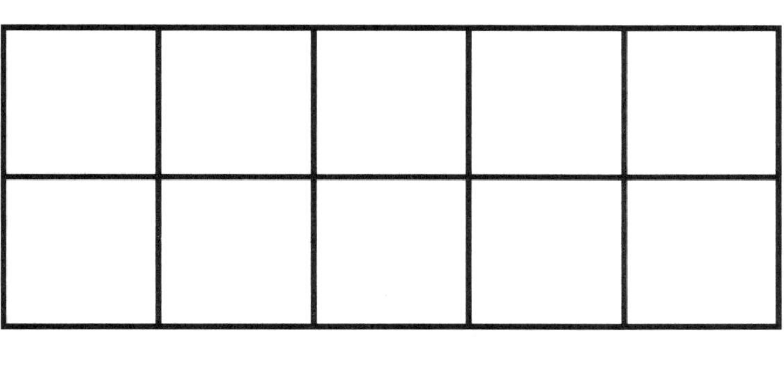

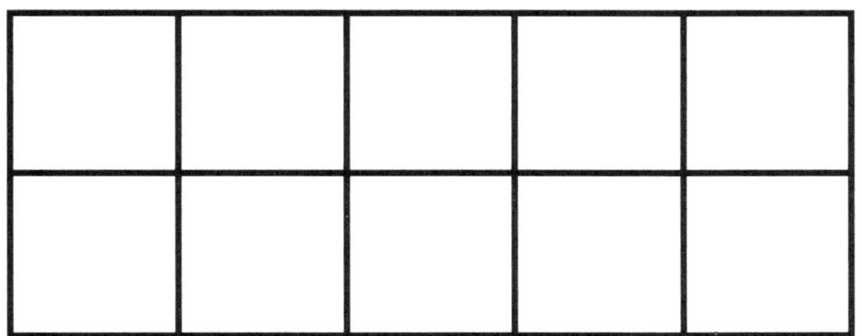

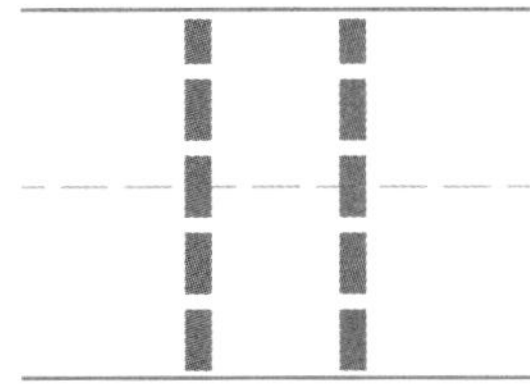

Directions:

- Place 11 linking cubes on the ten frames. Trace the number.
- Place another cube on the ten frames. Write the number to tell how many.
- Place 1 more cube on the ten frames. Write the number to tell how many.

Think and Grow

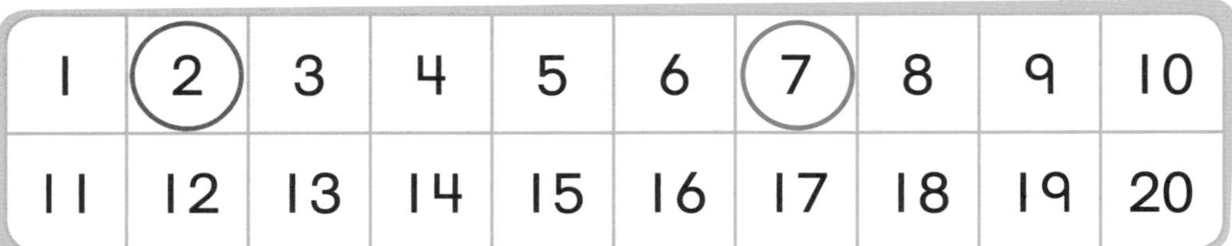

1	2	3	4	5	6	7	8	9	10
11	12	13	14	15	16	17	18	19	20

2 3 4 5 6 7

1	2	3	4	5	6	7	8	9	10
11	12	13	14	15	16	17	18	19	20

8 ____ ____ ____ ____ 13

1	2	3	4					9	10
11	12	13	14	15	16	17	18	19	20

4 ____ ____ ____ ____ 9

Directions: Count forward from the number in the blue circle to the number in the red circle. Write the numbers you count.

Name ______________________________

Apply and Grow: Practice

1	2	3	4	5	6	7	8	(9)	
			(14)	15	16	17	18	19	20

9 ______ ______ ______ ______ 14

1	2	3	4	5	(6)				
(11)	12	13	14	15	16	17	18	19	20

6 ______ ______ ______ ______ ______

3

11 ______ ______ ______ ______ 16

Directions: 1 and 2 Count forward from the number in the blue circle to the number in the red circle. Write the numbers you count. 3 Count forward from 11 and stop at 16. Write the numbers you count.

Think and Grow: Modeling Real Life

7

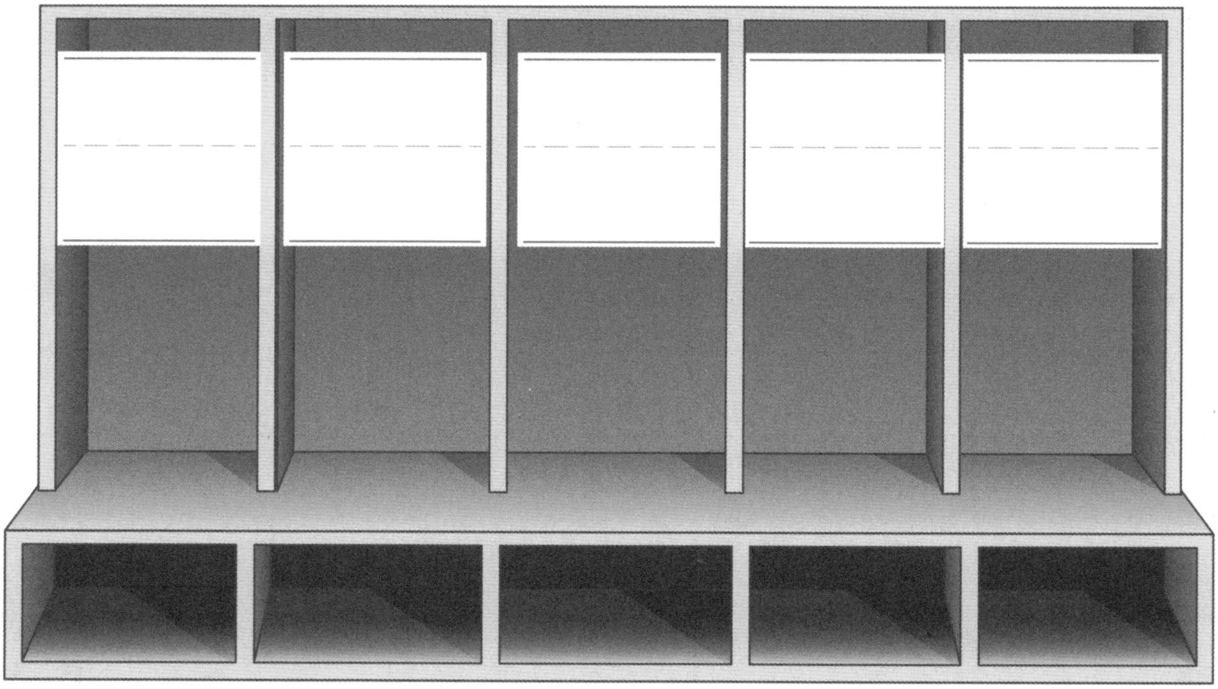

Directions:

- Your teacher labels the class cubbies and stops at 7. Count forward to finish labeling the cubbies. Write the numbers you count.
- Label the first cubby with a number from 1 to 16. Count forward from your number to finish labeling the cubbies. Write the numbers you count.

Name ________________________

Learning Target: Count forward from any number.

1	2	3	4	5	6	7	8	9	10
11	12	13	14	15	16	17	18	19	20

1 2 3 4 5 6

Directions: Count forward from the number in the blue circle to the number in the red circle. Write the numbers you count.

1	2	3	4	5	6	7	8	9	10
11	12	13	14	15	16	17	18	19	20

7 ____ ____ ____ ____ 12

2

1	2	3					8	9	10
11	12	13	14	15	16	17	18	19	20

3 ____ ____ ____ ____ 8

Directions: 1 and 2 Count forward from the number in the blue circle to the number in the red circle. Write the numbers you count.

3

1	2	3	4	5	6	7	8	9	(10)
				(15)	16	17	18	19	20

10

14 ______ ______ ______ ______ 19

12

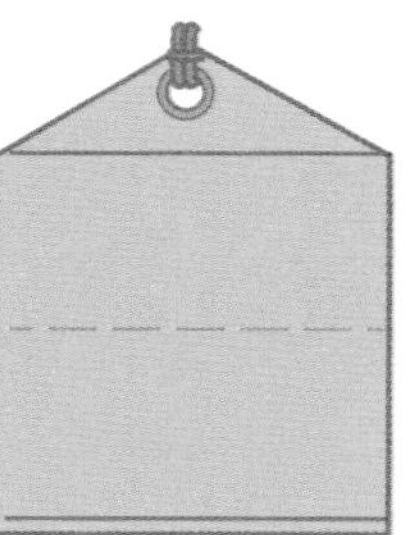

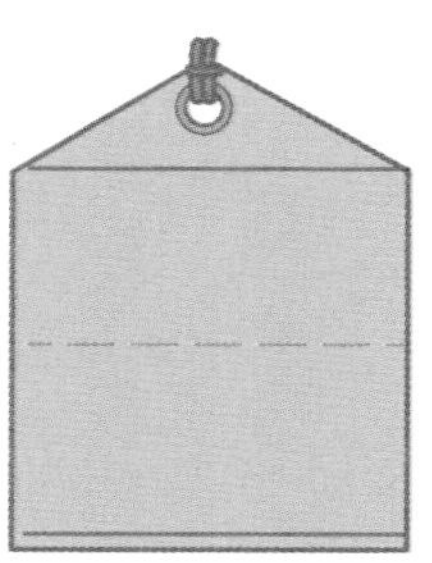

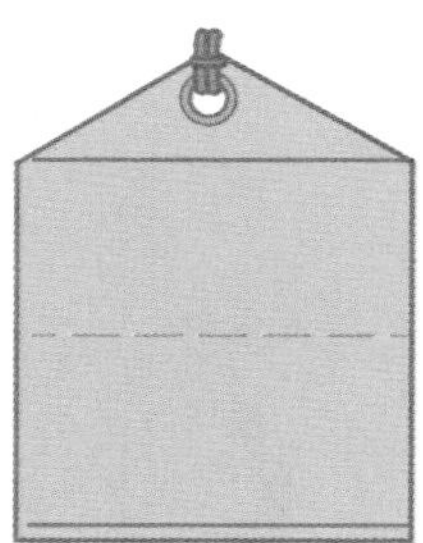

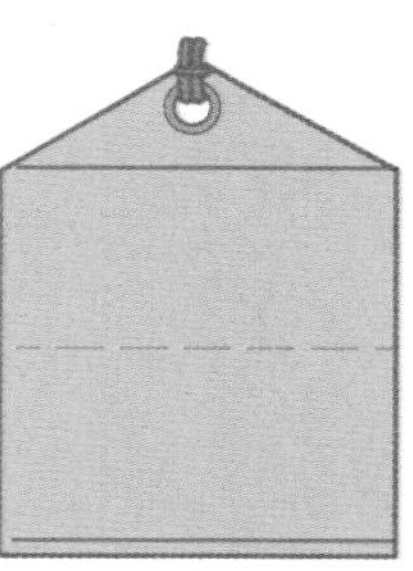

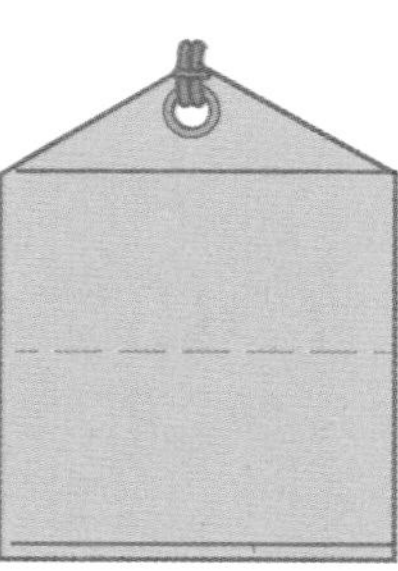

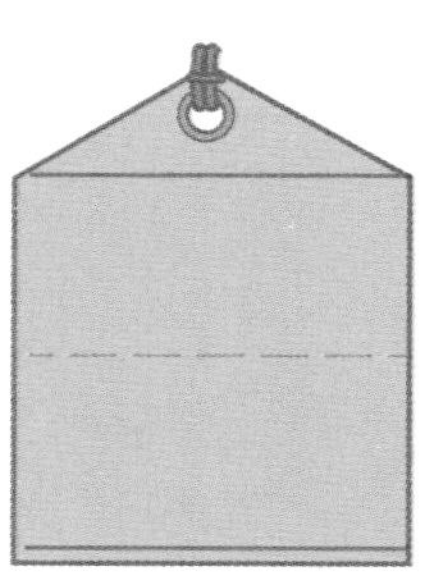

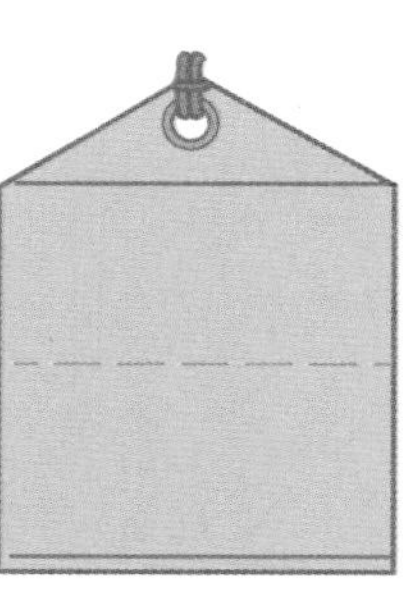

Directions: 3 Count forward from the number in the blue circle to the number in the red circle. Write the numbers you count. 4 Count forward from 14 and stop at 19. Write the numbers you count. 5 Your teacher is numbering tags and stops at 12. Count forward to finish numbering the tags. Write the numbers you count. 6 Write a number from 1 to 16 on the first tag. Count forward from your number to finish numbering the tags. Write the numbers you count.

Name ___

Order Numbers to 20

9.5

Learning Target: Order numbers to 20.

Explore and Grow

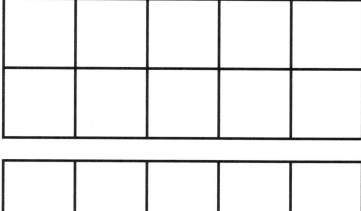

11 12 13 14 ___

16 17 ___ 19 20

Directions: Place 11 linking cubes on the ten frames. Place more cubes on the ten frames as you count forward to 20. Trace or write the missing numbers.

Think and Grow

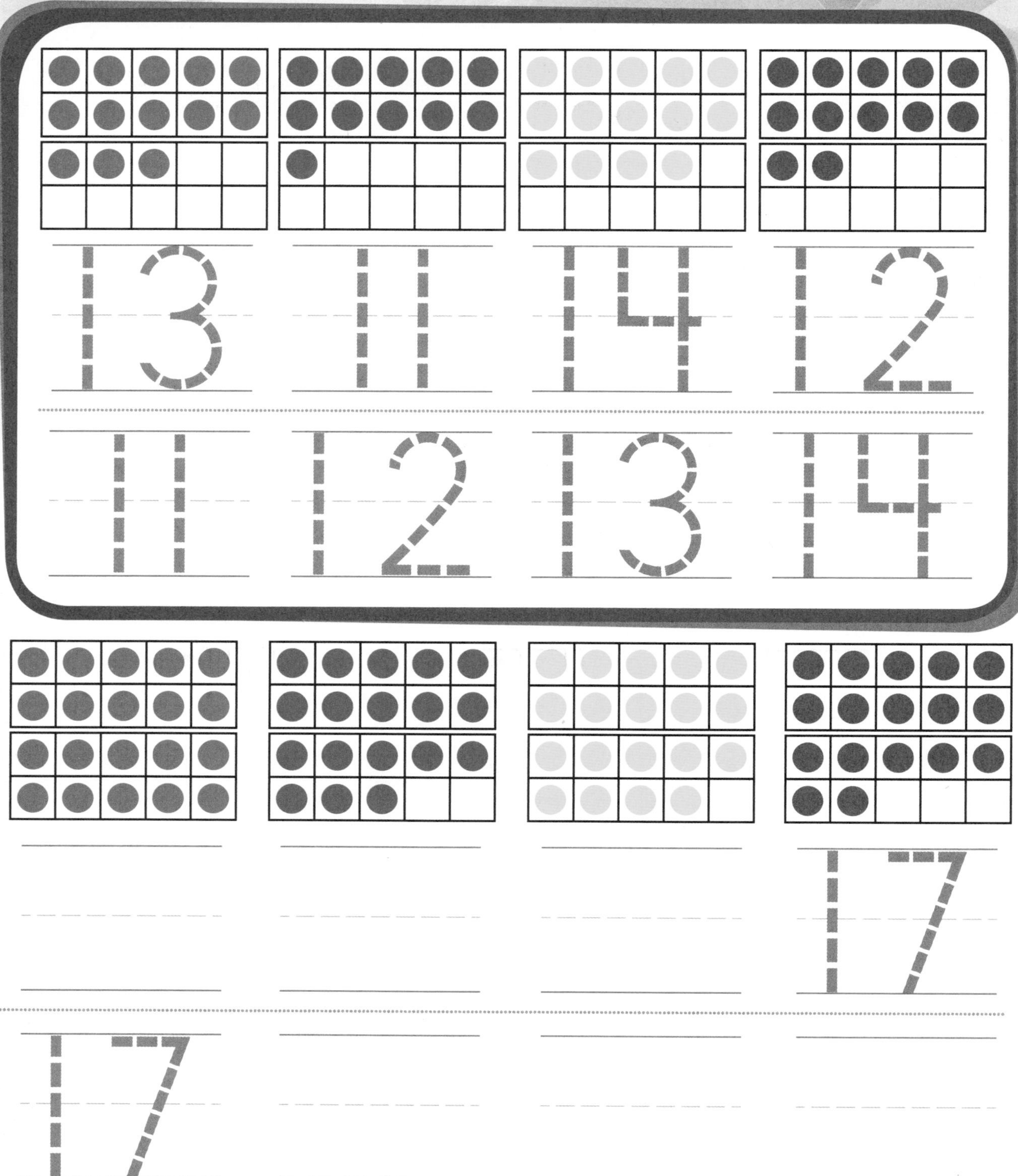

17

17

Directions: Count the dots in each set of ten frames. Say each number. Write each number. Then write the numbers in order.

Name ______________________

Apply and Grow: Practice

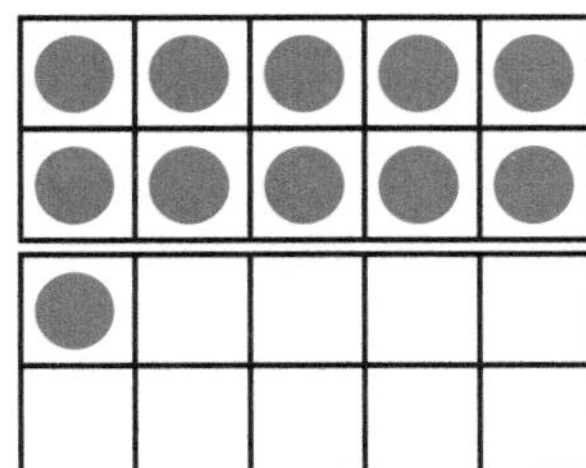

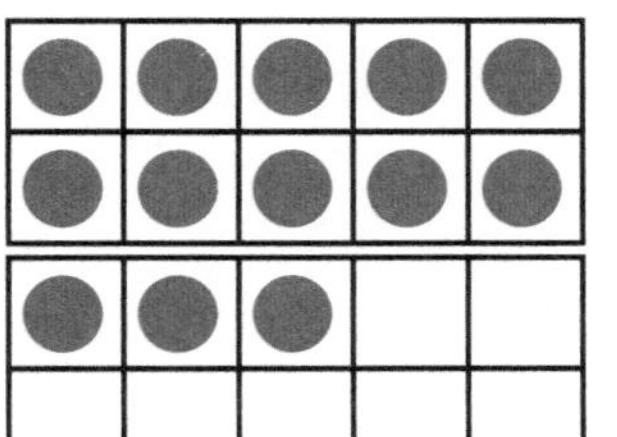

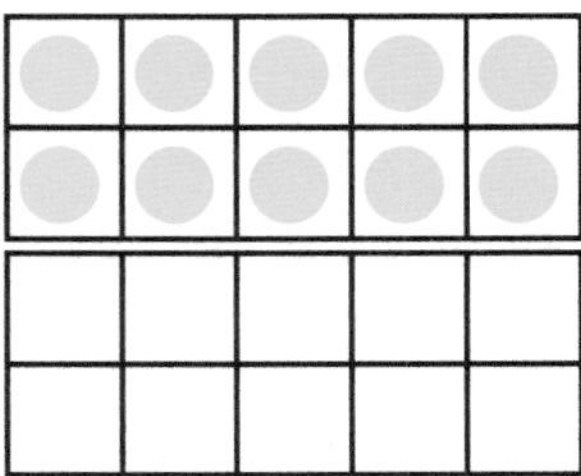

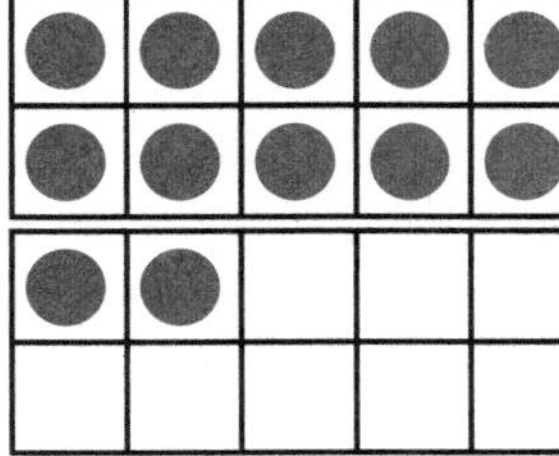

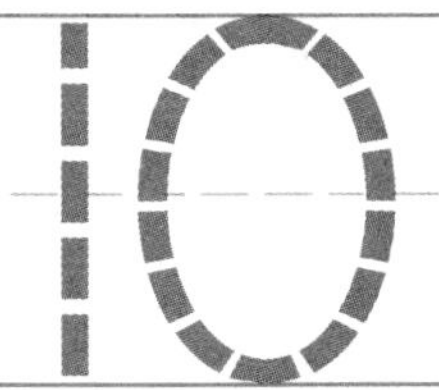

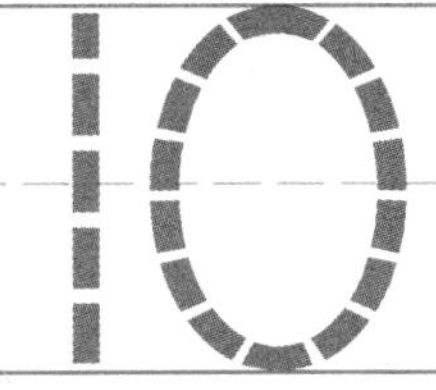

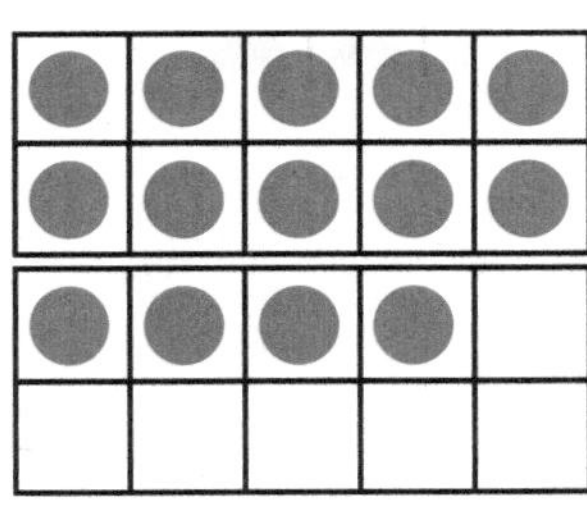

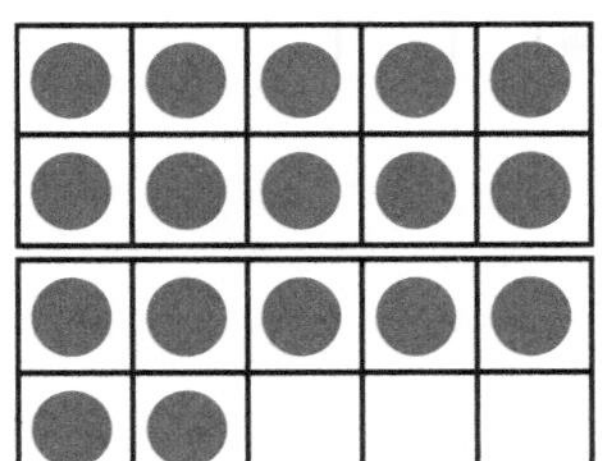

Directions: 1 and 2 Count the dots in each set of ten frames. Say each number. Write each number. Then write the numbers in order.

Think and Grow: Modeling Real Life

Directions: Line up the students for lunch by writing the numbers in order. Circle the student who is first. Underline the student who is last.

Name ______________________

Practice 9.5

Learning Target: Order numbers to 20.

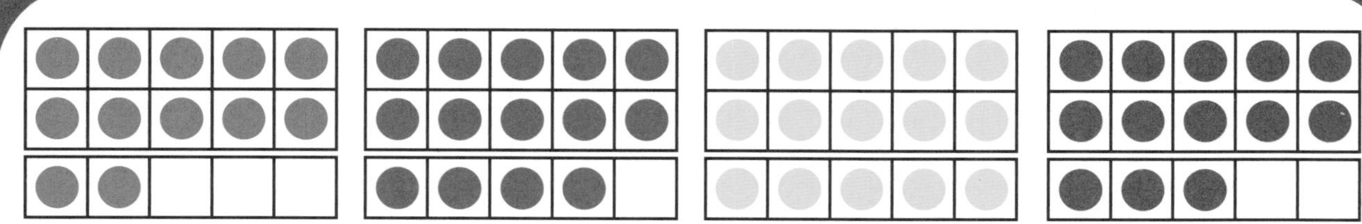

12 14 15 13

12 13 14 15

Directions: Count the dots in each set of ten frames. Say each number. Write each number. Then write the numbers in order.

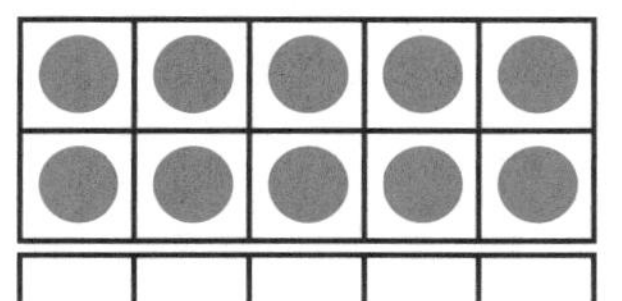
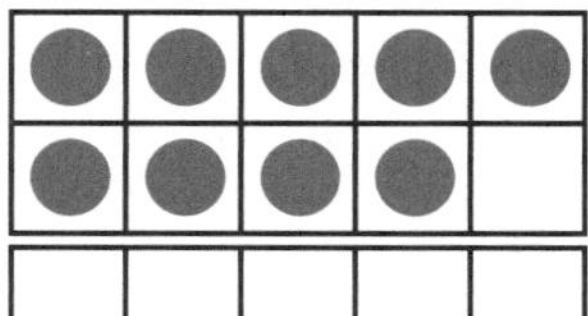
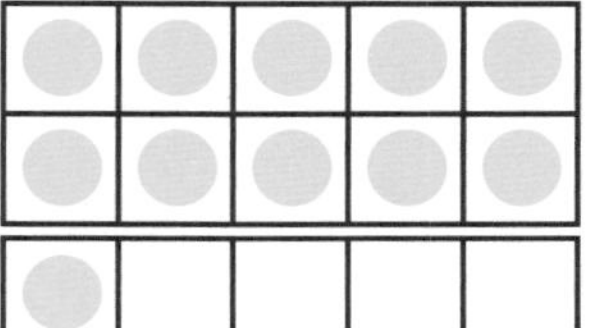
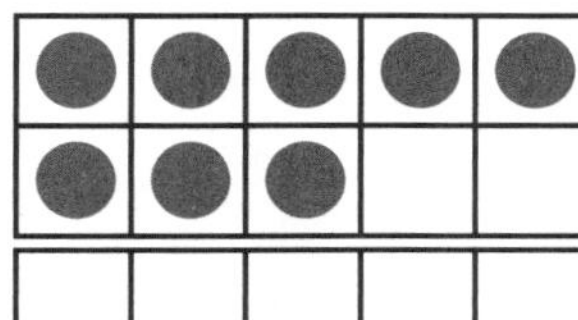

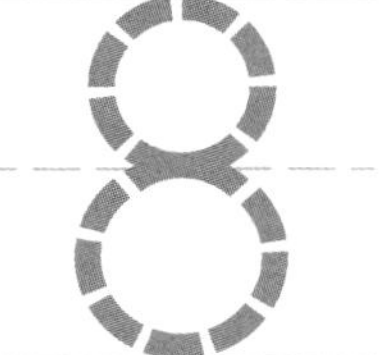

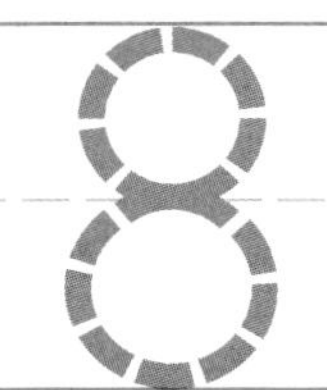

Directions: 1 Count the dots in each set of ten frames. Say each number. Write each number. Then write the numbers in order.

2

3

Directions: 2 Count the dots in each set of ten frames. Say each number. Write each number. Then write the numbers in order. 3 Line up the train cars by writing the numbers in order. Circle the train car that is first. Underline the train car that is last.

Name ____________________

Compare Numbers to 20

9.6

Learning Target: Use counting to compare the numbers of objects in two groups.

Explore and Grow

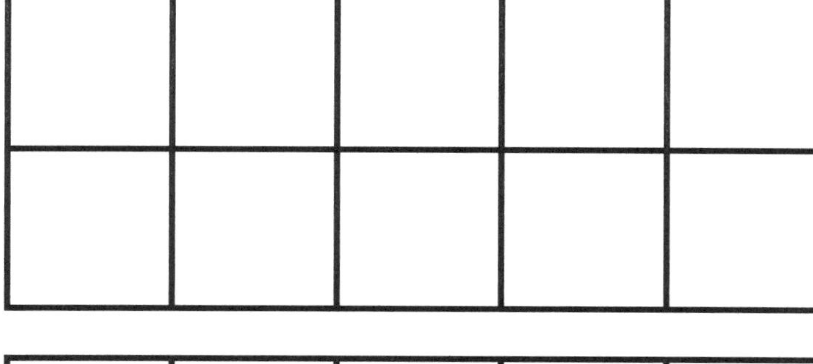

13

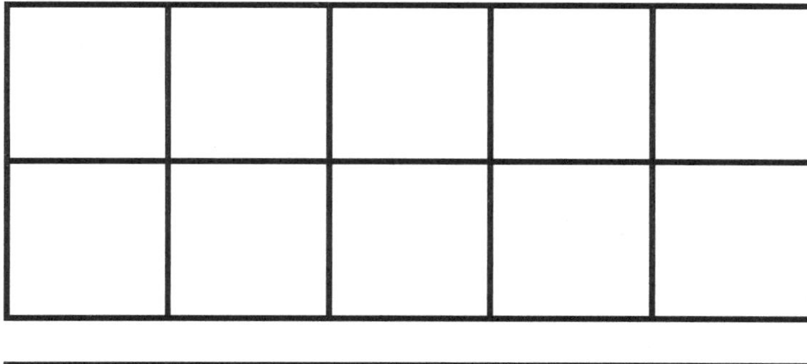

15

Directions: Place linking cubes on the ten frames to show the numbers. Which number is greater than the other number? Which number is less than the other number?

Think and Grow

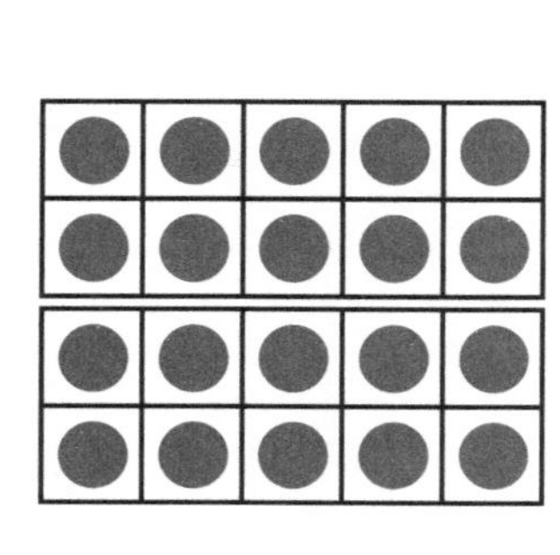
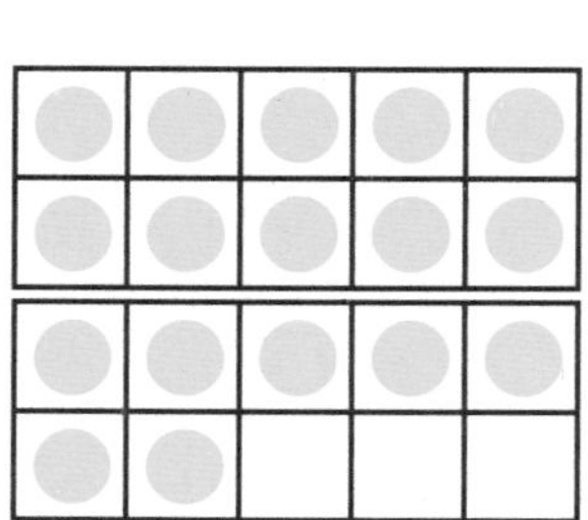
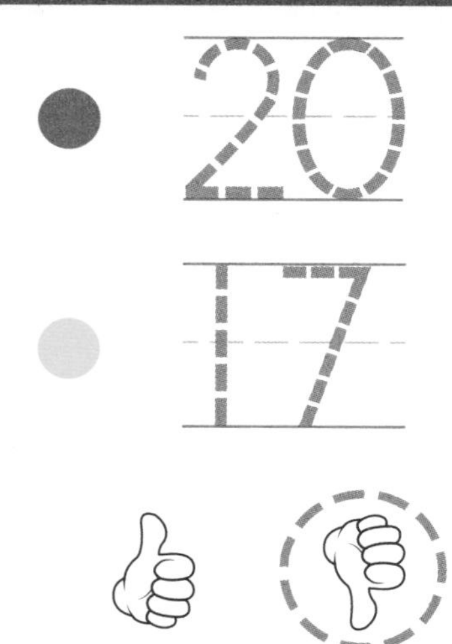

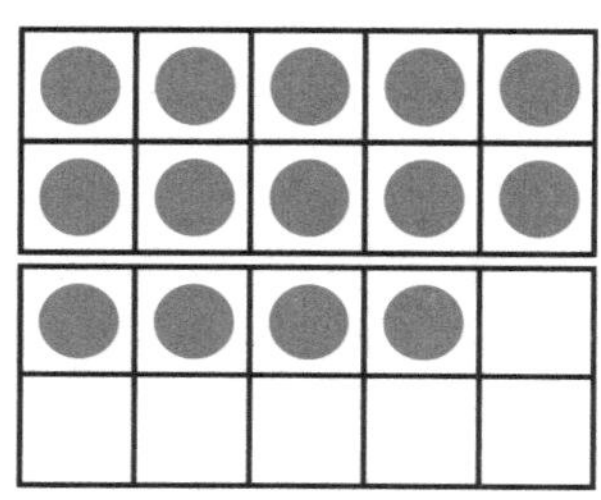
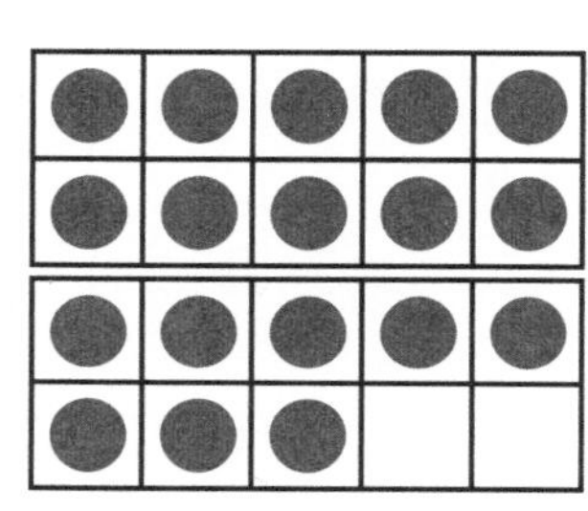
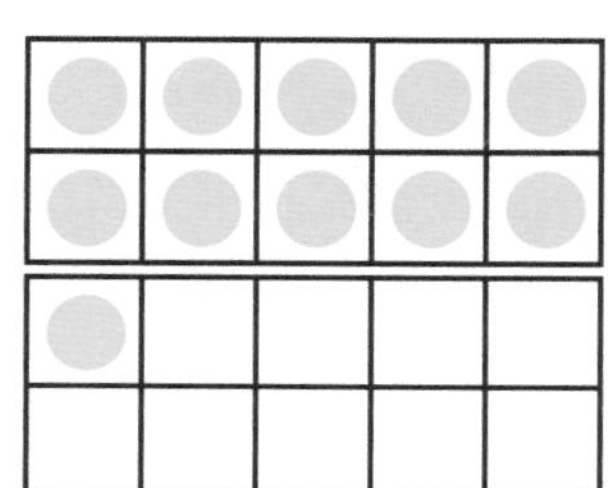

Directions: Count the dots in each set of ten frames. Write each number.

- Is the number of green dots equal to the number of yellow dots? Circle the thumbs up for *yes* or the thumbs down for *no*.
- Compare the numbers of red dots and blue dots. Circle the number that is greater than the other number.
- Compare the numbers of yellow dots and red dots. Draw a line through the number that is less than the other number.

Name ___________________________

Apply and Grow: Practice

1

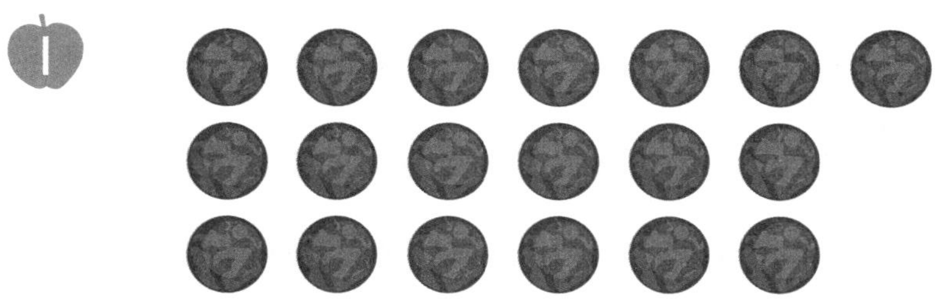

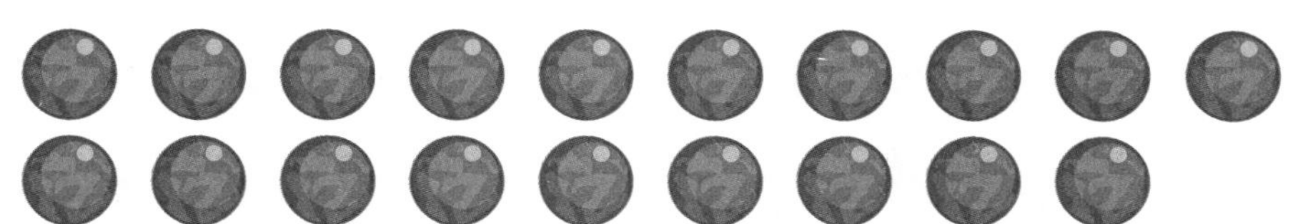

2

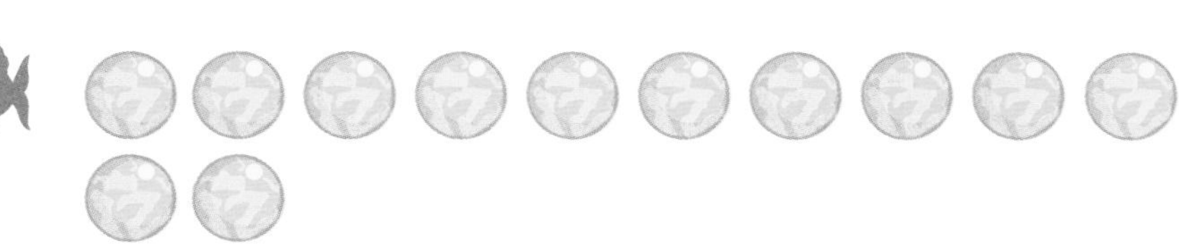

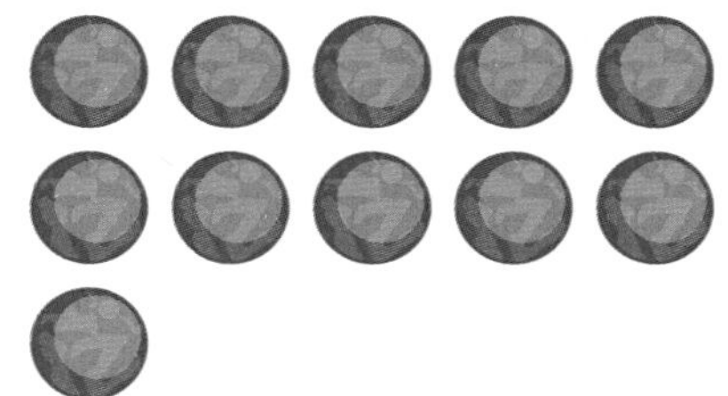

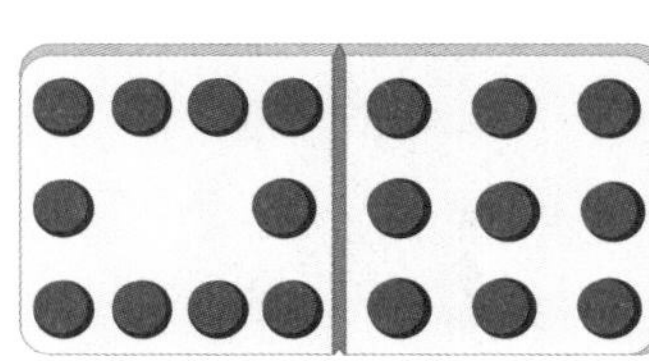

Directions: Count the objects in each group. Write each number. 1 Is the number of blue bouncy balls equal to the number of green bouncy balls? Circle the thumbs up for *yes* or the thumbs down for *no*. 2 Circle the number that is greater than the other number. 3 Draw a line through the number that is less than the other number.

Think and Grow: Modeling Real Life

Who has more?

Who has less?

Directions:

- You have 14 balls. Your friend has a number of balls that is 1 more than 12. Draw the balls. Write the numbers. Circle the number that is greater than the other number.
- You have 18 balls. Your friend has a number of balls that is greater than 15 and less than 17. Draw the balls. Write the numbers. Draw a line through the number that is less than the other number.

Name ______________________

Learning Target: Use counting to compare the numbers of objects in two groups.

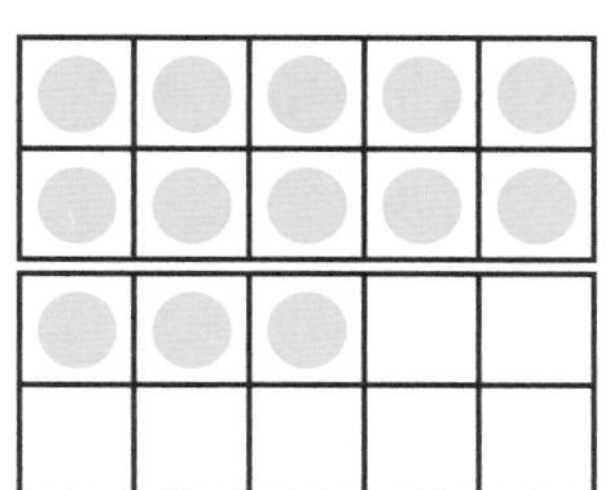

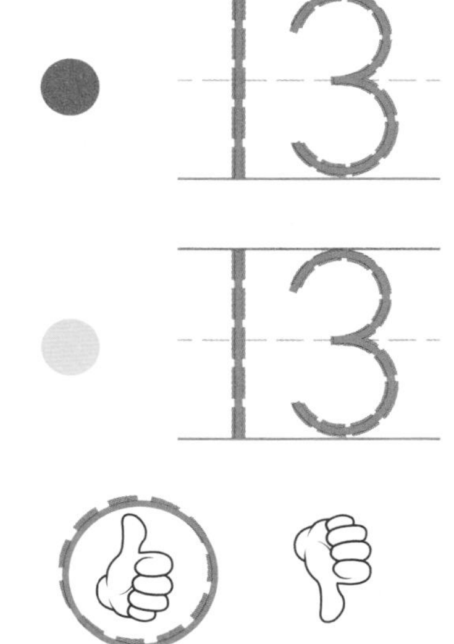

Directions: Count the dots in each set of ten frames. Write each number. Is the number of green dots equal to the number of yellow dots? Circle the thumbs up for *yes* or the thumbs down for *no*.

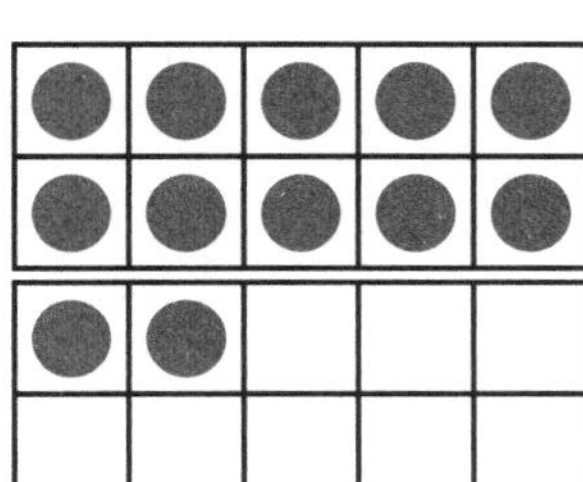

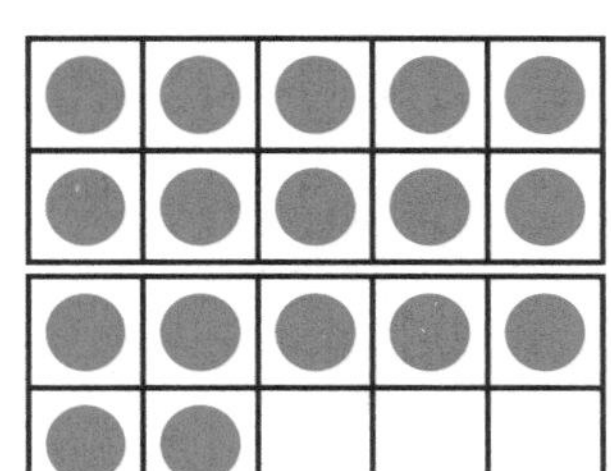

Directions: 1 Count the dots in each set of ten frames. Write each number. Is the number of blue dots equal to the number of red dots? Circle the thumbs up for *yes* or the thumbs down for *no*.

2

3

4

Who has less?

Directions: 2 Count the bouncy balls in each group. Write each number. Circle the number that is greater than the other number. 3 Count the dots on each domino. Write each number. Draw a line through the number that is less than the other number. 4 You have 13 balls. Your friend has a number of balls that is 1 more than 19. Draw the balls. Write the numbers. Draw a line through the number that is less than the other number.

Name ______

Performance Task 9

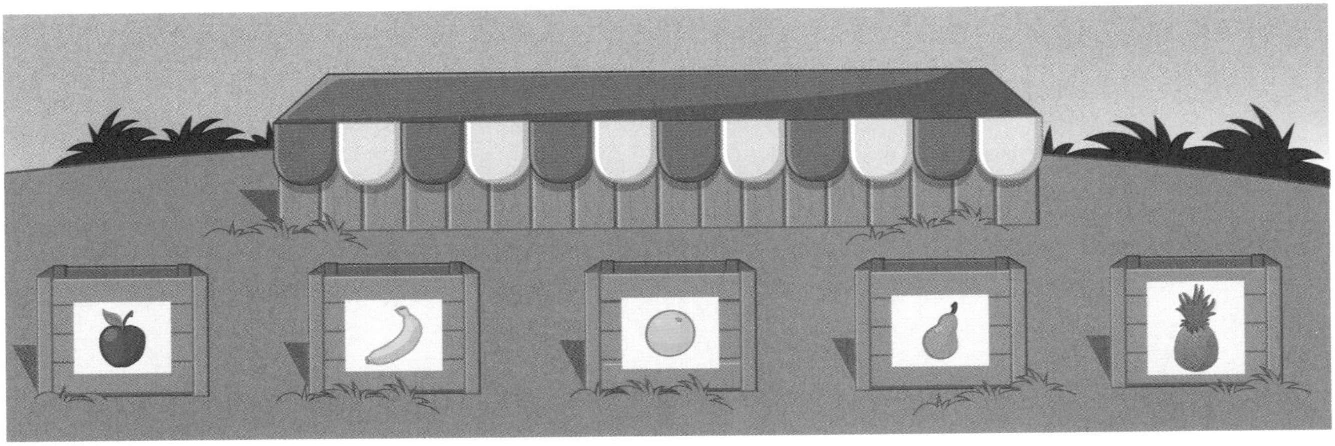

Directions: Use the clues to find the number of fruit in each crate. Write each number.

- The number of apples is more than 16 but less than 18.
- The number of bananas is more than 15 but less than 17.
- The number of oranges is more than 18 but less than 20.
- The number of pears is 1 more than the number of oranges.
- The number of pineapples is 1 less than the number of oranges.
- Write the numbers in order.

Number Boss

Player 1	Player 2

Directions: Each player flips a card and places it on the page. Compare the numbers. The player with the greater number takes both cards. If the numbers are equal, flip the cards again. The player with the greater number takes all the cards. Repeat until all cards have been used.

Name ______________________

Chapter Practice 9

9.1 Model and Count 20

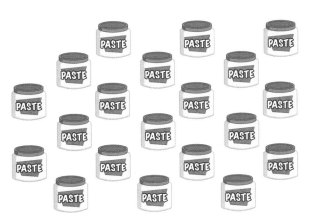

1

9.2 Count and Write 20

______

______

Directions: 1 Count the paste jars. Color the boxes to show how many. 2 Count the insects in the picture. Say the number. Write the number.

9.3 Count to Find How Many

3

11

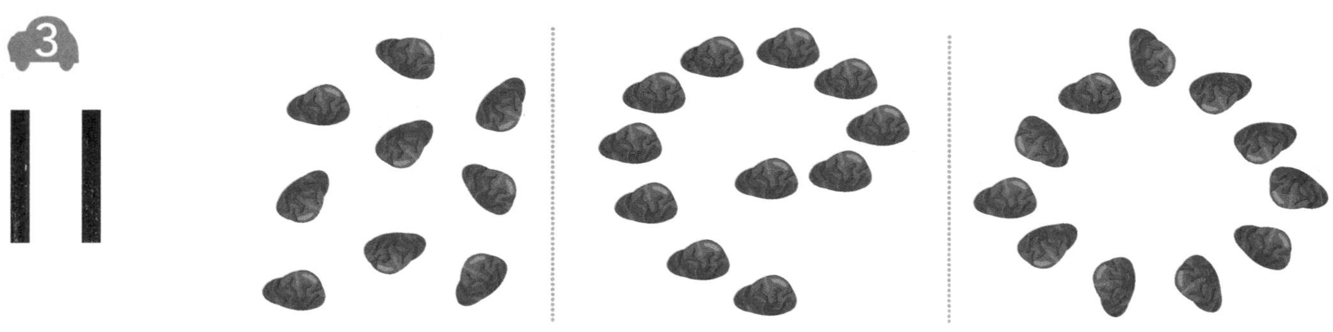

4

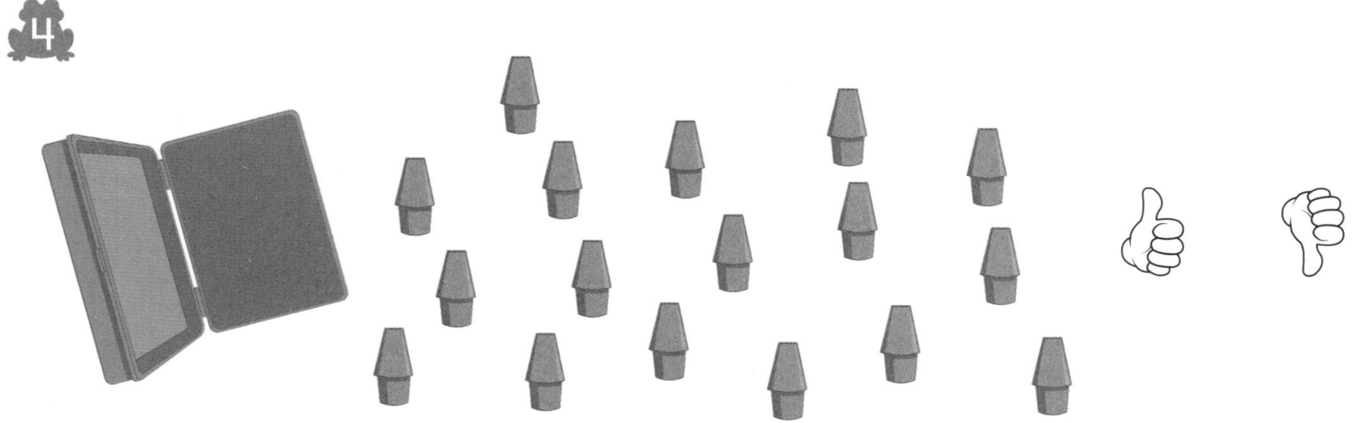

9.4 Count Forward from Any Number to 20

1	2	3	4	5	6	7	8	9	10
11	12	13	14	15	16	17	18	19	20

5 ____ ____ ____ ____ 10

Directions: 3 Circle any group that has the given number of objects. 4 You have 20 erasers in your box. You drop your box. Did you find all of your erasers? Circle the thumbs up for *yes* or the thumbs down for *no*. 5 Count forward from the number in the blue circle to the number in the red circle. Write the numbers you count.

6

1	2	3	4	5	6	7	8	9	10
11	12	13	14	15	16	17	18	19	20

15

9.5 Order Numbers to 20

Directions: 6 Count forward from the number in the blue circle to the number in the red circle. Write the numbers you count. 7 Line up the students for recess by writing the numbers in order. Circle the student who is first. Underline the student who is last.

9.6 Compare Numbers to 20

8

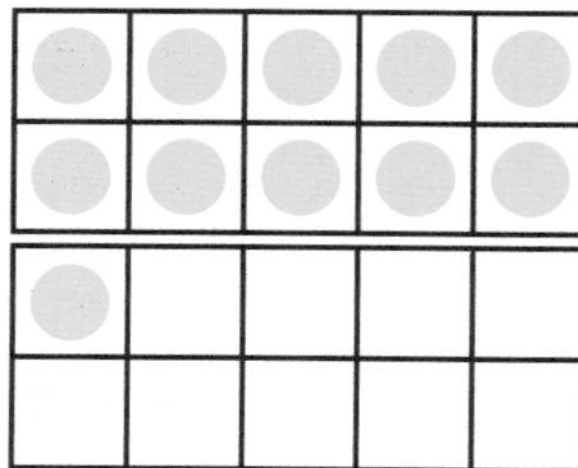

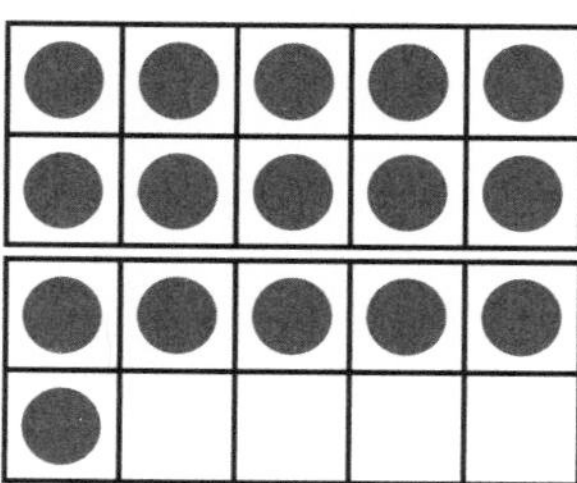

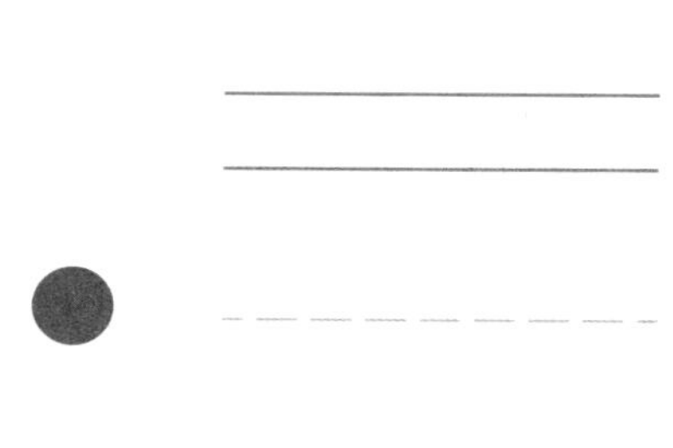

9

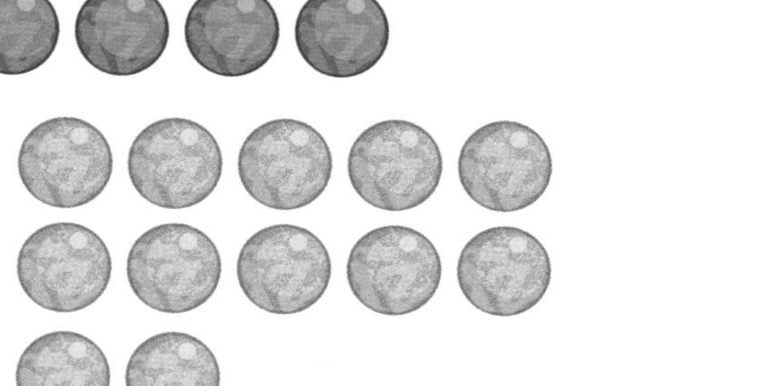

Directions: Count the objects in each group. Write each number. 8 Is the number of yellow dots equal to the number of blue dots? Circle the thumbs up for *yes* or the thumbs down for *no*. 9 Circle the number that is greater than the other number. 10 Draw a line through the number that is less than the other number.

10 Count to 100

- What events do you celebrate?
- How many presents are in the picture?

Chapter Learning Target:
Understand counting to 100.

Chapter Success Criteria:
- I can identify numbers.
- I can name numbers.
- I can describe numbers on a chart.
- I can explain counting numbers with patterns.

Name ______________________

10 Vocabulary

Review Words
ten
addition sentence

______ + ______ = ______

Directions: Circle 10 balloons. Then write an addition sentence to tell how many balloons there are in all.

Chapter 10 Vocabulary Cards

column

decade number

hundred chart

row

1	2	3	4	5	6	7	8	9	10
11	12	13	14	15	16	17	18	19	20
21	22	23	24	25	26	27	28	29	30
31	32	33	34	35	36	37	38	39	40
41	42	43	44	45	46	47	48	49	50
51	52	53	54	55	56	57	58	59	60
61	62	63	64	65	66	67	68	69	70
71	72	73	74	75	76	77	78	79	80
81	82	83	84	85	86	87	88	89	90
91	92	93	94	95	96	97	98	99	100

1	2	3	4	5	6	7	8	9	10
11	12	13	14	15	16	17	18	19	20
21	22	23	24	25	26	27	28	29	30
31	32	33	34	35	36	37	38	39	40
41	42	43	44	45	46	47	48	49	50
51	52	53	54	55	56	57	58	59	60
61	62	63	64	65	66	67	68	69	70
71	72	73	74	75	76	77	78	79	80
81	82	83	84	85	86	87	88	89	90
91	92	93	94	95	96	97	98	99	100

1	2	3	4	5	6	7	8	9	10
11	12	13	14	15	16	17	18	19	20
21	22	23	24	25	26	27	28	29	30
31	32	33	34	35	36	37	38	39	40
41	42	43	44	45	46	47	48	49	50
51	52	53	54	55	56	57	58	59	60
61	62	63	64	65	66	67	68	69	70
71	72	73	74	75	76	77	78	79	80
81	82	83	84	85	86	87	88	89	90
91	92	93	94	95	96	97	98	99	100

1	2	3	4	5	6	7	8	9	10
11	12	13	14	15	16	17	18	19	20
21	22	23	24	25	26	27	28	29	30
31	32	33	34	35	36	37	38	39	40
41	42	43	44	45	46	47	48	49	50
51	52	53	54	55	56	57	58	59	60
61	62	63	64	65	66	67	68	69	70
71	72	73	74	75	76	77	78	79	80
81	82	83	84	85	86	87	88	89	90
91	92	93	94	95	96	97	98	99	100

Name ___________________________

Count to 30 by Ones 10.1

Learning Target: Count to 30 by ones.

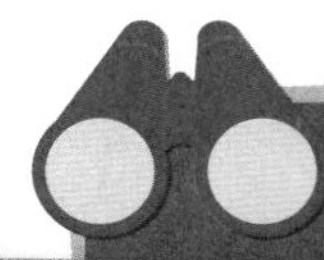

Explore and Grow

1	2	3	4	5	6	7	8	9	10
11	12	13	14	15	16	17	18	19	20
21	22	23	24	25	26	27	28	29	30

Directions: Point to each number as you count to 30. Color the number 30.

Think and Grow

1	2	3	4	5	6	7	8	9	10	7
11	12	13	14	15		17	18	19	20	14
21	22	23	24	25	26	27	28	29	30	16

1	2	3	4	5	6	7	8	9	10	14
11	12	13	14	15	16	17	18	19	20	23
21	22		24	25	26	27	28	29	30	12

1	2	3	4	5	6	7	8		10	9
11	12	13	14	15	16	17	18	19	20	18
21	22	23	24	25	26	27	28	29	30	6

1	2	3	4	5	6	7	8	9	10	11
11	12	13	14	15	16	17	18	19		20
21	22	23	24	25	26	27	28	29	30	29

Directions: Circle the missing number. Count to 30 starting with that number. Color the boxes as you count.

Name ______________________________

Apply and Grow: Practice

1	2	3	4	5	6	7	8	9	10
11	12	13		15	16	17	18	19	20
21	22	23	24	25	26	27	28	29	30

14

15

24

1	2	3	4	5	6	7	8	9	10
11	12	13	14	15	16	17	18	19	20
21	22	23	24	25				29	30

16, 17, 18 | 26, 27, 28 | 17, 18, 19

1	2	3	4	5	6	7	8	9	10
11	12	13	14	15	16	17	18	19	20
21	22	23	24	25	26	27	28	29	30

Directions: 1 Circle the missing number. Count to 30 starting with that number. Color the boxes as you count. 2 Circle the missing numbers. Tell how the missing numbers are alike. 3 Find and circle the number *twenty-three*.

Think and Grow: Modeling Real Life

JUNE

Sunday	Monday	Tuesday	Wednesday	Thursday	Friday	Saturday
			1	2		4
5	6	7	8	9	10	11
12	13		15	16	17	18
19	20	21	22	23	24	25
26	27	28		30		

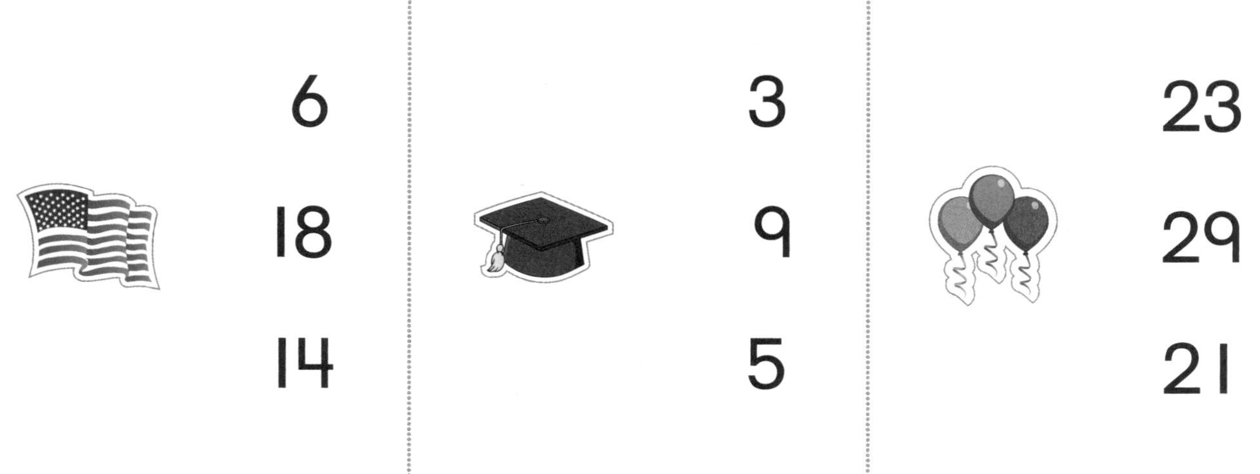

Directions: Circle the missing date for each sticker on the calendar. Circle the sticker that covers the earliest missing date. Underline the sticker that covers the latest missing date.

Name ______________________

Practice 10.1

Learning Target: Count to 30 by ones.

1	2	3	4	5	6	7	8	9	10
11	12	13	14	15	16	17		19	20
21	22	23	24	25	26	27	28	29	30

(18) 27 9

Directions: Circle the missing number. Count to 30 starting with that number. Color the boxes as you count.

1

1	2	3	4	5	6	7	8	9	10
11	12	13	14	15	16	17	18	19	20
21	22	23	24	25	26	27		29	30

26
19
28

1	2	3	4	5	6	7	8	9	10
11	12		14	15	16	17	18	19	20
21	22	23	24	25	26	27	28	29	30

4
22
13

Directions: 1 and 2 Circle the missing number. Count to 30 starting with that number. Color the boxes as you count.

1	2	3	4	5	6	7	8	9	10
11	12	13	14	15	16				20
21	22	23	24	25	26	27	28	29	30

27, 28, 29 | 8, 9, 10 | 17, 18, 19

1	2	3	4	5	6	7	8	9	10
11	12	13	14	15	16	17	18	19	20
21	22	23	24	25	26	27	28	29	30

5

FEBRUARY

Sunday	Monday	Tuesday	Wednesday	Thursday	Friday	Saturday
8	9	10	11	12		14
15		17	18	19	20	21

 10 15 16 |  19 13 14

Directions: 3 Circle the missing numbers. Tell how the missing numbers are alike. 4 Find and circle the number *fourteen*. 5 Circle the missing date for each sticker on the calendar. Circle the sticker that covers the earliest missing date. Underline sticker that covers the latest missing date.

Name ____________________

Count to 50 by Ones 10.2

Learning Target: Count to 50 by ones.

Explore and Grow

1	2	3	4	5	6	7	8	9	10
11	12	13	14	15	16	17	18	19	20
21	22	23	24	25	26	27	28	29	30
31	32	33	34	35	36	37	38	39	40
41	42	43	44	45	46	47	48	49	50

Directions: Point to each number as you count to 50. Color the number 50.

Think and Grow

1	2	3	4	5	6	7	8	9	10
11	12	13	14	15	16	17	18	19	20
21	22	23	24	25	26	27	28	29	30
31		33	34	35	36	37	38	39	40
41	42	43	44	45	46	47	48	49	50

23

32

41

1	2	3	4	5	6	7	8	9	10
11	12	13	14	15	16	17	18	19	20
21	22	23	24	25	26		28	29	30
31	32	33	34	35	36	37	38	39	40
41	42	43	44	45	46	47	48	49	50

36

18

27

1	2	3	4	5	6	7	8	9	10
11	12	13	14	15	16	17	18	19	20
21	22	23	24	25	26	27	28	29	30
31	32	33	34	35	36	37	38	39	40
41	42	43		45	46	47	48	49	50

44

35

33

Directions: Circle the missing number. Count to 50 starting with that number. Color the boxes as you count.

Name ____________________

Apply and Grow: Practice

1	2	3	4	5	6	7	8	9	10
11	12	13	14	15	16	17	18	19	20
	22	23	24	25	26	27	28	29	30
31	32	33	34	35	36	37	38	39	40
41	42	43	44	45	46	47	48	49	50

12

21

30

1	2	3	4	5	6	7	8	9	10
11	12	13	14	15	16	17	18	19	20
21	22	23	24	25	26	27	28	29	30
31	32	33	34	35	36				40
41	42	43	44	45	46	47	48	49	50

37, 38, 39 | 46, 47, 48 | 26, 27, 28

1	2	3	4	5	6	7	8	9	10
11	12	13	14	15	16	17	18	19	20
21	22	23	24	25	26	27	28	29	30
31	32	33	34	35	36	37	38	39	40
41	42	43	44	45	46	47	48	49	50

Directions: 1 Circle the missing number. Count to 50 starting with that number. Color the boxes as you count. 2 Circle the missing numbers. Tell how the missing numbers are alike. 3 Find and circle the numbers *thirty-two* and *forty-seven*.

Think and Grow: Modeling Real Life

1	2	3	4	5
6	7	8	9	10
11	12	13	14	15
16	17		19	20
21	22	23	24	25
26	27	28	29	30
	32	33	34	
36	37	38	39	40
41	42	43	44	45
46	47	48	49	50

35

27

31

18

14

22

40

31

35

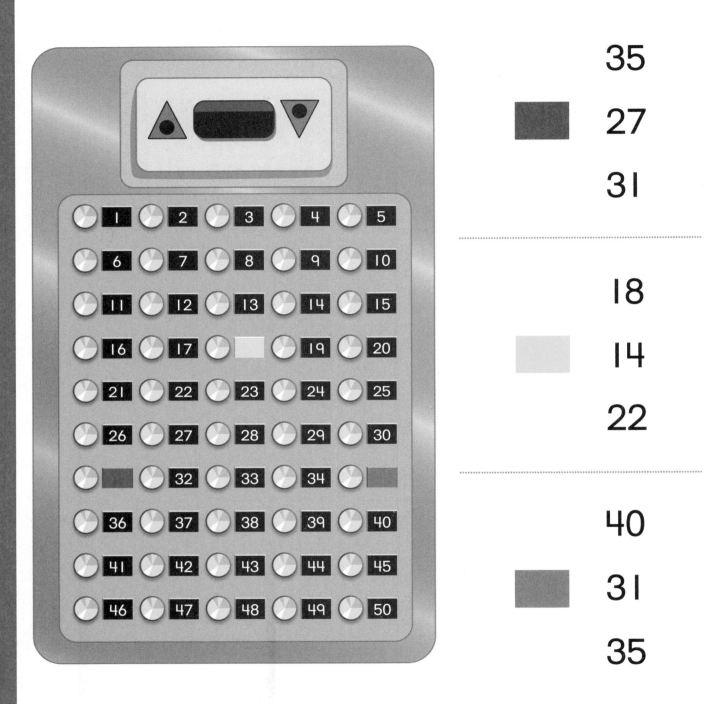

Directions: Circle the missing floor number for each color on the elevator keypad. Circle the color that covers the lowest missing floor number. Underline the color that covers the highest missing floor number.

Name ___________________________

Practice 10.2

Learning Target: Count to 50 by ones.

1	2	3	4	5	6	7	8	9	10
11	12	13	14	15	16	17	18	19	20
21	22	23	24	25	26	27	28	29	30
31	32	33	34	35		37	38	39	40
41	42	43	44	45	46	47	48	49	50

27

45

36

Directions: Circle the missing number. Count to 50 starting with that number. Color the boxes as you count.

1

1	2	3	4	5	6	7	8	9	10
11	12	13	14	15	16	17	18	19	20
21	22	23	24	25	26	27	28	29	30
31	32	33		35	36	37	38	39	40
41	42	43	44	45	46	47	48	49	50

34

25

43

1	2	3	4	5	6	7	8	9	10
11	12	13	14	15	16	17	18	19	20
21	22	23	24	25	26	27	28	29	
31	32	33	34	35	36	37	38	39	40
41	42	43	44	45	46	47	48	49	50

21

30

39

Directions: 1 and 2 Circle the missing number. Count to 50 starting with that number. Color the boxes as you count.

1	2	3	4	5	6	7	8	9	10
11	12	13	14	15	16	17	18	19	20
21	22	23	24	25	26	27	28	29	30
31	32	33	34	35	36	37	38	39	40
			44	45	46	47	48	49	50

43, 44, 45 | 32, 33, 34 | 41, 42, 43

1	2	3	4	5	6	7	8	9	10
11	12	13	14	15	16	17	18	19	20
21	22	23	24	25	26	27	28	29	30
31	32	33	34	35	36	37	38	39	40
41	42	43	44	45	46	47	48	49	50

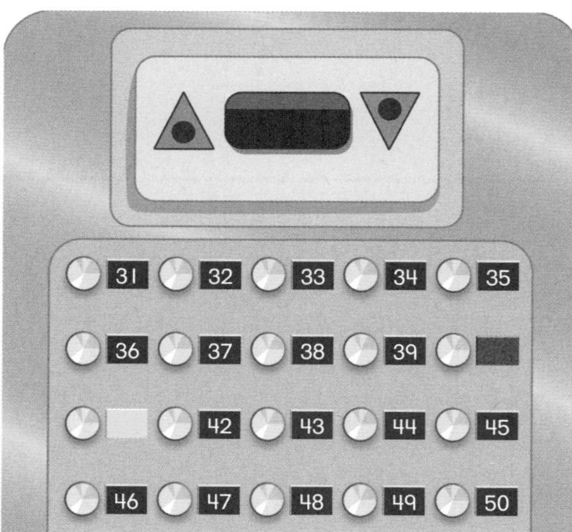

36

40

44

45

37

41

Directions: 3 Circle the missing numbers. Tell how the missing numbers are alike. 4 Find and circle the numbers *twenty-six* and *forty-two*. 5 Circle the missing floor number for each color on the elevator keypad. Circle the color that covers the lowest missing floor number. Underline the color that covers the highest missing floor number.

Name ______________________

Count to 100 by Ones 10.3

Learning Target: Count to 100 by ones.

Explore and Grow

1	2	3	4	5	6	7	8	9	10
11	12	13	14	15	16	17	18	19	20
21	22	23	24	25	26	27	28	29	30
31	32	33	34	35	36	37	38	39	40
41	42	43	44	45	46	47	48	49	50
51	52	53	54	55	56	57	58	59	60
61	62	63	64	65	66	67	68	69	70
71	72	73	74	75	76	77	78	79	80
81	82	83	84	85	86	87	88	89	90
91	92	93	94	95	96	97	98	99	100

Directions: Point to each number as you count to 100. Color the numbers 30, 50, and 100.

Think and Grow

1	2	3	4	5	6	7	8	9	10
11	12	13	14	15	16	17	18	19	20
21	22	23	24	25	26	27	28	29	30
31	32	33	34	35		37	38	39	40
41	42	43	44	45	46	47	48	49	50
51	52	53	54	55	56	57	58		60
61	62	63	64	65	66	67	68	69	70
71	72		74	75	76	77	78	79	80
81	82	83	84	85	86	87	88	89	90
91	92	93	94	95	96	97	98	99	100

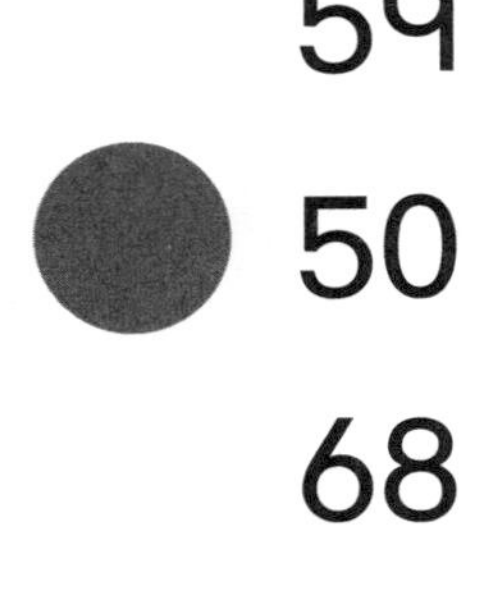

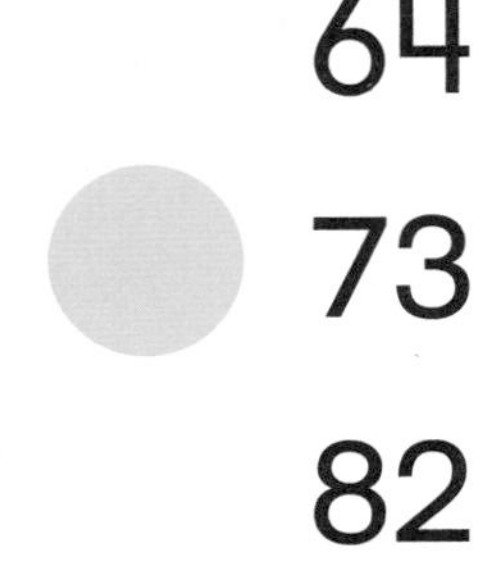

Directions: Circle the first missing number. Count to 100 starting with that number. Color the boxes as you count. Circle the other missing numbers as you count and color to 100.

Name ______________________________

Apply and Grow: Practice

1	2	3	4	5	6	7	8	9	10
11	12	13	14	15	16	17	18	19	20
21	22	23	24	25	26	27	28	29	30
31	32	33	34	35	36	37	38	39	40
41	42	43	44	45	46		48	49	50
51	52	53	54	55	56	57	58	59	60
	62	63	64	65	66	67	68	69	70
71	72	73	74	75	76	77	78	79	80
81	82	83	84	85	86	87	88	89	90
91	92		94	95	96	97	98	99	100

1

47
 56
38

70
 52
61

82
93
84

Directions: 1 Circle the first missing number. Count to 100 starting with that number. Color the boxes as you count. Circle the other missing numbers as you count and color to 100.

Think and Grow: Modeling Real Life

61 62 63 64 65 66 68 69 70

71 72 73 74 75 76 77 79 80

81 82 83 84 85 87 88 89 90

78

67

86

Directions: Your friend, Newton, and Descartes each have 10 prize tickets. They each lose 1 ticket.

- Circle the owner of each lost ticket.
- The winning ticket number is 1 more than 70. Circle the winning ticket number. Who is the winner? Circle the face of the winning ticket holder.

Name ______________________________

Practice 10.3

Learning Target: Count to 100 by ones.

1	2	3	4	5	6	7	8	9	10
11	12	13	14	15	16	17	18	19	20
21	22	23	24	25	26	27	28	29	30
31	32	33	34	35	36	37	38	39	40
41	42	43	44	45	46	47	48	49	50
51	52	53	54	55	●	57	58	59	60
61	62	63	64	65	66	67	68	69	70
71	72	73	74	75	76	77	●	79	80
81	82	83	84	85	86	87	88	89	90
91	92	93	94	95	96	97	98	99	100

● 65 (56) 47

● 55 68 (78)

Directions: Circle the missing number. Count to 100 starting with that number. Color the boxes as you count. Circle the other missing number as you count and color to 100.

1	2	3	4	5	6	7	8	9	10
11	12	13	14	15	16	17	18	19	20
21	22	23	24	25	26	27	28	29	30
31	32	33	34	35	36	37	38	39	40
41	42	43	44	45	46	47	48	49	50
51	52	●	54	55	56	57	58	59	60
61	62	63	64	65	66	67	68	69	70
71	72	73	74	75	76	77	78	79	80
81	82	●	84	85	86	87	88	89	90
91	92	93	94	95	96	97	98	99	100

1 ● 53 44 83 ● 74 92 83

Directions: 1 Circle the first missing number. Count to 100 starting with that number. Color the boxes as you count. Circle the other missing number as you count and color to 100.

1	2	3	4	5	6	7	8	9	10
11	12	13	14	15	16	17	18	19	20
21	22	23	24	25	26	27	28	29	30
31	32	33	34	35	36	37	38	39	40
41	42	43	44	45	46	47	48	49	50
51	52	53	54	55	56	57	58	59	60
61	62	63	64	65	66	67	68	69	70
71	72	73	74	75	76	77	78		
	82	83	84	85	86	87	88	89	90
91	92	93	94	95	96	97	98	99	100

68, 69, 70 | 79, 80, 81 | 86, 87, 88

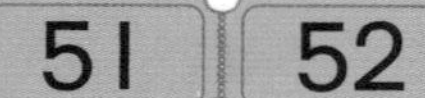

51 52

54 55 56 57 58 59 60

61 62 63 64 65 66 67 69 70

53

68

Directions: Circle the missing numbers. Newton and Descartes both have 10 prize tickets. They both lose 1 ticket. Circle the owner of each lost ticket. The winning ticket number is 1 more than 50. Circle the winning ticket number. Who is the winner? Circle the face of the winning ticket holder.

Name ______________________

Count to 100 by Tens 10.4

Learning Target: Count to 100 by tens.

Explore and Grow

1	2	3	4	5	6	7	8	9	10
11	12	13	14	15	16	17	18	19	20
21	22	23	24	25	26	27	28	29	30
31	32	33	34	35	36	37	38	39	40
41	42	43	44	45	46	47	48	49	50
51	52	53	54	55	56	57	58	59	60
61	62	63	64	65	66	67	68	69	70
71	72	73	74	75	76	77	78	79	80
81	82	83	84	85	86	87	88	89	90
91	92	93	94	95	96	97	98	99	100

Directions: Count to 10. Circle the number. Count 10 more. Circle the number. Repeat this process until you reach 100.

Think and Grow

1	2	3	4	5	6	7	8	9	10
11	12	13	14	15	16	17	18	19	20
21	22	23	24	25	26	27	28	29	30
31	32	33	34	35	36	37	38	39	40
41	42	43	44	45	46	47	48	49	50
51	52	53	54	55	56	57	58	59	
61	62	63	64	65	66	67	68	69	70
71	72	73	74	75	76	77	78	79	80
81	82	83	84	85	86	87	88	89	90
91	92	93	94	95	96	97	98	99	100

20 40 60

50 60 70

1	2	3	4	5	6	7	8	9	10
11	12	13	14	15	16	17	18	19	20
21	22	23	24	25	26	27	28	29	30
31	32	33	34	35	36	37	38	39	40
41	42	43	44	45	46	47	48	49	50
51	52	53	54	55	56	57	58	59	60
61	62	63	64	65	66	67	68	69	70
71	72	73	74	75	76	77	78	79	80
81	82	83	84	85	86	87	88	89	
91	92	93	94	95	96	97	98	99	100

60 70 90

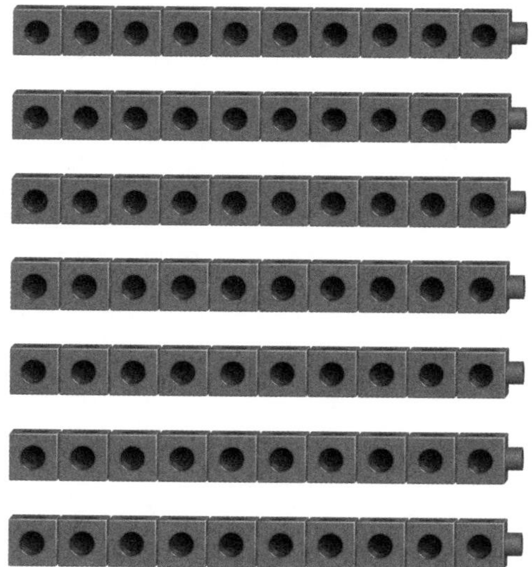

70 80 90

Directions:

- Count to 100 by tens. Color the boxes as you count. Circle the missing decade number.
- Count the linking cubes. Circle the number that tells how many.

Name ________________________________

Apply and Grow: Practice

20 30 50

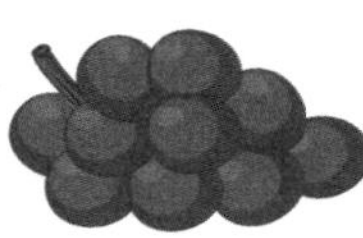

40 80 100

1	2	3	4	5	6	7	8	9	10
11	12	13	14	15	16	17	18	19	
21	22	23	24	25	26	27	28	29	
31	32	33	34	35	36	37	38	39	
41	42	43	44	45	46	47	48	49	50
51	52	53	54	55	56	57	58	59	60
61	62	63	64	65	66	67	68	69	70
71	72	73	74	75	76	77	78	79	80
81	82	83	84	85	86	87	88	89	90
91	92	93	94	95	96	97	98	99	100

15, 25, 35

20, 30, 40

40, 50, 60

Directions: 1 and 2 Count the objects. Circle the number that tells how many. 3 Count to 100 by tens. Color the boxes as you count. Circle the missing decade numbers.

Think and Grow: Modeling Real Life

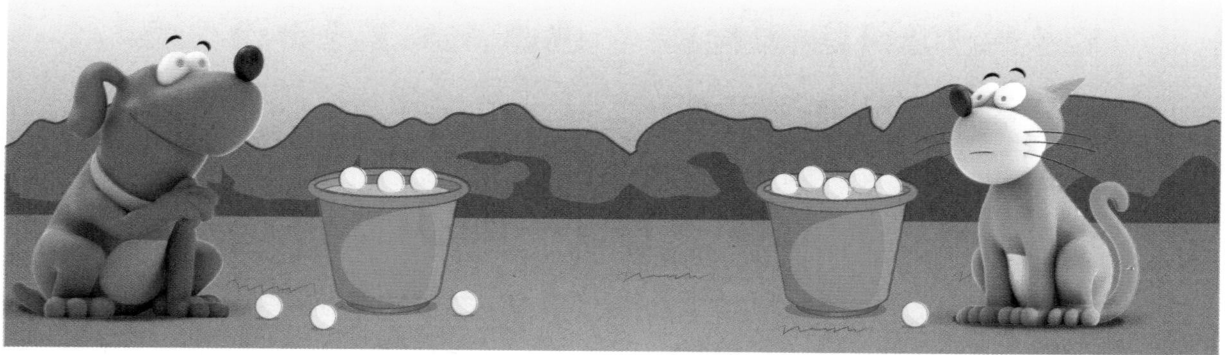

10 20 30 40 50 60

10 20 30 40 50 60

Directions: Newton and Descartes each toss 6 balls. Each time a ball lands in their bucket, they earn 10 points. The player with the most points wins.

- Newton gets 3 balls in his bucket. Circle the number of points Newton earns. Draw a picture to show how you found your answer.
- Descartes gets 5 balls in his bucket. Circle the number of points Descartes earns. Draw a picture to show how you found your answer.
- Who earns more points? Circle the face of the winning player.

Name ______________________________

Practice 

Learning Target: Count to 100 by tens.

1	2	3	4	5	6	7	8	9	10
11	12	13	14	15	16	17	18	19	20
21	22	23	24	25	26	27	28	29	30
31	32	33	34	35	36	37	38	39	
41	42	43	44	45	46	47	48	49	50
51	52	53	54	55	56	57	58	59	60
61	62	63	64	65	66	67	68	69	70
71	72	73	74	75	76	77	78	79	80
81	82	83	84	85	86	87	88	89	90
91	92	93	94	95	96	97	98	99	100

(40) 20 70

50 (40)  70

Directions:

- Count to 100 by tens. Color the boxes as you count. Circle the missing decade number.
- Count the linking cubes. Circle the number that tells how many.

30 60 50

50 65 70

Directions: 1 and 2 Count the objects. Circle the number that tells how many.

3

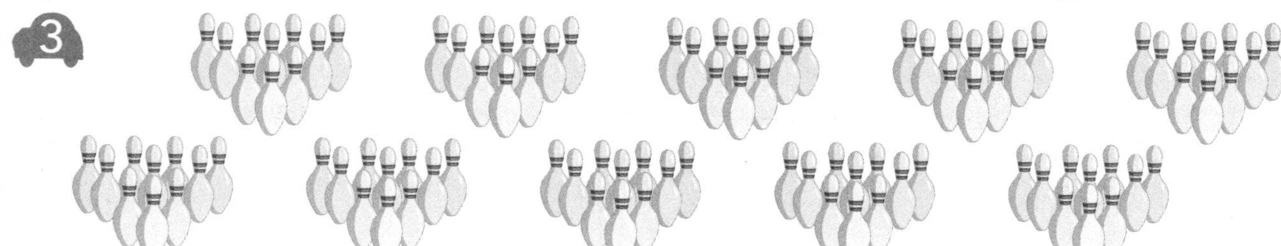

10 90 100

1	2	3	4	5	6	7	8	9	10
11	12	13	14	15	16	17	18	19	20
21	22	23	24	25	26	27	28	29	30
31	32	33	34	35	36	37	38	39	40
41	42	43	44	45	46	47	48	49	50
51	52	53	54	55	56	57	58	59	60
61	62	63	64	65	66	67	68	69	
71	72	73	74	75	76	77	78	79	
81	82	83	84	85	86	87	88	89	
91	92	93	94	95	96	97	98	99	100

70, 75, 80

50, 40, 30

70, 80, 90

50

4

40

Directions: 3 Count the bowling pins. Circle the number that tells how many. 4 Count to 100 by tens. Color the boxes as you count. Circle the missing decade numbers. 5 Each time a ball sticks to the wall you earn 10 points. Four of your balls stick to the wall. Circle the number of points you earn. Draw a picture to show how you found your answer.

Name ______________________

Learning Target: Count by tens and ones within 100.

Explore and Grow

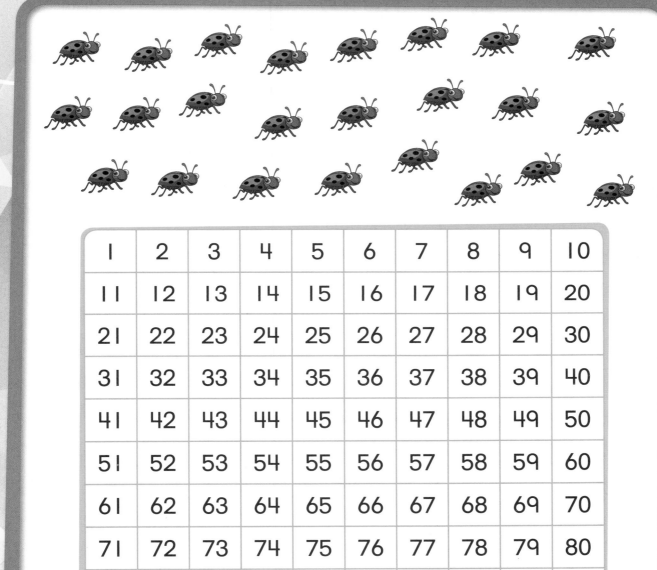

1	2	3	4	5	6	7	8	9	10
11	12	13	14	15	16	17	18	19	20
21	22	23	24	25	26	27	28	29	30
31	32	33	34	35	36	37	38	39	40
41	42	43	44	45	46	47	48	49	50
51	52	53	54	55	56	57	58	59	60
61	62	63	64	65	66	67	68	69	70
71	72	73	74	75	76	77	78	79	80
81	82	83	84	85	86	87	88	89	90
91	92	93	94	95	96	97	98	99	100

Directions: Circle groups of 10 ladybugs. Count the ladybugs. Circle the number in the chart that tells how many. Color to show how you counted.

Think and Grow

1	2	3	4	5	6	7	8	9	10
11	12	13	14	15	16	17	18	19	20
21	22	23	24	25	26	27	28	29	30
31	32	33	34	35	36	37	38	39	40
41	42	43	44	45	46	47	48	49	50
51	52	53	54	55	56	57	58	59	60
61	62	63	64	65	66	67	68	69	70
71	72	73	74	75	76	77	78	79	80
81	82	83	84	85	86	87	88	89	90
91	92	93	94	95	96	97	98	99	100

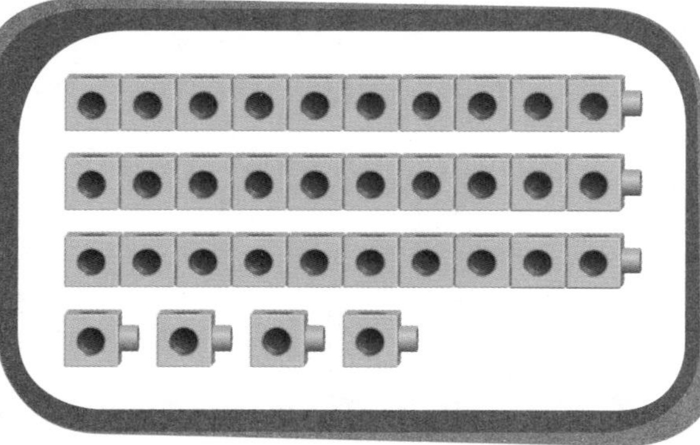

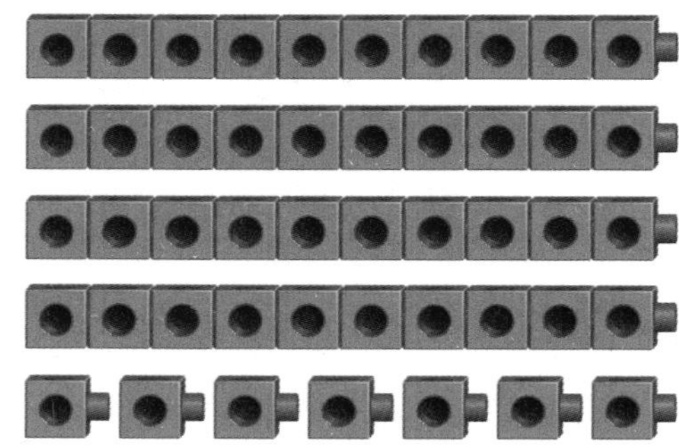

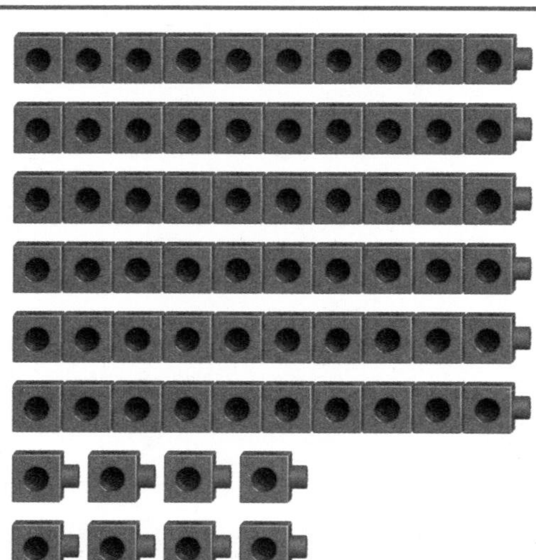

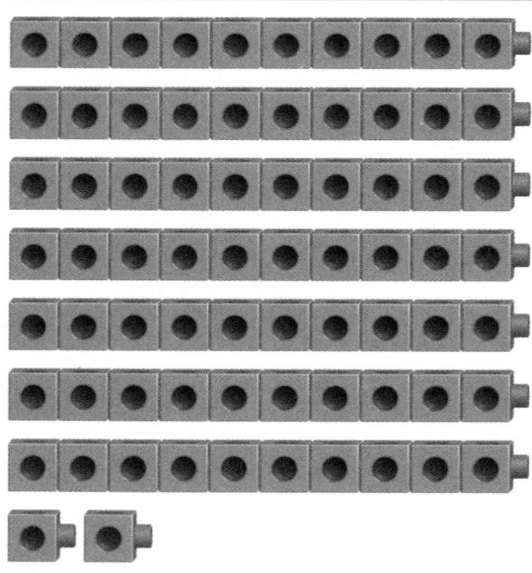

Directions: Count the linking cubes. Find the number in the hundred chart that tells how many. Color the number. Tell how you counted.

Name ______________________________

Apply and Grow: Practice

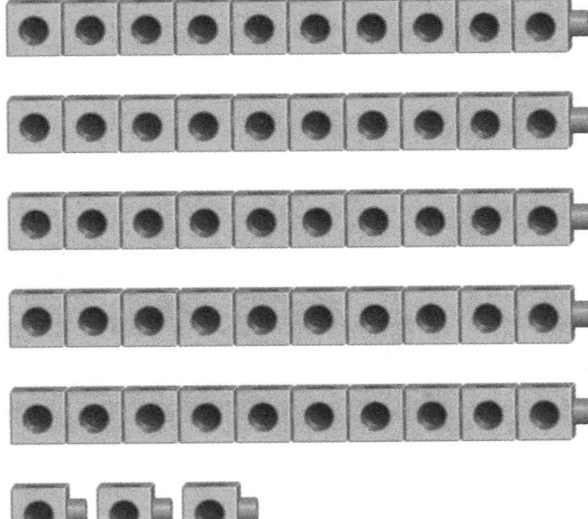

43

35

53

29

11

38

84

48

12

Directions: 1–3 Count the objects. Circle the number that tells how many. Tell how you counted.

Think and Grow: Modeling Real Life

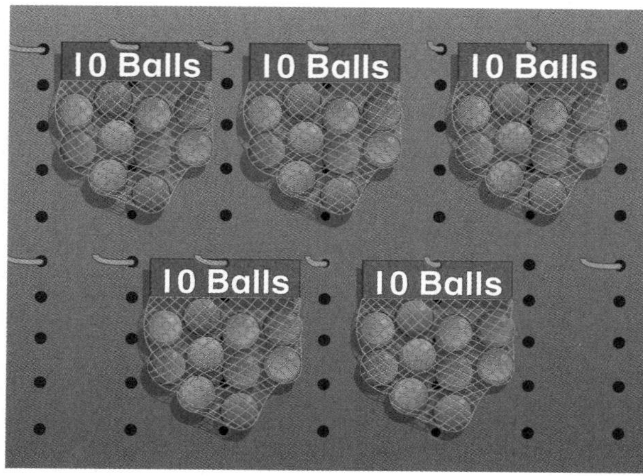

6 14 59 60 95

8 20 61 79 80

Directions: A toy store sells bouncy balls individually and in bags of 10.

- Count the bouncy balls. Circle the number that tells how many.
- The store orders 2 more bags of bouncy balls. Draw the new bags of balls.
- Circle the number that tells how many bouncy balls the store has now.

Name ______________________

Learning Target: Count by tens and ones within 100.

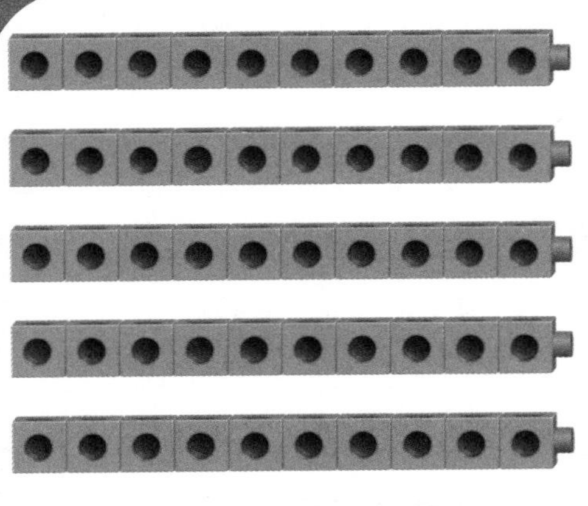

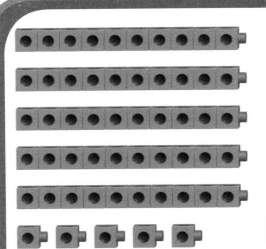

1	2	3	4	5	6	7	8	9	10
11	12	13	14	15	16	17	18	19	20
21	22	23	24	25	26	27	28	29	30
31	32	33	34	35	36	37	38	39	40
41	42	43	44	45	46	47	48	49	50
51	52	53	54	55	56	57	58	59	60
61	62	63	64	65	66	67	68	69	70
71	72	73	74	75	76	77	78	79	80
81	82	83	84	85	86	87	88	89	90
91	92	93	94	95	96	97	98	99	100

by tens and by ones

Directions: Count the linking cubes. Find the number in the chart that tells how many. Color the number. Tell how you counted.

10

19

20

11

47

56

Directions: 1 and 2 Count the objects. Circle the number that tells how many. Tell how you counted.

3

29

90

92

4

36

9

63

5

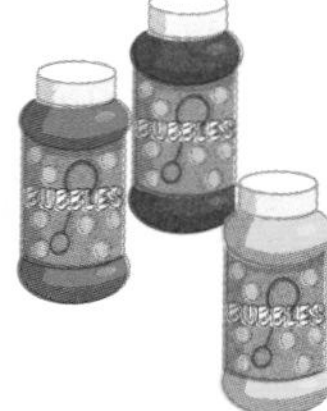

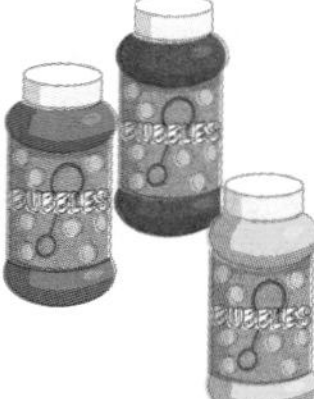

9		66
21		62
32		39
36		12

Directions: 3 and 4 Count the objects. Circle the number that tells how many. Tell how you counted. 5 Count the bottles of bubbles. Circle the number that tells how many. Draw 3 more packs of bubbles. Circle the number that tells how many bottles of bubbles there are now.

Name ___________________________

Learning Target: Count by tens from a given number within 100.

Count by Tens from a Number 10.6

Explore and Grow

1	2	3	4	5	6	7	8	9	10
11	12	13	14	15	16	17	18	19	20
21	22	23	24	25	26	27	28	29	30
31	32	33	34	35	36	37	38	39	40
41	42	43	44	45	46	47	48	49	50
51	52	53	54	55	56	57	58	59	60
61	62	63	64	65	66	67	68	69	70
71	72	73	74	75	76	77	78	79	80
81	82	83	84	85	86	87	88	89	90
91	92	93	94	95	96	97	98	99	100

Directions: Count each group of linking cubes. Circle the numbers in the chart that tell how many for each group. What is the same in each number? What is different in each number?

Think and Grow

1	2	3	(4)	5	6	7	8	9	10
11	12	13		15	16	17	18	19	20
21	22	23		25	26	27	28	29	30
31	32	33		35	36	37	38	39	40
41	42	43	44	45	46	47	(48)	49	50
(51)	52	53	54	55	56	57		59	60
	62	63	64	65	66	67		69	70
	72	73	74	75	76	77		79	80
	82	83	84	85	86	87	88	89	90
91	92	93	94	95	96	97	98	99	100

(51)	52, 53, 54	61, 62, 63	(61, 71, 81)
(4)	14, 24, 34	5, 6, 7	14, 15, 16
(48)	38, 28, 18	58, 68, 78	49, 50, 51

Directions: Count by tens starting with the circled number. Circle the correct group of missing numbers.

Name ______________________________

Apply and Grow: Practice

1	2	3	4	5	6	7	8	9	10
11	12	13	14	15	16	(17)	18	19	20
21	22	23	24	25	26		28	29	30
31	32	33	(34)	35	36		38	39	40
41	42	43		45	(46)		48	49	50

(17) 18, 19, 20 | 26, 36, 46 | 27, 37, 47

(34) 23, 33, 43 | 44, 54, 64 | 35, 36, 37

(46) 56, 66, 76 | 47, 48, 49 | 26, 36, 46

19, 29, 39, 49, 59, ____, 79, 89, 99

60 69 78

Directions: 1–3 Count by tens starting with the circled number. Circle the numbers that tell how you counted. 4 Circle the missing number. Tell how you counted.

Think and Grow: Modeling Real Life

5 7 20 25 50

Directions: A grocery store sells milk cartons individually and in boxes of 10.

- Count the milk cartons. Circle the number that tells how many.
- You need 75 milk cartons in all. Draw to show how many more boxes of milk cartons you need.

Name ______________________

Practice 

Learning Target: Count by tens from a given number within 100.

1	2	3	4	5	6	7	8	9	10
11	12	13	14	(15)	16	17	18	19	20
21	22	23	24		26	27	28	29	30
31	32	33	34		36	37	38	39	40
41	42	43	44		46	47	48	49	50

(25, 35, 45) | 16, 17, 18 | 4, 14, 24

Directions: Count by tens starting with the circled number. Circle the missing numbers.

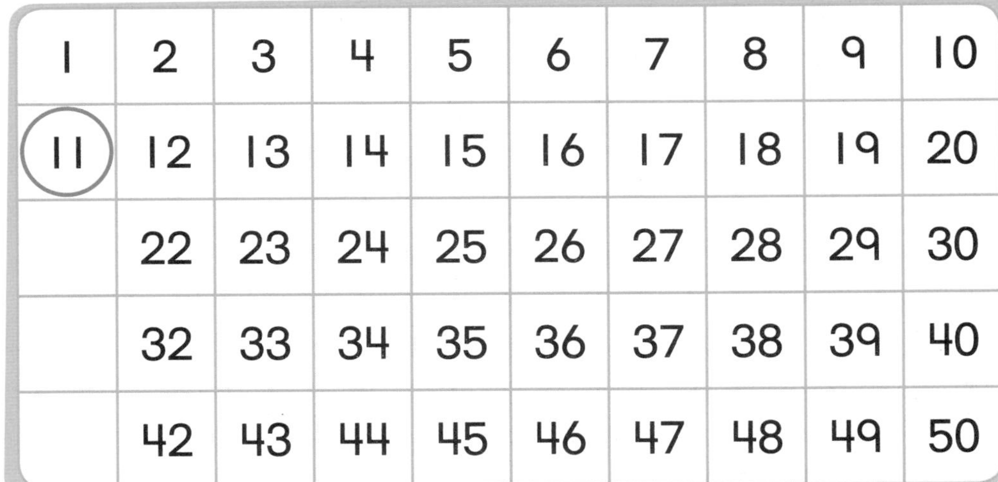

1	2	3	4	5	6	7	8	9	10
(11)	12	13	14	15	16	17	18	19	20
	22	23	24	25	26	27	28	29	30
	32	33	34	35	36	37	38	39	40
	42	43	44	45	46	47	48	49	50

1 12, 13, 14 | 21, 31, 41 | 20, 30, 40

Directions: 1 Count by tens starting with the circled number. Circle the missing numbers.

(62) 63, 64, 65 | 72, 82, 92 | 61, 71, 81

3

(19) 29, 39, 49 | 20, 21, 22 | 20, 30, 40

4

(53) 54, 55, 56 | 55, 57, 59 | 63, 73, 83

5

27, 37, 47, 57, 67, 77, ____, 97

78 96 87

16

26

10

Directions: 2–4 Count by tens starting with the circled number. Circle the numbers that tell how you counted. 5 Circle the missing number. Tell how you counted. 6 Count the cups of applesauce. Circle the number that tells how many. You need 36 cups of applesauce in all. Draw to show how many more boxes you need.

Name ____________________

Performance Task 10

65

11

56

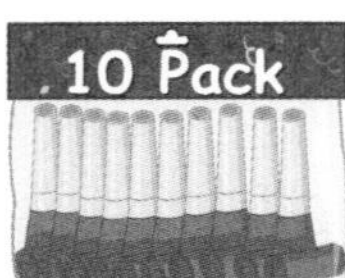

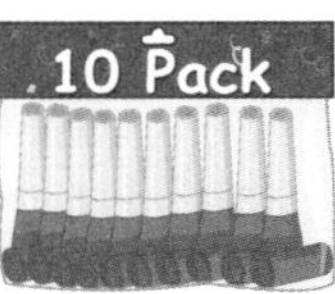

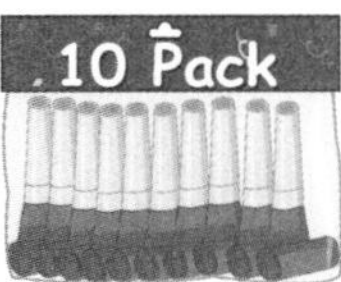

59

77 66, 76, 86 57, 58, 59 57, 67, 77

86

Directions: A store sells gift bags and party blowers in packages of 10 and individually. 1 Count the gift bags. Circle the number that tells how many. 2 You buy an equal number of party blowers and gift bags. Draw more party blowers to complete the picture. 3 You buy 3 more packages of party blowers for the adults. Circle the number that tells how many party blowers there are in all. Circle the group of numbers that tells how you counted.

Hundred Chart Puzzle

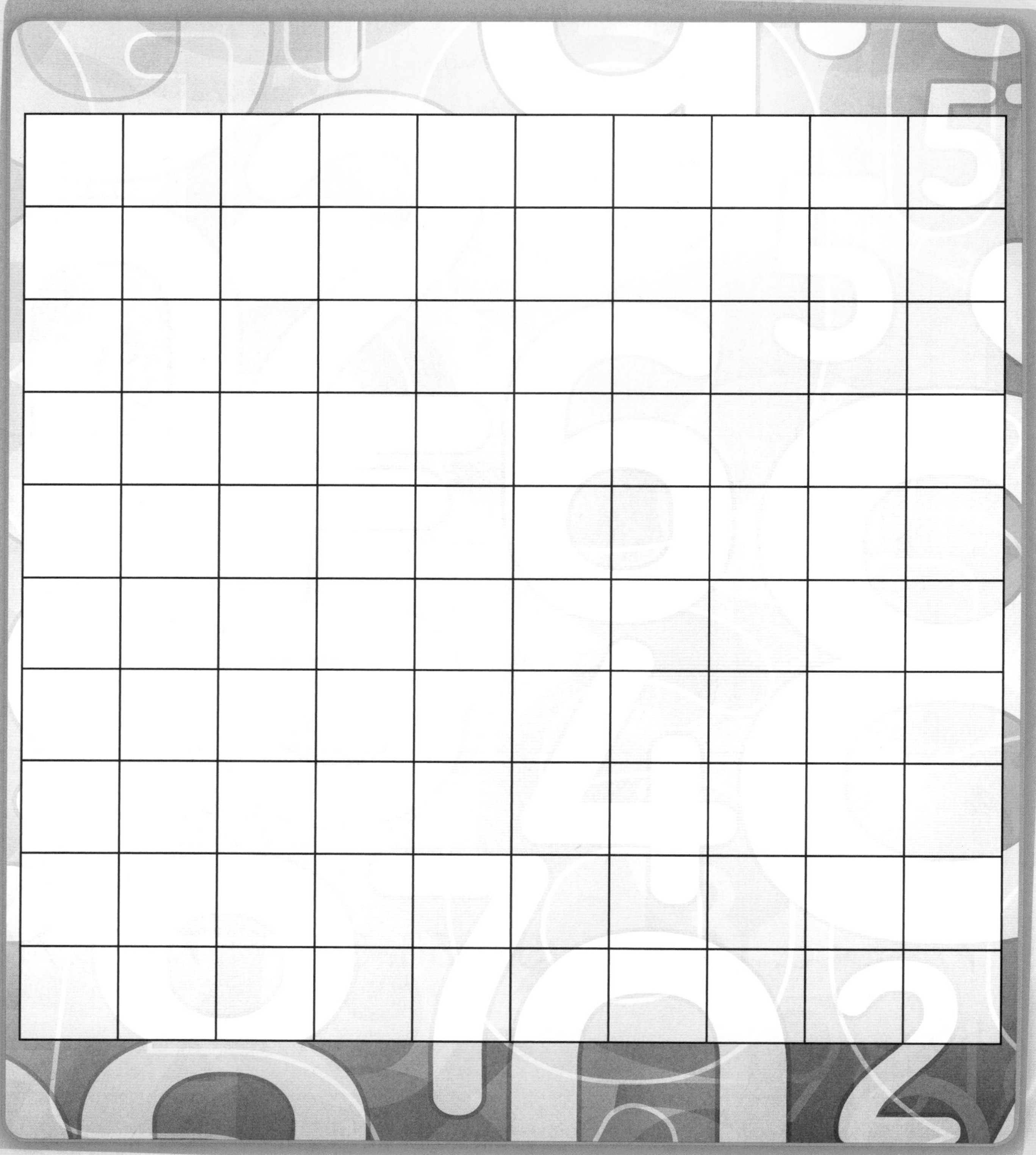

Directions: Cut out the Hundred Chart Puzzle Pieces. Put the pieces together to complete the hundred chart.

Name ______________________________

Chapter Practice 10

10.1 Count to 30 by Ones

1	2	3	4	5	6	7	8	9	10
11	12	13	14	15	16		18	19	20
21	22	23	24	25	26	27	28	29	30

8

17

26

2

1	2	3	4	5	6	7	8	9	10
11	12	13	14	15	16	17	18	19	20
21	22	23	24	25	26	27	28	29	30

10.2 Count to 50 by Ones

1	2	3	4	5	6	7	8	9	10
11	12	13	14	15	16	17	18	19	20
			24	25	26	27	28	29	30
31	32	33	34	35	36	37	38	39	40
41	42	43	44	45	46	47	48	49	50

21, 22, 23 | 28, 29, 30 | 12, 13, 14

Directions: 1 Circle the missing number. Count to 30 starting with that number. Color the boxes as you count. 2 Find and circle the number *twenty-nine*. 3 Circle the missing numbers. Tell how the missing numbers are alike.

10.3 Count to 100 by Ones

1	2	3	4	5	6	7	8	9	10
11	12	13	14	15	16	17	18	19	20
21	●	23	24	25	26	27	28	29	30
31	32	33	34	35	36	37	38	39	40
41	42	43	44	45	46	47	48	49	50
51	52	53	54	●	56	57	58	59	60
61	62	63	64	65	66	67	68	69	70
●	72	73	74	75	76	77	78	79	●
81	82	83	84	85	86	87	88	89	90
91	92	93	94	95	96	97	98	99	100

4

22	46	62	71
● 13	● 64	● 71	● 80
31	55	80	89

Directions: 4 Circle the first missing number. Count to 100 starting with that number. Color the boxes as you count. Circle the other missing numbers as you count and color to 100.

10.4 Count to 100 by Tens

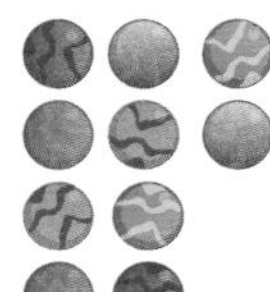 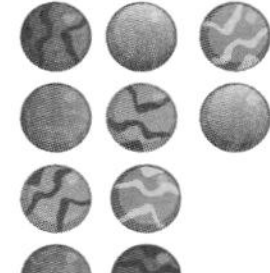 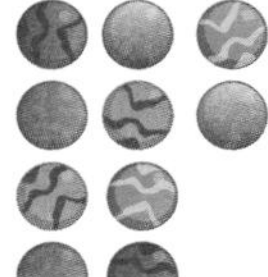 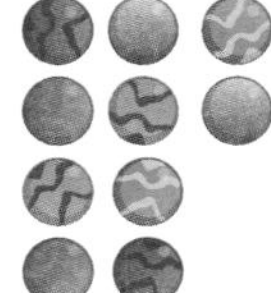

40 65 70

60 70 90

10.5 Count by Tens and Ones

18 88 99

Directions:  and  Count the objects. Circle the number that tells how many.
 Count the crayons. Circle the number that tells how many. Tell how you counted.

8

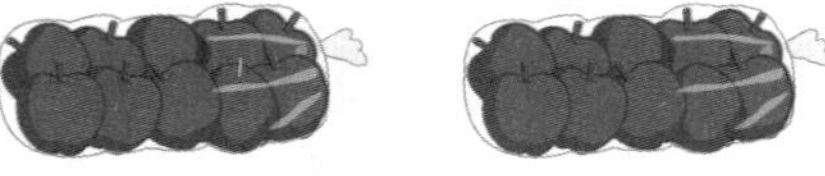

7		90
34		72
70		54

10.6 Count by Tens from a Number

9 — 19, 29, 39 | 10, 20, 30 | 62, 73, 84

10 — 46 — 29, 39, 49 | 56, 66, 76 | 3, 40, 51

11

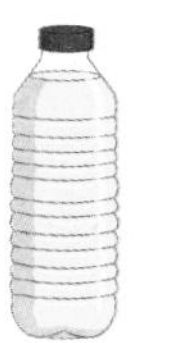
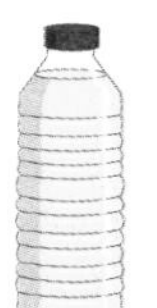

32

42

50

Directions: 8 Count the apples. Circle the number that tells how many. Draw 2 more bags of apples. Circle the number that tells how many apples there are now. 9 and 10 Count by tens starting with the circled number. Circle the numbers that tell how you counted. 11 Count the water bottles. Circle the number that tells how many. You need 42 water bottles in all. Draw to show how many more cases you need.

Name ______________________________

Cumulative Practice 1–10

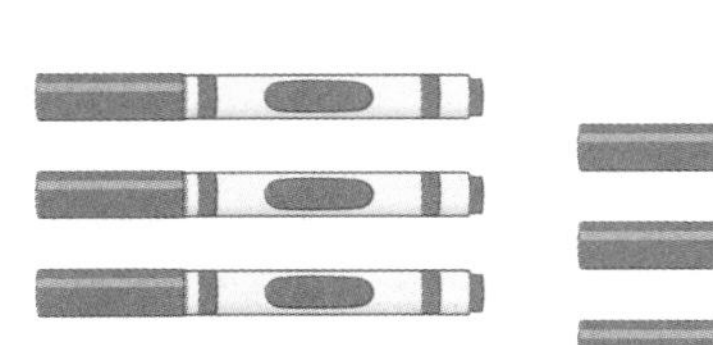

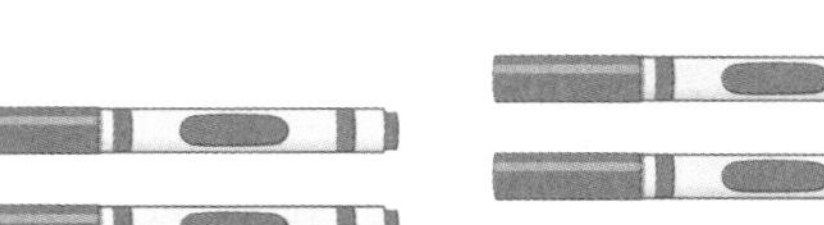

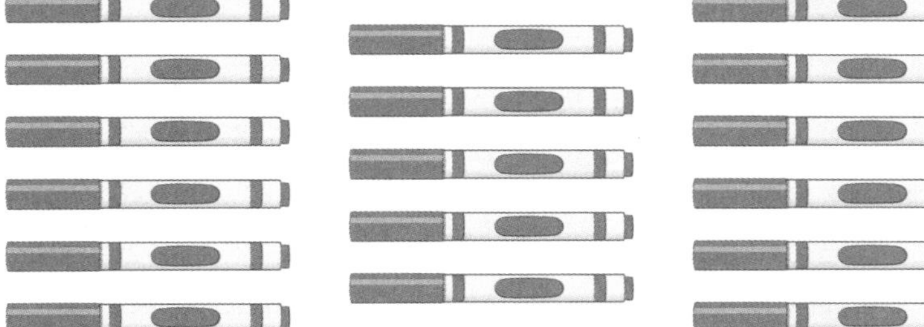

○ 17

○ 18

○ 19

○ 20

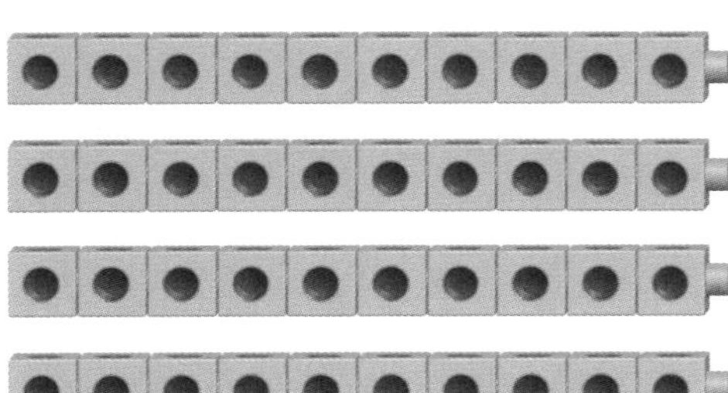

○ 60 ○ 90 ○ 80 ○ 100

3

$$3 + 1 = ?$$

○ 3

○ 1

○ 2

○ 4

Directions: Shade the circle next to the answer. 1 and 2 Which number tells how many? 3 Which number completes the addition sentence?

- ○ $15 = 10 + 5$
- ○ $15 - 10 = 5$
- ○ $10 + 5 = 15$
- ○ $5 + 10 = 15$

7

- ○ 9
- ○ 8
- ○ 6
- ○ 10

○ 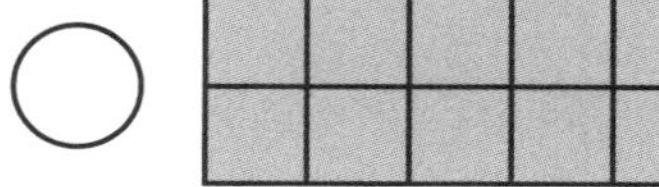

○ 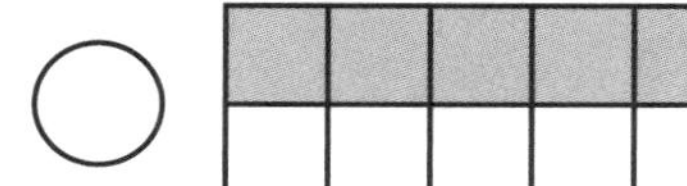

○ 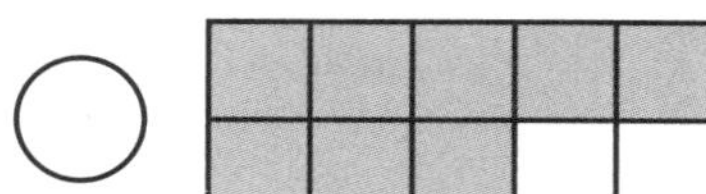

○ 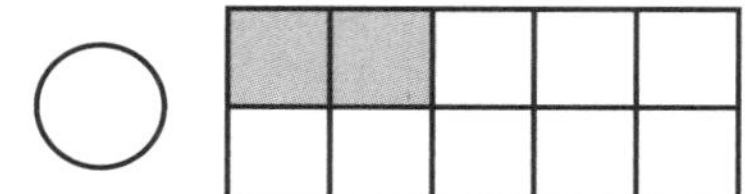

Directions: Shade the circle next to the answer. 4 Which number sentence does *not* tell how many flowers there are in all? 5 Which number is *not* greater than 7? 6 Which ten frame shows the number of tomatoes?

7

8

61	62	63	64	65	66	67	68	69	70
71	72	73	74	75	76	77	78	79	80
81	82	83		85	86	87	88	89	90
91	92	93	94	95	96	97	98	99	100

93

75

84

9

Directions: 7 Count the peaches. Say the number. Write the number. 8 Circle the missing number. Count to 100 starting with that number. Color boxes as you count. Then circle a number in the chart that is greater than the missing number. 9 Draw 19 leaves on the ground. Write the number.

10

9 ______ ______ ______ ______ 14

______ ___ ______ = ______

8

9

18

Directions: 10 Count forward from 9 and stop at 14. Write the numbers you count. 11 Take apart the linking cubes. Circle the parts. Then write a subtraction sentence by taking one of the parts from the whole. 12 Count the granola bars. Circle the number that tells how many. You need 48 granola bars in all. Draw to show how many more boxes you need.

11 Identify Two-Dimensional Shapes

- Do you have any pets?
- What shapes can you see in the picture?

Chapter Learning Target:
Understand two-dimensional shapes.

Chapter Success Criteria:
- I can identify two-dimensional shapes.
- I can describe two-dimensional shapes.
- I can compare two-dimensional shapes.
- I can build two-dimensional shapes.

Name ____________________

Vocabulary

Review Words
classify
category
less than

spots	 no spots
______	______

Directions: Classify the animals into the categories shown. Write the marks in the chart. Count the marks and write the numbers to tell how many animals are in each category. Draw a line through the number that is less than the other number.

Chapter 11 Vocabulary Cards

circle	curve
hexagon	rectangle
side	sort
square	triangle

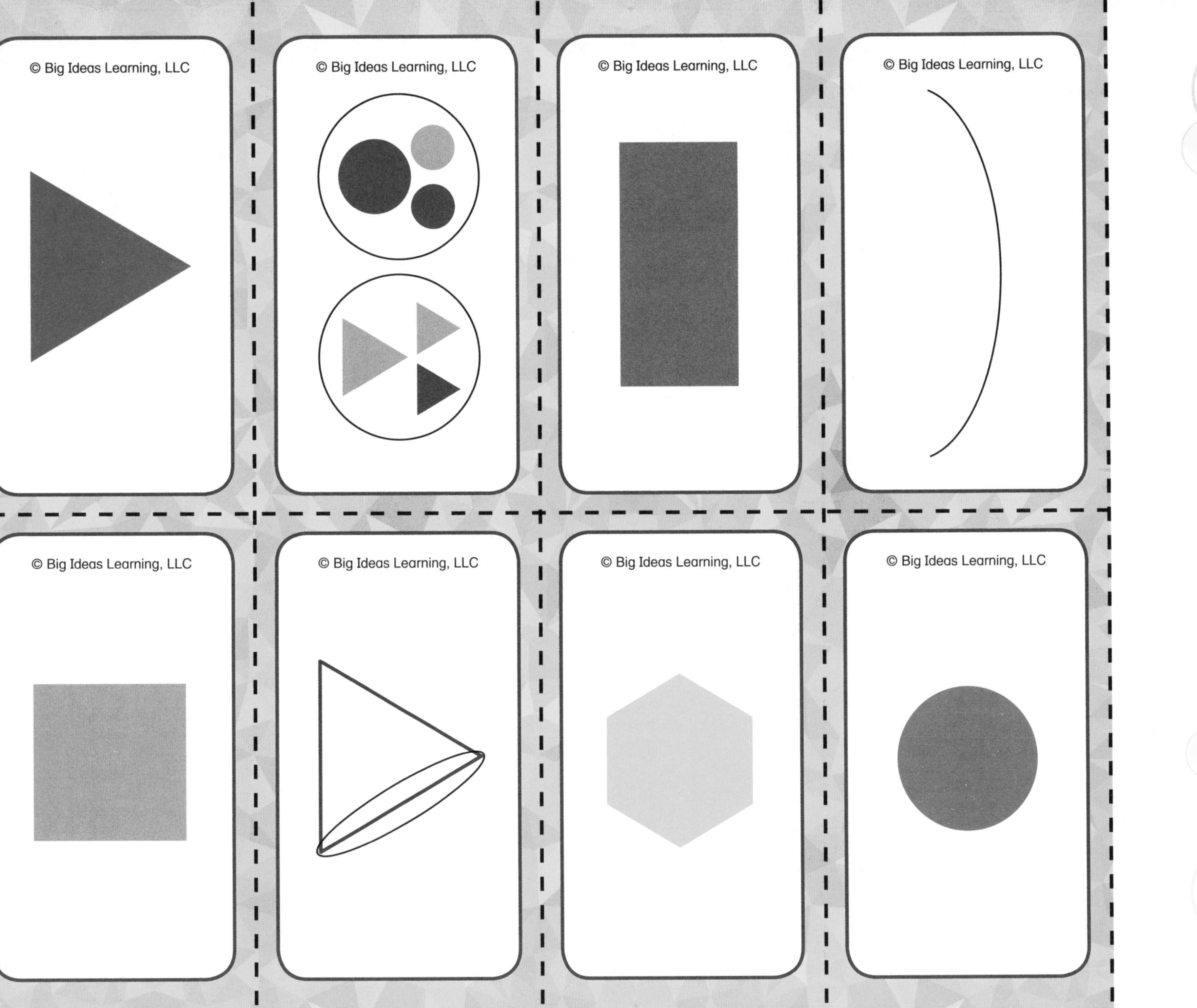
© Big Ideas Learning, LLC
© Big Ideas Learning, LLC
© Big Ideas Learning, LLC
© Big Ideas Learning, LLC
© Big Ideas Learning, LLC
© Big Ideas Learning, LLC
© Big Ideas Learning, LLC
© Big Ideas Learning, LLC

Chapter 11 Vocabulary Cards

two-dimensional shape

vertex

vertices

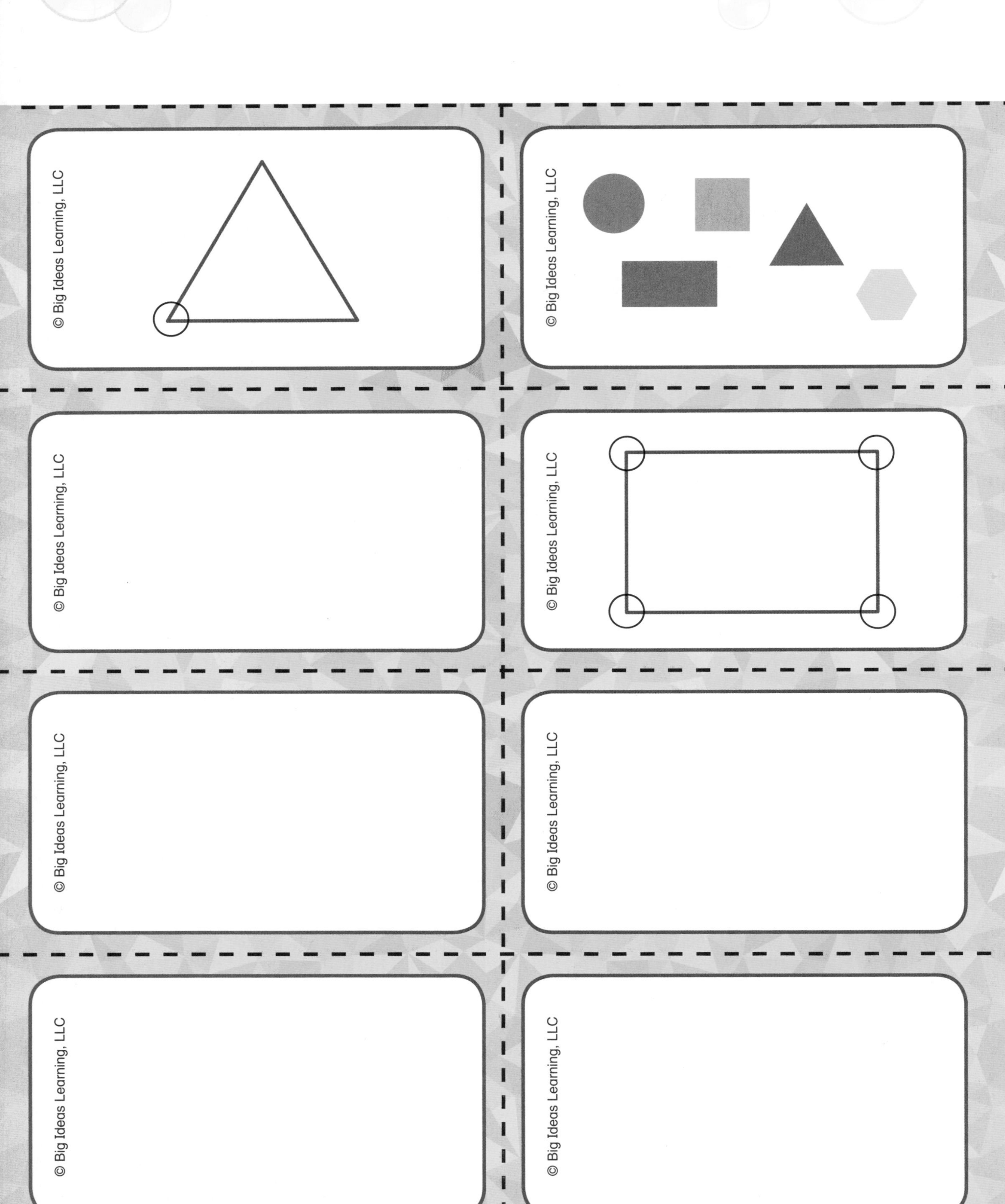
© Big Ideas Learning, LLC
© Big Ideas Learning, LLC
© Big Ideas Learning, LLC
© Big Ideas Learning, LLC
© Big Ideas Learning, LLC
© Big Ideas Learning, LLC
© Big Ideas Learning, LLC
© Big Ideas Learning, LLC

Name ______________________________

Describe Two-Dimensional Shapes

Learning Target: Describe two-dimensional shapes.

Explore and Grow

curves	no curves

Directions: Cut out the Two-Dimensional Shape Cards. Sort the cards into the categories shown.

Think and Grow

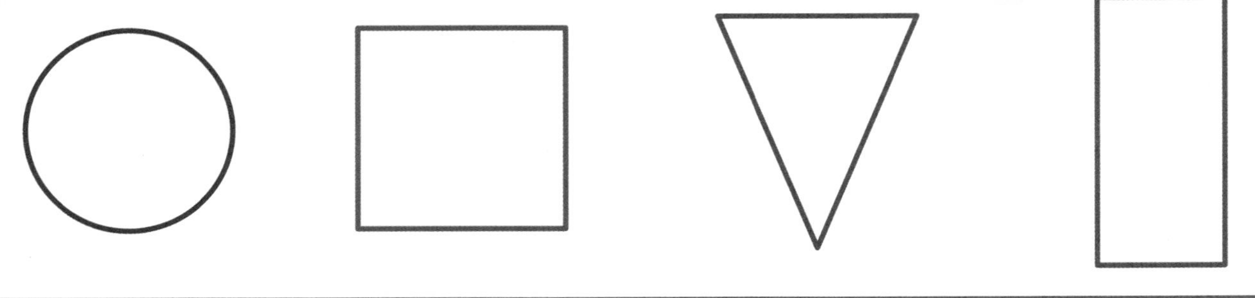

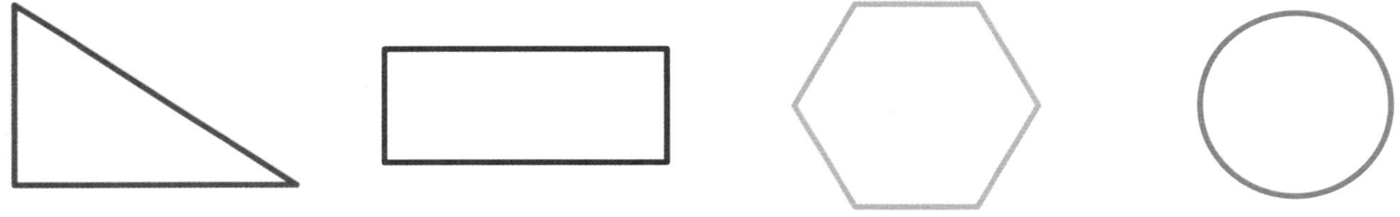

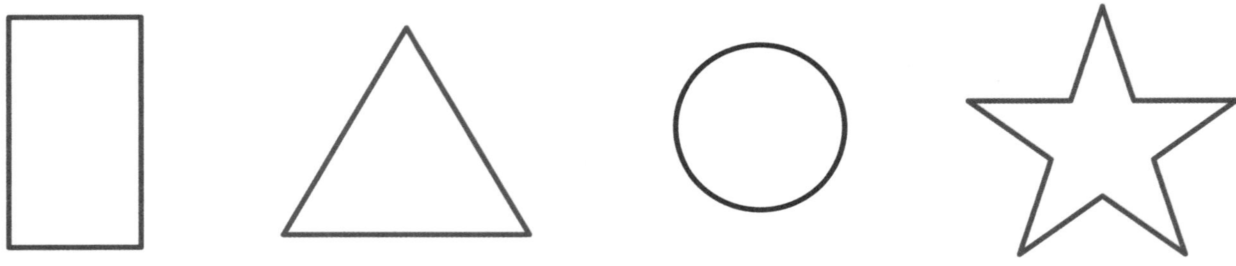

Directions:

- Color the shape that has a curve.
- Color the shape that does not have any vertices.
- Color the shape that has more than 4 vertices.
- Color the shape that has only 3 sides.

Name ______________________________

Apply and Grow: Practice

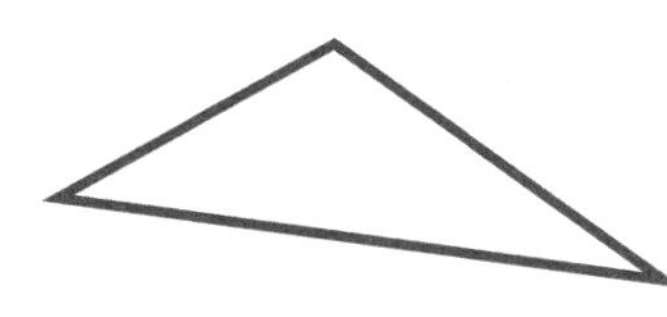  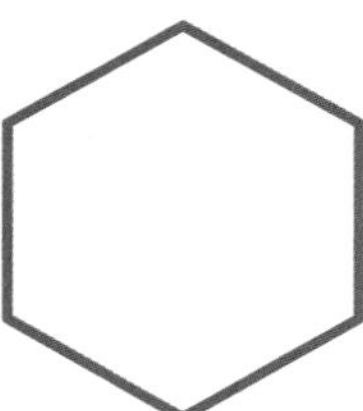 

 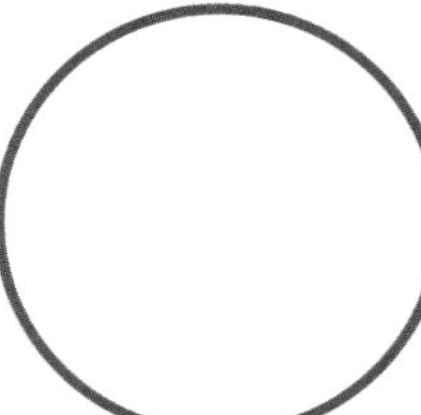  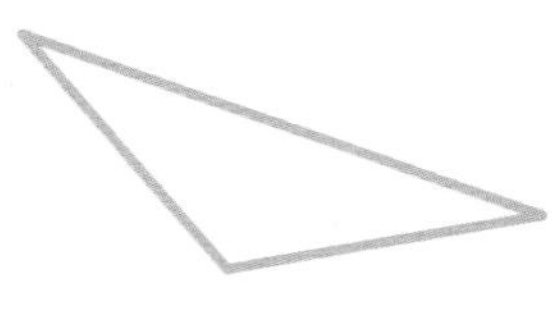

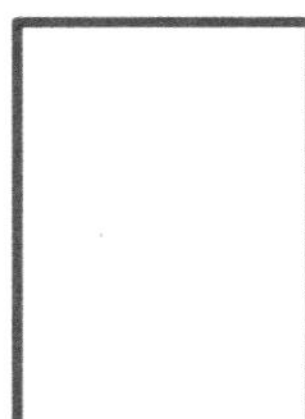 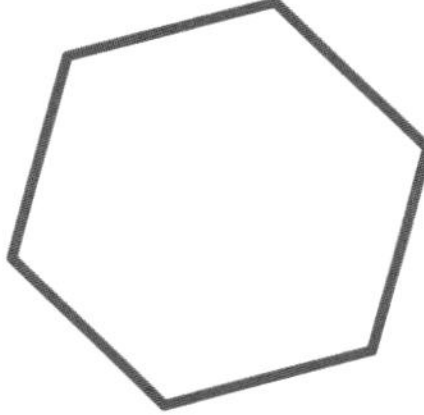 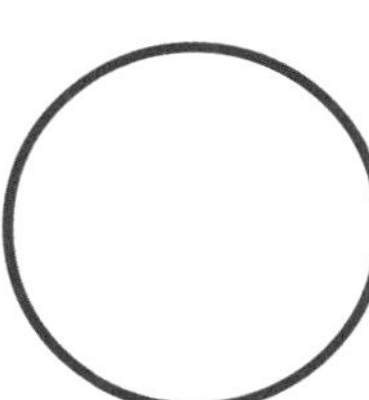 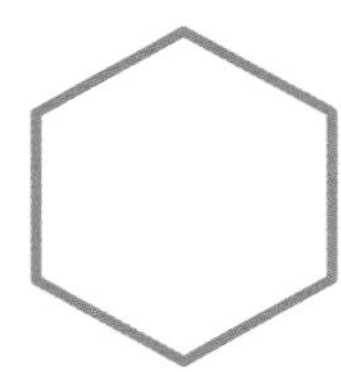

 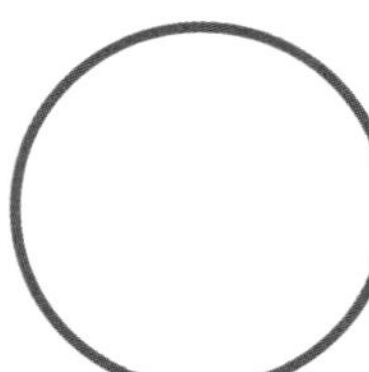 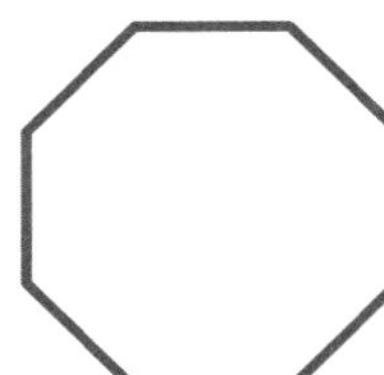 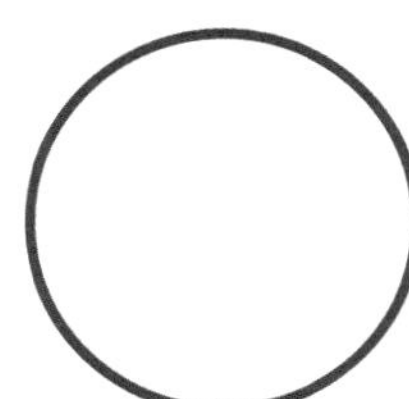

Directions: 1 Color the shapes that have only 4 sides. 2 Color the shapes that have only 3 vertices. 3 Color the shapes that have 6 vertices. 4 Color the shapes that have curves.

Think and Grow: Modeling Real Life

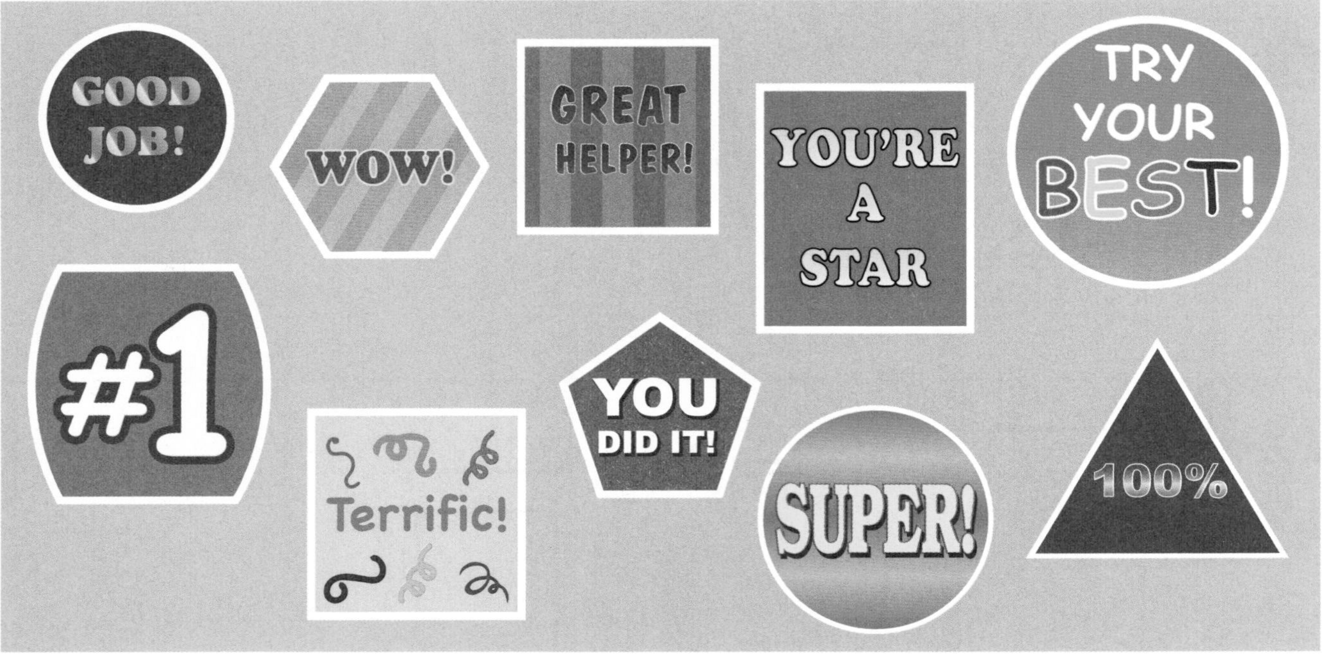

more than 4 vertices ______

all straight sides ______

curves and straight sides ______

Directions: Write the number that answers the question.

- How many stickers in the picture have more than 4 vertices?
- How many stickers in the picture have all straight sides?
- How many stickers in the picture have both curves and straight sides?

Name ____________________

Practice 

Learning Target: Describe two-dimensional shapes.

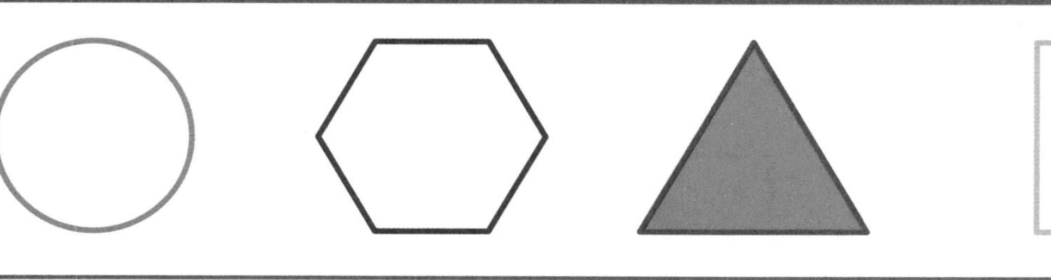

Directions:
- Color the shape that has only 3 vertices.
- Color the shape that has more than 4 sides.

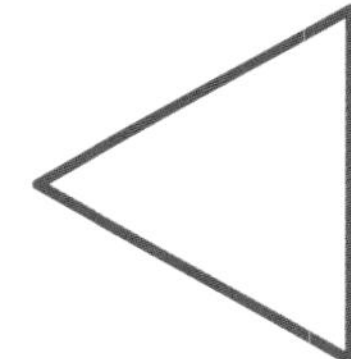 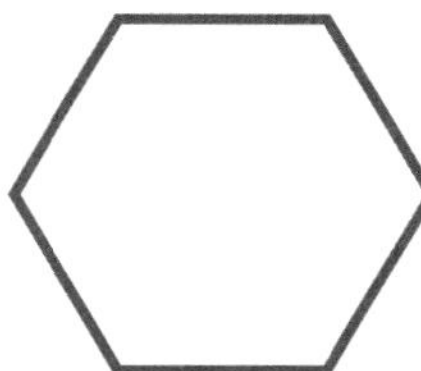 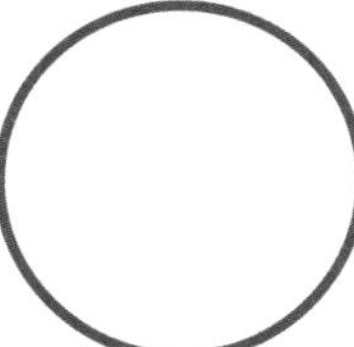 

 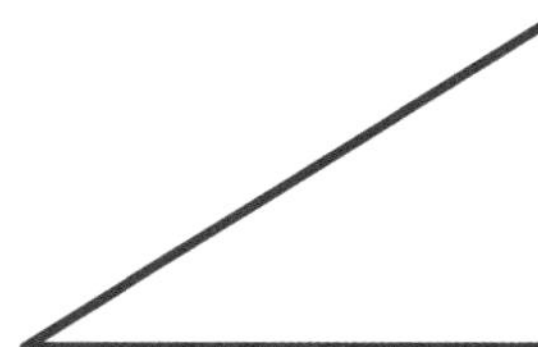  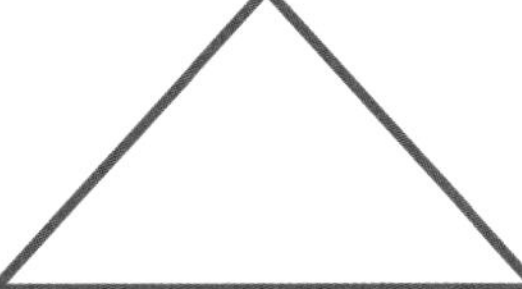

Directions: 1 Color the shape that has 6 sides. 2 Color the shape that has more than 3 straight sides.

3

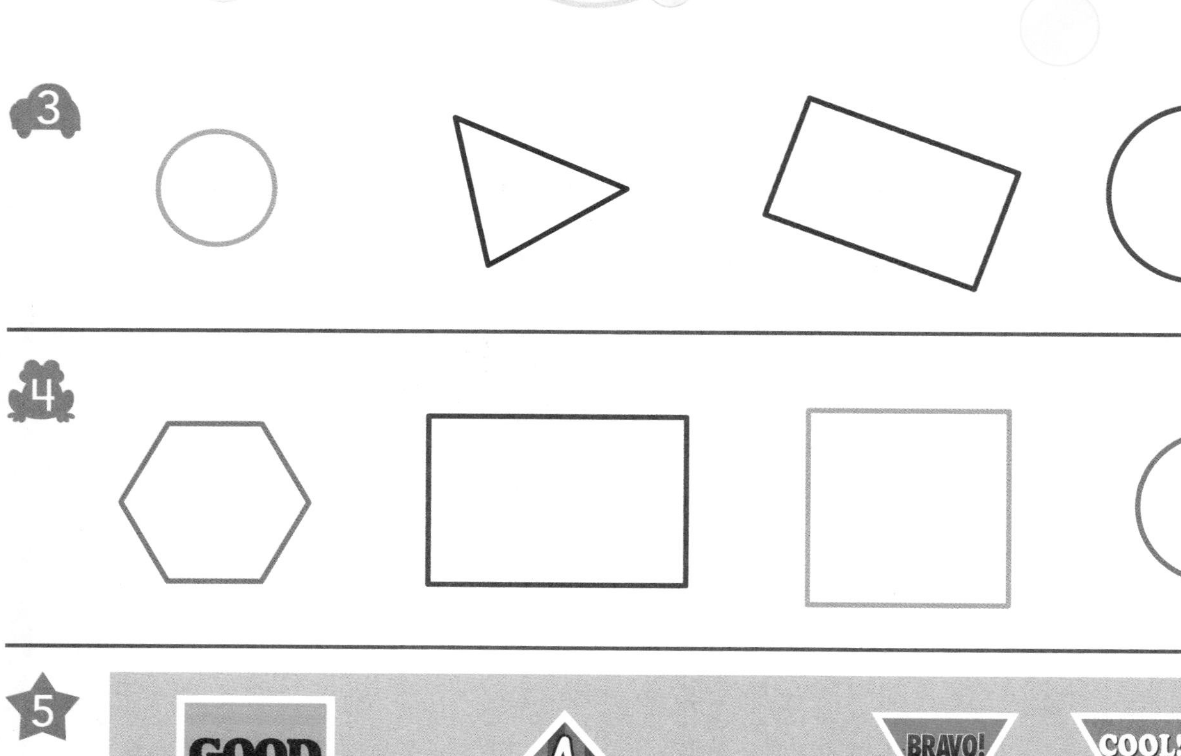

4

5 

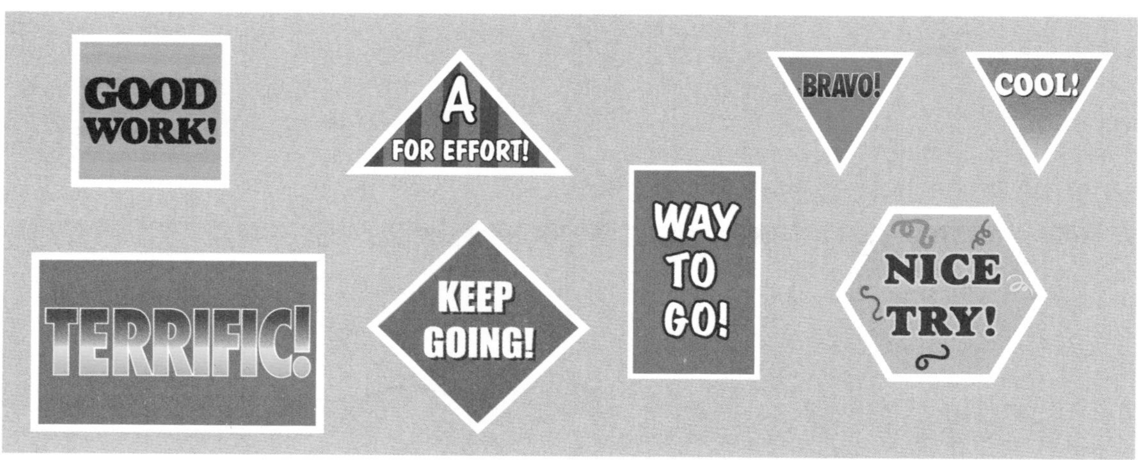

less than 4 vertices ______

more than 3 sides ______

Directions: 3 Color the shapes that have curves. 4 Color the shapes that have only 4 vertices. 5 How many stickers have less than 4 vertices? Write the number. How many stickers have more than 3 sides? Write the number.

Name ______________________

Learning Target: Identify and describe triangles.

Explore and Grow

triangle	not a triangle

Directions: Cut out the Triangle or Not a Triangle Sort Cards. Sort the cards into the categories shown.

Think and Grow

Directions: Color any triangles. Tell why your answers are correct.

Name ___________________________

Apply and Grow: Practice

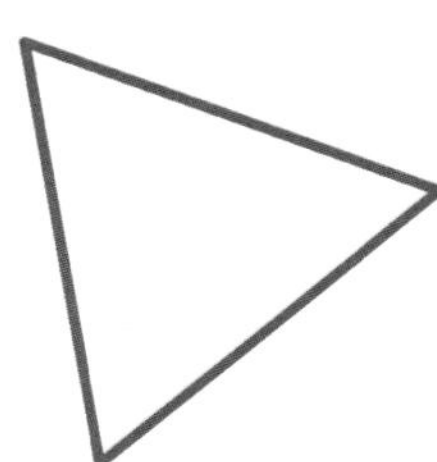 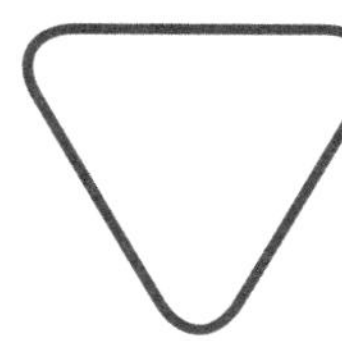 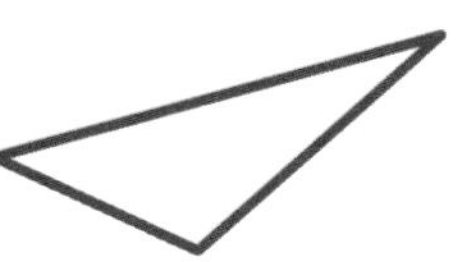 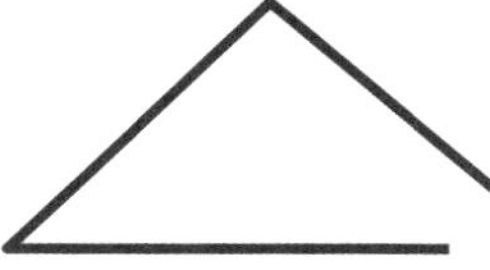

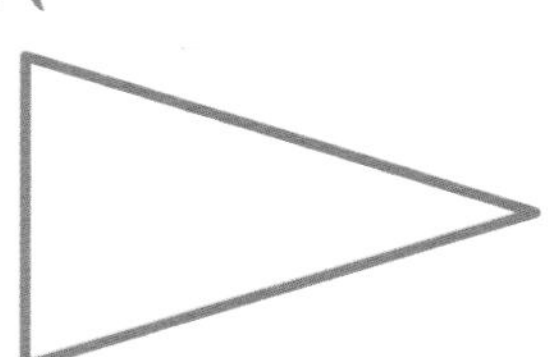  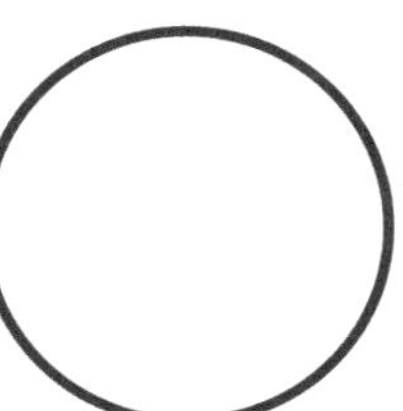 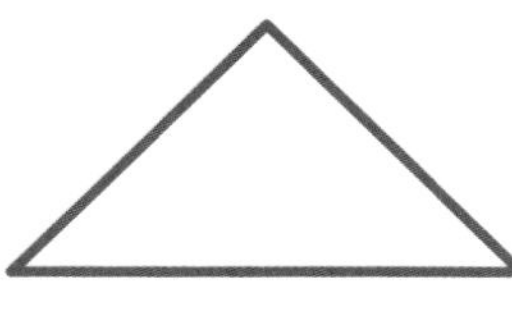

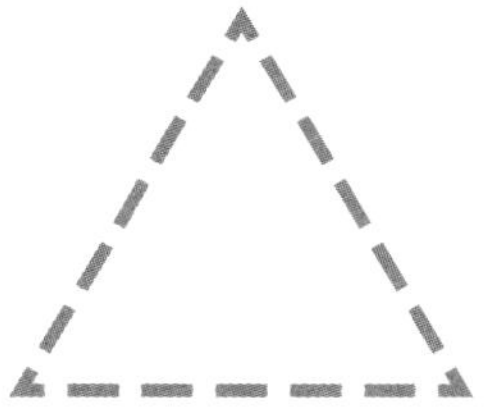  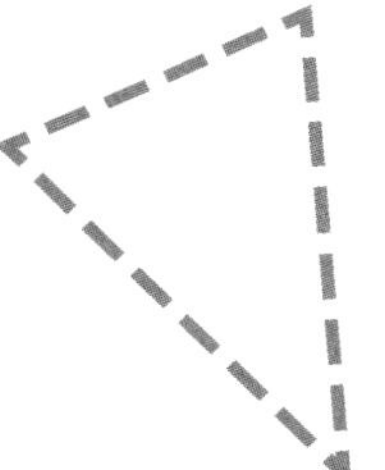 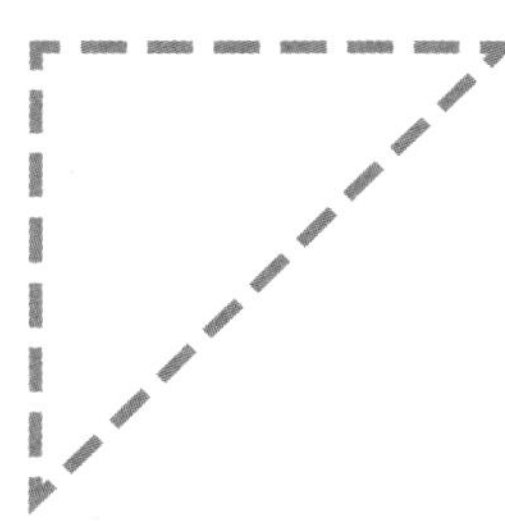

_______ sides _______ vertices

Directions: 1 and 2 Color any triangles. Tell why your answers are correct. 3 Trace the shapes that are triangles. Write the number of sides and the number of vertices of a triangle.

Think and Grow: Modeling Real Life

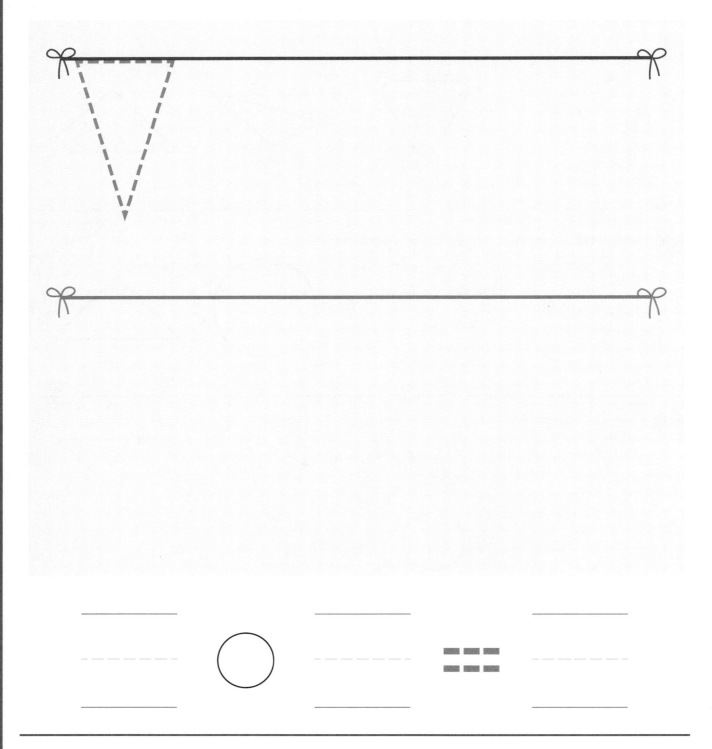

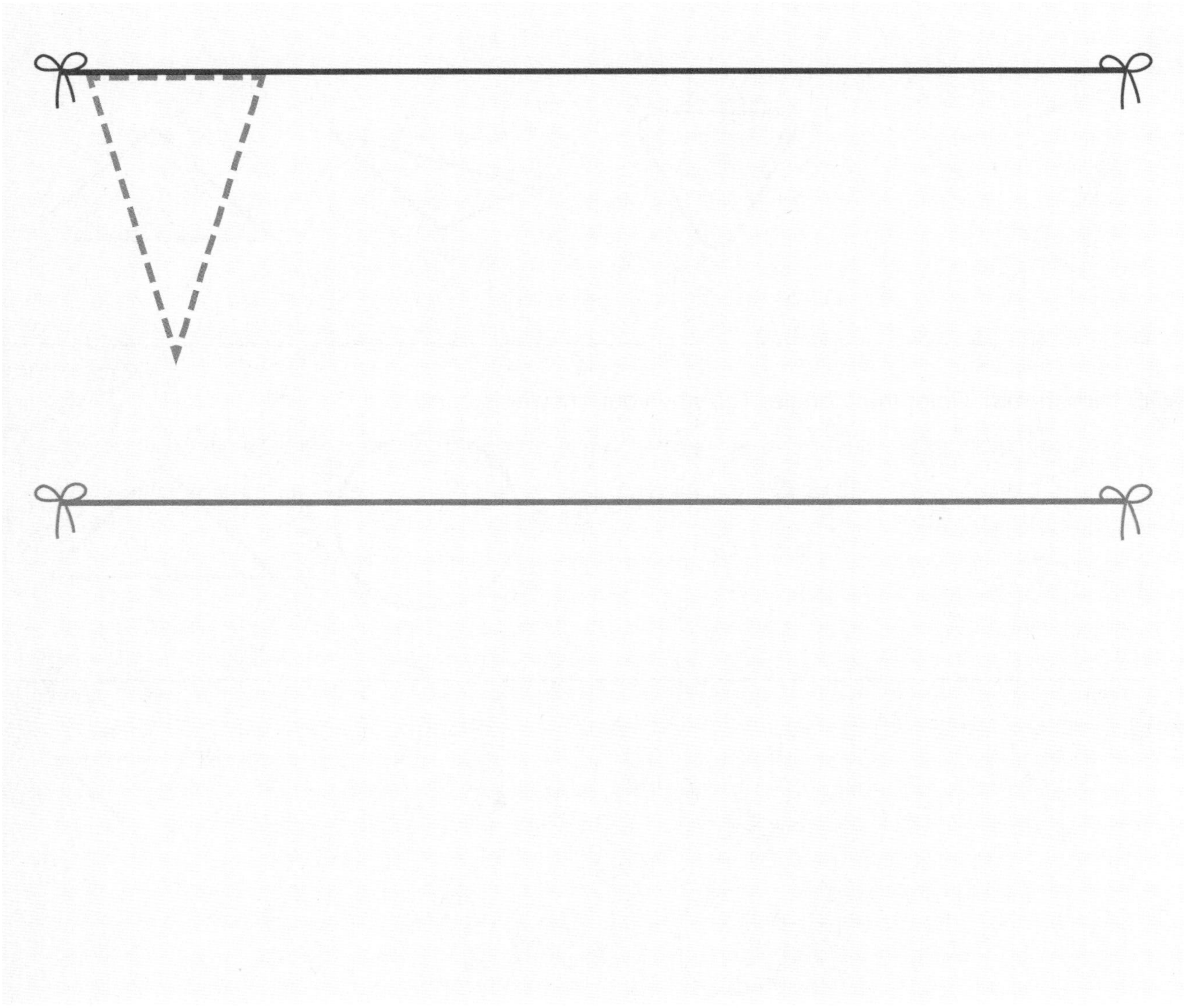

Directions: You use triangle-shaped flags to make two banners for a party. You use 10 flags in all.

- Draw and color flags to make the banners.
- Write an addition sentence to match your picture.

Name ______________________

Practice 11.2

Learning Target: Identify and describe triangles.

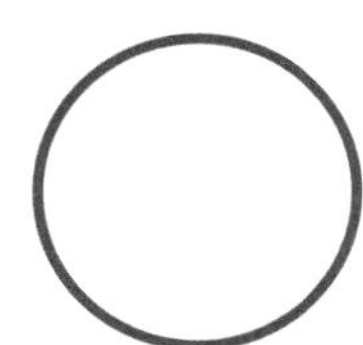

3 sides,
3 vertices
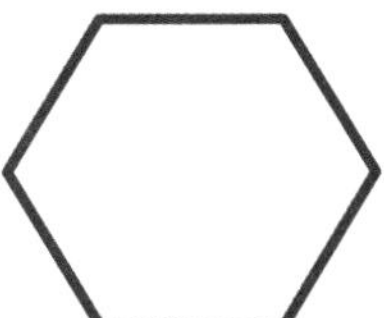

Directions: Color the triangle. Tell why your answer is correct.

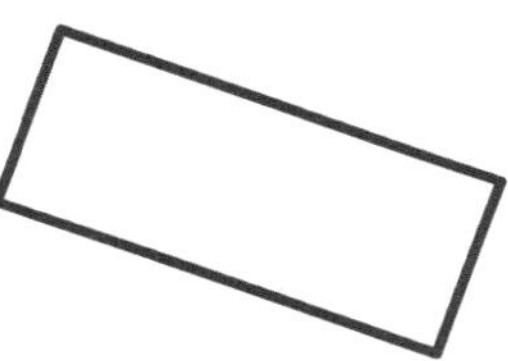
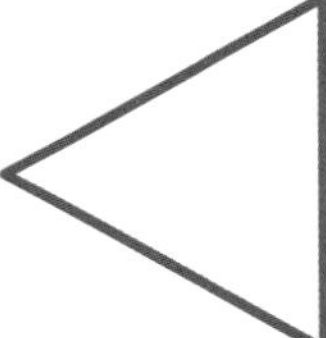
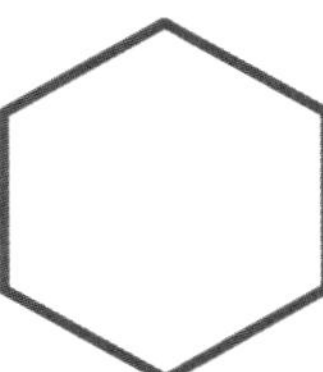

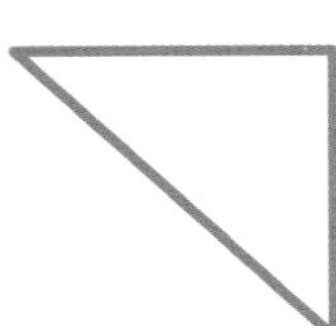

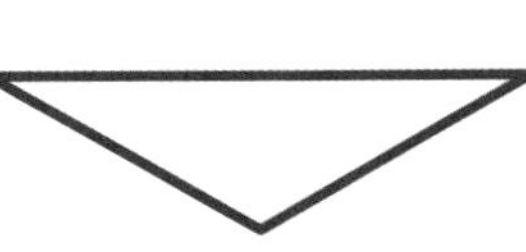

Directions: 1–3 Color any triangles. Tell why your answers are correct.

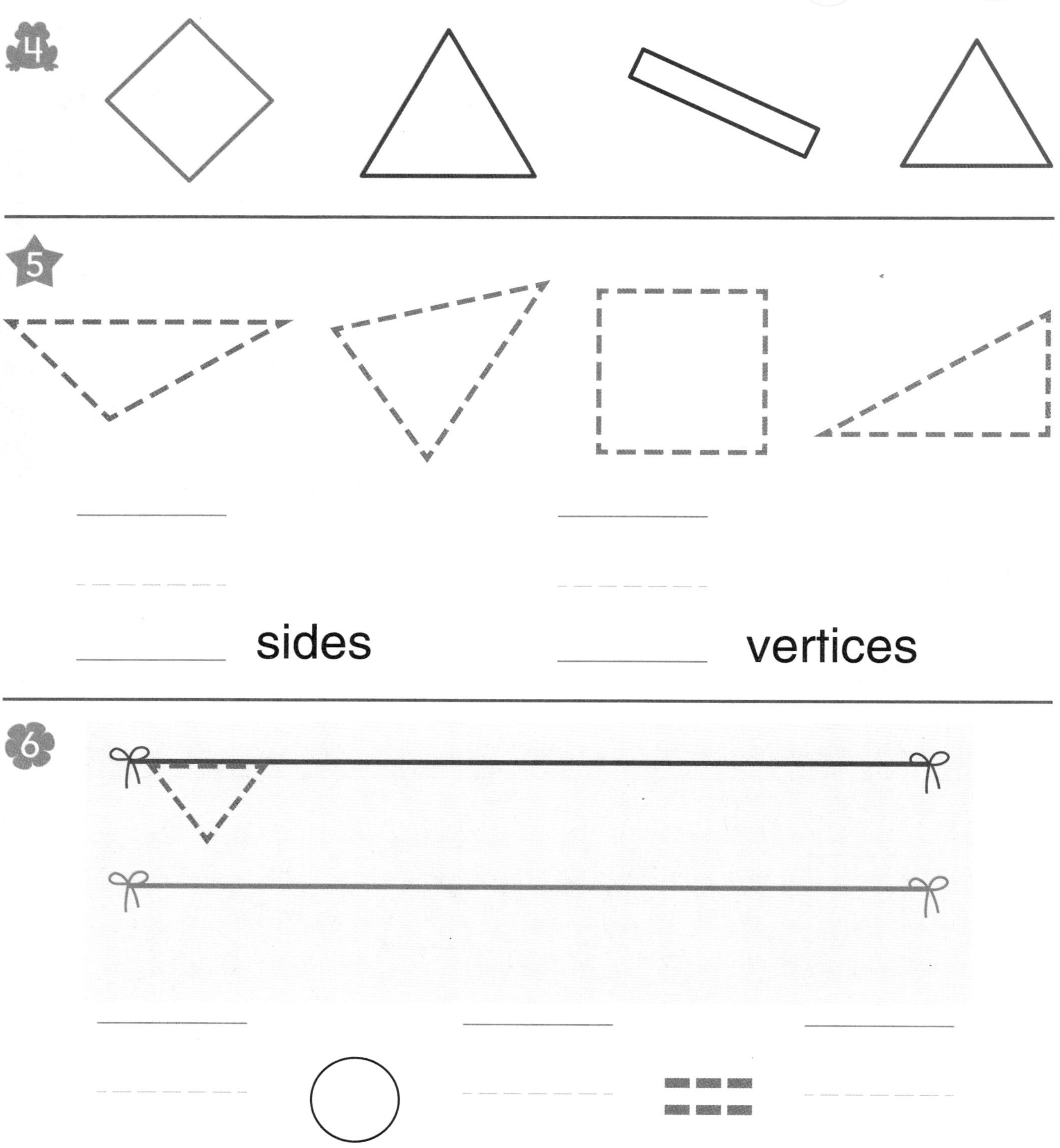

Directions: 4 Color any triangles. Tell why your answers are correct. 5 Trace the shapes that are triangles. Write the number of sides and the number of vertices of a triangle. 6 You use triangle-shaped flags to make two banners for a party. You use 8 flags in all. Draw and color flags to make the banners. Then write an addition sentence to match your picture.

Name ______________________________

Rectangles 11.3

Learning Target: Identify and describe rectangles.

Explore and Grow

rectangle	not a rectangle

Directions: Cut out the Rectangle or Not a Rectangle Sort Cards. Sort the cards into the categories shown.

Think and Grow

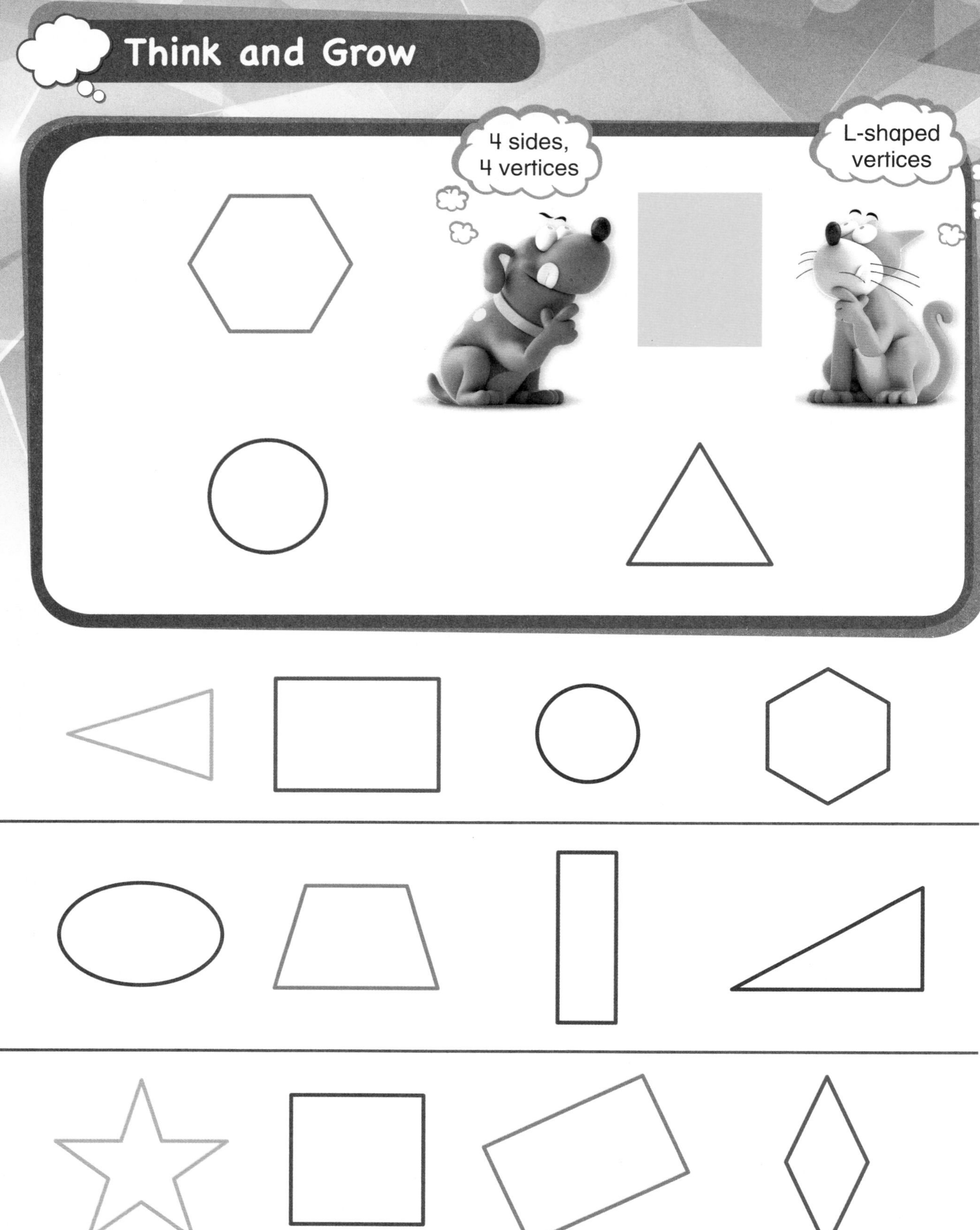

Directions: Color any rectangles. Tell why your answers are correct.

Name ______________________________

Apply and Grow: Practice

 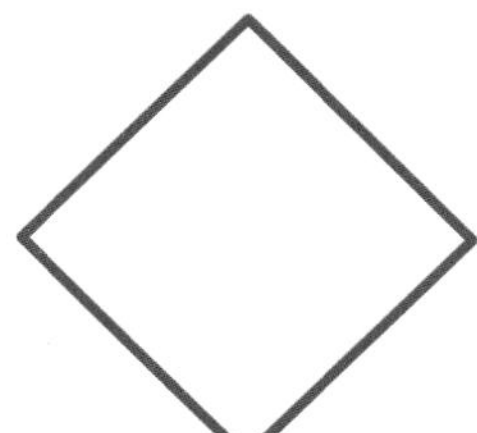  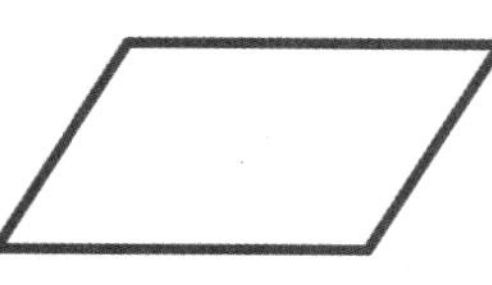

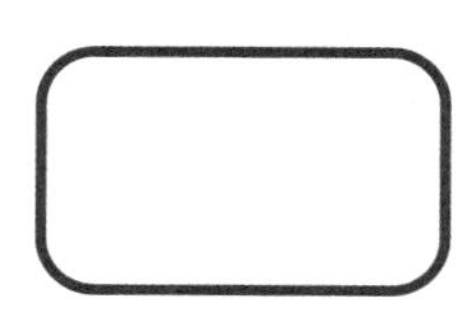  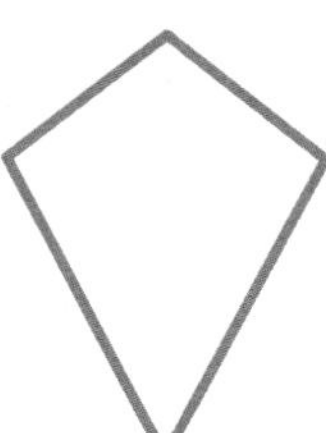 

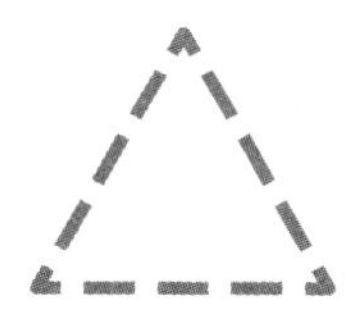   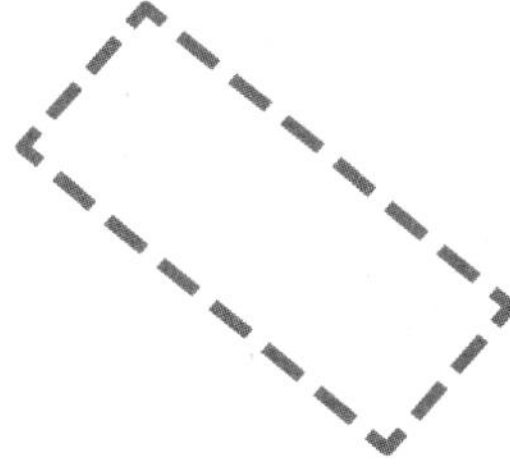

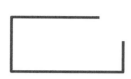

______ sides ______ vertices

Directions: 1 and 2 Color any rectangles. Tell why your answers are correct. 3 Trace the shapes that are rectangles. Write the number of sides and the number of vertices of a rectangle.

Think and Grow: Modeling Real Life

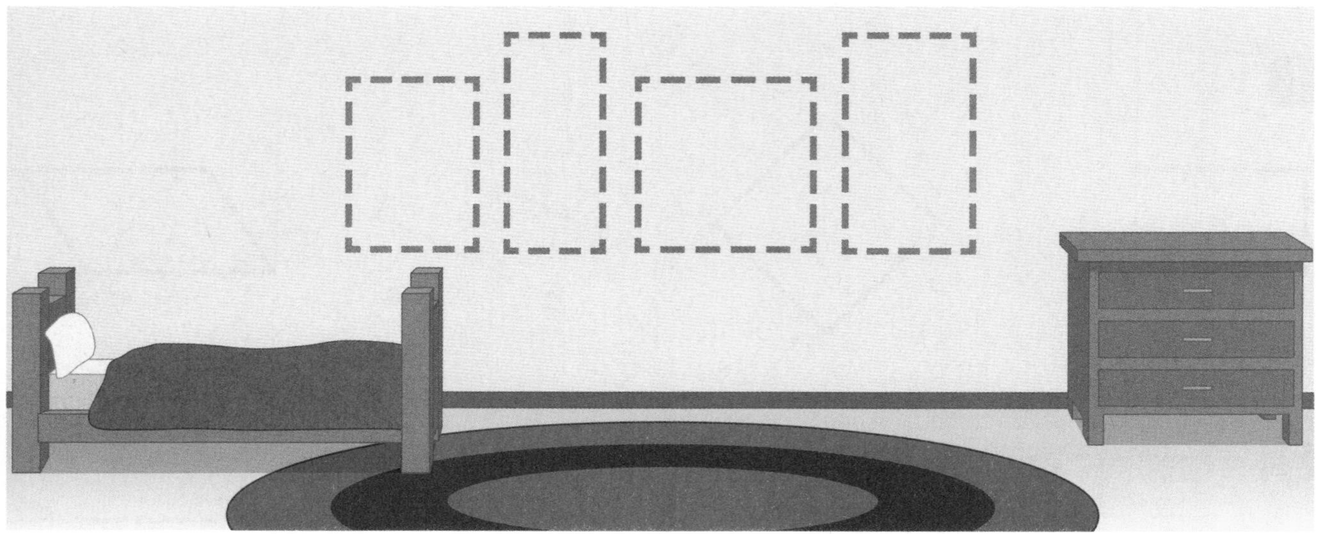

Directions:

- Trace and color 4 rectangular posters on the wall.
- You put 3 more posters on another wall. Draw and color 3 rectangular posters on the wall.
- Write an addition sentence to tell how many posters are on the walls in all.

Name ______________________________

Learning Target: Identify and describe rectangles.

 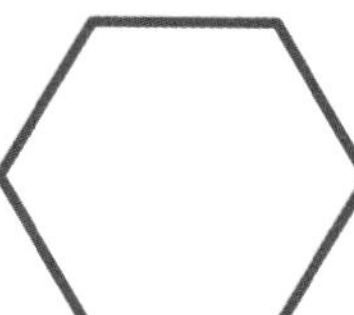  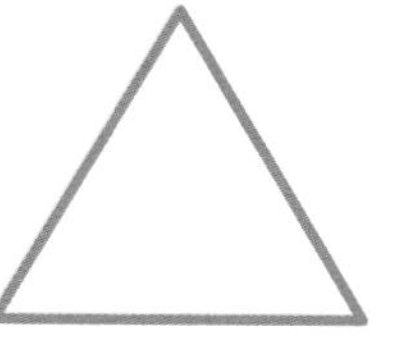

4 sides,
4 L-shaped
vertices

Directions: Color the rectangle. Tell why your answer is correct.

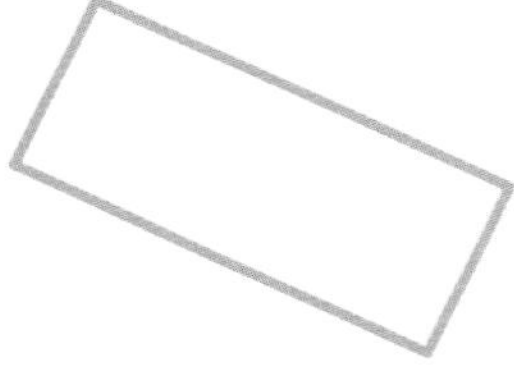 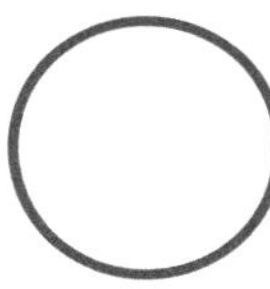 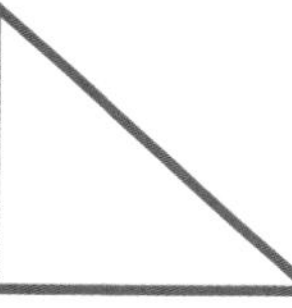 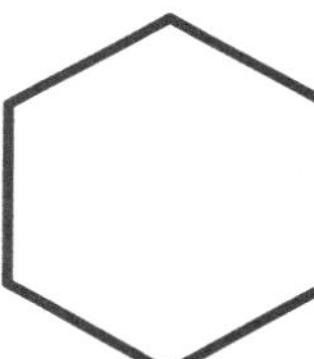

 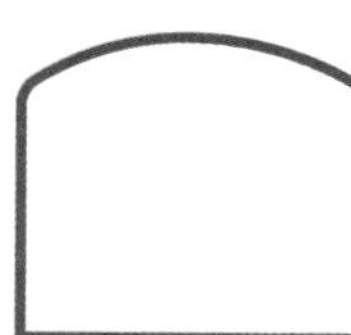 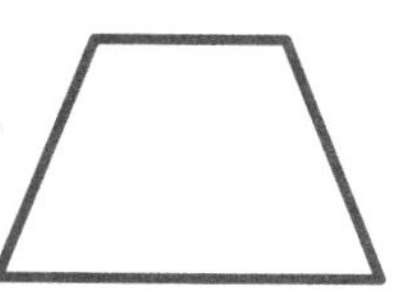 

Directions: 1–3 Color any rectangles. Tell why your answers are correct.

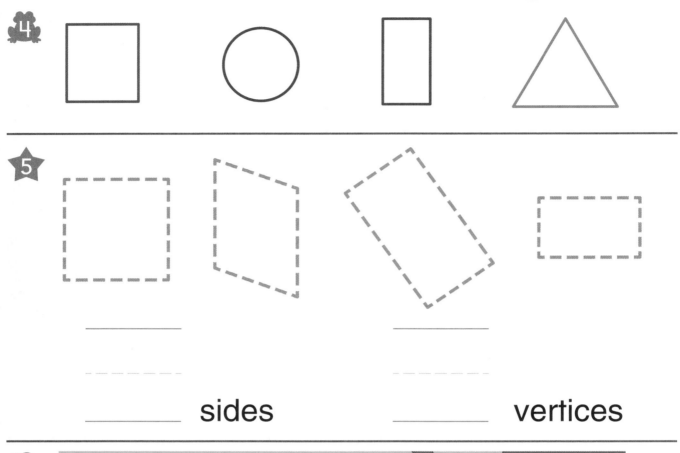

4

5

sides

vertices

6

Directions: 4 Color any rectangles. Tell why your answers are correct. 5 Trace the shapes that are rectangles. Write the number of sides and the number of vertices of a rectangle. 6 You make rectangular picture frames. Draw 1 large frame and 4 small frames. Then write an addition sentence to tell how many frames you make in all.

Name ______________________________

Squares 11.4

Learning Target: Identify and describe squares.

Explore and Grow

square	not a square

Directions: Cut out the Square or Not a Square Sort Cards. Sort the cards into the categories shown.

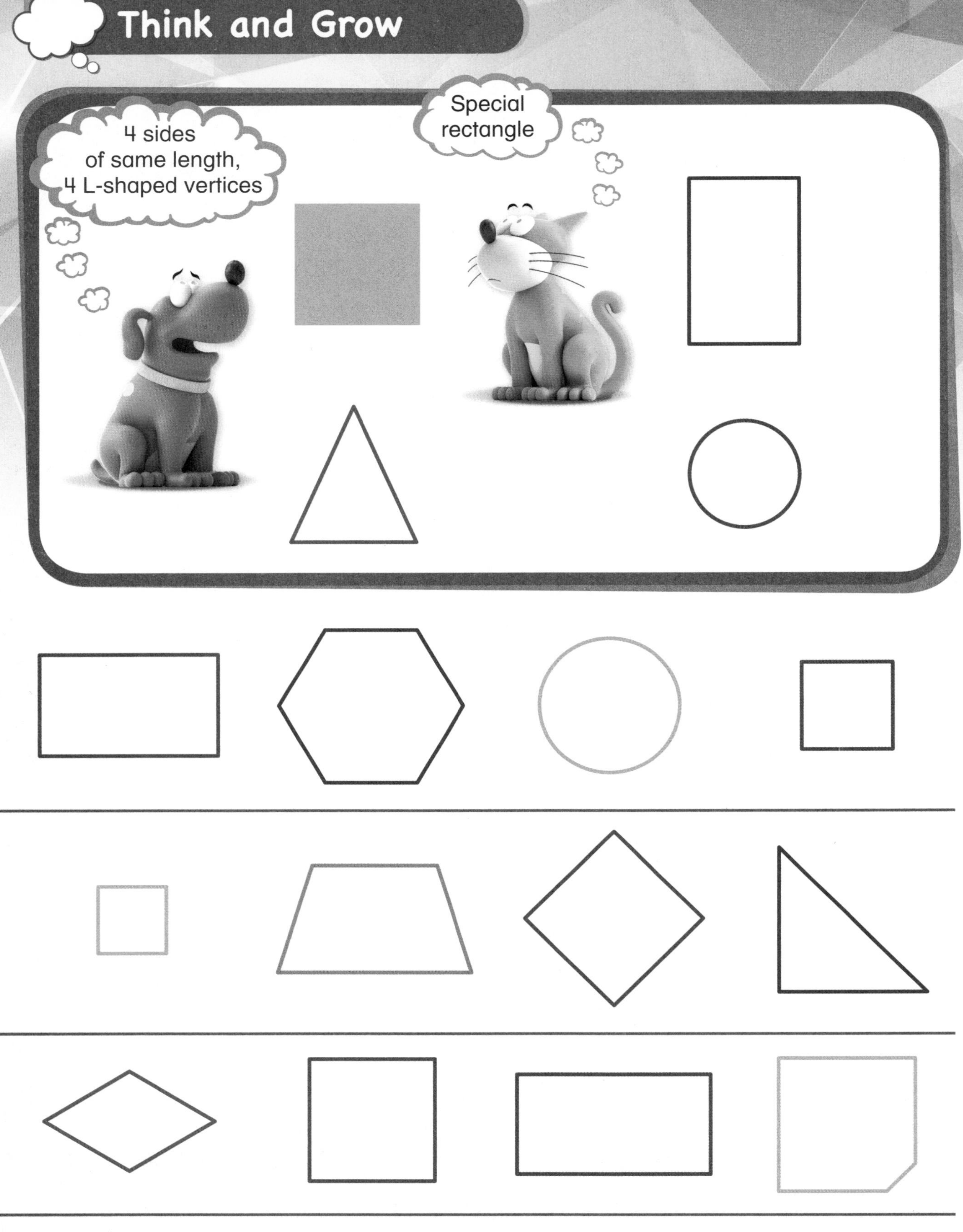

Think and Grow
4 sides
of same length,
4 L-shaped vertices
Special
rectangle

Directions: Color any squares. Tell why your answers are correct.

Name ______________________

Apply and Grow: Practice

1

 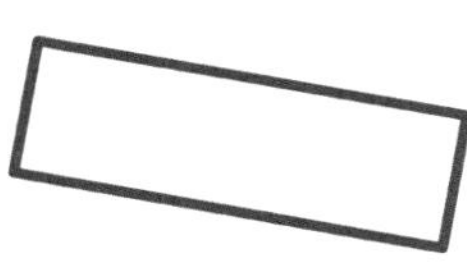  

2

3

 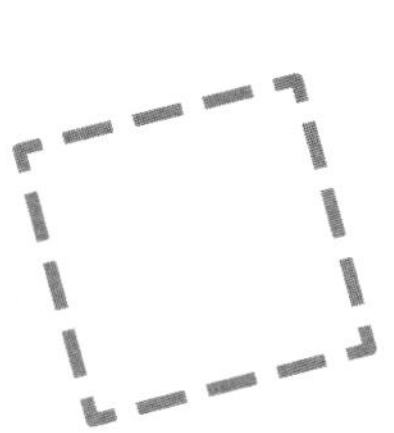 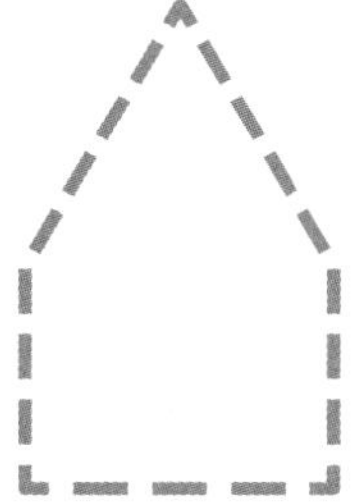 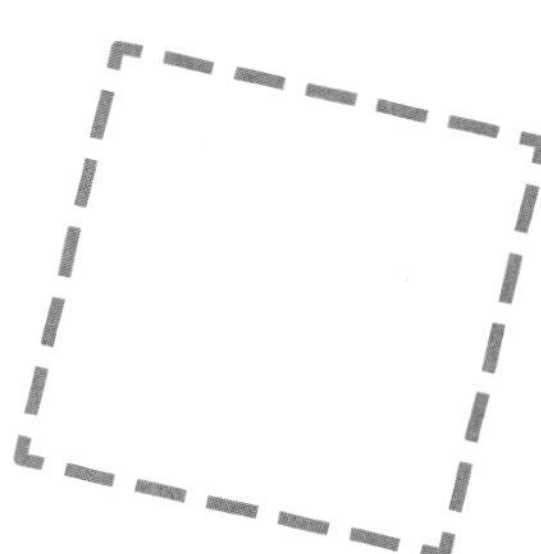

______ sides ______ vertices

Directions: 1 and 2 Color any squares. Tell why your answers are correct.
3 Trace the shapes that are squares. Write the number of sides and the number of vertices of a square.

Think and Grow: Modeling Real Life

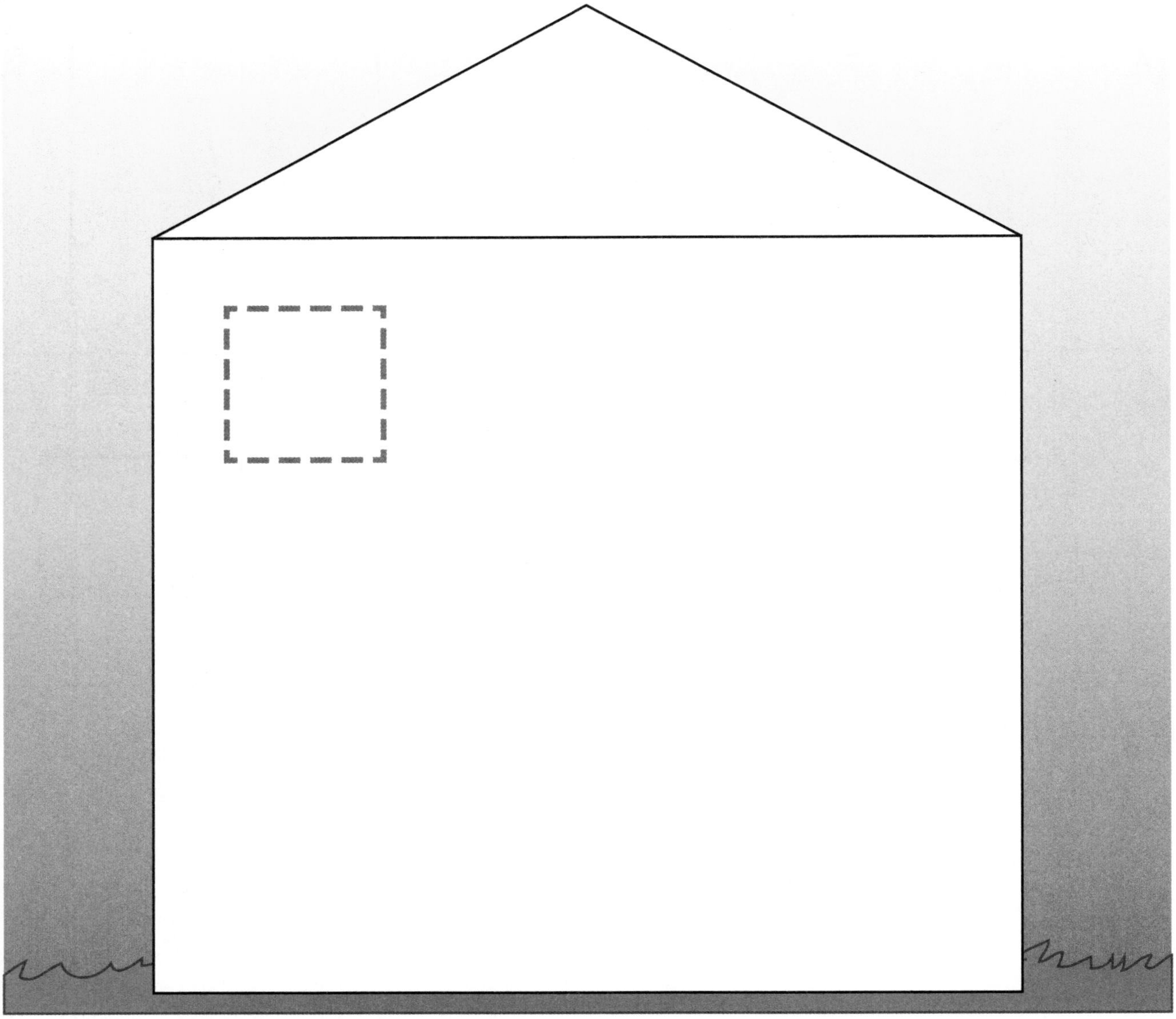

Directions:

- Use squares and rectangles to draw 6 windows and 1 door on the house. Color the house.
- Write an addition sentence to tell how many squares and how many rectangles you draw in all.

Name ______________________________

Practice 

Learning Target: Identify and describe squares.

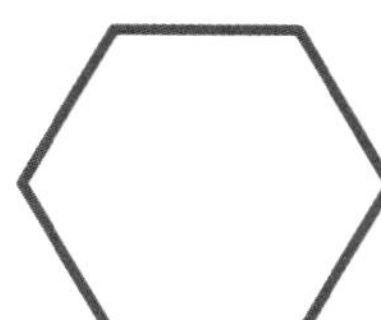

4 sides of same length, 4 L-shaped vertices

Directions: Color the square. Tell why your answer is correct.

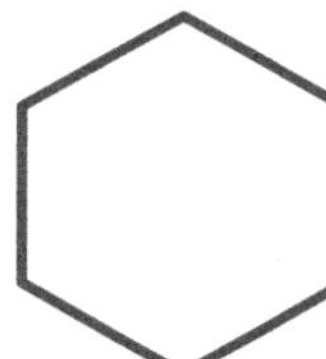

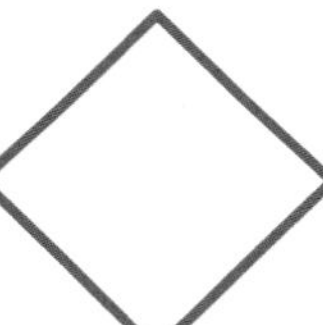
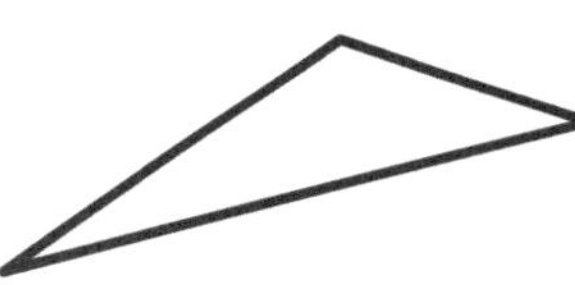

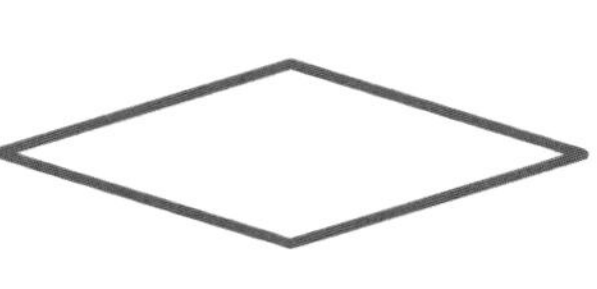
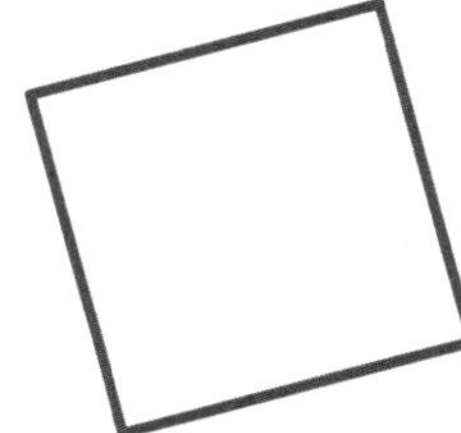

Directions: 1–3 Color any squares. Tell why your answers are correct.

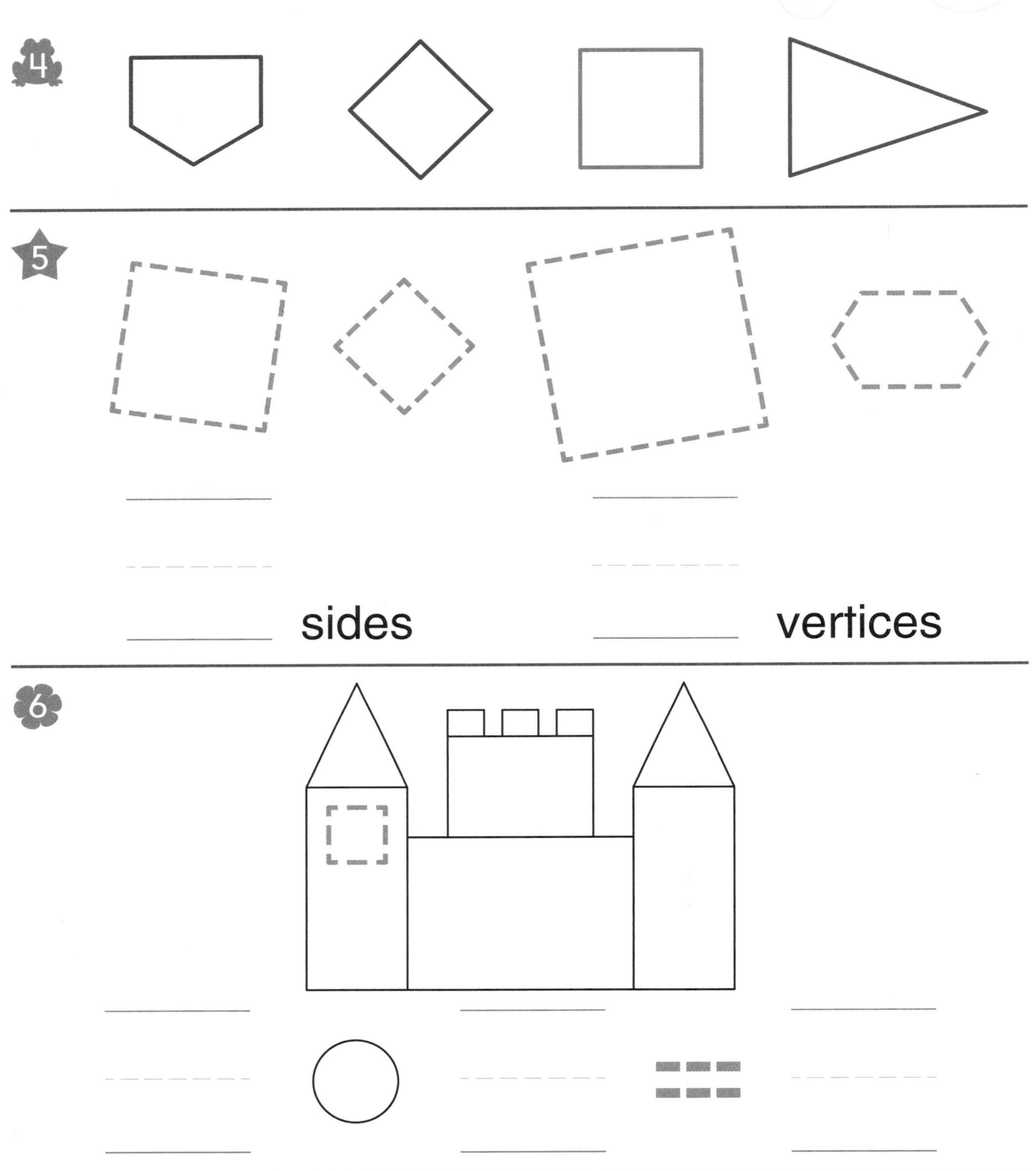

Directions: 4 Color any squares. Tell why your answers are correct. 5 Trace the shapes that are squares. Write the number of sides and the number of vertices of a square. 6 Use squares and rectangles to draw 4 windows and 1 door on the castle. Color the castle. Then write an addition sentence to tell how many squares and rectangles you draw in all.

Name ___________________________

Hexagons and Circles 11.5

Learning Target: Identify and describe hexagons and circles.

Explore and Grow

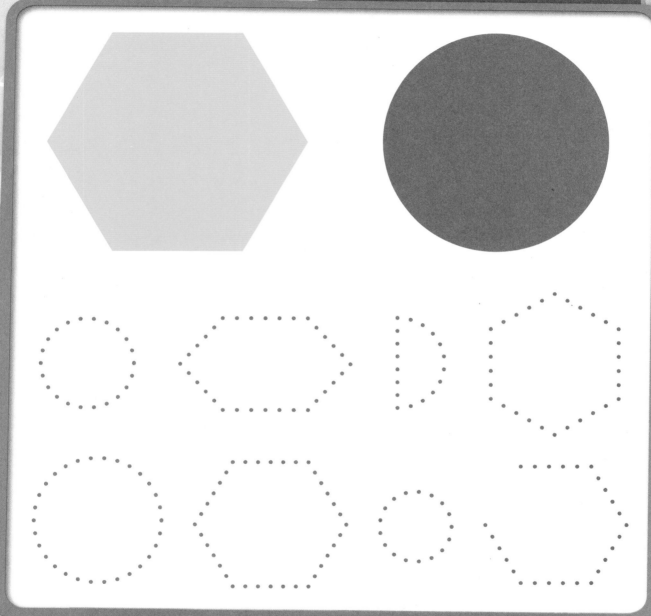

Directions:

- Use your finger to trace around the yellow hexagon. Trace and color the shapes that are hexagons.
- Use your finger to trace around the blue circle. Use a different color to trace and color the shapes that are circles.

Think and Grow
6 sides,
6 vertices
0 straight sides,
0 vertices

Directions: Color any hexagons red. Color any circles blue. Tell why your answers are correct.

Name ________________

Apply and Grow: Practice

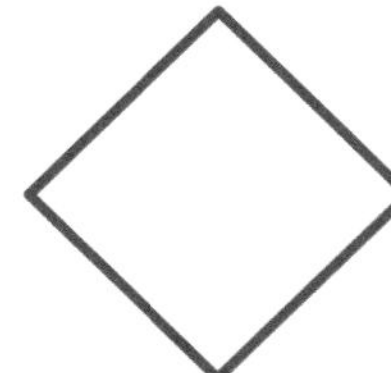   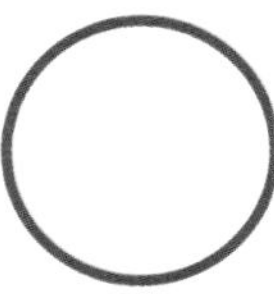

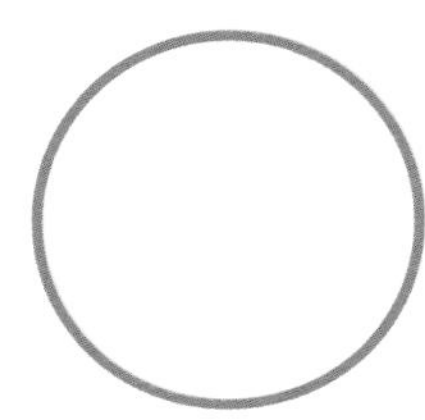 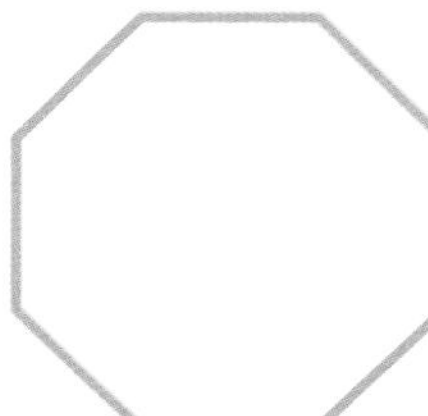 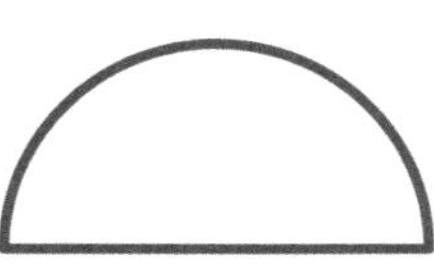 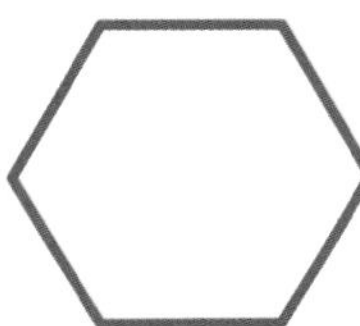

 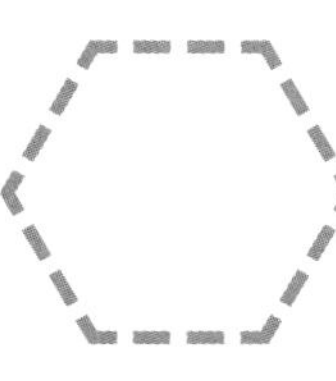 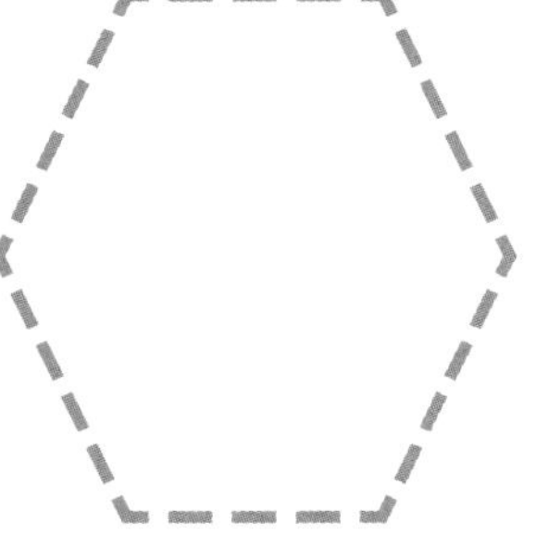 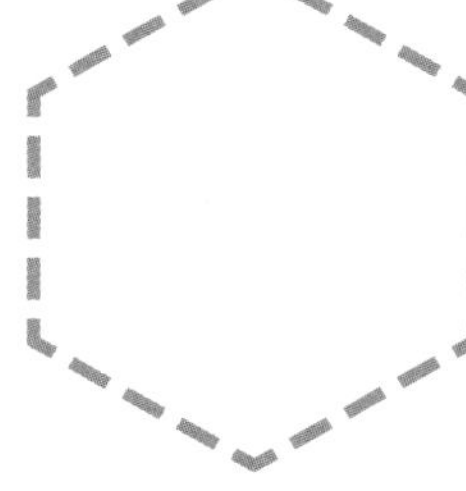

______ sides ______ vertices

Directions: 1 and 2 Color any hexagons red. Color any circles blue. Tell why your answers are correct. 3 Trace the shapes that are hexagons. Write the number of sides and the number of vertices of a hexagon.

Think and Grow: Modeling Real Life

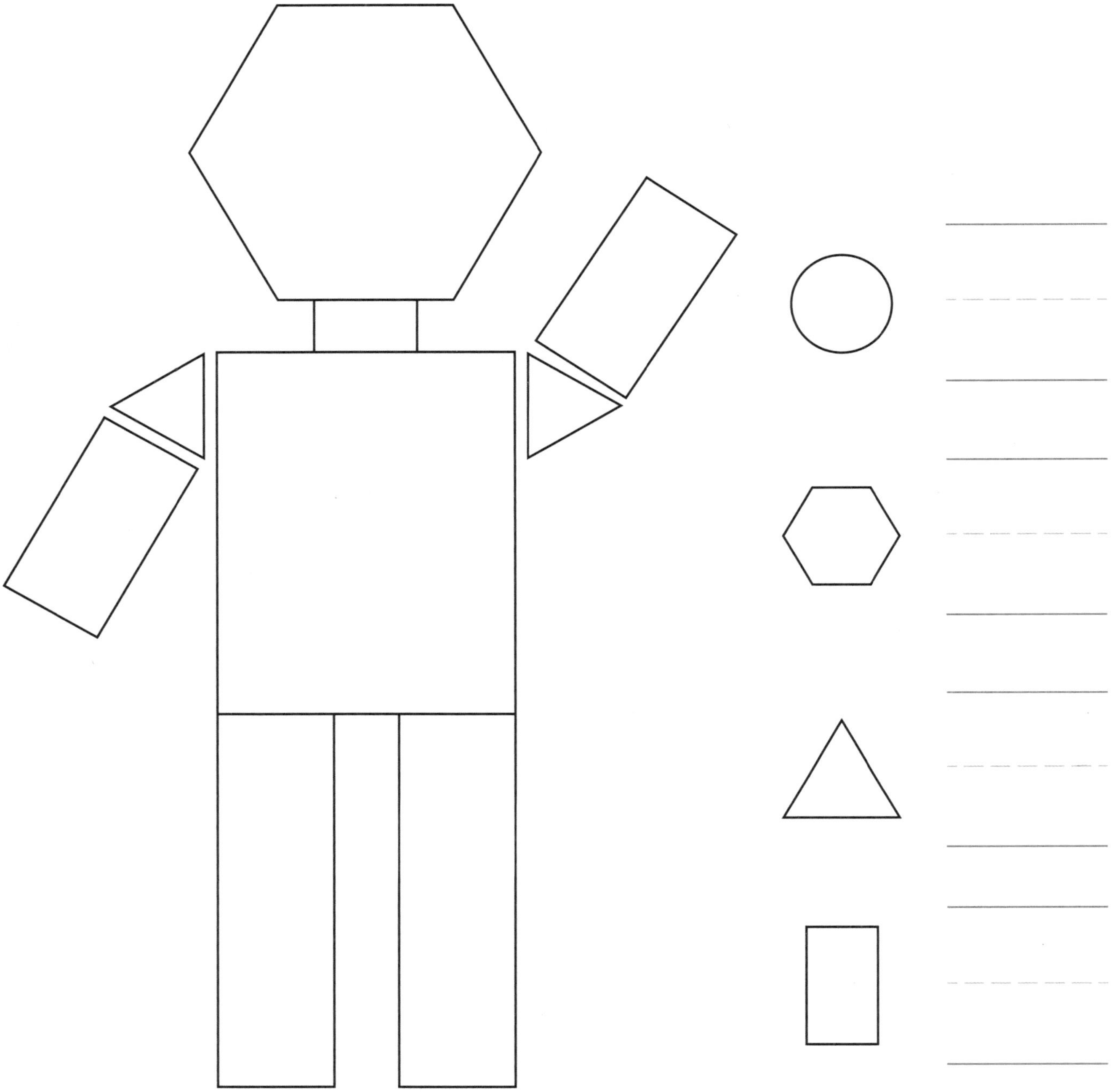

Directions: Follow the steps to complete the robot.

- Draw 2 circles for the robot's eyes, a triangle for the nose, and a rectangle for the mouth.
- Draw a hexagon for each of the robot's hands.
- How many of each shape is used for the whole robot? Write the number next to each shape.
- Color your robot.

Name ______________________________

Practice 11.5

Learning Target: Identify and describe hexagons and circles.

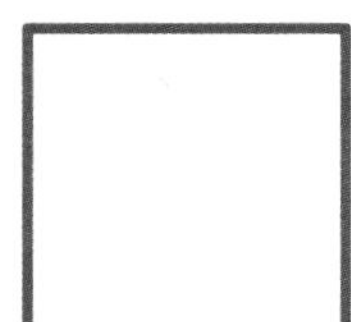

6 sides,
6 vertices

0 straight sides,
0 vertices

Directions: Color the hexagon red. Color the circle blue. Tell why your answers are correct.

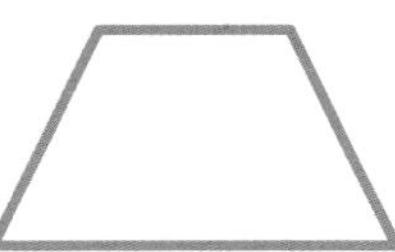
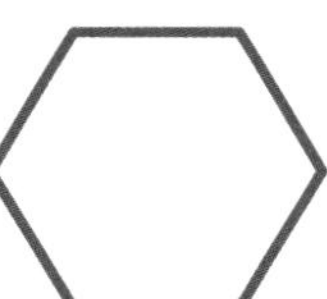
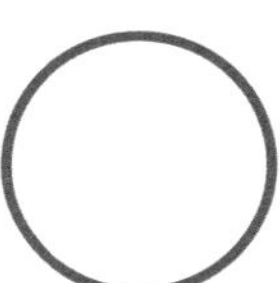
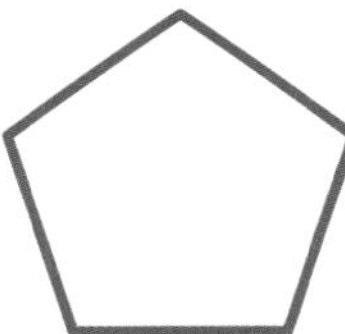

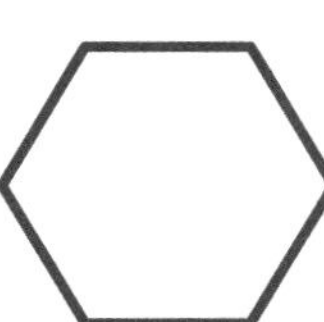
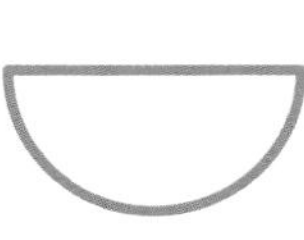

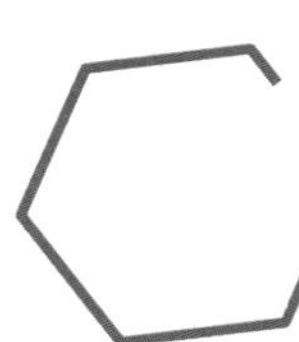

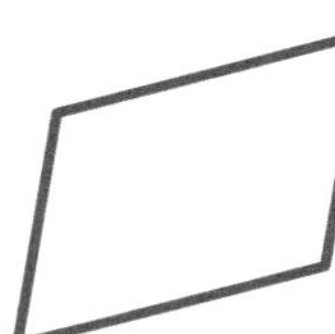
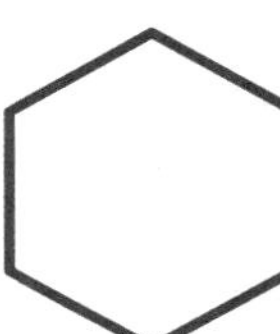

Directions: 1–3 Color any hexagons red. Color any circles blue. Tell why your answers are correct.

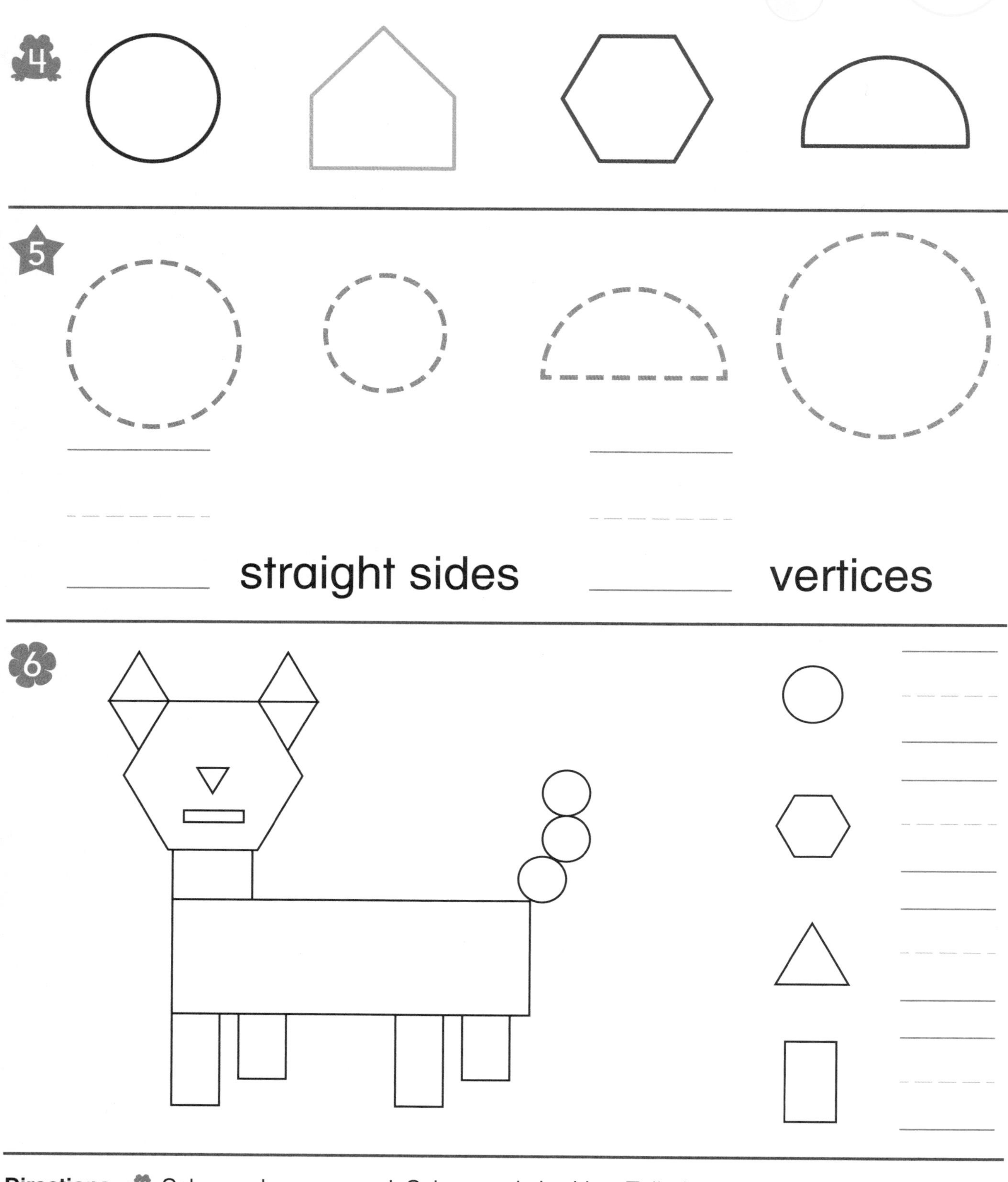

Directions: 4 Color any hexagons red. Color any circles blue. Tell why your answers are correct. 5 Trace the shapes that are circles. Write the number of straight sides and the number of vertices of a circle. 6 Draw a hexagon at the end of the cat's tail. Draw 2 circles for the eyes. How many of each shape is used for the cat? Write the numbers next to the shapes. Color your cat.

Name ____________________

Join Two-Dimensional Shapes 11.6

Learning Target: Join two-dimensional shapes to form a larger two-dimensional shape.

Explore and Grow

Directions:

- Use 2 squares to make a rectangle. Trace your shape.
- Add another square to make a larger rectangle. Trace your shape.
- Add another square to make a larger square. Trace your shape.

Think and Grow

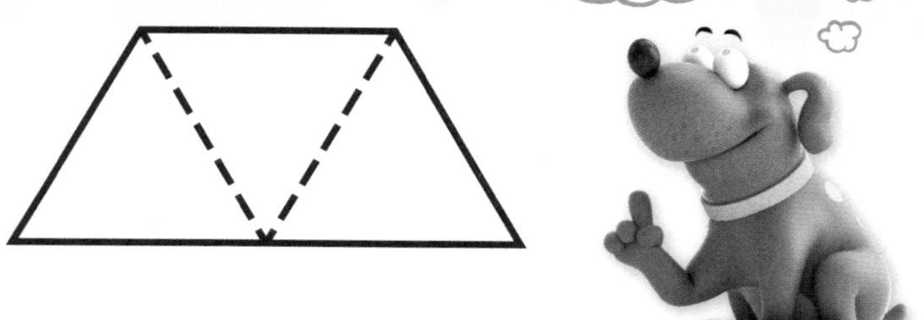

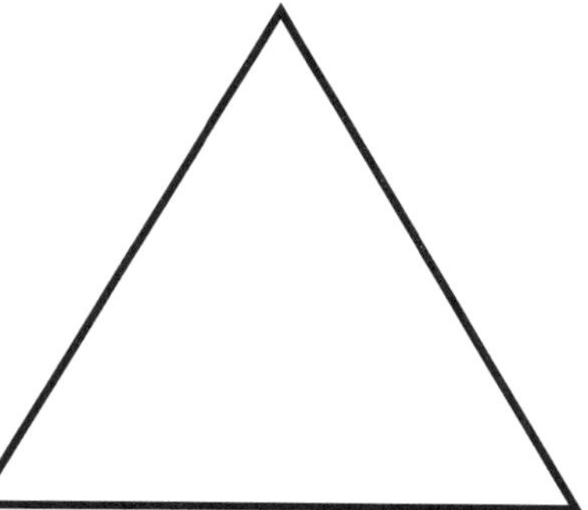

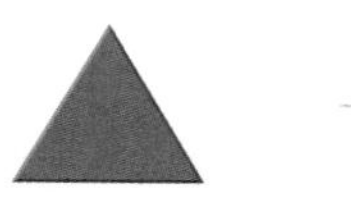

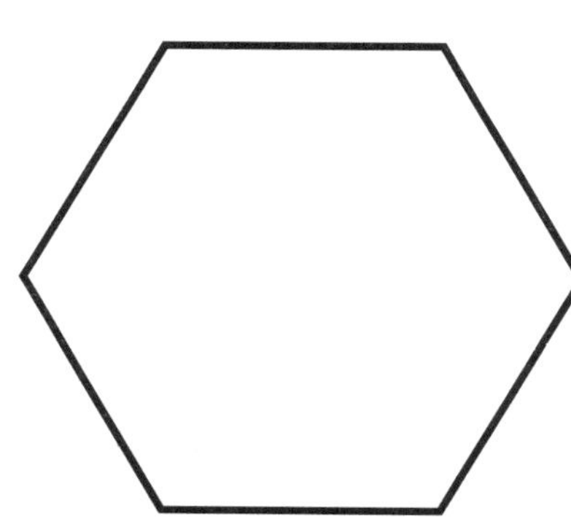

Directions: Use the pattern block shown to form the shape. Count and write how many pattern blocks you use.

Name ______________________

Apply and Grow: Practice

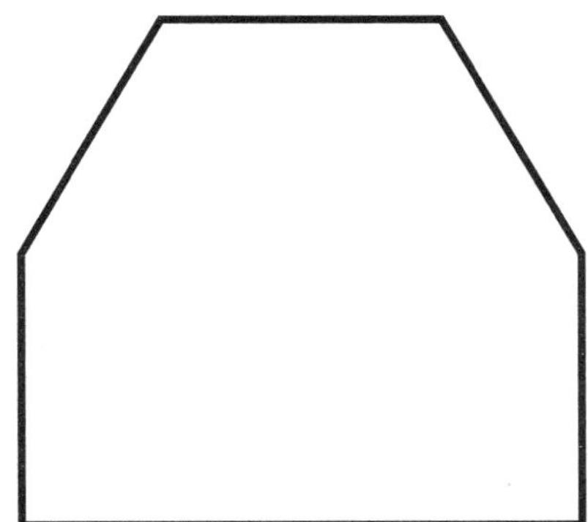

Directions: 1 and 2 Use the pattern blocks shown to form the shape. Count and write how many of each pattern block you use. 3 Draw a rectangle that can be formed by the 2 triangles shown.

Think and Grow: Modeling Real Life

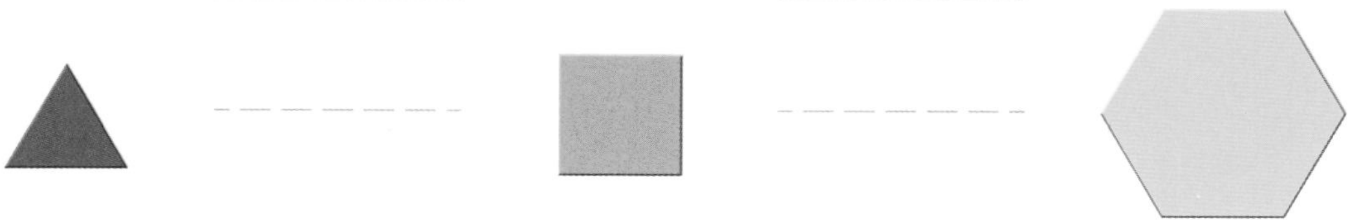

Directions: Use the pattern blocks shown to create the rocket ship. Count and write how many of each pattern block you use.

Name ______________________

Practice **11.6**

Learning Target: Join two-dimensional shapes to form a larger two-dimensional shape.

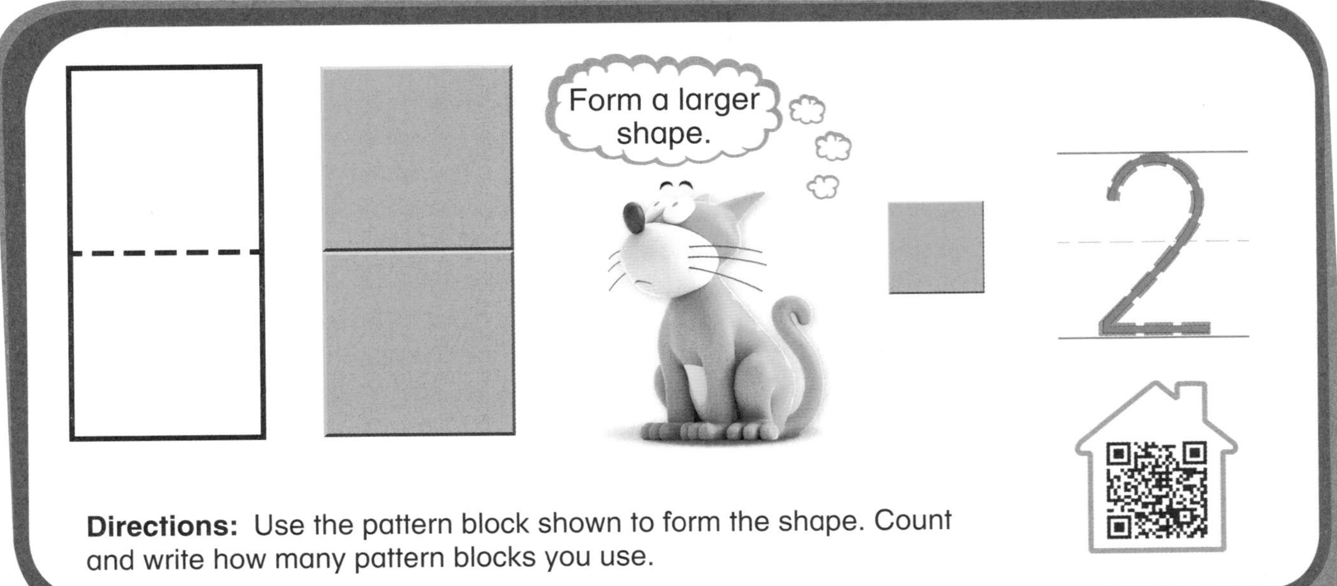

Directions: Use the pattern block shown to form the shape. Count and write how many pattern blocks you use.

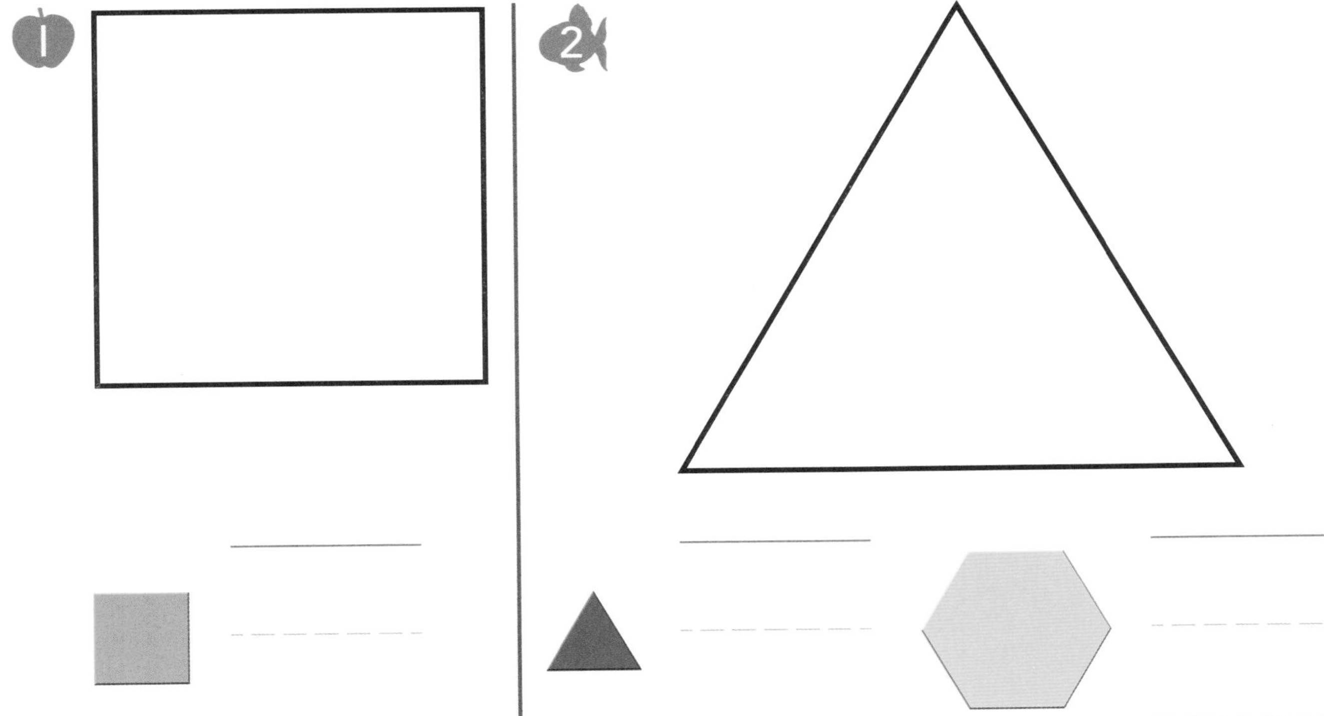

Directions: 1 and 2 Use the pattern blocks shown to form the shape. Count and write how many of each pattern block you use.

3

4

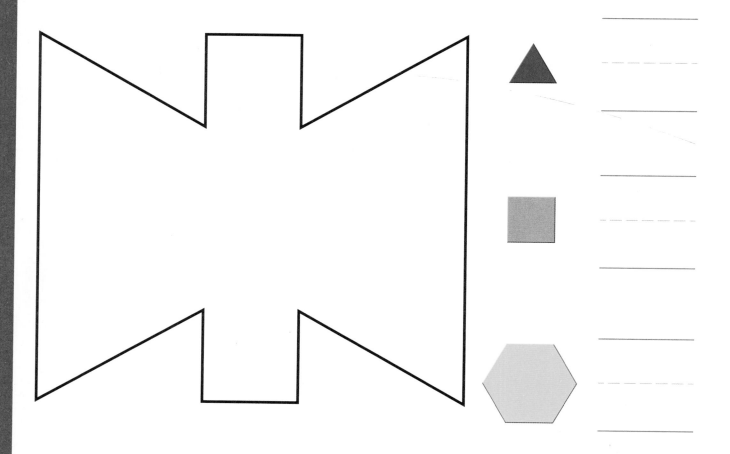

Directions: 3 Draw a square that can be formed by the 2 triangles shown. 4 Use the pattern blocks shown to create the butterfly. Count and write how many of each pattern block you use.

Name ______________________________

Build Two-Dimensional Shapes 11.7

Learning Target: Build and explore two-dimensional shapes.

Explore and Grow

Directions: Use your materials to build one of the two-dimensional shapes shown. Circle the two-dimensional shape that you make.

Think and Grow

Directions:

- Use your materials to build a triangle. Draw your triangle or attach it to the page.
- Use your materials to build a rectangle. Draw your shape or attach it to the page.

Name ______________________

Apply and Grow: Practice

Directions: 1 Use your materials to build a hexagon. Draw your hexagon or attach it to the page. 2 Use your materials to build a circle. Draw your circle or attach it to the page. 3 Use your materials to build a two-dimensional shape that has 4 vertices. Then build a different shape that has 4 vertices. Draw your shapes or attach them to the page.

Think and Grow: Modeling Real Life

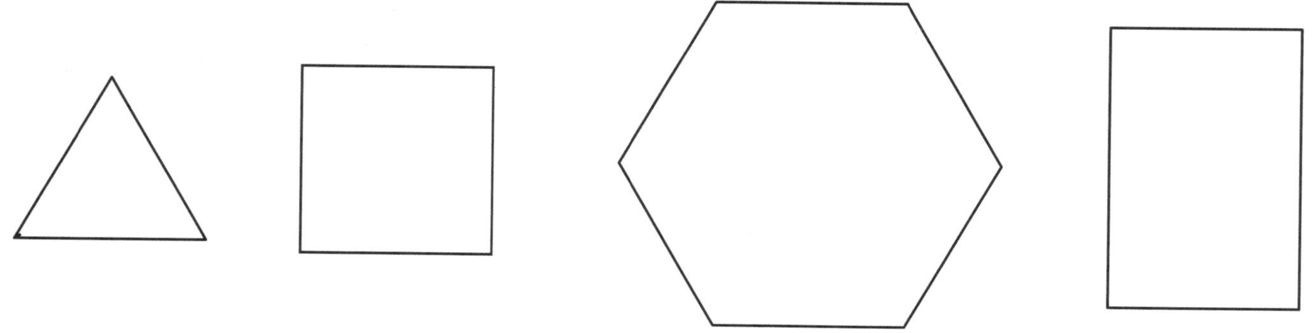

Directions:

- Use your materials to build the front of the house in the picture. Draw your shape or attach it to the page.
- Circle the shapes that you use to make the front of the house.

Name ______________________________

Practice 11.7

Learning Target: Build and explore two-dimensional shapes.

Directions: Use your materials to build a square. Draw your square or attach it to the page.

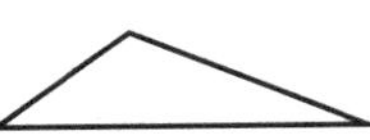

Directions: 1–3 Use your materials to build the shape shown. Draw your shape or attach it to the page. 4 Use your materials to build a two-dimensional shape that has 6 vertices. Draw your shape or attach it to the page.

5

6

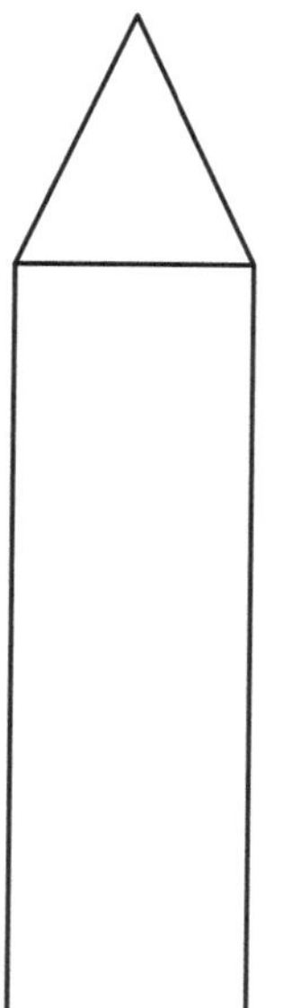

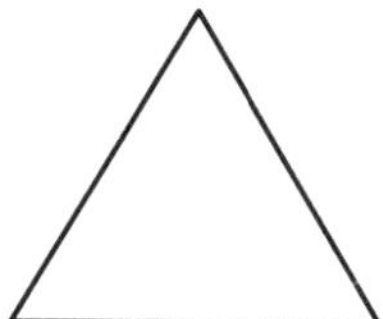

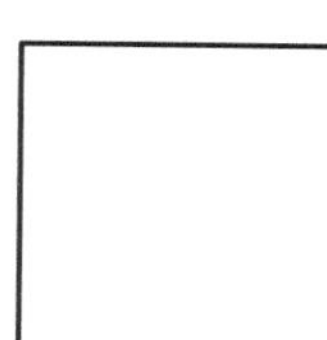

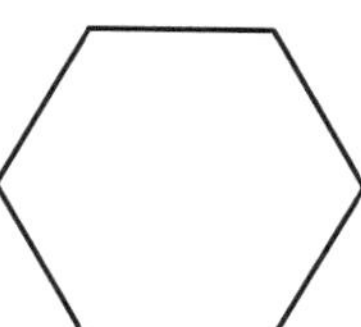

Directions: 5 Use your materials to build a two-dimensional shape that is not a rectangle. Then build a different two-dimensional shape that is not a rectangle. Draw your shapes or attach them to the page. 6 Use your materials to build the front of the sand castle tower in the picture. Draw your shape or attach it to the page. Circle the shapes that you use to make the front of the tower.

Name ___________________________________

Performance Task

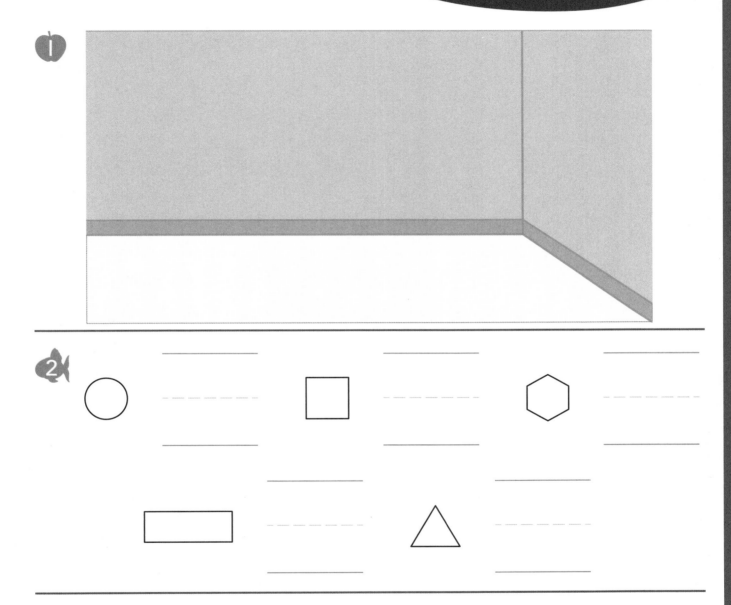

1

2

○ ______

□ ______

⬡ ______

▭ ______

△ ______

Directions: 1 Use the clues to draw each two-dimensional shape to make an animal.

- The face is a shape that has 1 more than 5 sides.
- The eyes are shapes that are curved and have no vertices.
- The nose and ears are shapes that have 1 more than 2 vertices.
- The mouth, the body, and the tail are shapes that have more than 3 sides, but less than 5 sides and have L-shaped vertices.
- The 4 legs are shapes that have 1 less than 5 sides and have all equal side lengths.

2 Count and write how many of each shape you draw.

Shape Flip and Find

Directions: Place the Shape Flip and Find Cards facedown in the boxes. Take turns flipping 2 cards. If your cards show the same shape, keep the cards. If your cards show different shapes, flip the cards back over. Repeat until all cards have been used.

Name ____________________

Chapter Practice

11.1 Describe Two-Dimensional Shapes

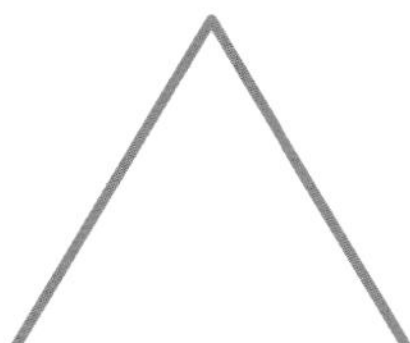

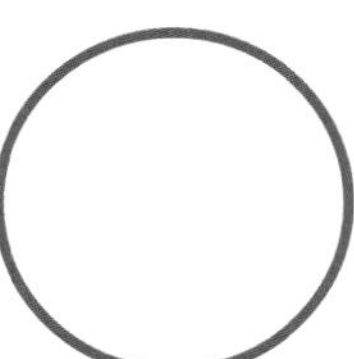

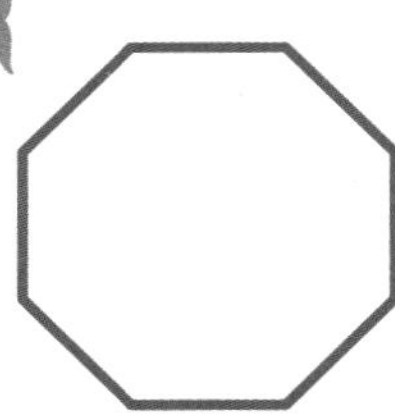
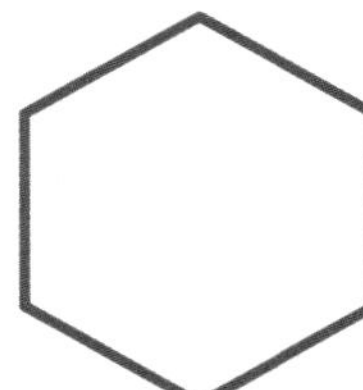

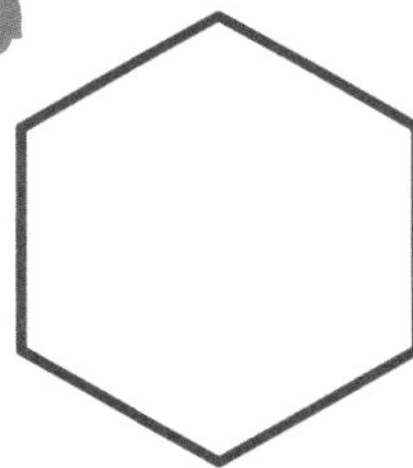
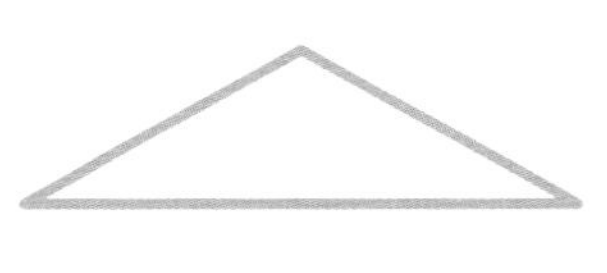

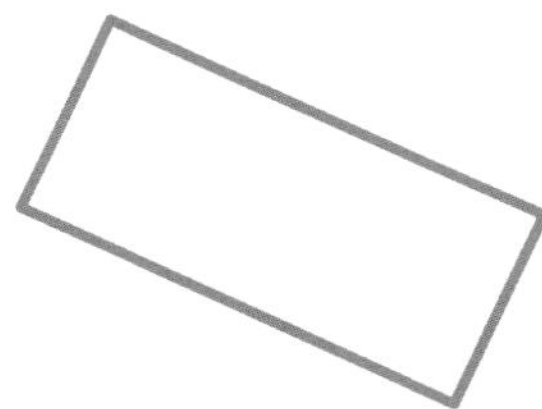

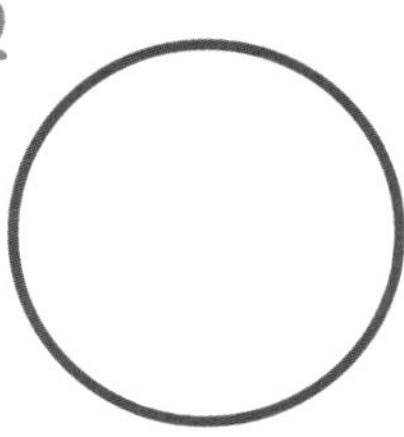

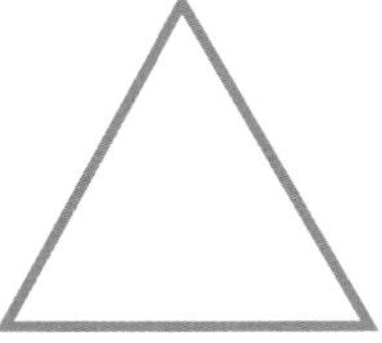

Directions: 1 Color the shape that has only 3 vertices. 2 Color the shape that has a curve. 3 Color the shapes that have 6 sides. 4 Color the shapes that have 4 vertices.

11.2 Triangles

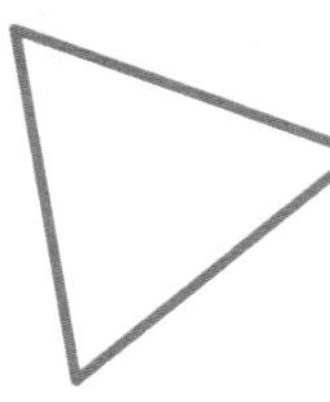 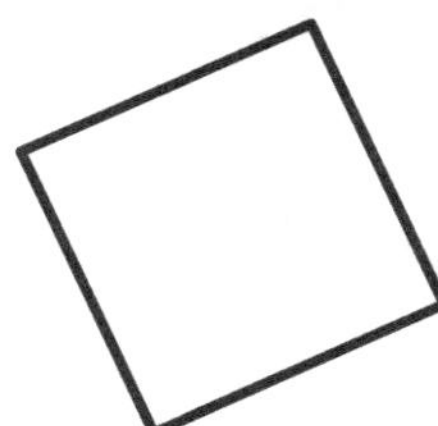 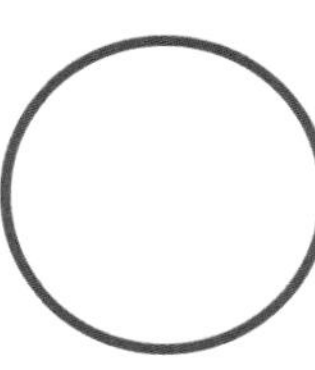 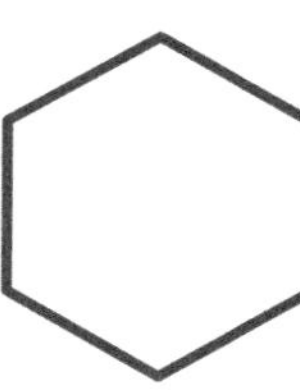

  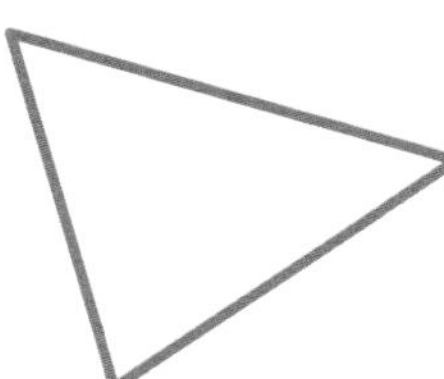 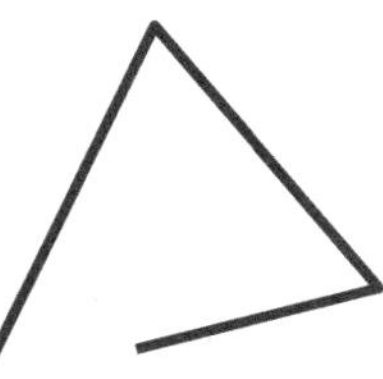

11.3 Rectangles

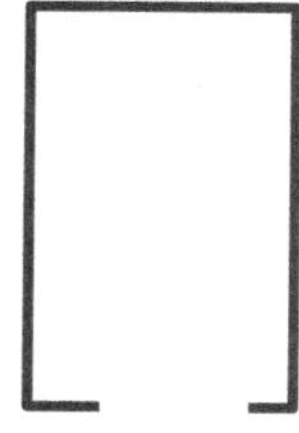 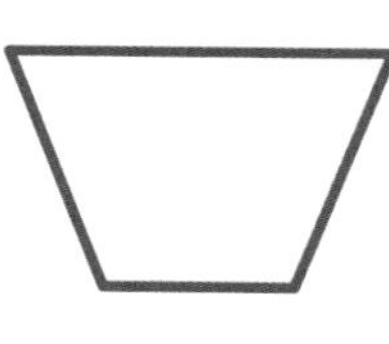  

8

 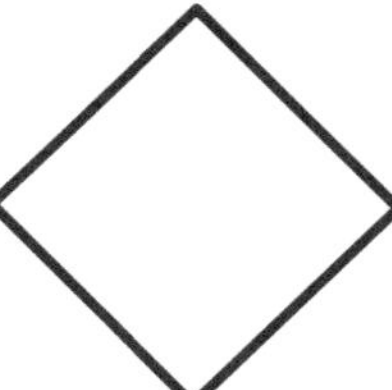 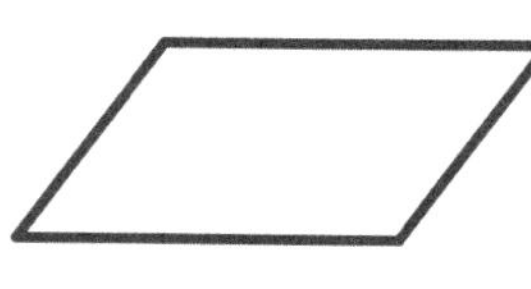 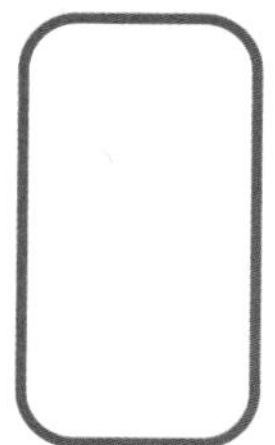

Directions: 5 and 6 Color the triangle. Tell why your answer is correct.
7 and 8 Color any rectangles. Tell why your answers are correct.

11.4 Squares

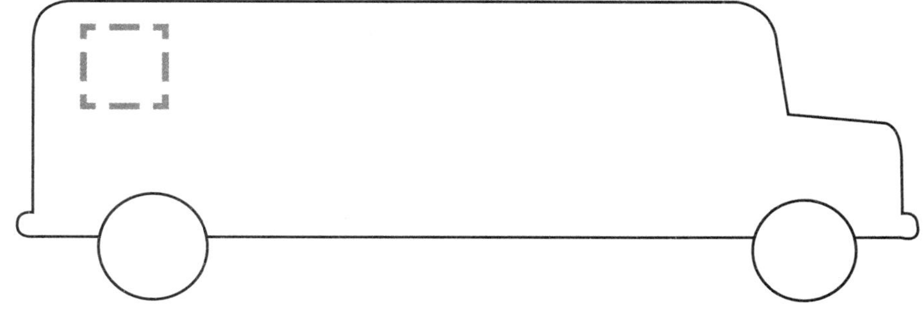

11.5 Hexagons and Circles

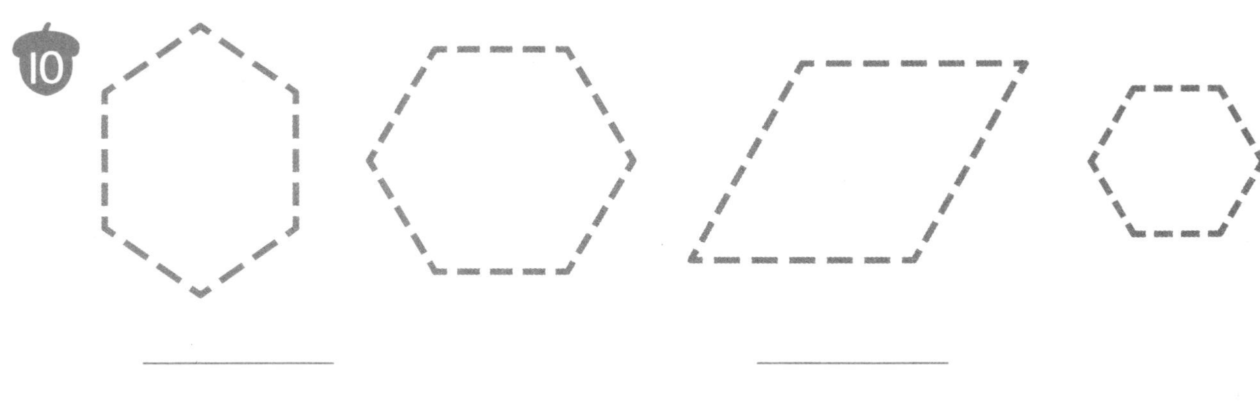

_______ sides _______ vertices

Directions: 9 Use squares and rectangles to draw 5 windows and 1 door on the bus. Color the bus. Then write an addition sentence to tell how many squares and rectangles you draw in all. 10 Trace the shapes that are hexagons. Write the number of sides and the number of vertices of a hexagon.

11.6 Join Two-Dimensional Shapes

11

12

11.7 Build Two-Dimensional Shapes

13

14

15

Directions: 11 Use the pattern block shown to form the shape. Count and write how many pattern blocks you use. 12 Draw a larger triangle that can be formed by the 2 triangles shown. 13 Use your materials to build the shape. Draw your shape or attach it to the page. 14 Use your materials to build a two-dimensional shape that has 4 sides of the same length. Draw your shape or attach it to the page. 15 Use your materials to build a two-dimensional shape that is *not* a hexagon. Draw your shape or attach it to the page.

12 Identify Three-Dimensional Shapes and Positions

- What items do you recycle?
- What three-dimensional shapes do you see in the picture?

Chapter Learning Target:
Understand three-dimensional shapes.

Chapter Success Criteria:

- I can identify three-dimensional shapes.
- I can describe three-dimensional shapes.
- I can compare three-dimensional shapes.
- I can build three-dimensional shapes.

Name ______________________

12 Vocabulary

Review Words
circle
square
two-dimensional shape

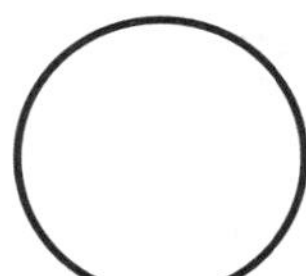

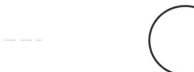

Directions: Circle each can. Draw a square around each box. Count and write how many of each two-dimensional shape you draw.

Chapter 12 Vocabulary Cards

above

behind

below

beside

cone

cube

curved surface

cylinder

© Big Ideas Learning, LLC
© Big Ideas Learning, LLC
© Big Ideas Learning, LLC
© Big Ideas Learning, LLC
© Big Ideas Learning, LLC
© Big Ideas Learning, LLC
© Big Ideas Learning, LLC
© Big Ideas Learning, LLC

Chapter 12 Vocabulary Cards

flat surface	in front of
next to	roll
slide	sphere
stack	three-dimensional shape

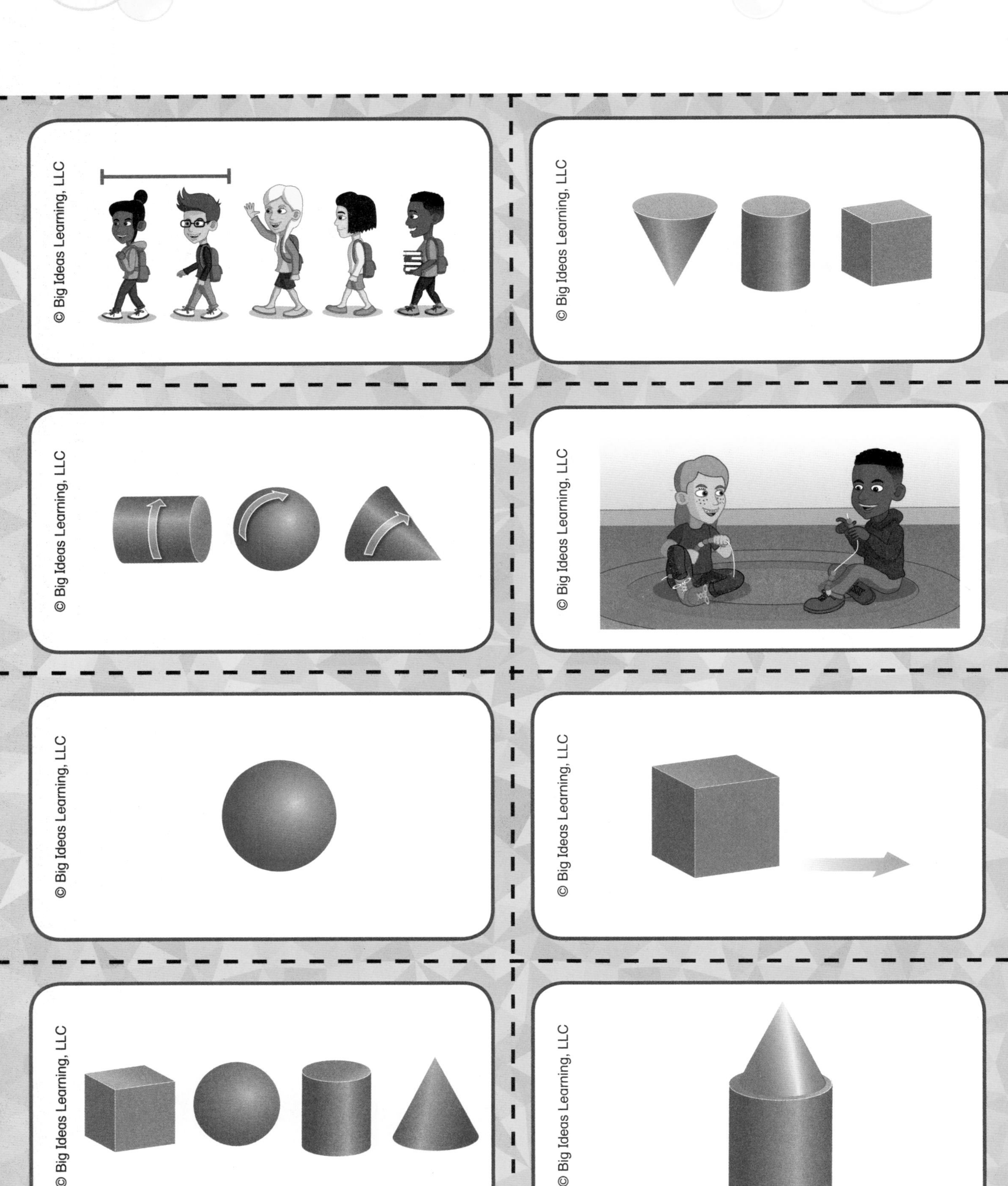
© Big Ideas Learning, LLC
© Big Ideas Learning, LLC
© Big Ideas Learning, LLC
© Big Ideas Learning, LLC
© Big Ideas Learning, LLC
© Big Ideas Learning, LLC
© Big Ideas Learning, LLC
© Big Ideas Learning, LLC

Chapter 12 Vocabulary Cards

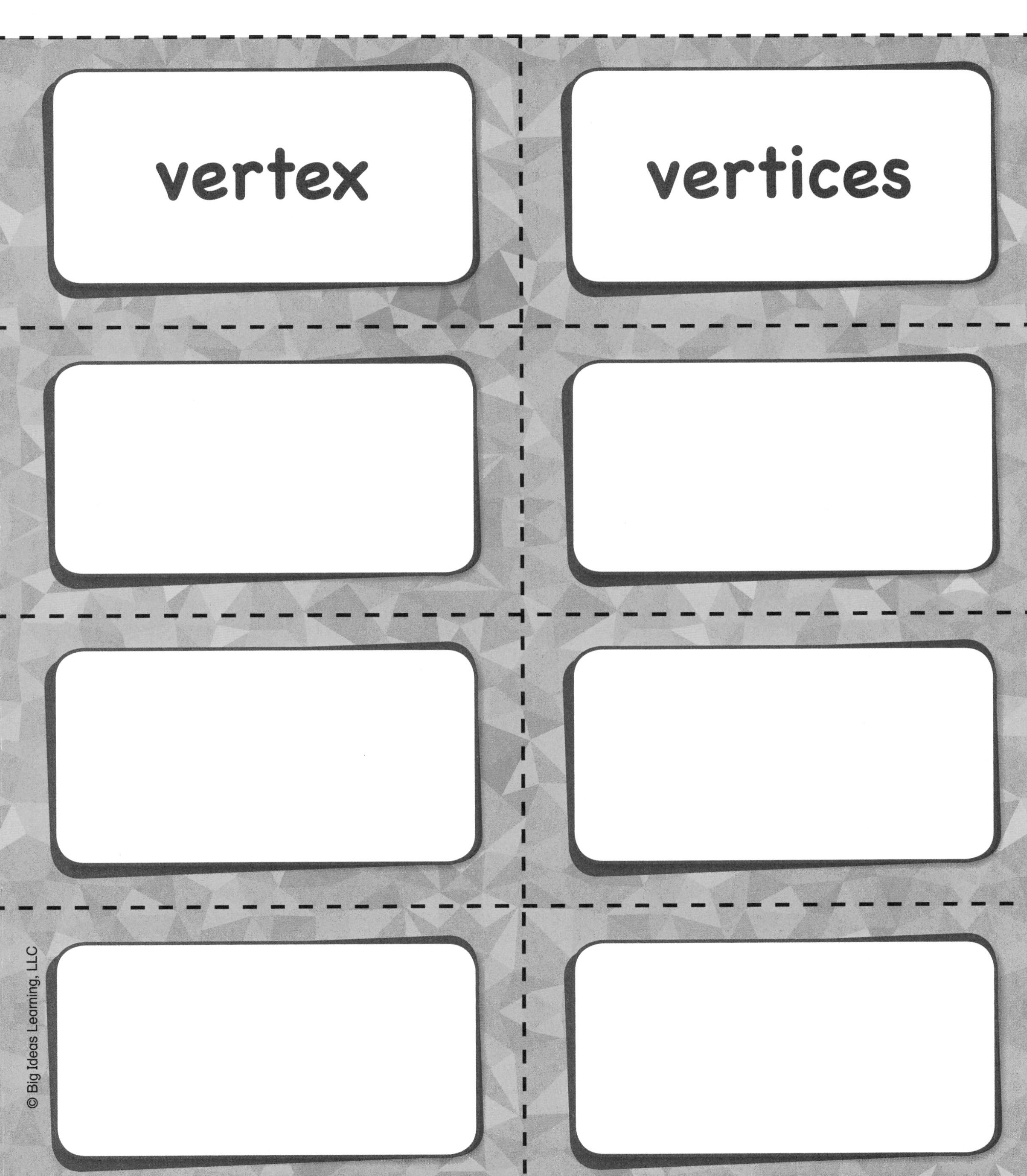

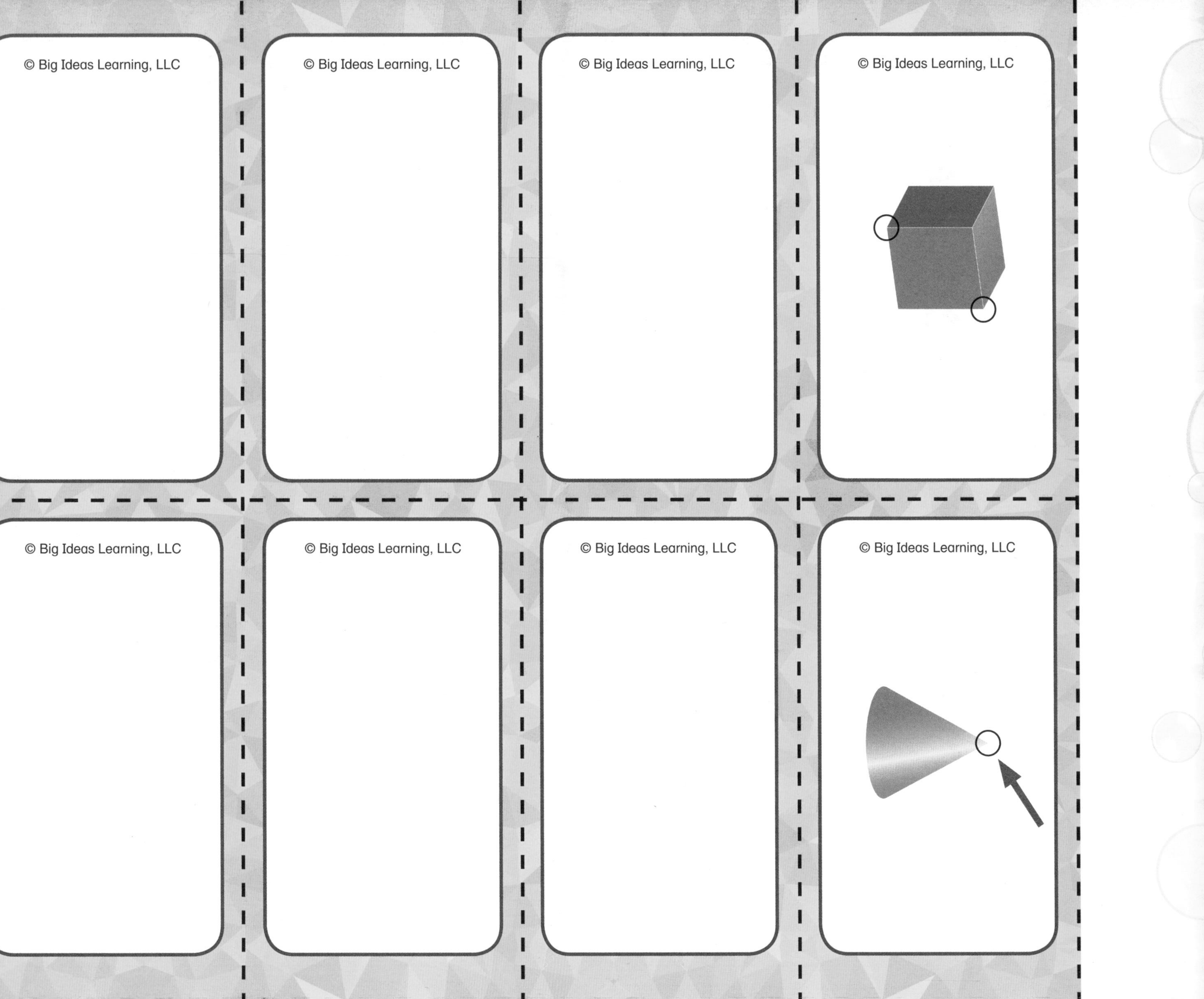

© Big Ideas Learning, LLC
© Big Ideas Learning, LLC
© Big Ideas Learning, LLC
© Big Ideas Learning, LLC
© Big Ideas Learning, LLC
© Big Ideas Learning, LLC
© Big Ideas Learning, LLC

Name ______________________________

Two- and Three-Dimensional Shapes 12.1

Learning Target: Identify and describe two-dimensional and three-dimensional shapes.

Explore and Grow

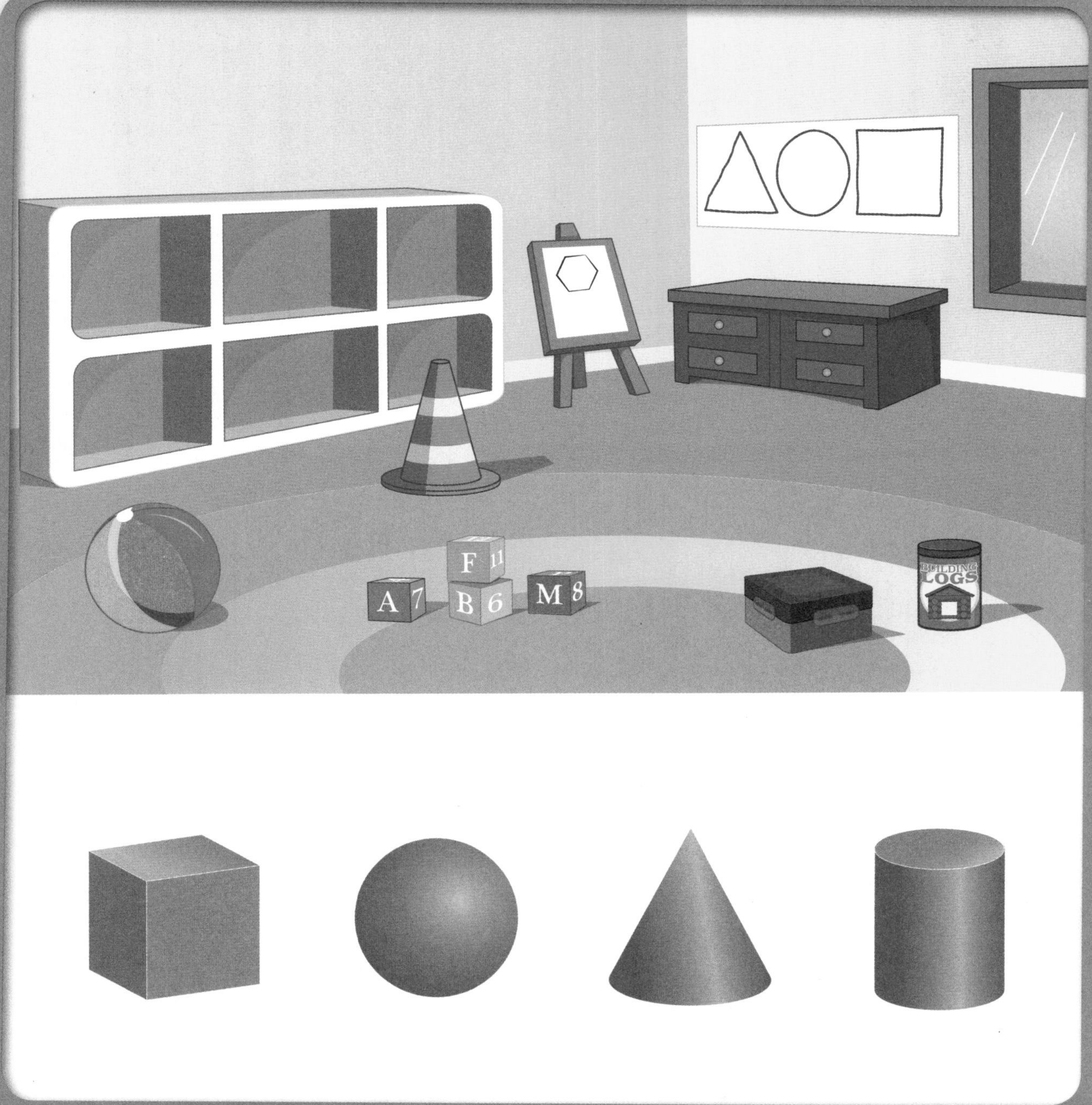

Directions: Circle any triangles, rectangles, squares, hexagons, and circles you see in the picture. Use another color to circle any objects in the picture that match the blue shapes shown. Tell what you notice about each shape.

Think and Grow

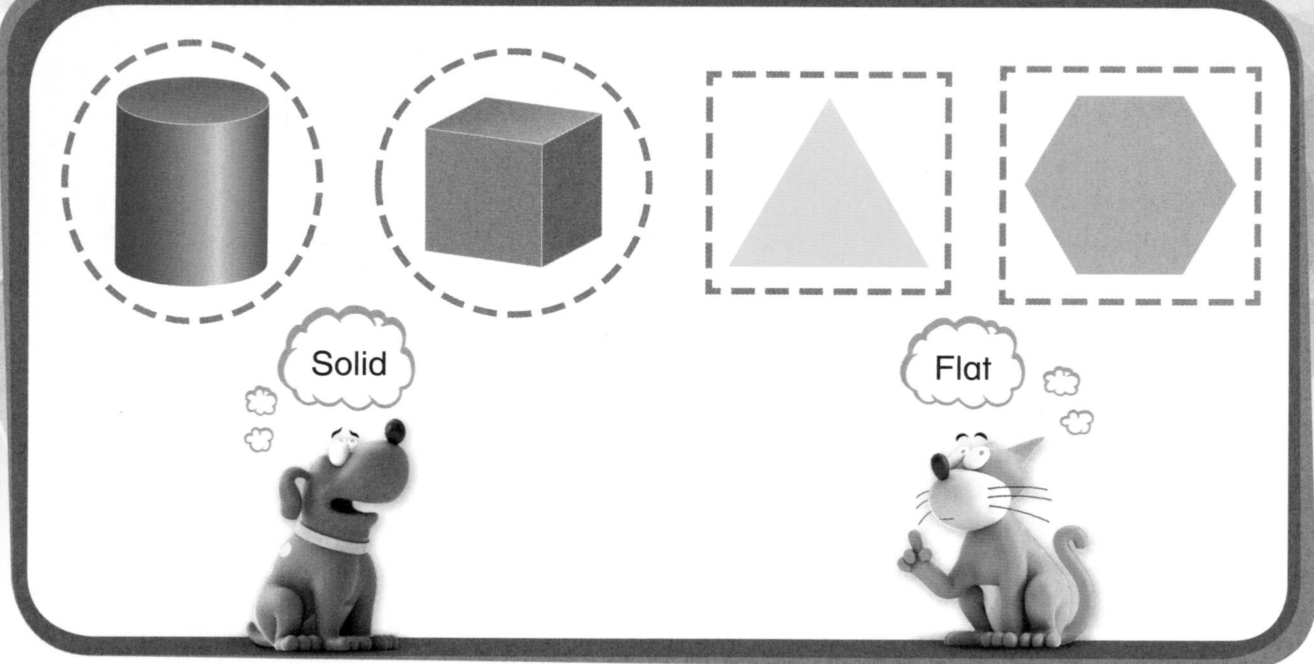

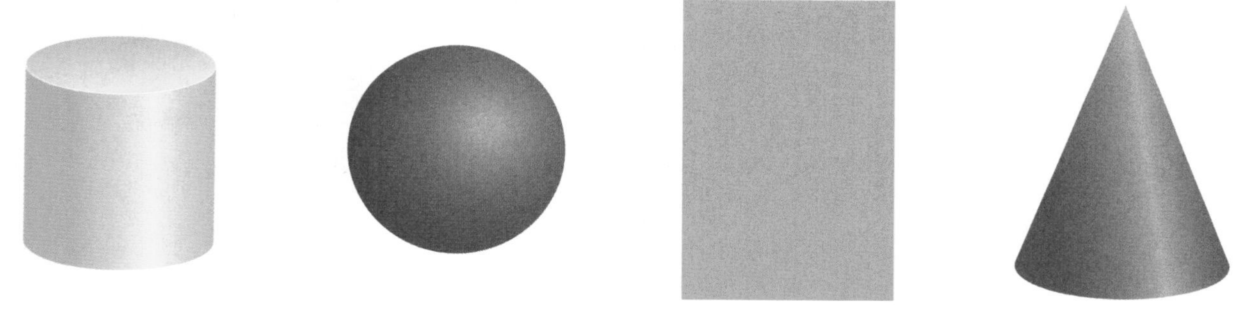

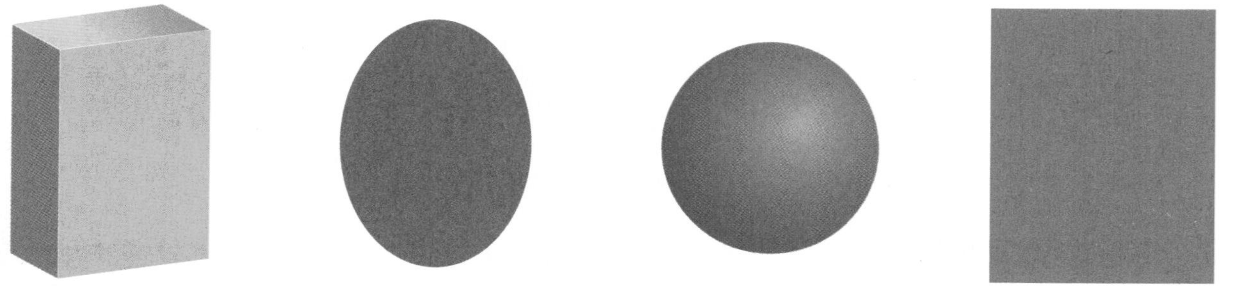

Directions: Circle any three-dimensional shapes. Draw rectangles around any two-dimensional shapes. Tell why your answers are correct.

Name ______________________________

Apply and Grow: Practice

 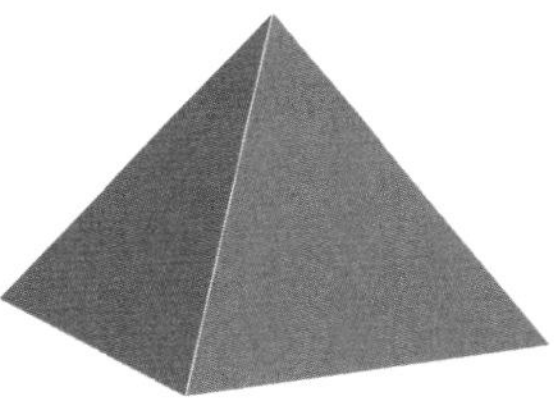  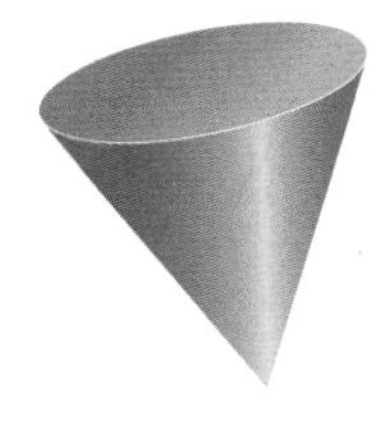

4

 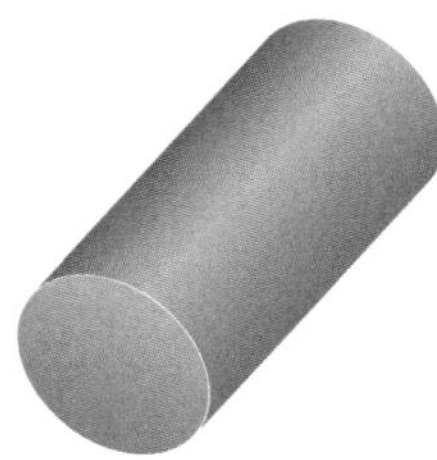  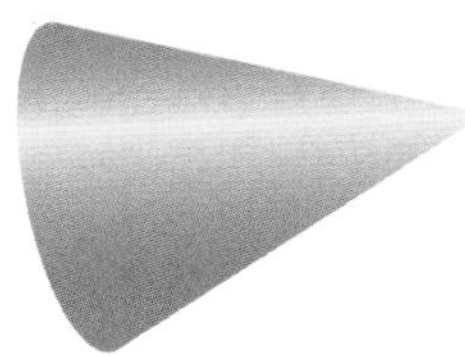

Directions: 1–4 Circle any three-dimensional shapes. Draw rectangles around any two-dimensional shapes. Tell why your answers are correct.

Think and Grow: Modeling Real Life

three-dimensional

____

two-dimensional

____

Directions: Circle any shapes in the picture that are solids. Draw rectangles around any shapes in the picture that are flats. Count and write how many solids and flats you find.

Name ________________________________

Learning Target: Identify and describe two-dimensional and three-dimensional shapes.

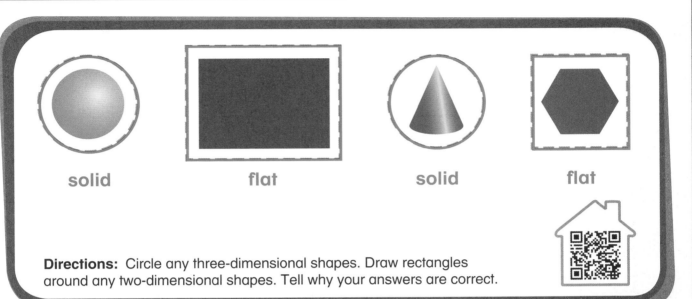

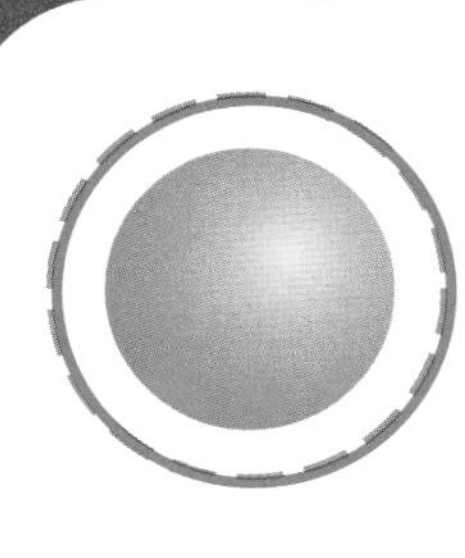
solid

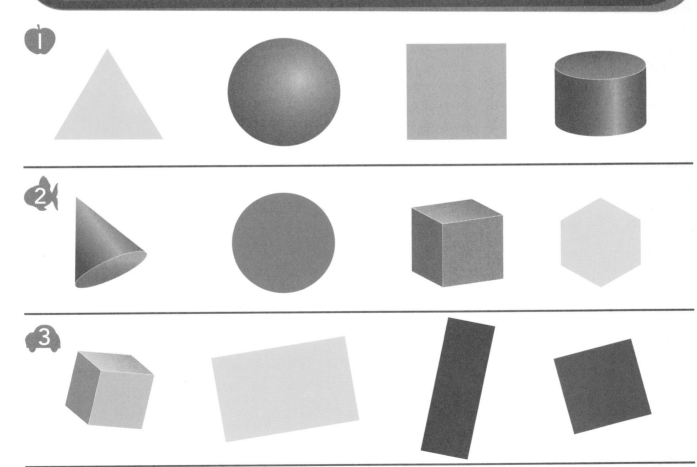
flat

solid

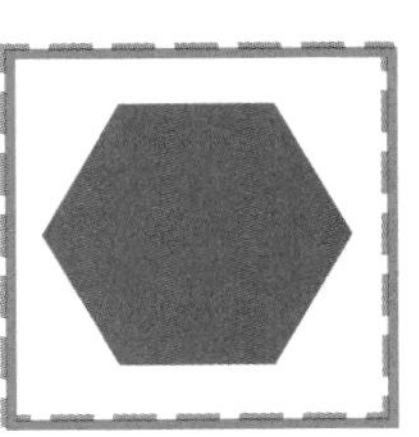
flat

Directions: Circle any three-dimensional shapes. Draw rectangles around any two-dimensional shapes. Tell why your answers are correct.

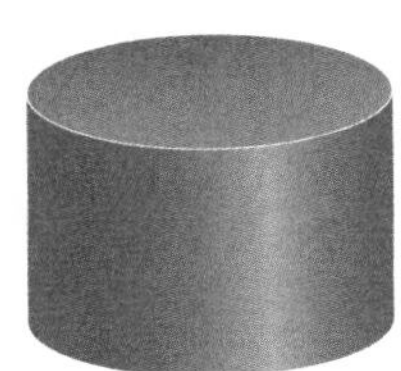

Directions: 1–3 Circle any three-dimensional shapes. Draw rectangles around any two-dimensional shapes. Tell why your answers are correct.

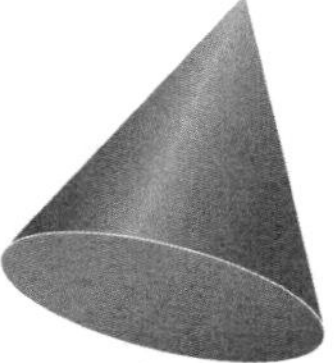   

three-dimensional

two-dimensional

Directions: 4 and 5 Circle any three-dimensional shapes. Draw rectangles around any two-dimensional shapes. Tell why your answers are correct. 6 Circle any three-dimensional shapes in the picture. Count and write the number. Draw rectangles around any two-dimensional shapes in the picture. Count and write the number.

Name ______________________

12.2 Describe Three-Dimensional Shapes

Learning Target: Describe three-dimensional shapes.

Explore and Grow

rolls

stacks

slides

Directions: Cut out the Roll, Stack, Slide Sort Cards. Sort the cards into the categories shown.

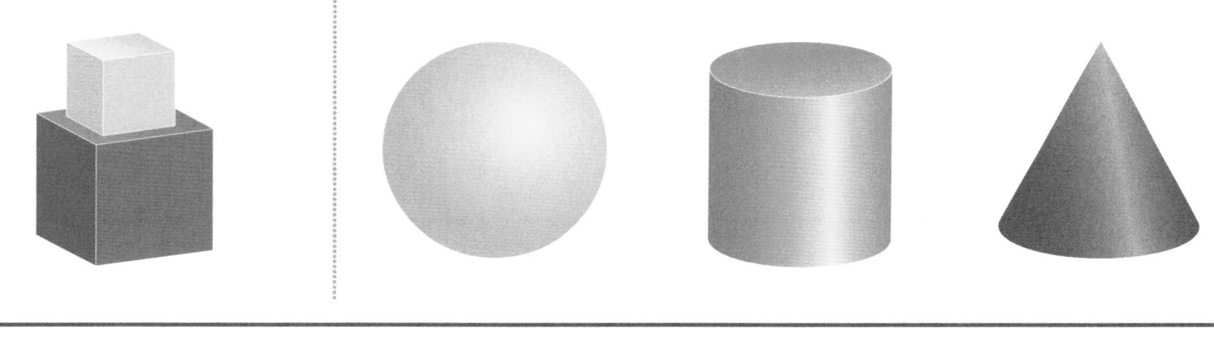

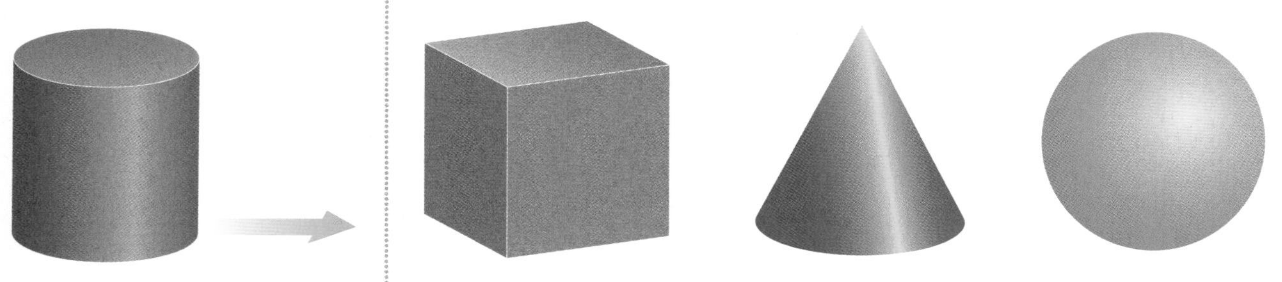

Directions:

- Look at the solid shape on the left that rolls. Circle the other solid shapes that roll.
- Look at the solid shapes on the left that stack. Circle the other solid shapes that stack.
- Look at the solid shape on the left that slides. Circle the other solid shapes that slide.

Name ____

Apply and Grow: Practice

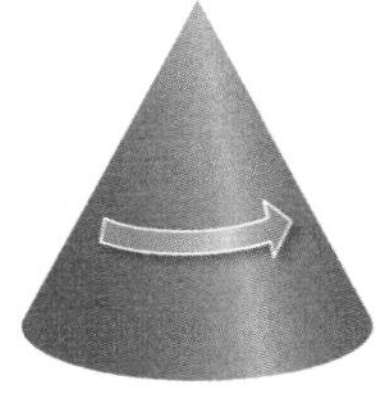
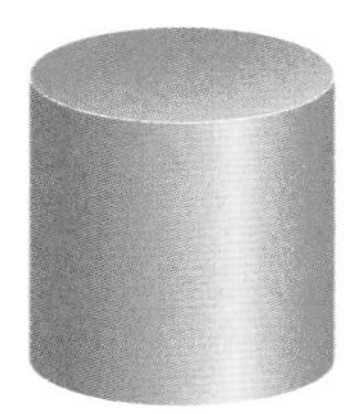

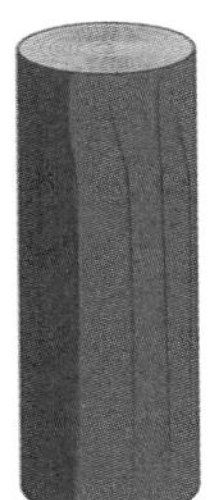

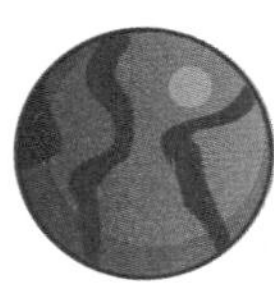
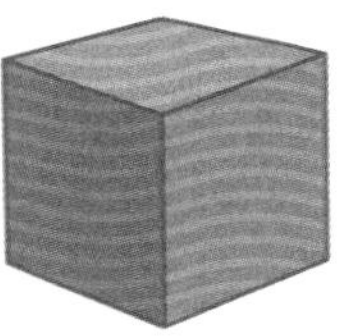

Directions: 1 Look at the solid shape on the left that rolls. Circle the other solid shapes that roll. 2 Circle the solid shapes that roll and slide. 3 Circle the solid shapes that stack and slide. 4 Circle the solid shape that does *not* stack or slide.

Think and Grow: Modeling Real Life

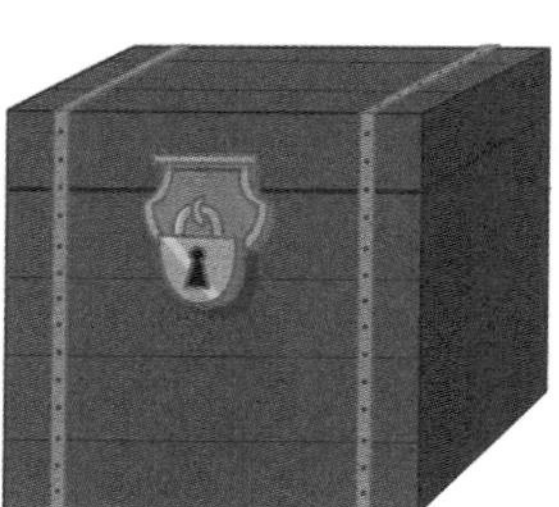

Directions: You stack the 3 objects shown. Write 1 below the object you place at the bottom of the stack, write 2 below the object you stack next, and write 3 below the object you stack last. Tell why you chose this order.

Name ______________________

Practice 12.2

Learning Target: Describe three-dimensional shapes.

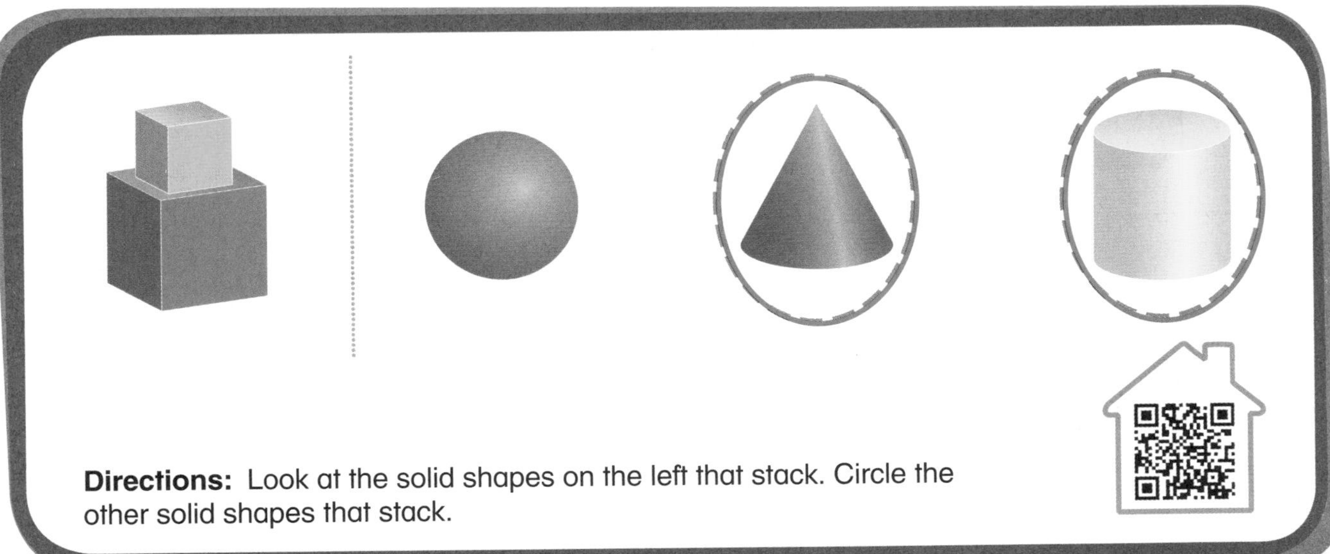

Directions: Look at the solid shapes on the left that stack. Circle the other solid shapes that stack.

1

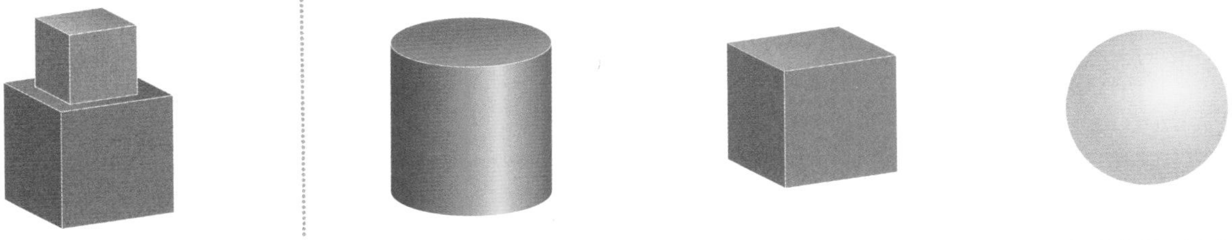

2

3

Directions: 1 Look at the solid shapes on the left that stack. Circle the other solid shapes that stack. 2 Look at the solid shape on the left that rolls. Circle the other solid shapes that roll. 3 Look at the solid shape on the left that slides. Circle the other solid shapes that slide.

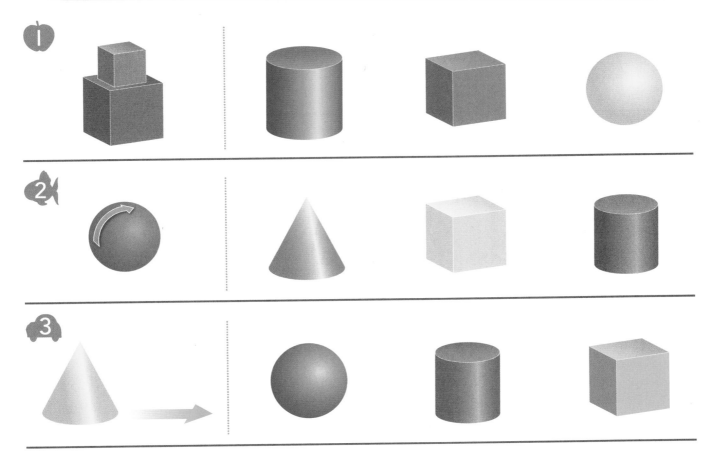

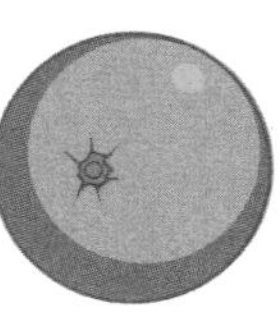

Directions: 4 Circle the solid shapes that roll and stack. 5 Circle the solid shapes that stack and slide. 6 Circle the solid shape that does *not* roll. 7 You stack the 3 objects shown. Write 1 below the object you place at the bottom of the stack, write 2 below the object you stack next, and write 3 below the object you stack last. Tell why you chose this order.

Name ______________________________

Learning Target: Identify and describe cubes and spheres.

Explore and Grow

 cube	 sphere

Directions: Cut out the Cube and Sphere Sort Cards. Sort the cards into the categories shown.

Think and Grow

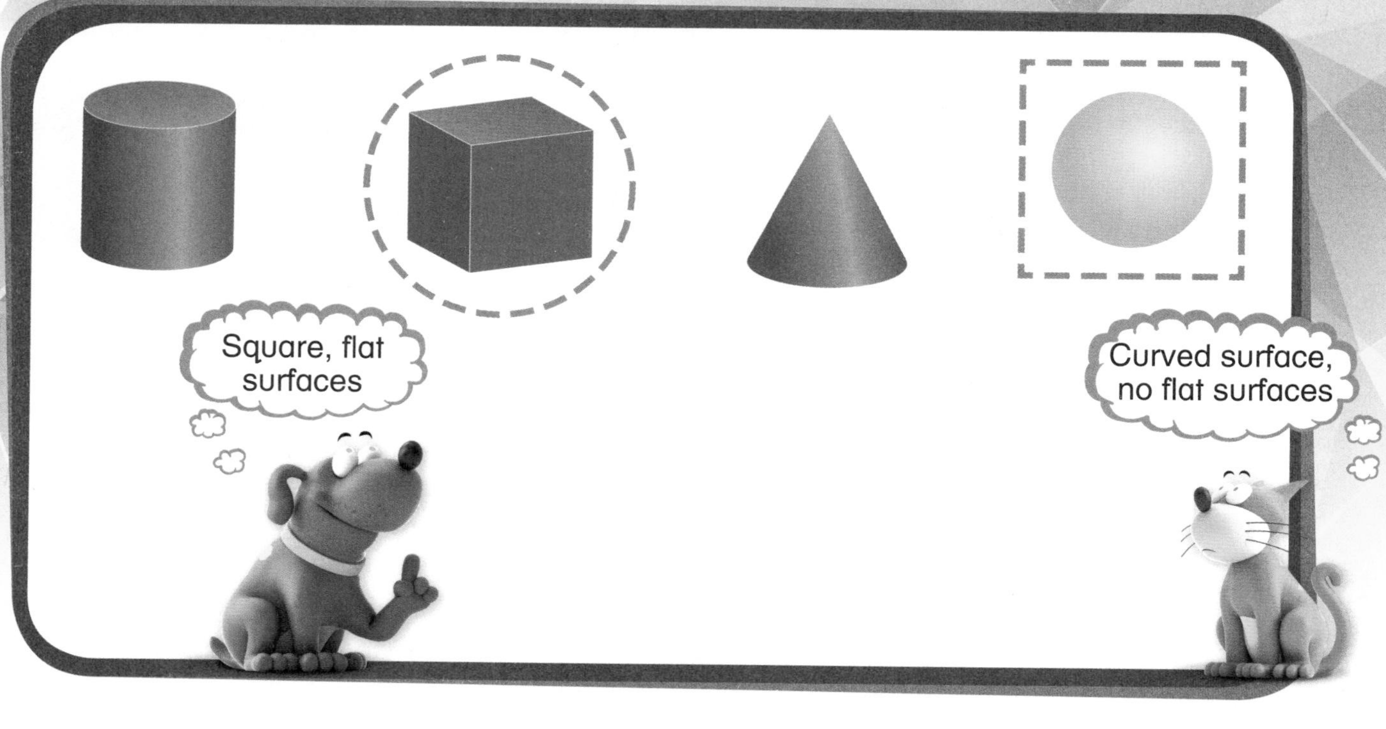

Square, flat surfaces
Curved surface, no flat surfaces

 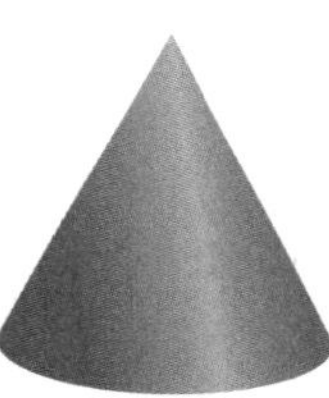  

   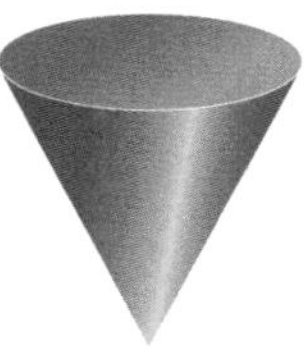

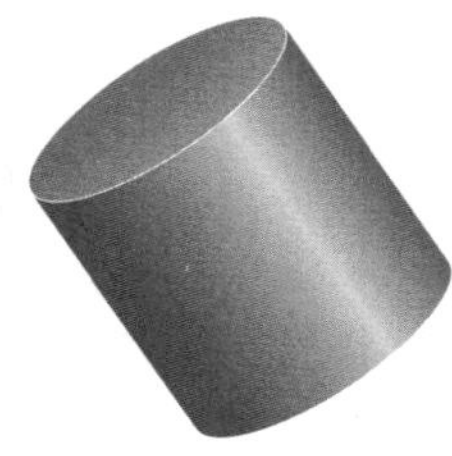   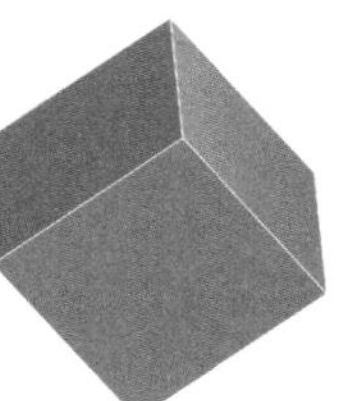

Directions: Circle the cube. Draw a rectangle around the sphere. Tell why your answers are correct.

Name ______________________________

Apply and Grow: Practice

  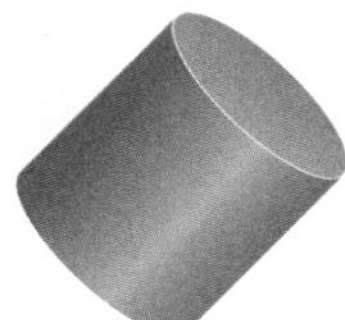 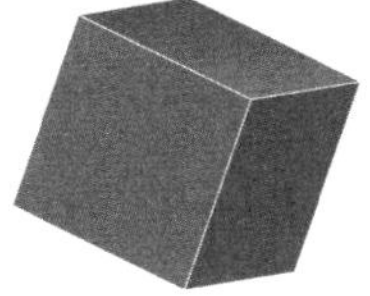

 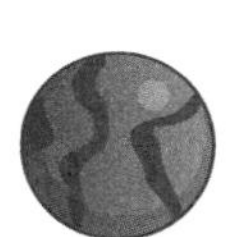 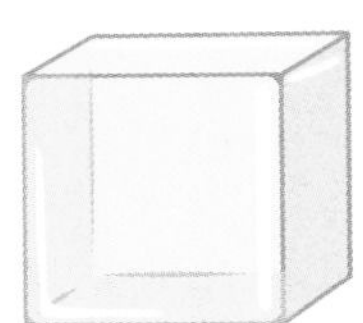 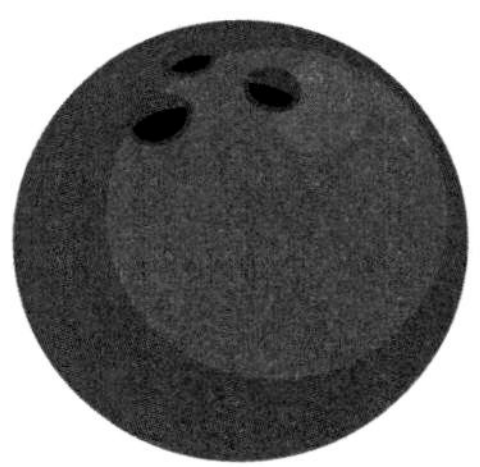

 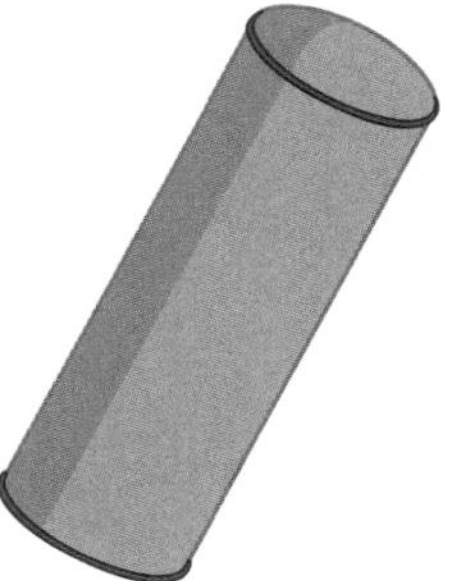 

Directions: 1 Circle the cube. Draw a rectangle around the sphere. Tell why your answers are correct. 2–4 Circle any object that looks like a cube. Draw a rectangle around any object that looks like a sphere. Tell why your answers are correct.

Think and Grow: Modeling Real Life

_______ flat surfaces

Directions: Use Make a Cube to build your own number cube. Draw the shape of the flat surfaces of your cube. Count and write the number of flat surfaces.

Name ______________________

Learning Target: Identify and describe cubes and spheres.

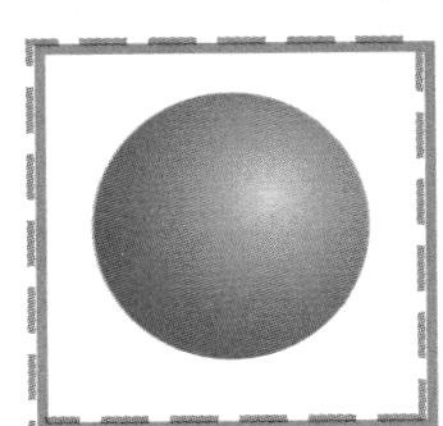
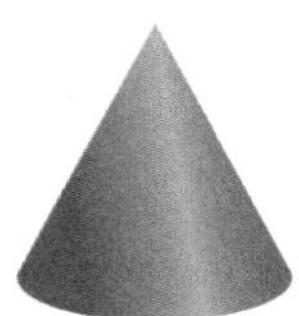
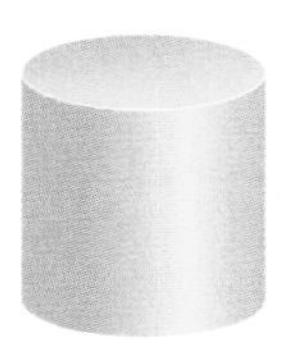
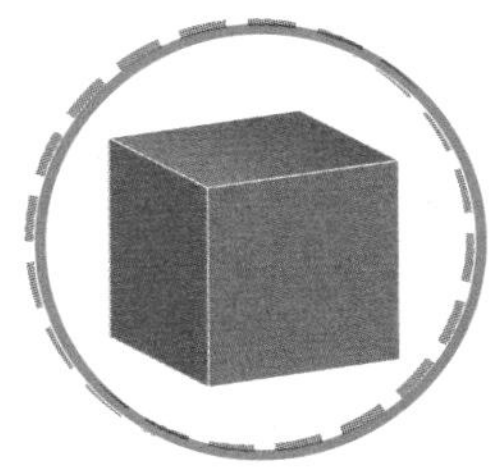

curved surface, no flat surfaces

square, flat surfaces

Directions: Circle the cube. Draw a rectangle around the sphere. Tell why your answers are correct.

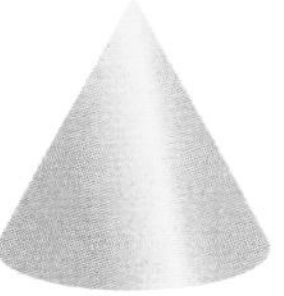

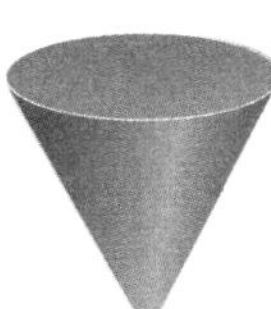

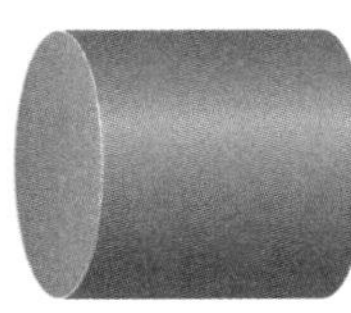

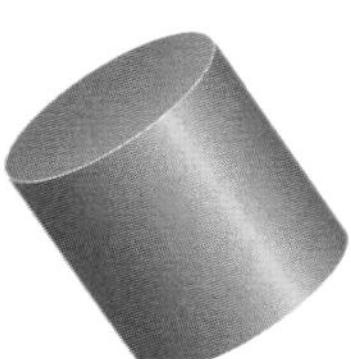

Directions: 1–3 Circle the cube. Draw a rectangle around the sphere. Tell why your answers are correct.

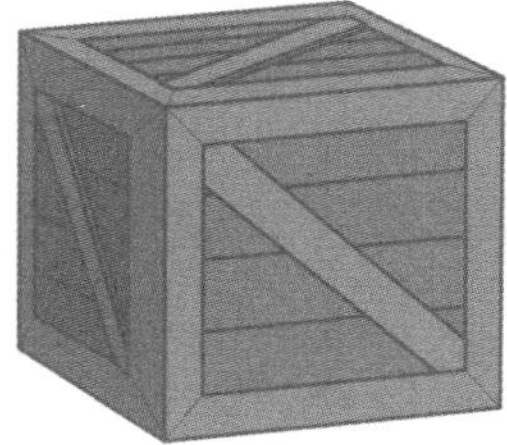

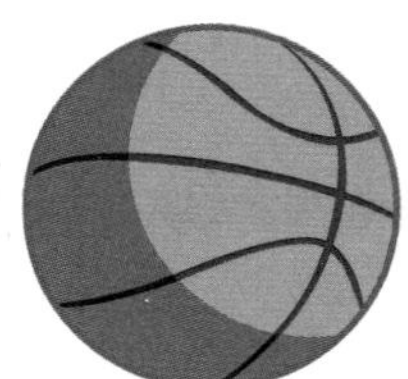

____

_______ flat surfaces

Directions: 4–6 Circle any object that looks like a cube. Draw a rectangle around any object that looks like a sphere. Tell why your answers are correct. 7 Draw the shape of the flat surfaces of a die. Count and write the number of flat surfaces.

Name ____________________

Learning Target: Identify and describe cones and cylinders.

Explore and Grow

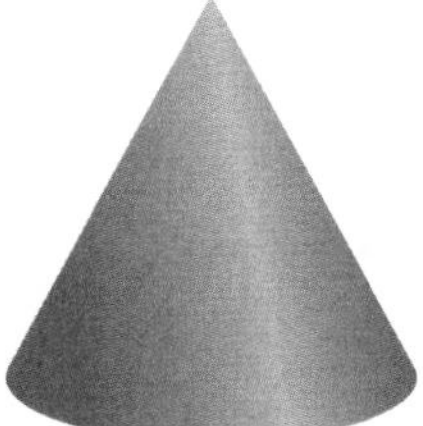 cone	 cylinder

Directions: Cut out the Cone and Cylinder Sort Cards. Sort the cards into the categories shown.

Think and Grow

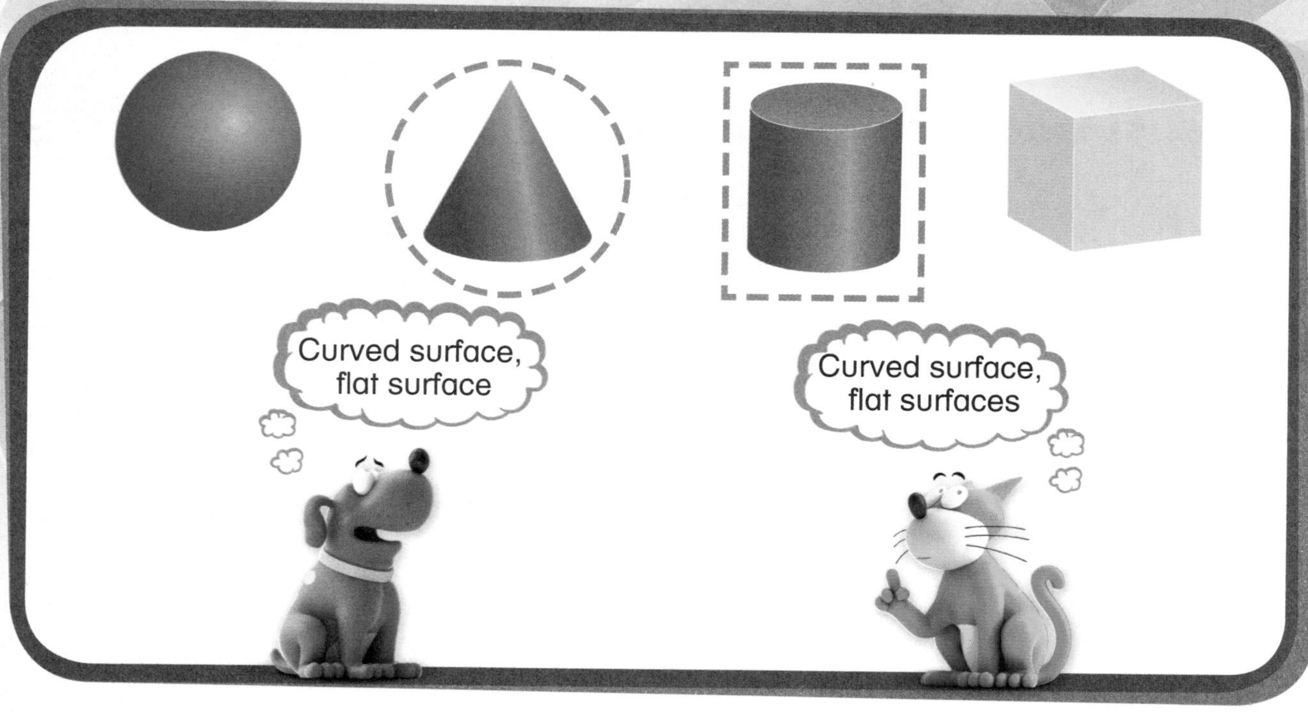

Curved surface,
flat surface
Curved surface,
flat surfaces

   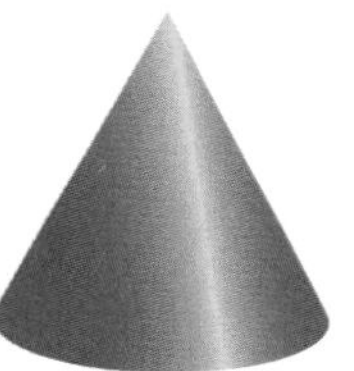

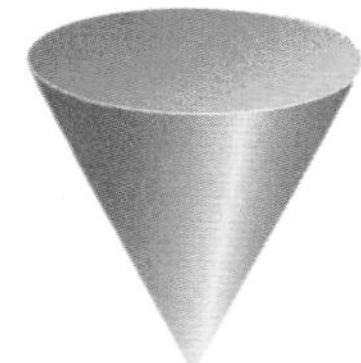   

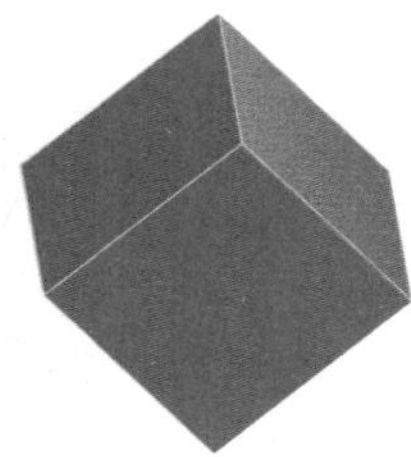  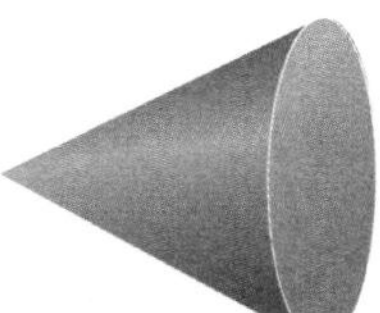 

Directions: Circle the cone. Draw a rectangle around the cylinder. Tell why your answers are correct.

Name ______________________________

Apply and Grow: Practice

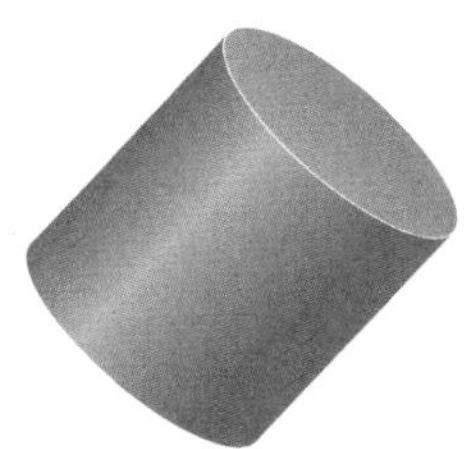 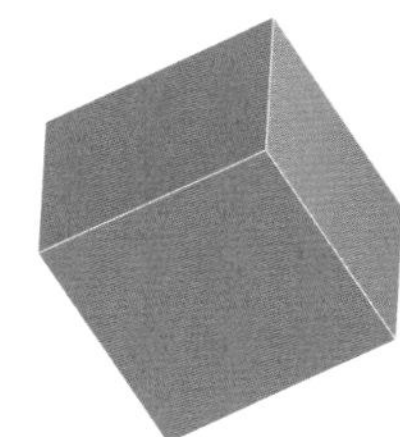 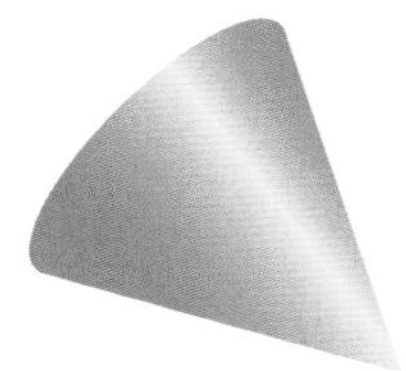 

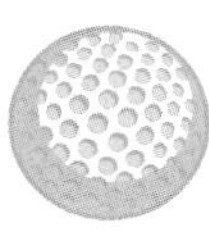   

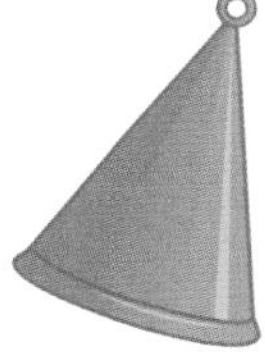 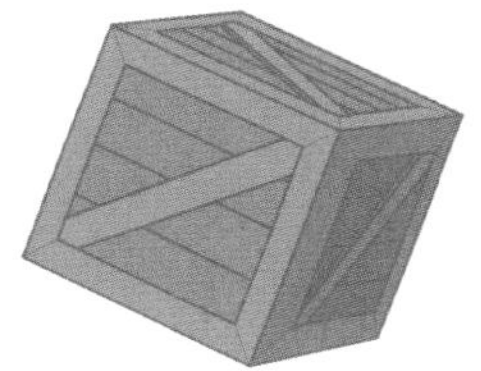  

Directions: 1 Circle the cone. Draw a rectangle around the cylinder. Tell why your answers are correct. 2–4 Circle any object that looks like a cone. Draw a rectangle around any object that looks like a cylinder. Tell why your answers are correct.

Think and Grow: Modeling Real Life

______

______ flat surfaces

Directions: Use Make a Cylinder to build a can of vegetables. Draw the shape of the flat surfaces of your can. Count and write the number of flat surfaces.

Name ______________________

Practice 

Learning Target: Identify and describe cones and cylinders.

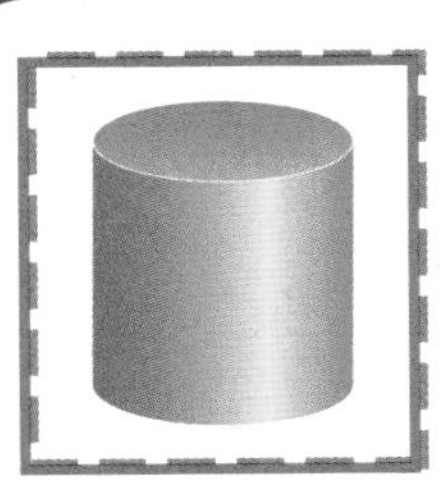
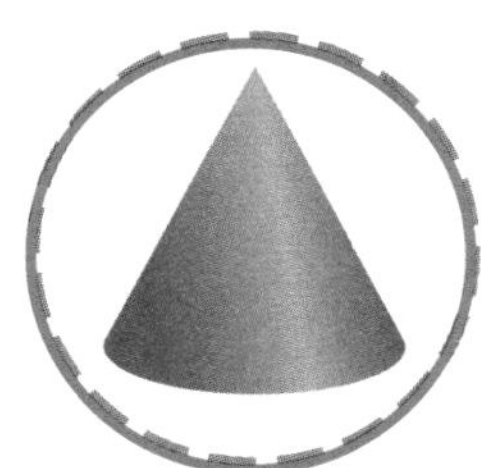

curved surface, flat surfaces

curved surface, flat surface

Directions: Circle the cone. Draw a rectangle around the cylinder. Tell why your answers are correct.

1

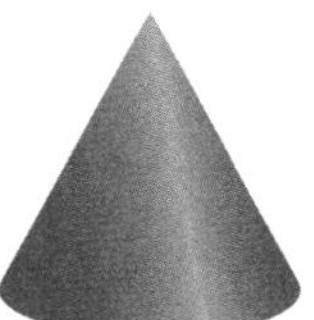

2

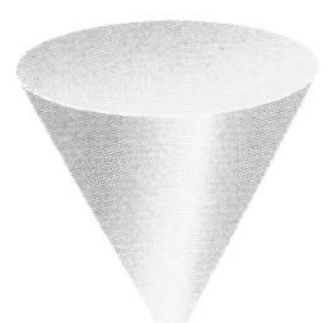

3

Directions: 1–3 Circle the cone. Draw a rectangle around the cylinder. Tell why your answers are correct.

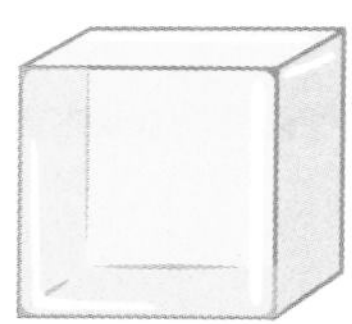   

  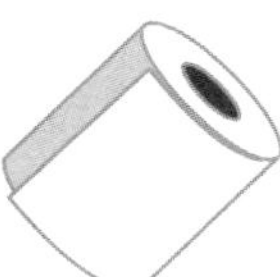 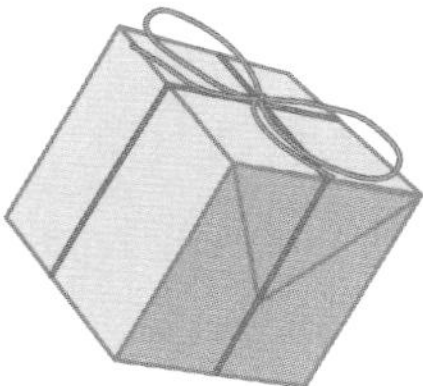

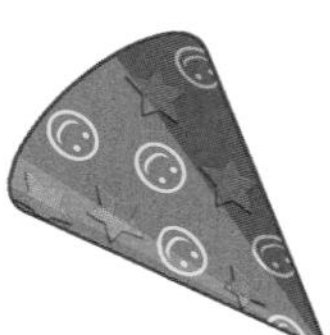   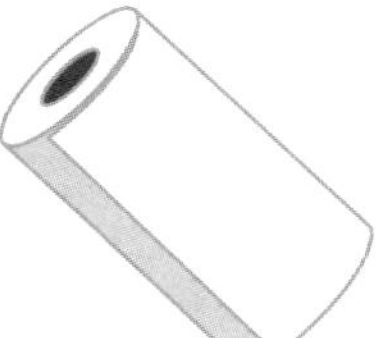

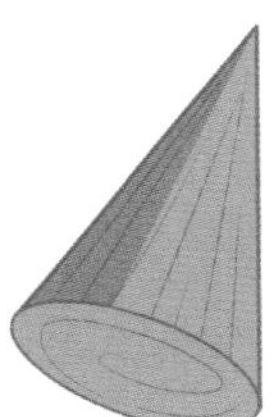

______ flat surface

Directions: 4–6 Circle any object that looks like a cone. Draw a rectangle around any object that looks like a cylinder. Tell why your answers are correct. 7 Draw the shape of the flat surface of a cone. Count and write the number of flat surfaces.

Name ______________________________

12.5 Build Three-Dimensional Shapes

Learning Target: Build and explore three-dimensional shapes.

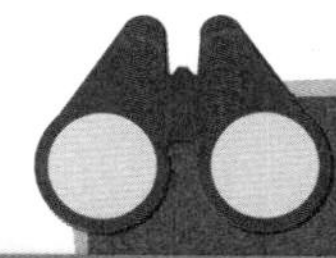

Explore and Grow

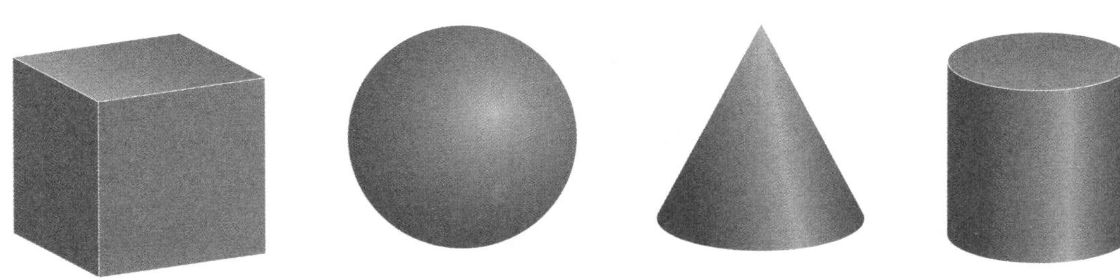

Directions: Use your materials to build one of the three-dimensional shapes shown. Circle the three-dimensional shape that you build.

Think and Grow

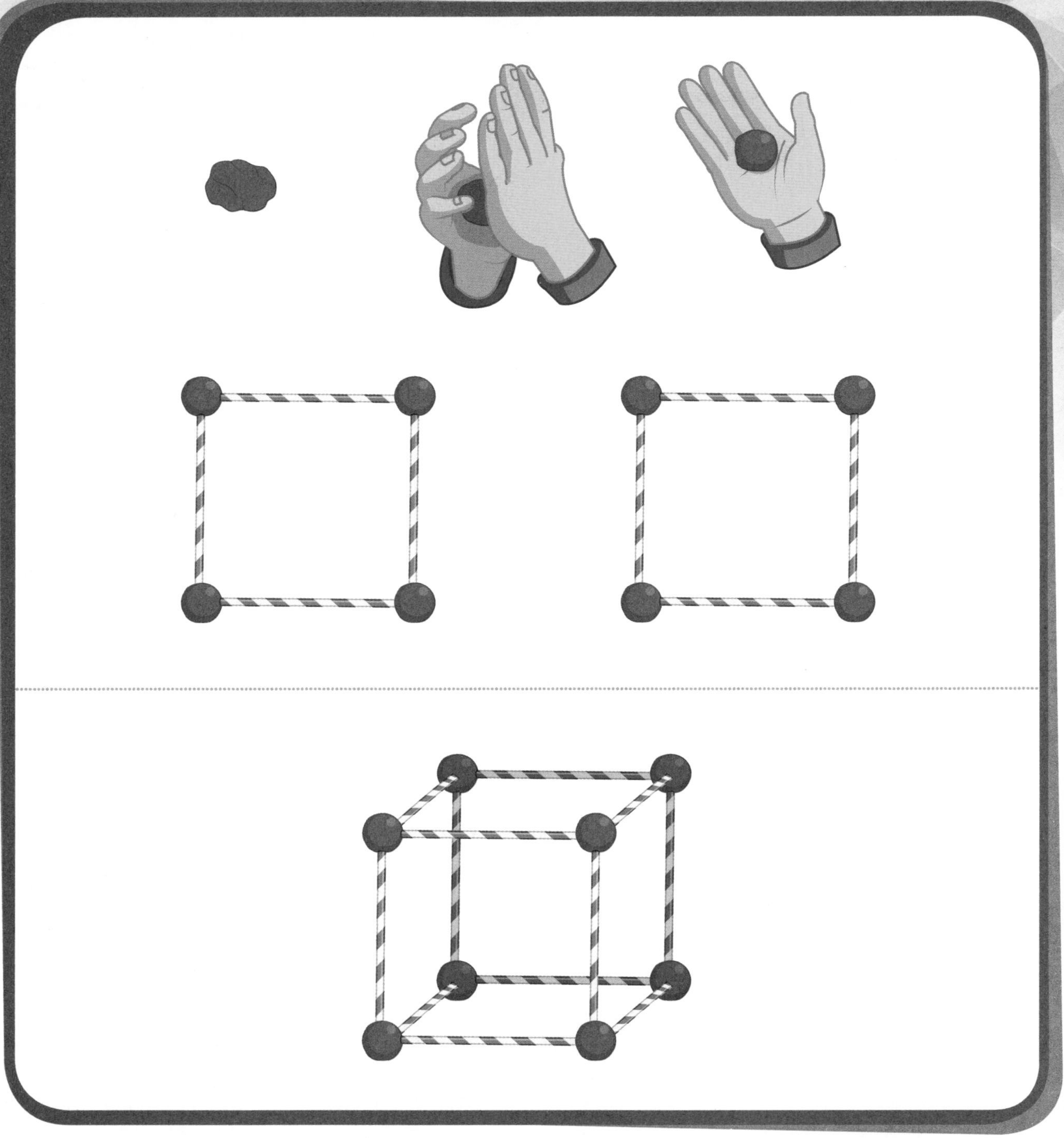

Directions:

- Use your materials to build the 2 shapes shown.
- Connect the 2 shapes that you build, as shown.
- Tell what solid shape you build.

Name ____________________

Apply and Grow: Practice

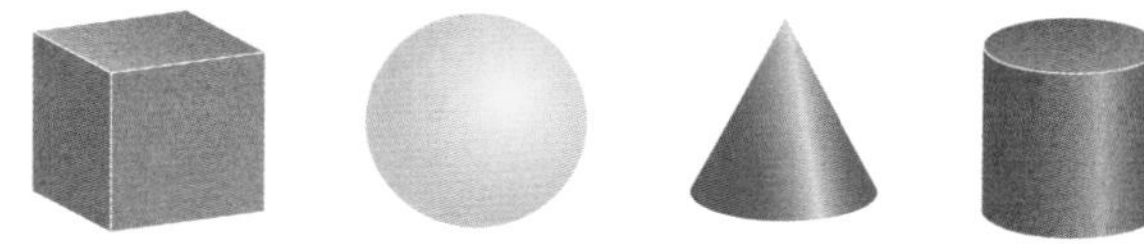

Directions: 1–3 Use your materials to build the solid shape shown. 4 Use your materials to build a solid shape that has 6 square, flat surfaces. Circle the shape you build.

Think and Grow: Modeling Real Life

Directions:

- Use your materials to build the castle tower in the picture.
- Circle the solid shapes that you use to build the tower.

Name ____________________

Learning Target: Build and explore three-dimensional shapes.

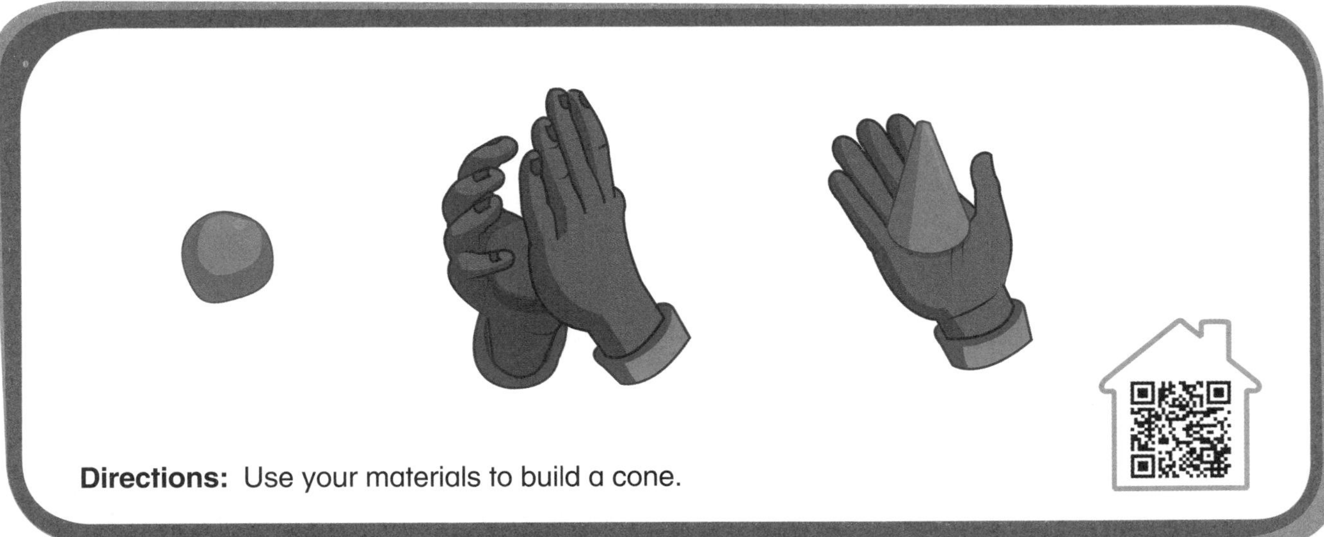

Directions: Use your materials to build a cone.

Directions: 1 and 2 Use your materials to build the solid shape shown. 3 Use your materials to build the solid shape that has a curved surface and only 1 flat surface. Circle the shape you build. 4 Use your materials to build a solid shape that has no flat surfaces. Circle the shape you build.

5

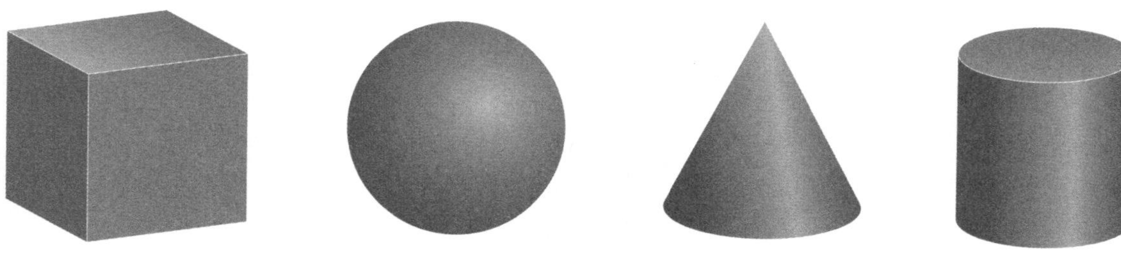

Directions: 5 Use your materials to build the totem pole in the picture. Circle the solid shapes that you use to make the totem pole.

Name ______________________________

Positions of Solid Shapes 12.6

Learning Target: Describe positions of solid shapes based on other objects.

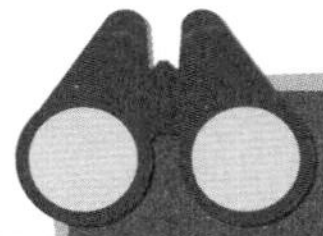

Explore and Grow

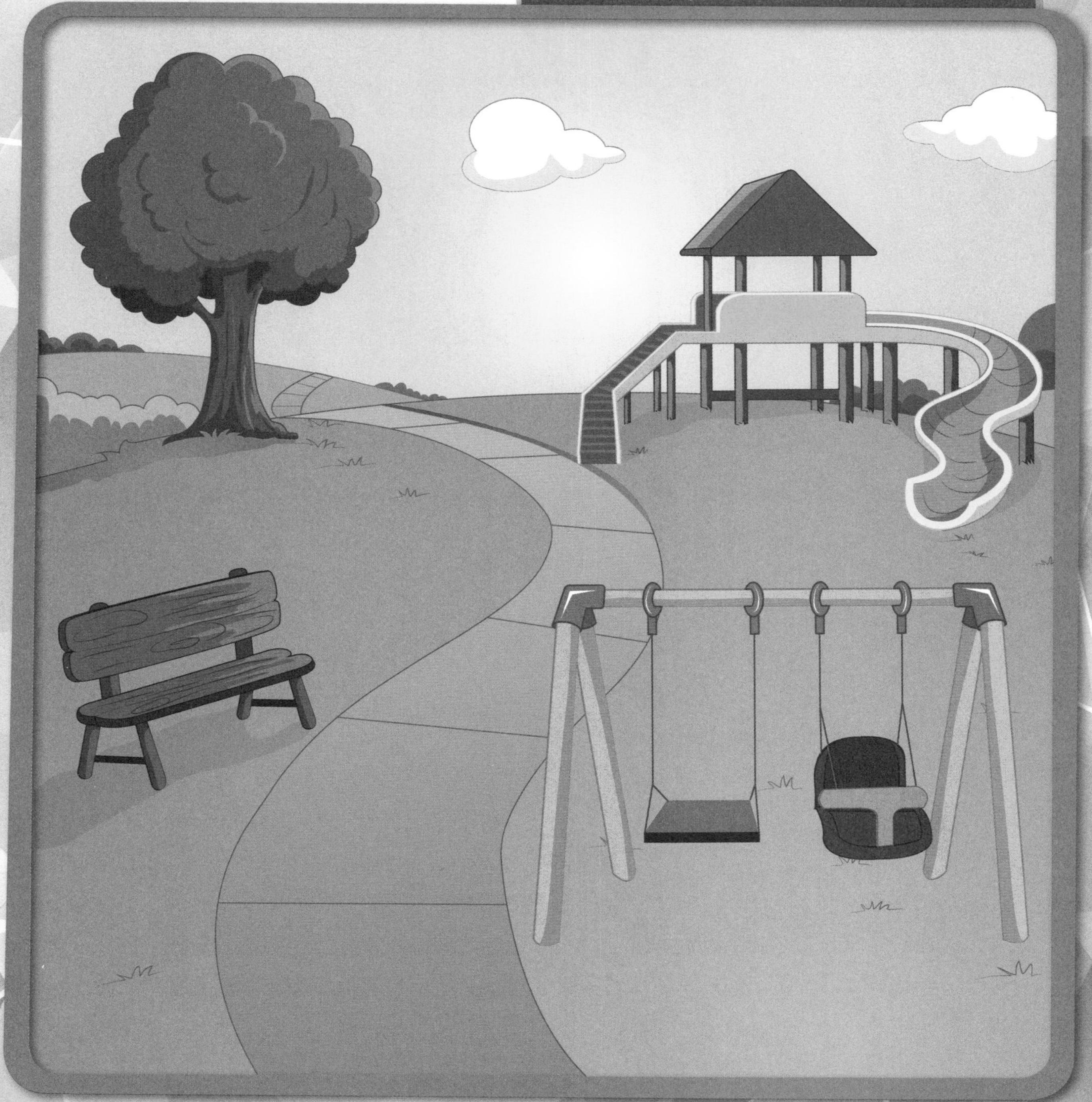

Directions: Place a counter *beside* the bench. Place a counter *in front of* the tree. Place a counter *next to* the stairs. Place a counter *below* the baby swing.

Think and Grow

Directions:

- Circle the object that looks like a cylinder that is *next to* the table. Draw a line through the object that looks like a cone that is *below* the shelf. Draw a rectangle around the object that looks like a sphere that is *above* the table.
- Circle the object that looks like a cube that is *behind* the shovel. Draw a line through the object that looks like a cylinder that is *beside* the tree. Draw a rectangle around the object that looks like a sphere that is *in front of* the tree.

Name ___________

Apply and Grow: Practice

Directions: 1 Circle the object that looks like a cylinder that is *behind* a paper cup. Draw a line through the object that looks like a sphere that is *above* the napkin dispenser. Draw a rectangle around the object that looks like a cone that is *below* a glass cup. 2 Circle the object that looks like a cone that is *beside* the log. Draw a line through the object that looks like a sphere that is *above* the log. Draw a rectangle around the object that looks like a cone that is *in front of* the log.

Think and Grow: Modeling Real Life

Directions: Use the City Scene Cards to place the objects on the picture.

- Place a dog *in front of* the boy crossing the street.
- Place a tree *beside* the building that looks like a cube.
- Place an object that looks like a sphere *above* the buildings. Place that object *behind* a cloud.
- Place an object that looks like a cone *below* the traffic light.
- Place a streetlight *next to* the girl on the sidewalk.

Name ______________________________

Practice 12.6

Learning Target: Describe positions of solid shapes based on other objects.

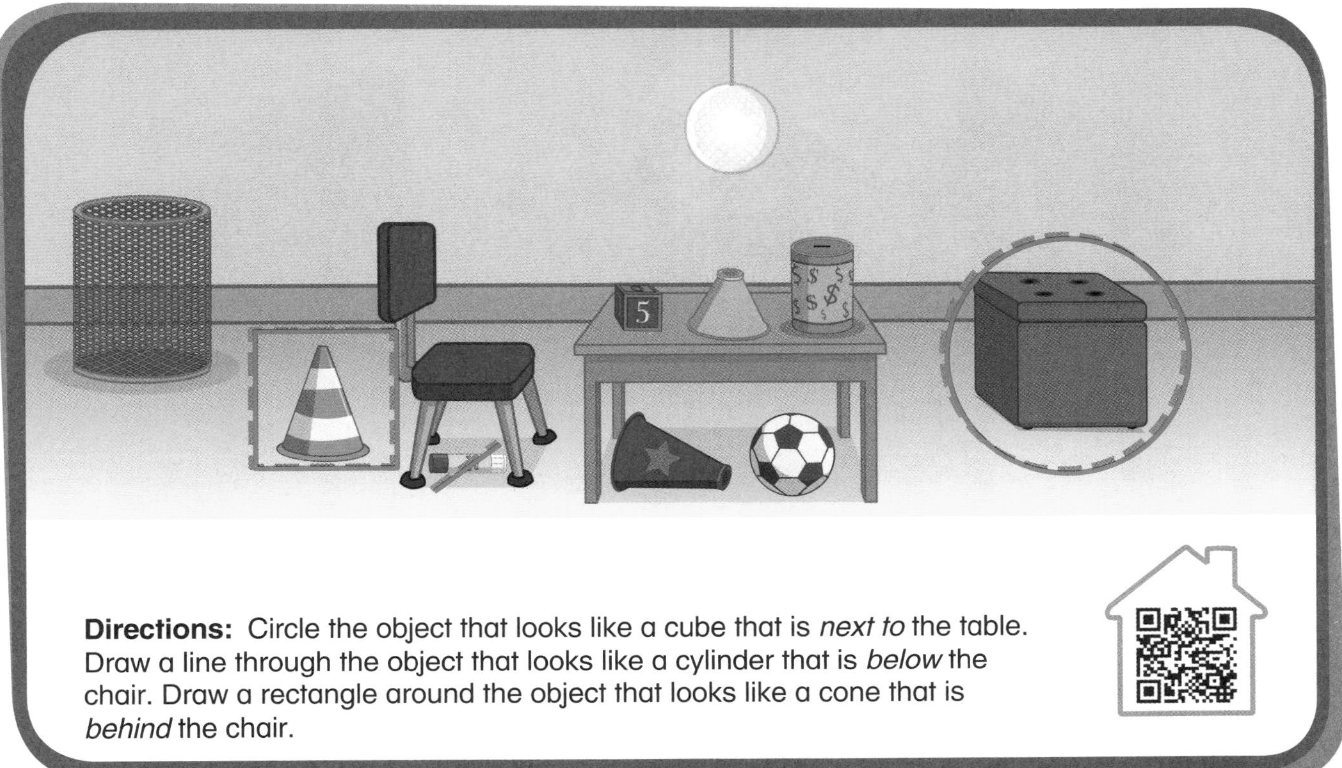

Directions: Circle the object that looks like a cube that is *next to* the table. Draw a line through the object that looks like a cylinder that is *below* the chair. Draw a rectangle around the object that looks like a cone that is *behind* the chair.

1

Directions: 1 Circle the object that looks like a sphere that is *beside* the pool. Draw a line through the object that looks like a cone that is *next to* the ball. Draw a rectangle around the object that looks like a cylinder that is *behind* the block.

Directions: Circle the object that looks like a cone that is *above* the stuffed animal. Draw a line through the object that looks like a cylinder that is *in front of* the stuffed animal. Draw a rectangle around the object that looks like a cube that is *below* the stuffed animal. Use the Construction Scene Cards to place the objects on the picture. Place a building *below* the object that is shaped like a cube. Place a tree *beside* that building. Place a blimp *above* the traffic cone. Place a truck *in front of* the traffic cone.

Name ______________________________

Performance Task

Directions: 1 You pick up trash in the park. Draw lines to match each item with its correct recycling bin.

- The object that rolls but does not stack that is *in front of* the lamppost goes in the yellow bin.
- The object *below* the bench that does not roll goes in the blue bin.
- The object that has 1 flat surface that is *behind* an object that looks like a cylinder goes in the green bin.
- The object that stacks, slides, and rolls that is *above* an object that looks like a cube goes in the orange bin.
- The object *in front of* the tree that rolls and has 2 flat surfaces goes in the green bin.
- The object *next to* the tree that stacks and slides and has only flat surfaces goes in the green bin.
- The object that has a curved surface that does not stack that is *beside* the tree goes in the blue bin.
- The object that slides and rolls that is *next to* an object that has 6 flat surfaces goes in the blue bin.

Solid Shapes: Spin and Cover

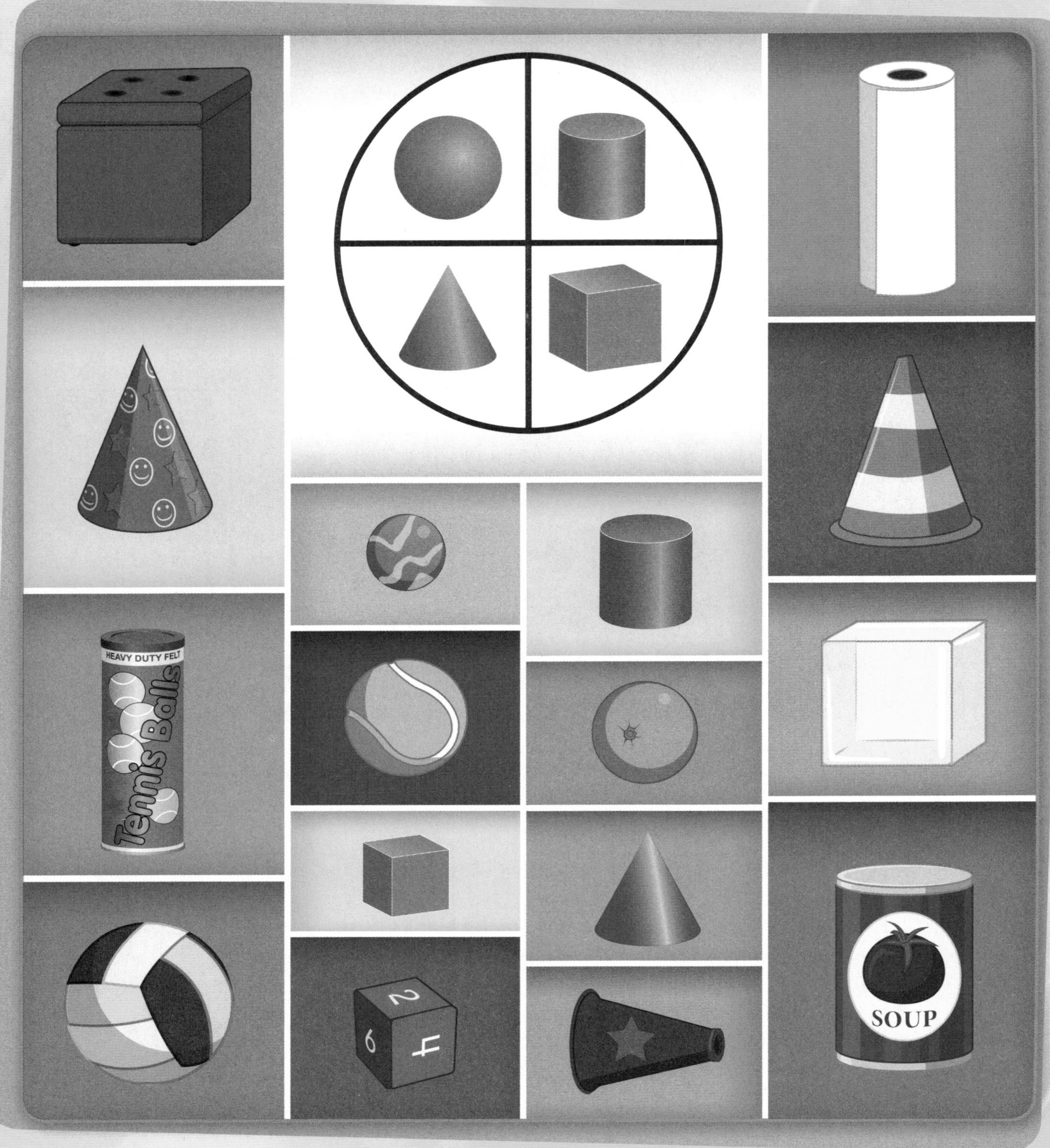

Directions: Take turns using the spinner to find which type of three-dimensional shape to cover. Use a counter to cover an object on the page. Repeat this process until you have covered all of the objects.

Name ________________________________

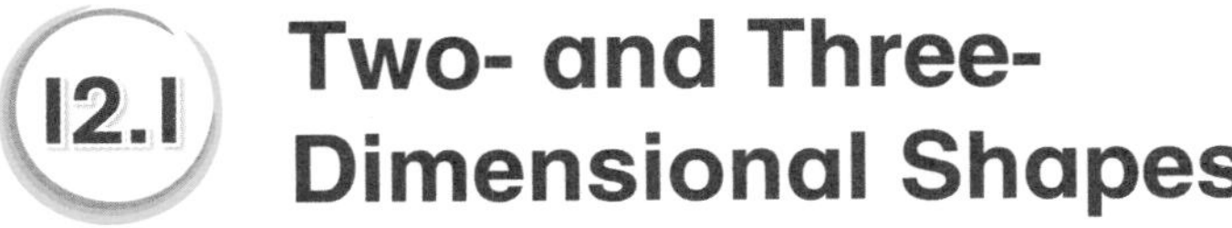

Chapter 12 Practice

12.1 Two- and Three-Dimensional Shapes

  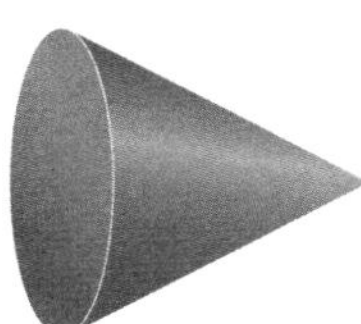 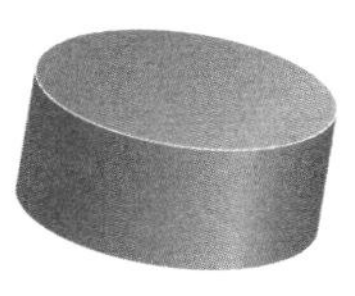

12.2 Describe Three-Dimensional Shapes

Directions: 1 and 2 Circle any three-dimensional shapes. Draw rectangles around any two-dimensional shapes. Tell why your answers are correct. 3 Look at the solid shape on the left that rolls. Circle the other solid shapes that roll. 4 Circle the solid shapes that stack and slide.

12.3 Cubes and Spheres

 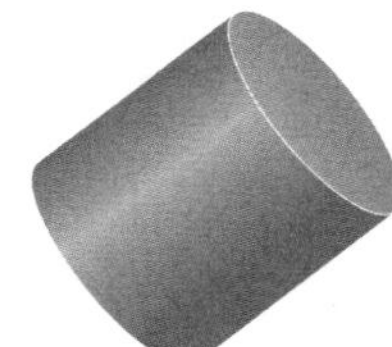  

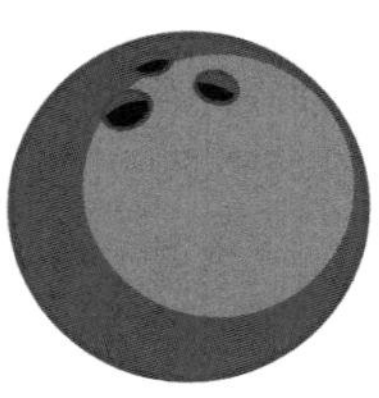   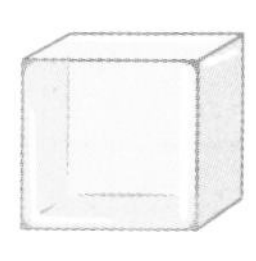

12.4 Cones and Cylinders

 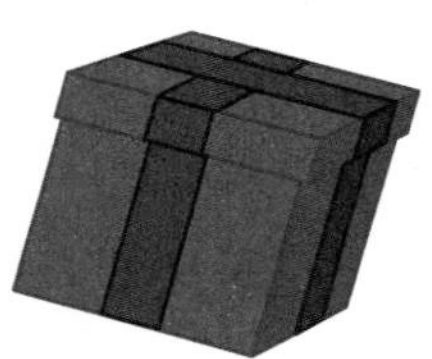 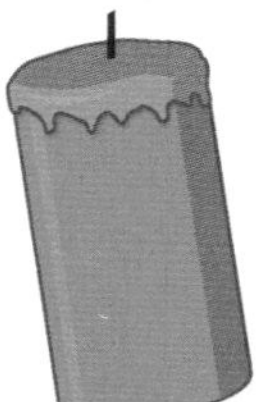 

8

 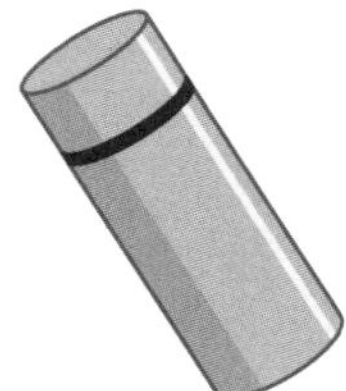

Directions: 5 Circle the cube. Draw a rectangle around the sphere. Tell why your answers are correct. 6 Circle any object that looks like a cube. Draw a rectangle around any object that looks like a sphere. Tell why your answers are correct. 7 and 8 Circle any object that looks like a cone. Draw a rectangle around any object that looks like a cylinder. Tell why your answers are correct.

12.5 Build Three-Dimensional Shapes

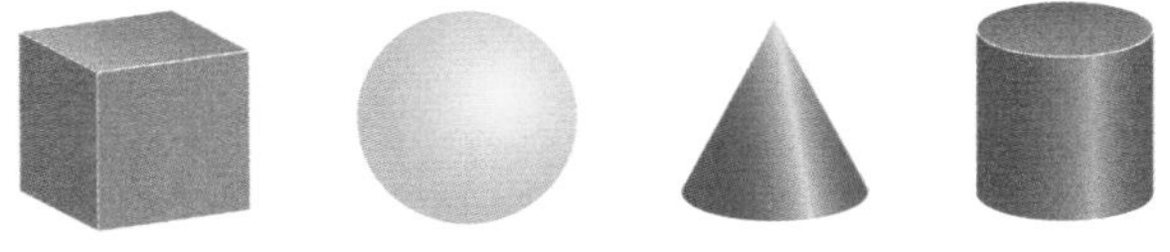

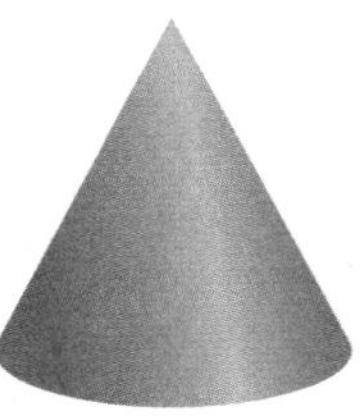

Directions: 9 Use your materials to build the solid shape shown. 10 Use your materials to build a shape that has a curved surface and 2 flat surfaces. Circle the shape you build. 11 Use your materials to build the elf in the picture. Circle the solid shapes that you use to make the elf.

12.6 Positions of Solid Shapes

Directions: 12 Circle the object that looks like a cylinder that is *below* the hat. Draw a line through the object that looks like a cone that is *beside* the cooler. Draw a rectangle around the object that looks like a cylinder that is *in front of* the hat. 13 Circle the object that looks like a sphere that is *above* the cone. Draw a line through the object that looks like a cylinder that is *next to* the cone. Draw a rectangle around the object that looks like a sphere that is *behind* the cone.

13 Measure and Compare Objects

Chapter Learning Target:
Understand measurement.

Chapter Success Criteria:

- I can describe height.
- I can describe weight.
- I can compare the capacities of objects.
- I can compare the heights of objects.

- Have you ever used a bucket to catch rainwater?
- Which bucket can hold the most rainwater?

Name ______________________

13 Vocabulary

Review Words
fewer
more

Directions: There are fewer clouds than umbrellas. There are more raindrops than puddles. Draw the clouds and the raindrops.

Chapter 13 Vocabulary Cards

balance scale

capacity

heavier

height

length

lighter

longer

measurable attribute

2 CUPS
1 CUP
Length or Height
Weight
Capacity
© Big Ideas Learning, LLC

Chapter 13 Vocabulary Cards

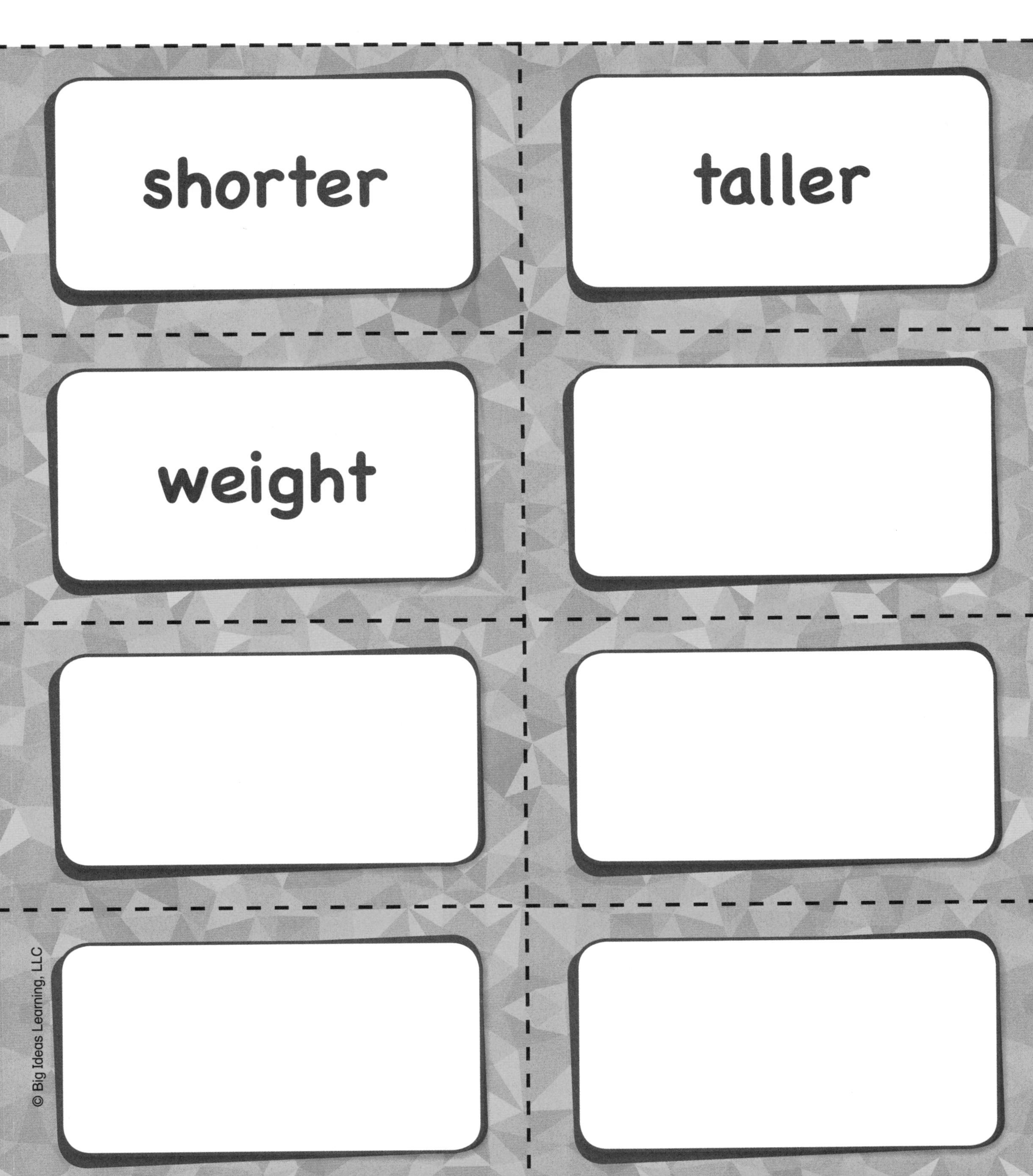

Name ________________________

Learning Target: Compare the heights of two objects.

Explore and Grow

shorter

taller

Directions: Cut out the Height Sort Cards. Compare the objects to the children shown. Then sort the cards into the categories shown.

Think and Grow

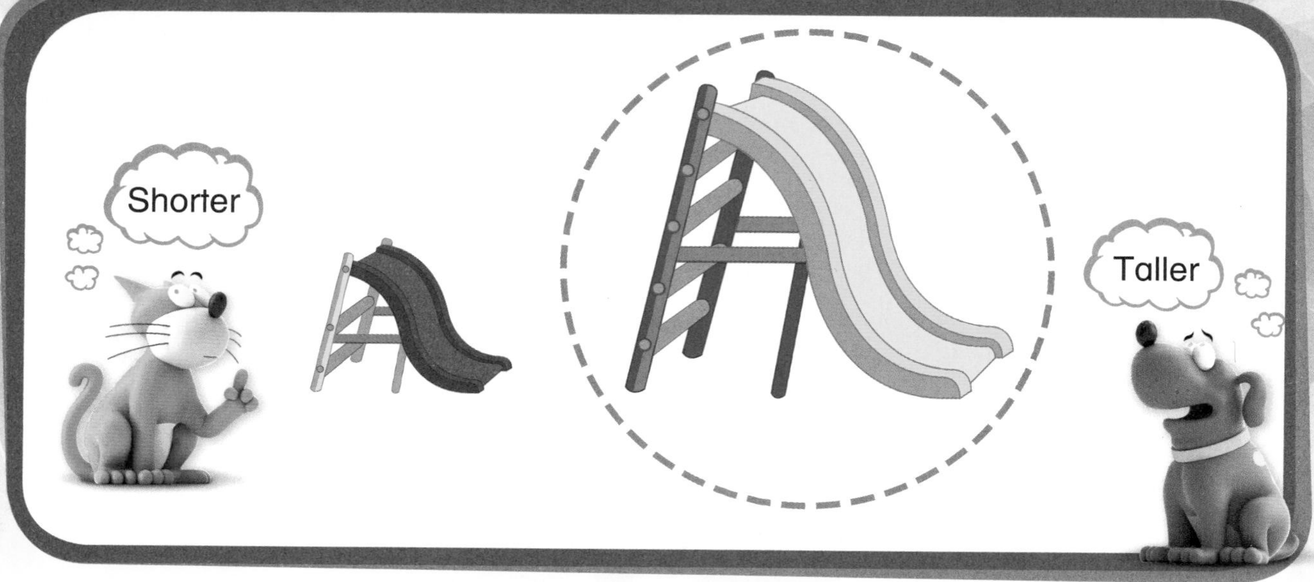

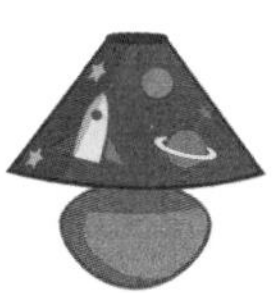

Directions: Compare the heights of the objects.

- Circle the taller slide.
- Draw a line through the shorter lamp.
- Are the mugs the same height? Circle the thumbs up for *yes* or the thumbs down for *no*.

Name ____________________

Apply and Grow: Practice

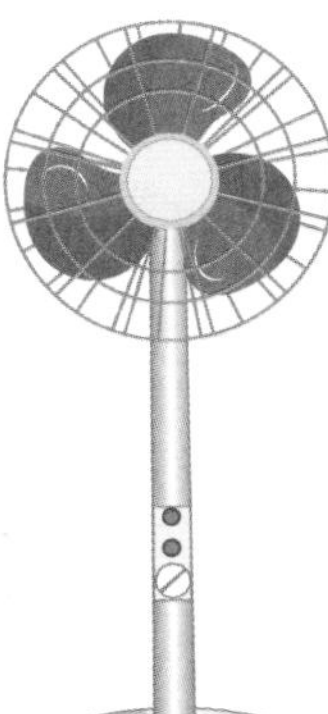

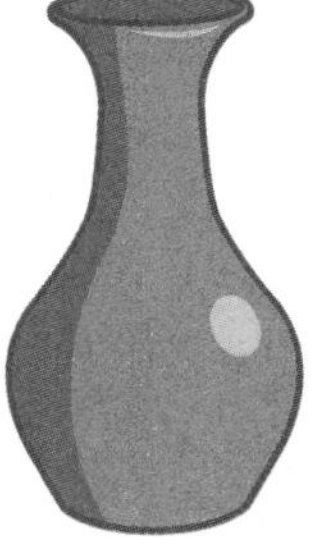

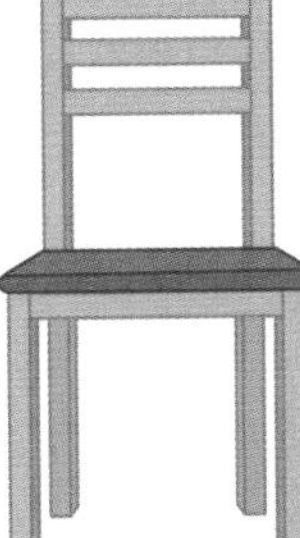

Directions: 1 and 2 Circle the taller object. 3 and 4 Draw a line through the shorter object. 5 Are the lion and the giraffe the same height? Circle the thumbs up for *yes* or the thumbs down for *no*.

Think and Grow: Modeling Real Life

Directions:

- Draw a building that is taller than the building shown.
- Draw a building that is shorter than the building shown.

Name ____________________

Practice 13.1

Learning Target: Compare the heights of two objects.

Directions:
- Circle the taller ladder.
- Draw a line through the shorter plant.

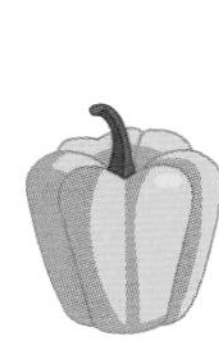

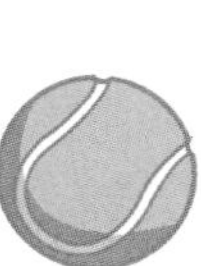

Directions: 1 and 2 Circle the taller object. 3 and 4 Draw a line through the shorter object.

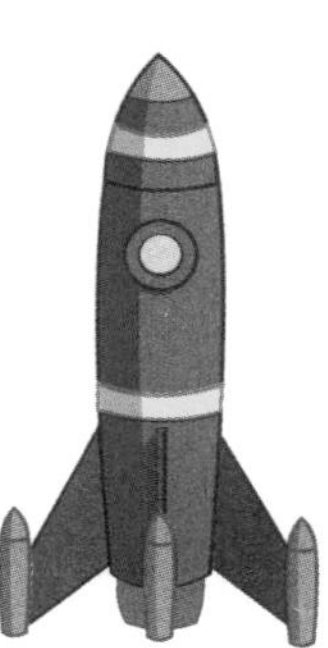

Directions: 5 and 6 Are the objects the same height? Circle the thumbs up for *yes* or the thumbs down for *no*. 7 Draw a building that is the same height as the building shown.

Name ______________________

Compare Lengths 13.2

Learning Target: Compare the lengths of two objects.

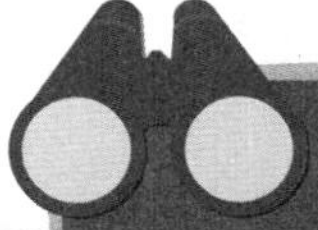

Explore and Grow

shorter	longer

Directions: Cut out the Length Sort Cards. Compare the objects to the pencil shown. Then sort the cards into the categories shown.

Think and Grow

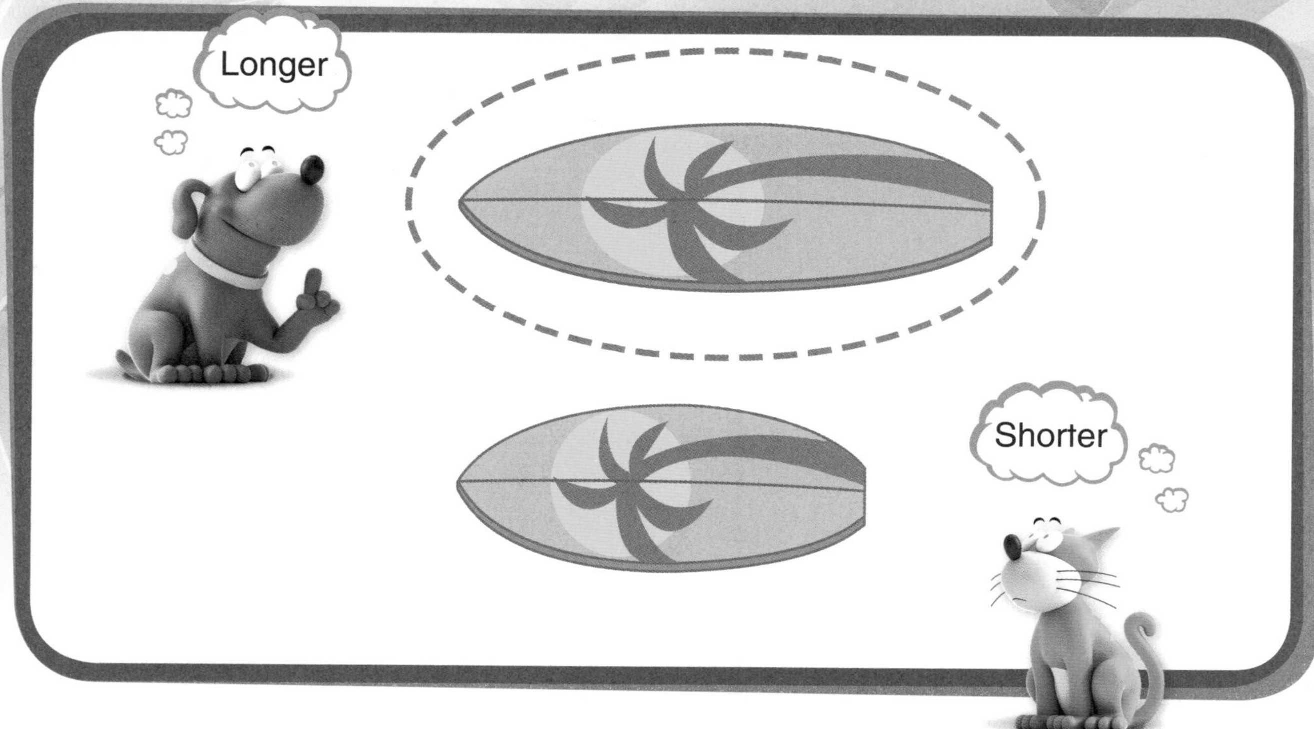

Directions: Compare the lengths of the objects.

- Circle the longer surfboard.
- Draw a line through the shorter watch.
- Are the shoes the same length? Circle the thumbs up for *yes* or the thumbs down for *no*.

Name ______________________________

Apply and Grow: Practice

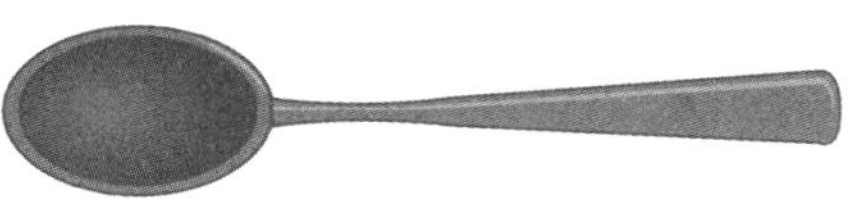

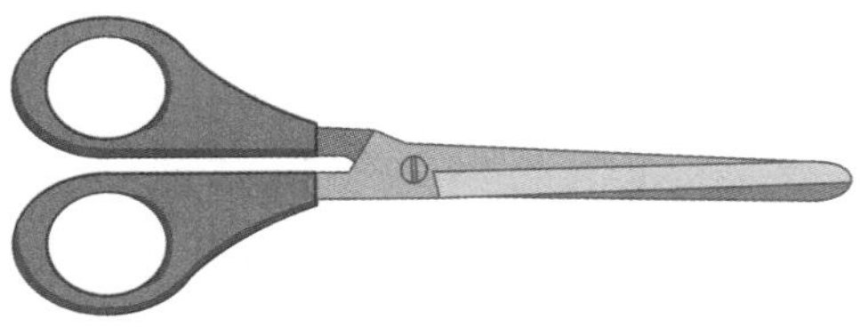

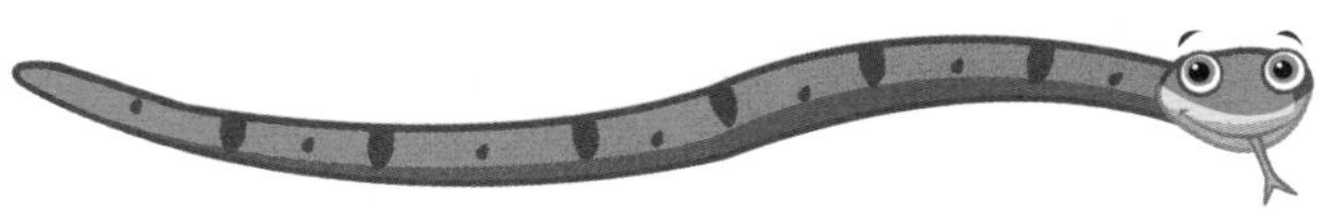

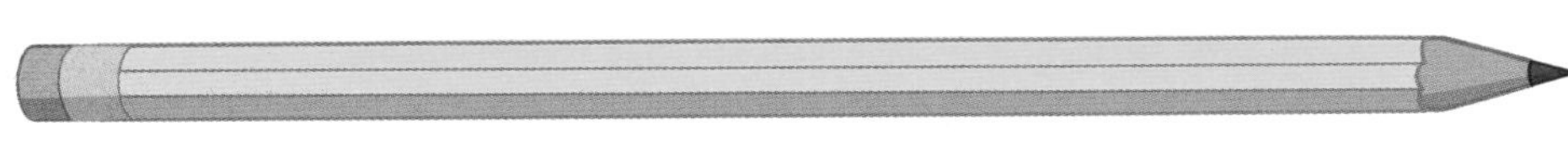

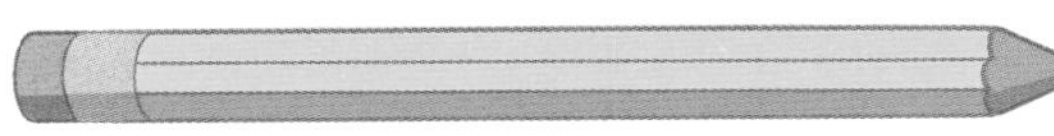

Directions: 1 and 2 Circle the longer object. 3 and 4 Draw a line through the shorter object.

Think and Grow: Modeling Real Life

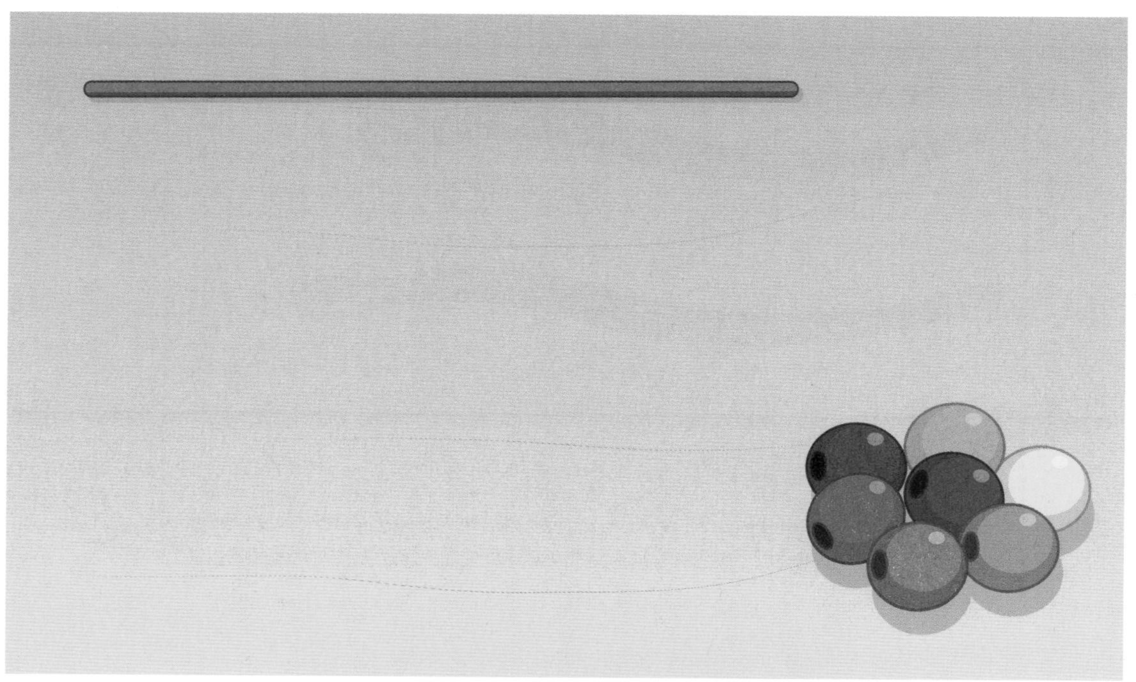

Directions:

- Draw a string that holds fewer beads than the string shown. Tell how you know.
- Draw a string that holds the same number of beads as the string shown. Tell how you know.

Name ______________________________

Practice 13.2

Learning Target: Compare the lengths of two objects.

Directions:

- Circle the longer caterpillar.
- Draw a line through the shorter branch.

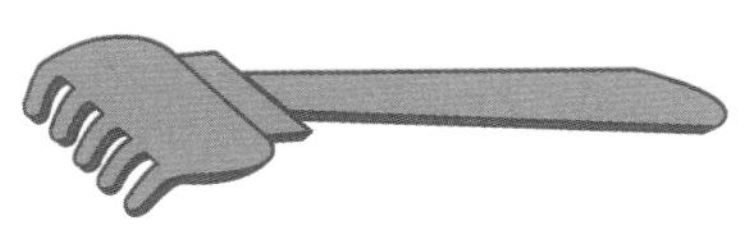

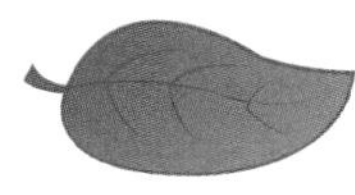

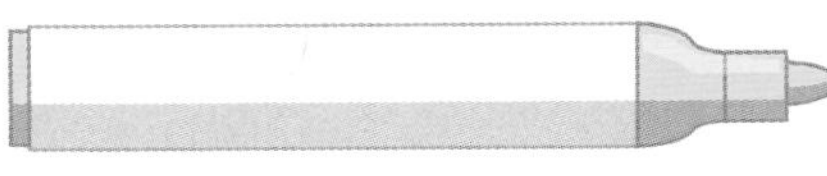

Directions: 1 and 2 Circle the longer object. 3 and 4 Draw a line through the shorter object.

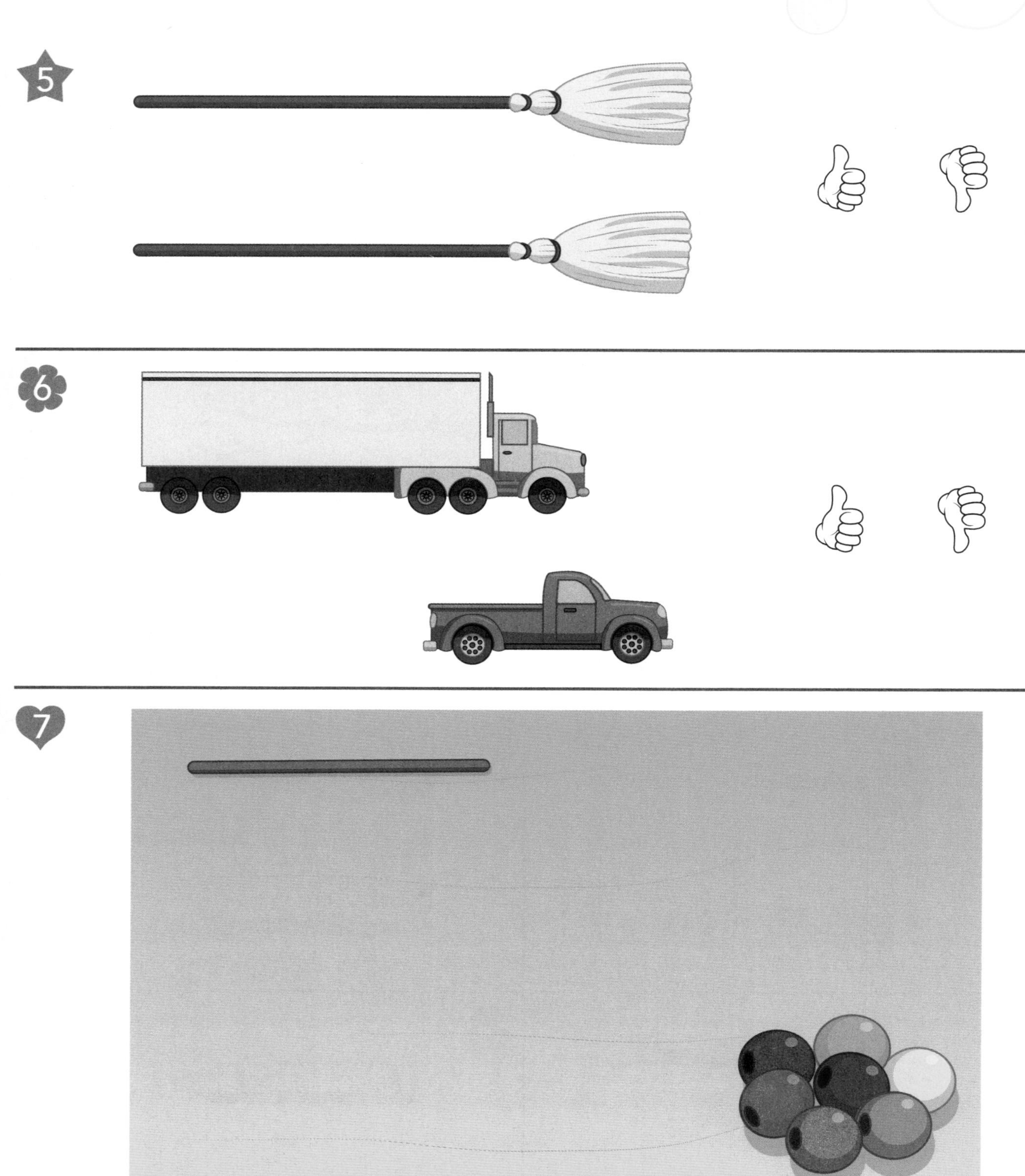

Directions: 5 and 6 Are the objects the same length? Circle the thumbs up for *yes* or the thumbs down for *no*. 7 Draw a string that holds more beads than the string shown. Tell how you know.

Name ______________________________

Use Numbers to Compare Lengths

13.3

Learning Target: Compare the lengths of two objects using numbers.

Explore and Grow

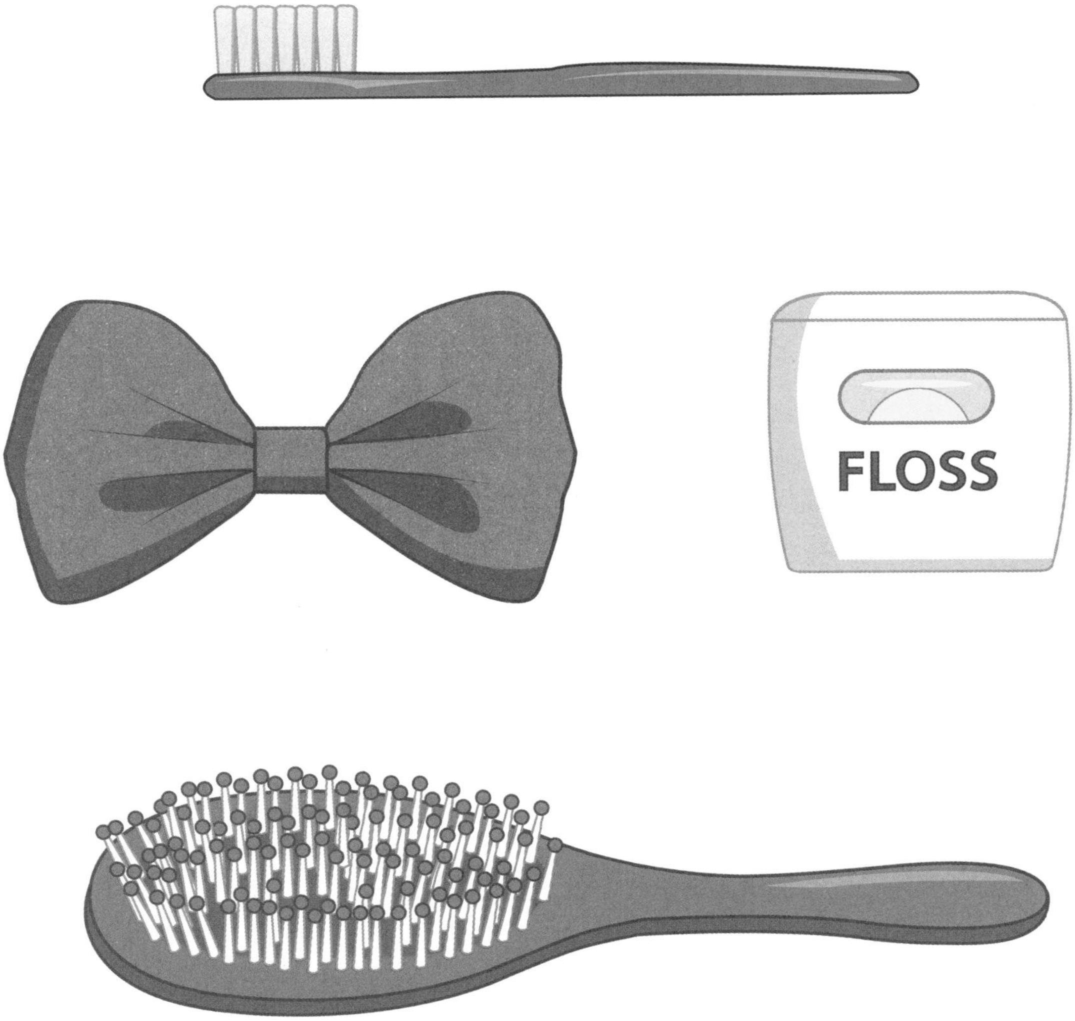

Directions: Build a linking cube train with 4 cubes. Circle the objects that are longer than the cube train.

Think and Grow

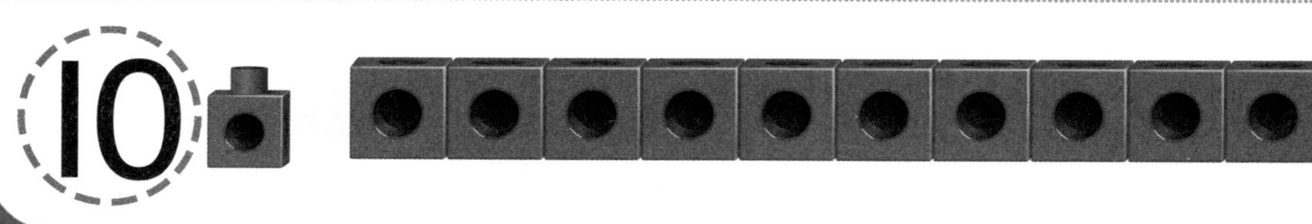

2

10

8

5

9

9

Directions: Compare the lengths of the cube trains with the given number of cubes.

- Circle the number of the train that is longer. Color to show how you know.
- Draw a line through the number of the train that is shorter. Color to show how you know.
- Are the cube trains the same length? Circle the thumbs up for *yes* or the thumbs down for *no*. Color to show how you know.

Name ______________________________

Apply and Grow: Practice

10

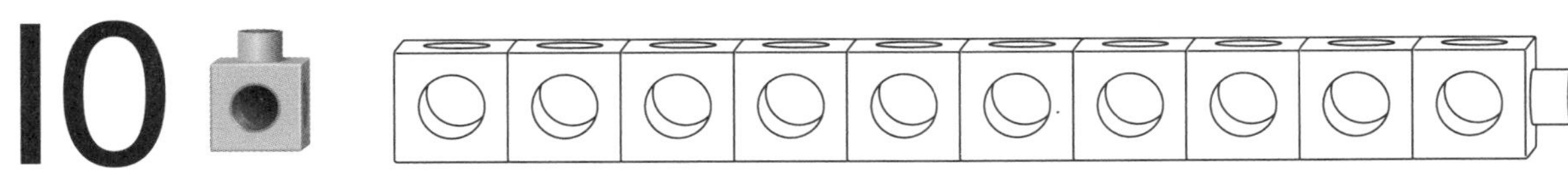

6

3

5

8

7

Directions: Compare the lengths of the cube trains with the given number of cubes. 1 and 2 Circle the number of the train that is longer. Color to show how you know. 3 Draw a line through the number of the train that is shorter. Color to show how you know.

Think and Grow: Modeling Real Life

Directions: Each car on a roller coaster holds 2 people.

- Do the roller-coaster trains hold the same number of people? Circle the thumbs up for *yes* or the thumbs down for *no*. Tell how you know.
- Circle the roller-coaster train that holds more people. Tell how you know.

Name ___________________________

Learning Target: Compare the lengths of two objects using numbers.

4  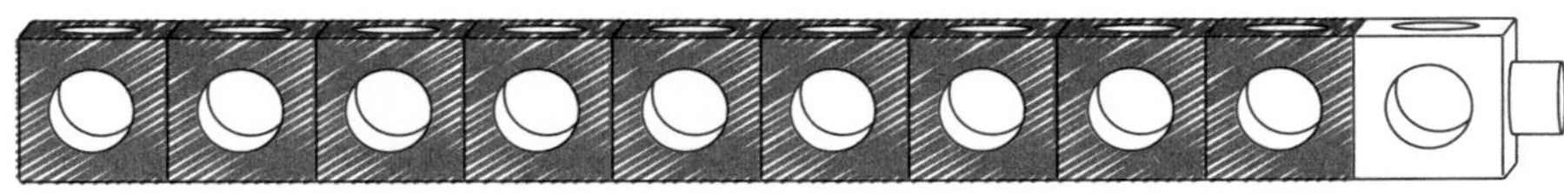

9

Directions: Compare the lengths of the cube trains with the given number of cubes. Circle the number of the train that is longer. Color to show how you know.

1

3

8 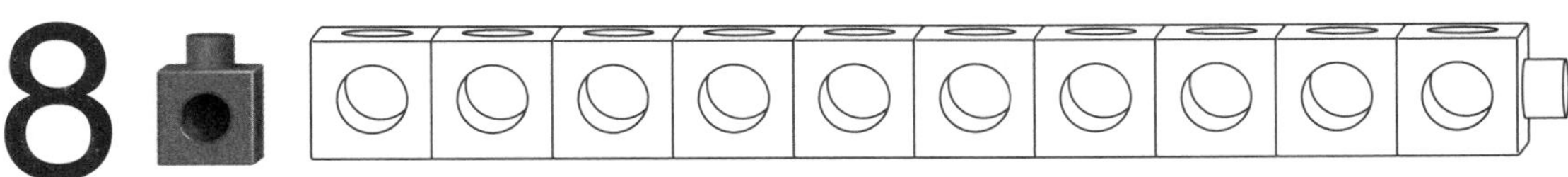

2

5

1 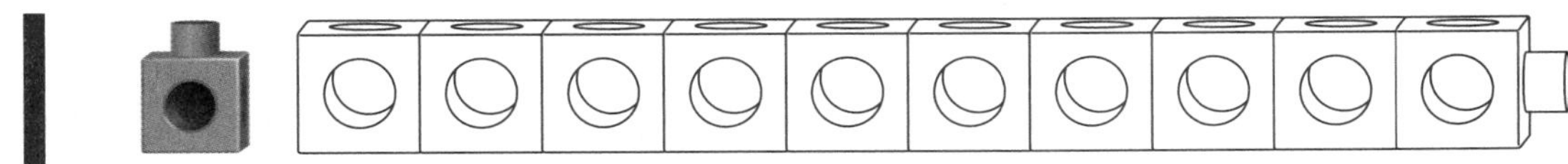

Directions: 1 and 2 Compare the lengths of the cube trains with the given number of cubes. Circle the number of the train that is longer. Color to show how you know.

3

5

7

4

3

Directions: 3 Compare the lengths of the cube trains with the given number of cubes. Draw a line through the number of the train that is shorter. Color to show how you know. 4 Compare the lengths of the cube trains with the given number of cubes. Are the cube trains the same length? Circle the thumbs up for *yes* or the thumbs down for *no*. Color to show how you know. 5 Each car on a roller coaster holds 2 people. Draw a line through the roller-coaster train that holds fewer people. Tell how you know.

Name ___________________

Learning Target: Compare the weights of two objects.

Explore and Grow

lighter

heavier

Directions: Cut out the Weight Sort Cards. Compare the objects to the lion shown. Then sort the cards into the categories shown.

Think and Grow

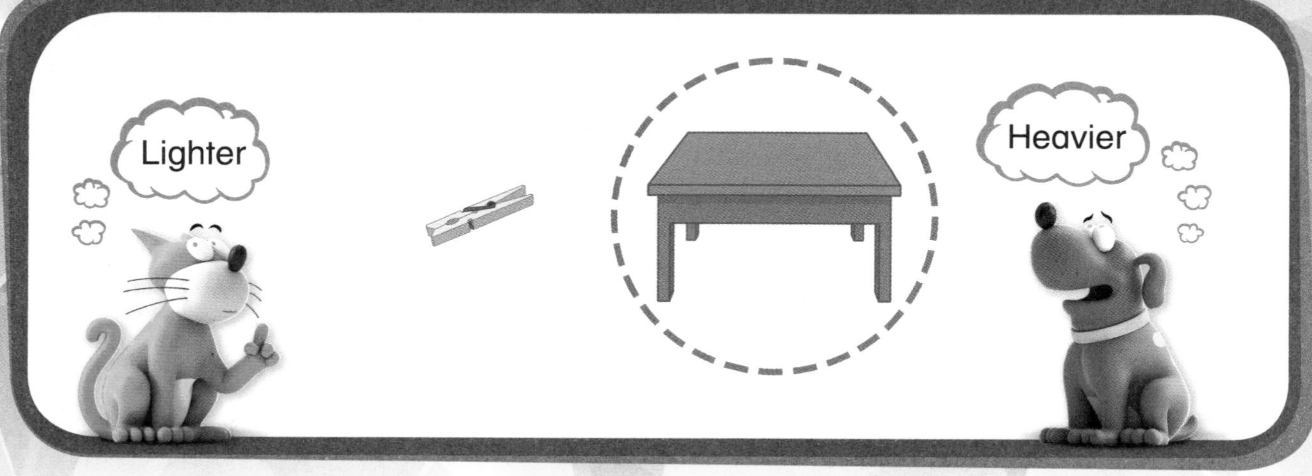

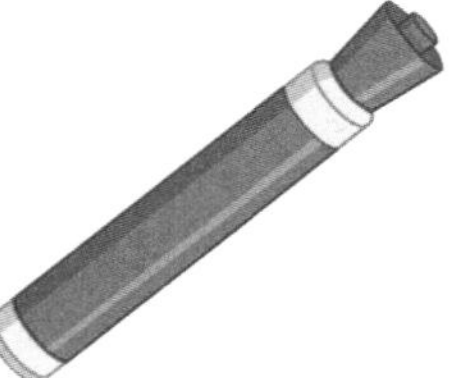

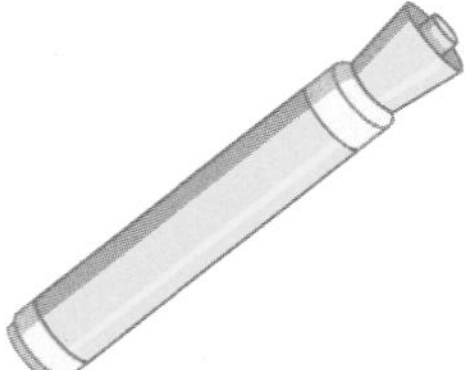

Directions: Compare the weights of the objects.

- Circle the heavier object.
- Draw a line through the lighter object.
- Are the markers the same weight? Circle the thumbs up for *yes* or the thumbs down for *no*.

Name ______________________________

Apply and Grow: Practice

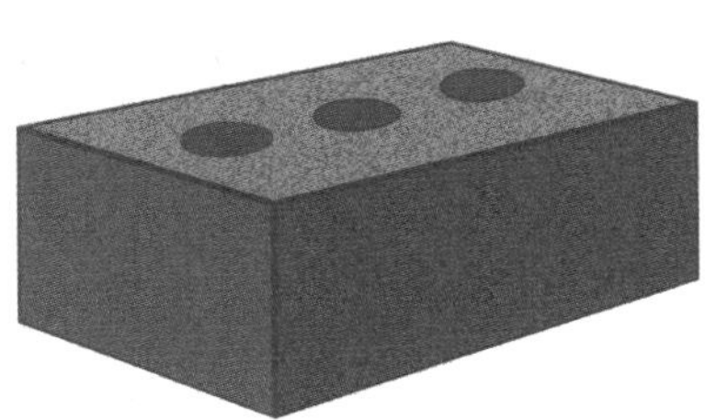

Directions: 1 and 2 Circle the heavier object. 3 and 4 Draw a line through the lighter object. 5 Are the objects the same weight? Circle the thumbs up for *yes* or the thumbs down for *no*.

Think and Grow: Modeling Real Life

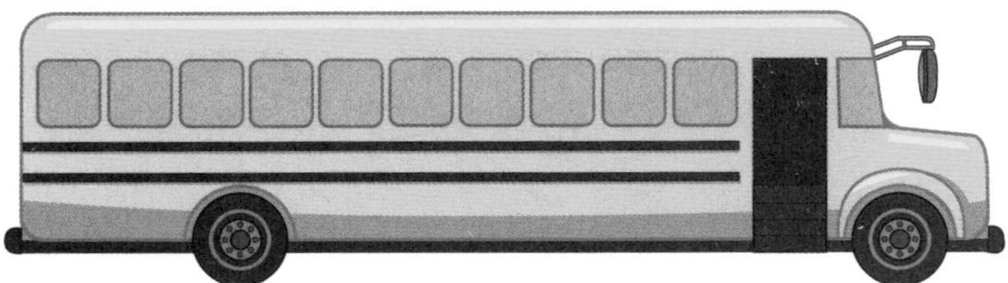

Directions:

- Circle the object you can carry. Tell why you can carry the object.
- Circle the object you *cannot* carry. Tell why you *cannot* carry the object.

Name ______________________

Practice **13.4**

Learning Target: Compare the weights of two objects.

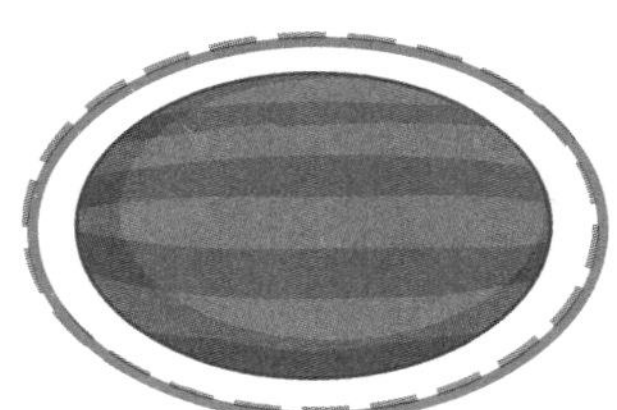

Directions:
- Circle the heavier fruit.
- Draw a line through the lighter toy.

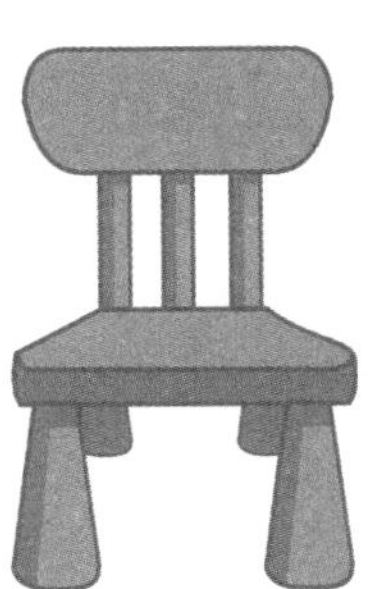

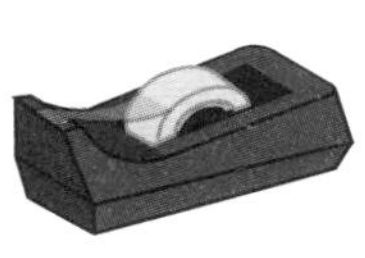
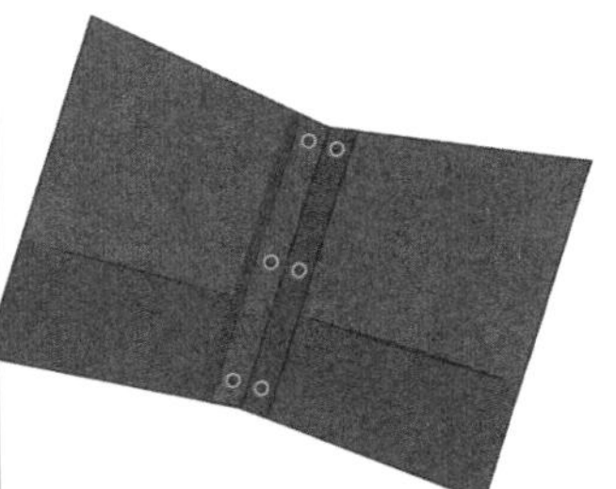

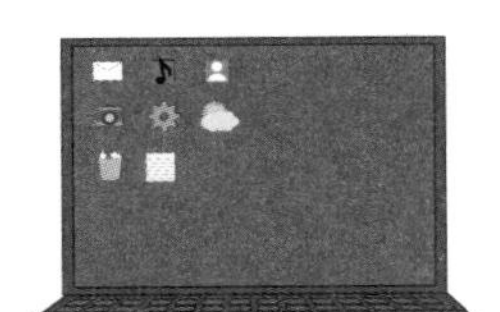

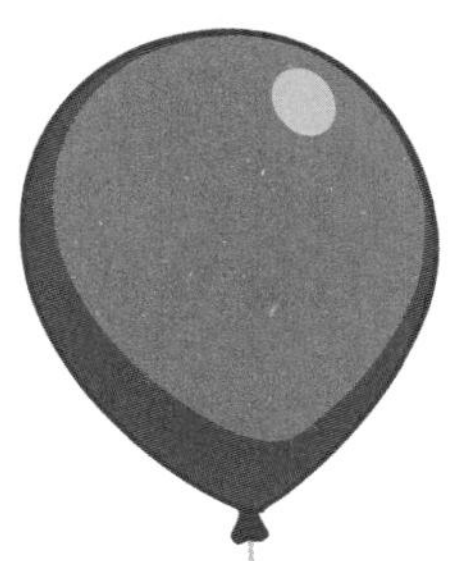

Directions: 1 and 2 Circle the heavier object. 3 and 4 Draw a line through the lighter object.

Directions: 5 and 6 Are the objects the same weight? Circle the thumbs up for *yes* or the thumbs down for *no*. 7 Circle the object you can carry. Tell why you can carry the object.

Name ________________________________

Use Numbers to Compare Weights 13.5

Learning Target: Compare the weights of two objects using numbers.

Explore and Grow

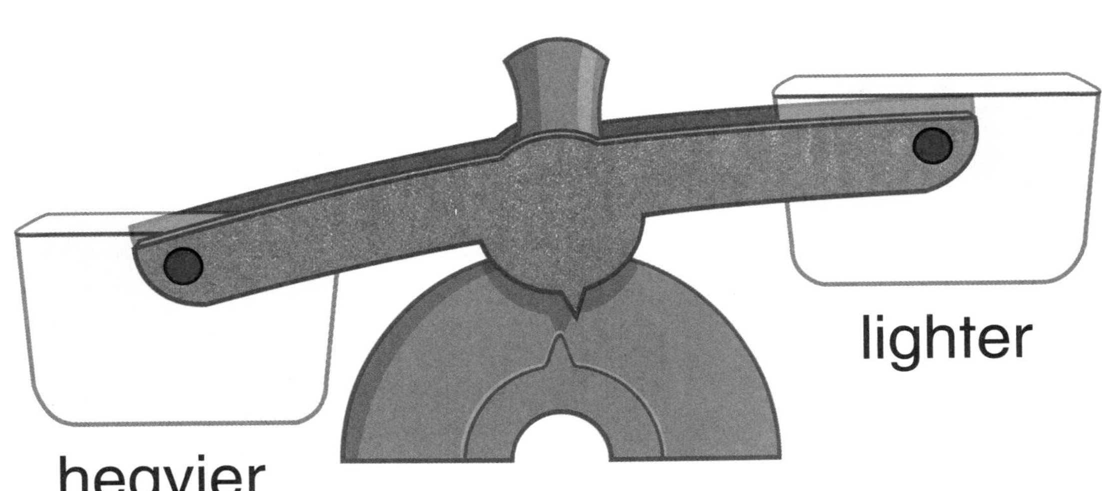

Directions: Hold some counting bears in one hand and a different amount of counting bears in your other hand. Place the groups of bears on the correct buckets on the scale.

Think and Grow

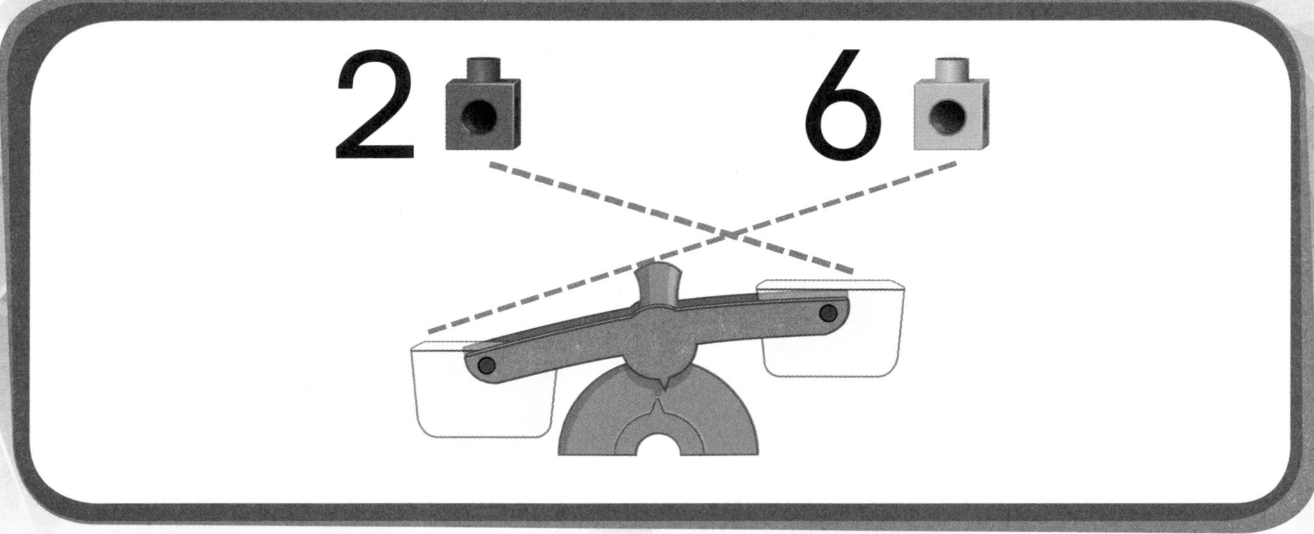

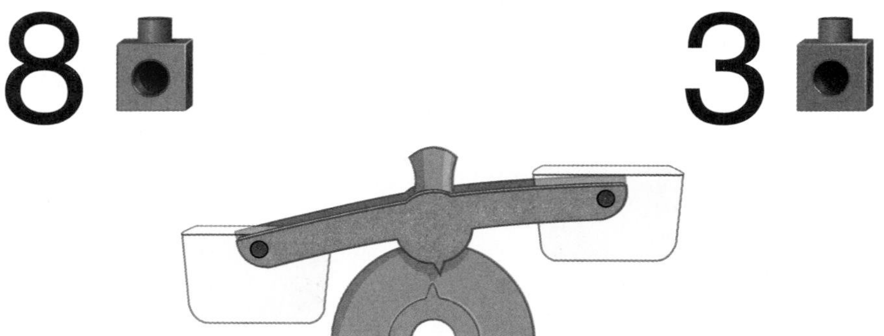

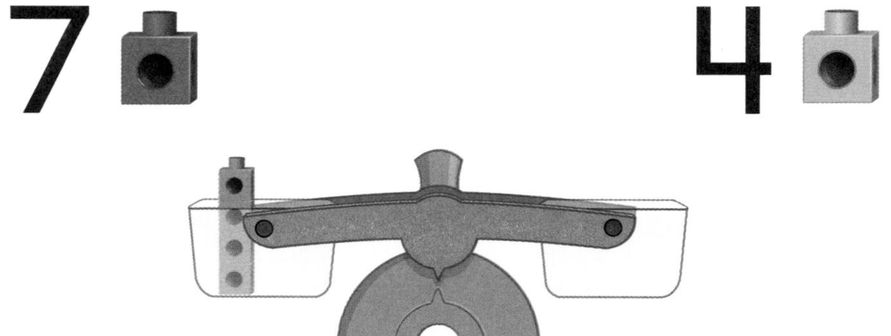

Directions:

- Compare the weights of the groups of linking cubes. Match each group of linking cubes with the correct side of the balance.
- Compare the weights of the groups of linking cubes. Match each group of linking cubes with the correct side of the balance.
- Circle the number of linking cubes that makes the balance scale even.

Name

Apply and Grow: Practice

7 ▢ 4 ▢

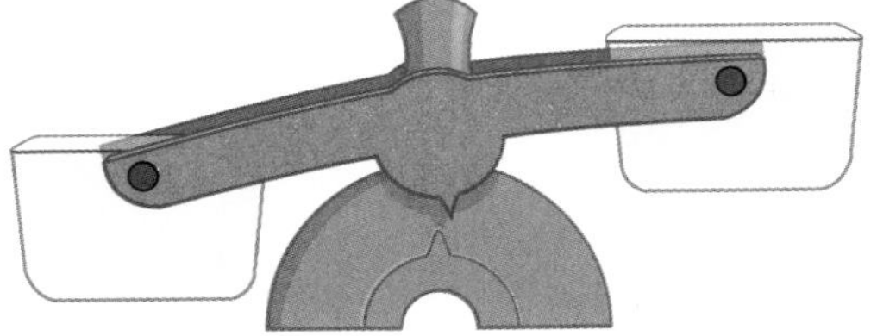

3 ▢ 6 ▢

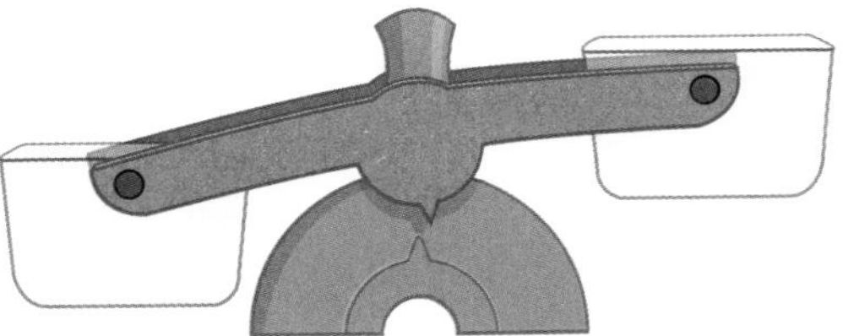

10 ▢ 3 ▢ + 1 ▢

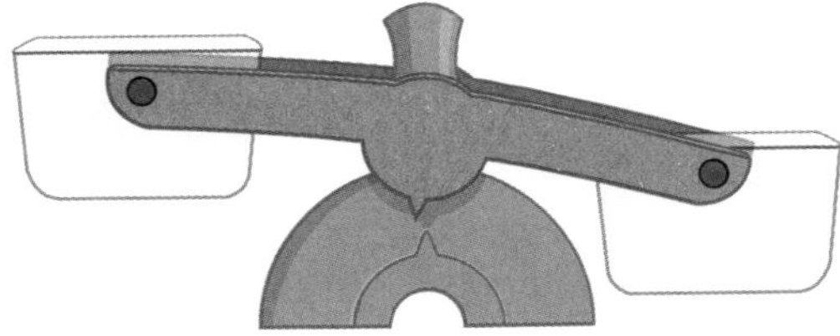

Directions: 1 – 3 Compare the weights of the groups of linking cubes. Match each group of linking cubes with the correct side of the balance scale.

Think and Grow: Modeling Real Life

Directions:

- Circle the basket that is lighter. Tell how you know.
- Circle the basket that is heavier. Tell how you know.

Name ______________________

Learning Target: Compare the weights of two objects using numbers.

10 6

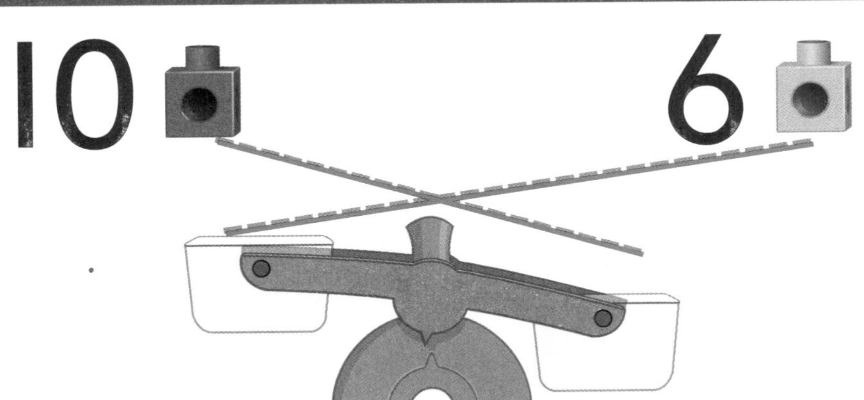

Directions: Compare the weights of the groups of linking cubes. Match each group of linking cubes with the correct side of the balance scale.

1

5 1

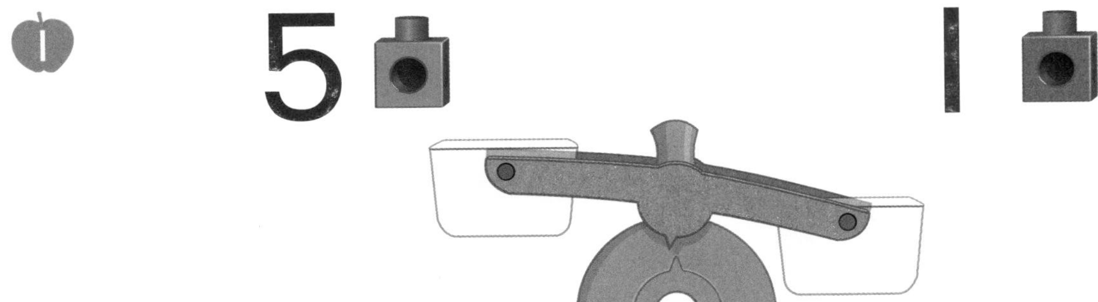

2

8 9

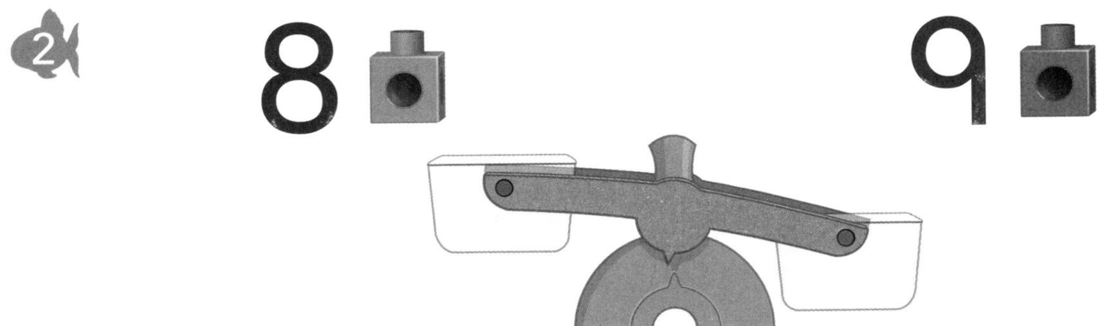

Directions: 1 and 2 Compare the weights of the groups of linking cubes. Match each group of linking cubes with the correct side of the balance scale.

2 + 2

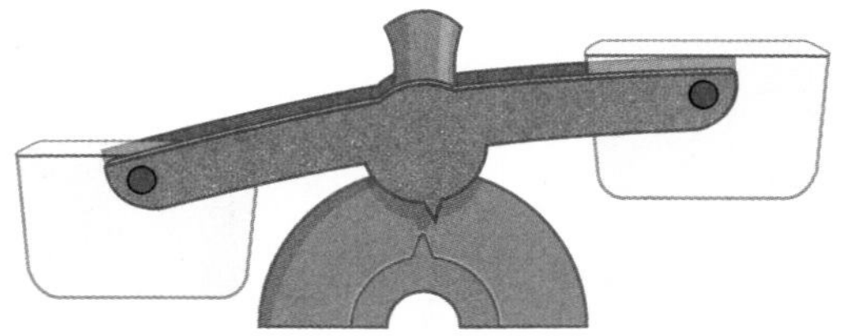

4

7 3

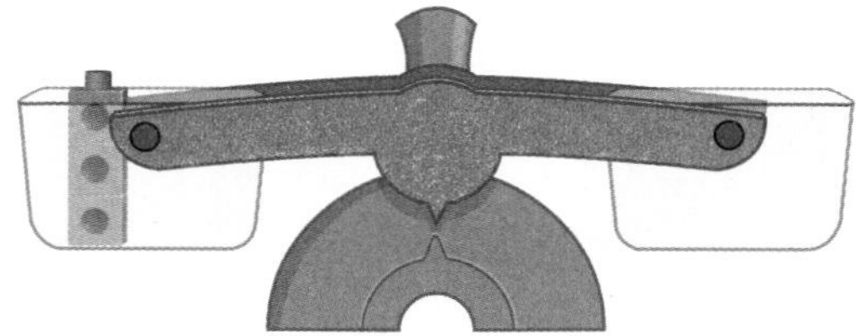

5

Directions: 3 Compare the weights of the groups of linking cubes. Match each group of linking cubes with the correct side of the balance scale. 4 Circle the number of linking cubes that makes the balance scale even. 5 Circle the basket that is heavier. Tell how you know.

Name ____________________

Compare Capacities **13.6**

Learning Target: Compare the capacities of two objects.

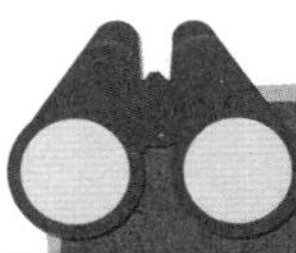

Explore and Grow

holds less

holds more

Directions: Cut out the Capacity Sort Cards. Compare the objects to the bucket shown. Then sort the cards into the categories shown.

Think and Grow

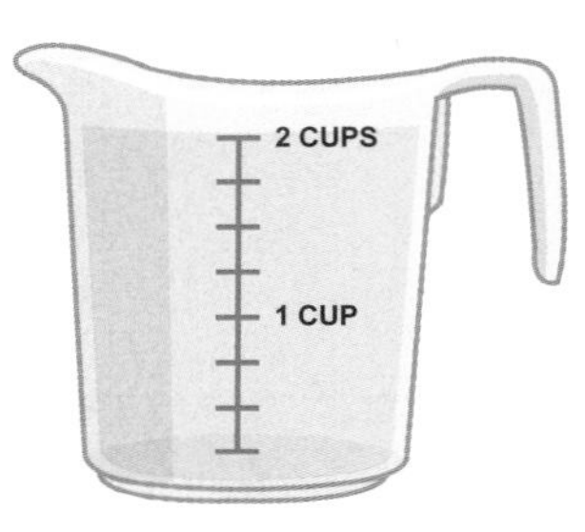

Directions: Compare the capacities of the objects.

- Circle the object that holds more.
- Draw a line through the object that holds less.
- Do the recycling bins hold the same amount? Circle the thumbs up for *yes* or the thumbs down for *no*.

Name ______________________________

Apply and Grow: Practice

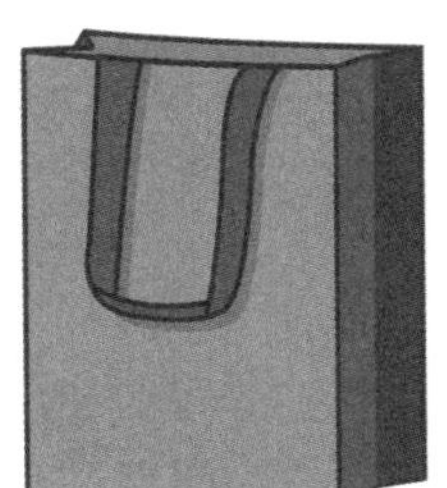

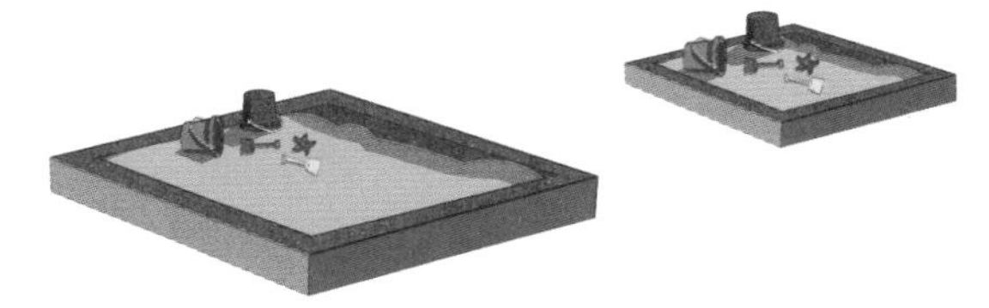

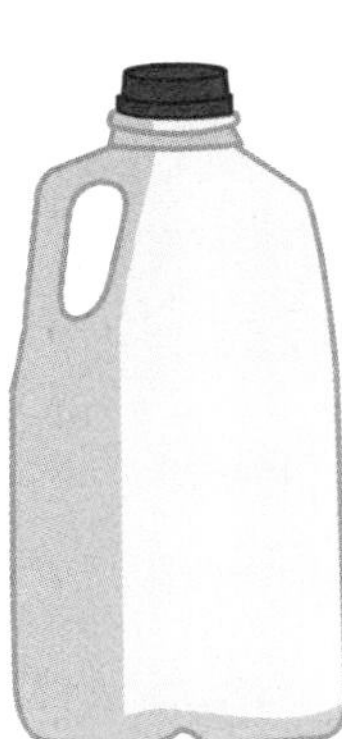

Directions: 1 and 2 Circle the object that holds more. 3 and 4 Draw a line through the object that holds less. 5 Do the milk containers hold the same amount? Circle the thumbs up for *yes* or the thumbs down for *no*.

Think and Grow: Modeling Real Life

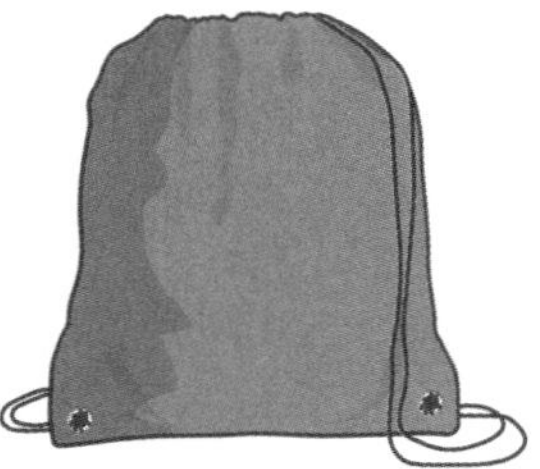

Directions:

- You are going camping. Circle the backpack that can hold all of your camping supplies. Tell how you know.
- You are going to school. Circle the bag that *cannot* hold all of your school supplies. Tell how you know.

Name ______________________________

Learning Target: Compare the capacities of two objects.

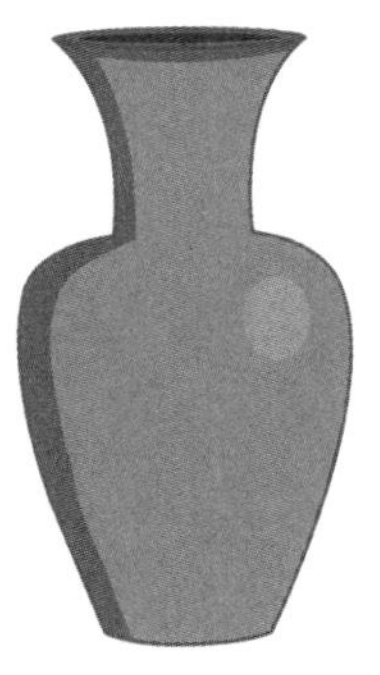
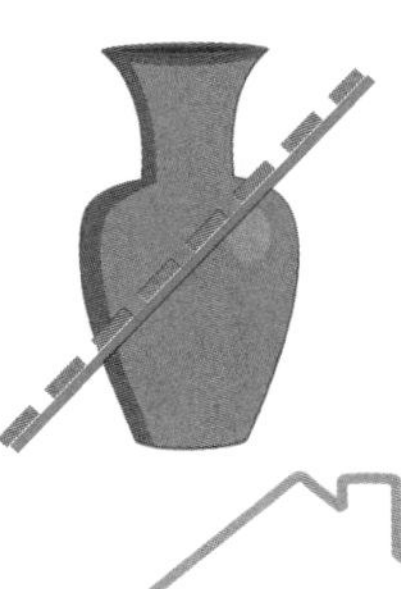

Directions:

- Circle the cup that holds more.
- Draw a line through the vase that holds less.

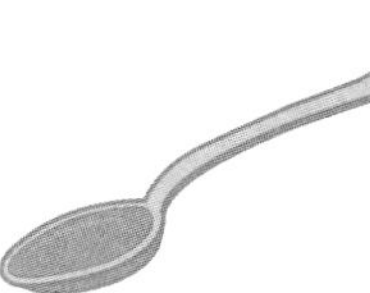

Directions: 1 and 2 Circle the object that holds more. 3 and 4 Draw a line through the object that holds less.

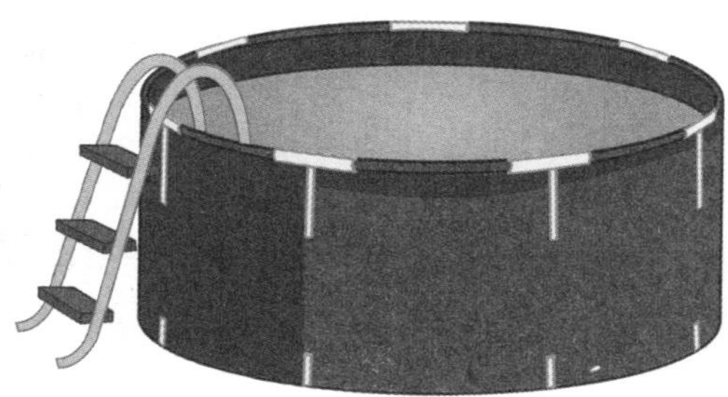

Directions: 5 and 6 Do the objects hold the same amount? Circle the thumbs up for *yes* or the thumbs down for *no*. 7 Your class is going on a field trip. Circle the vehicle that can hold your class. Tell how you know.

Name ____________________

Learning Target: Identify the measurable attributes of an object.

Explore and Grow

length or height

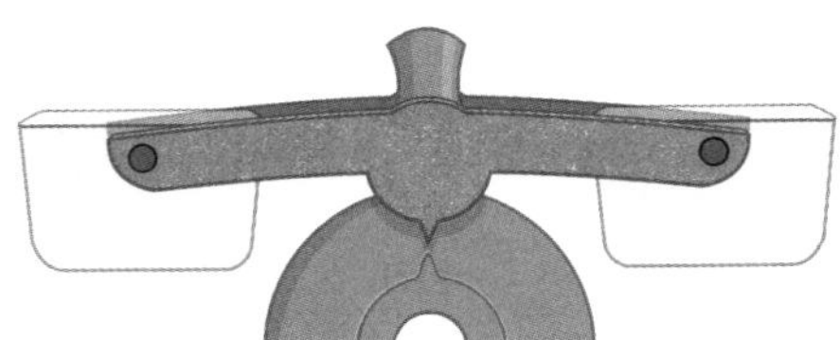

weight

capacity

Directions: Cut out the Measurable Attribute Sort Cards. Place the objects that you can measure using length or height into the length or height box. Then place the objects that you can measure using weight into the weight box. Then place the objects that you can measure using capacity into the capacity box.

Think and Grow

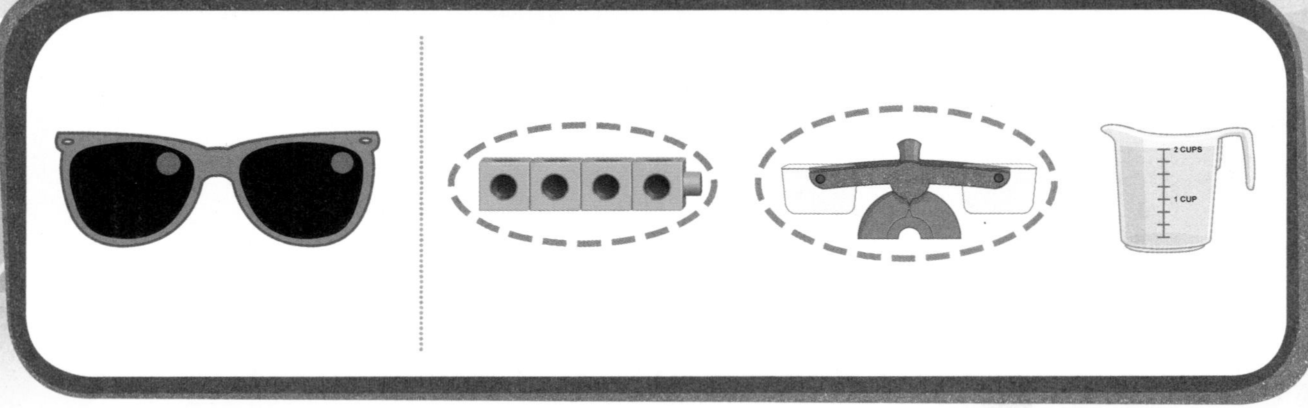

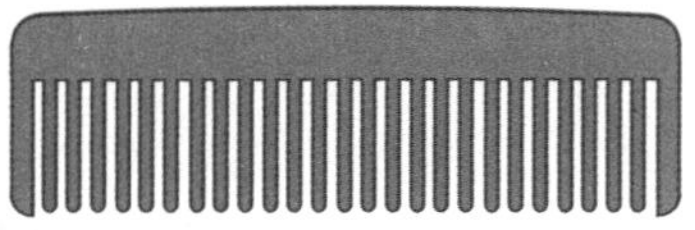

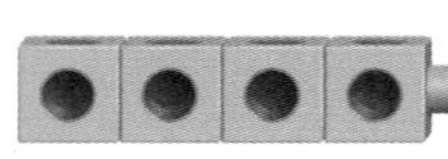

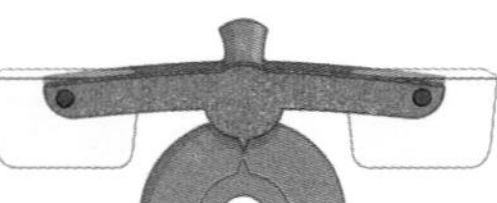

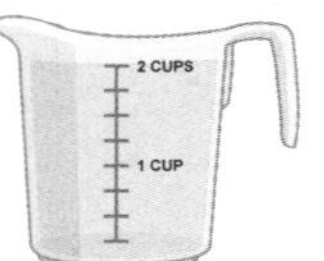

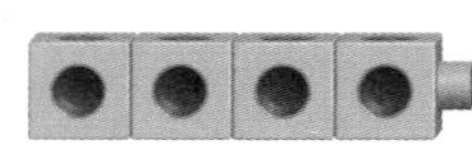

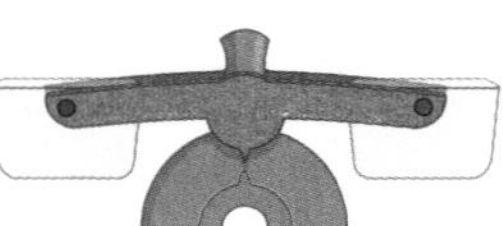

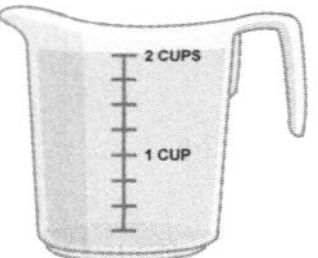

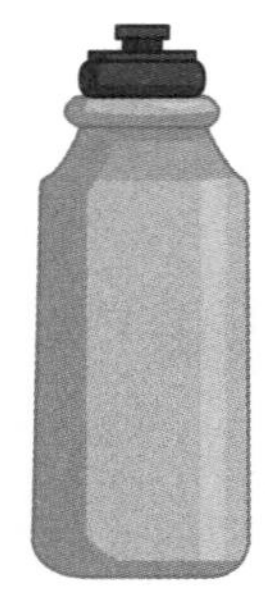

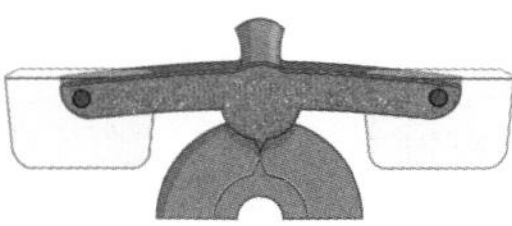

Directions: Circle the measurable attributes of the object.

Name ________________________________

Apply and Grow: Practice

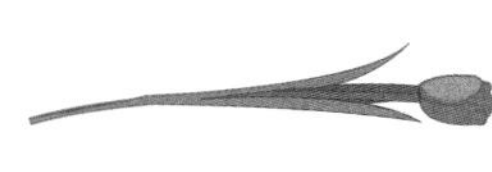
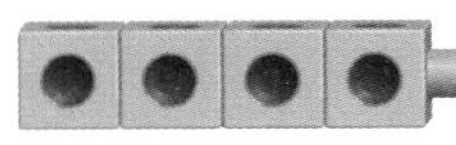

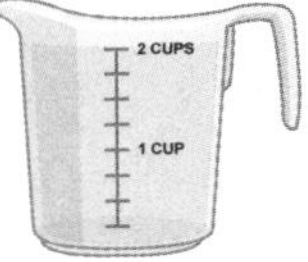

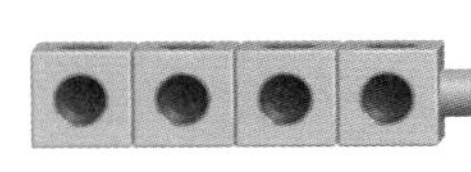
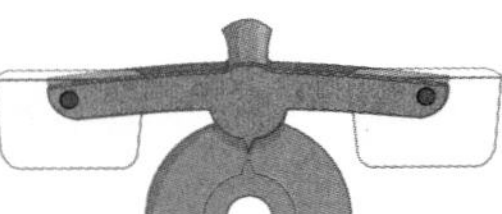
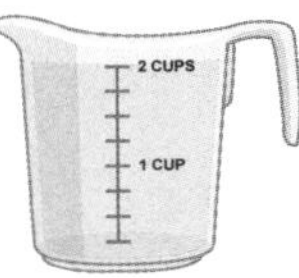

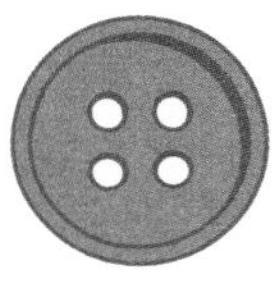
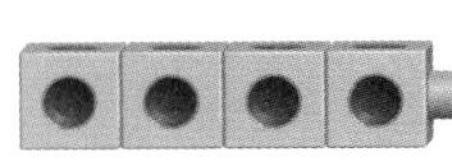
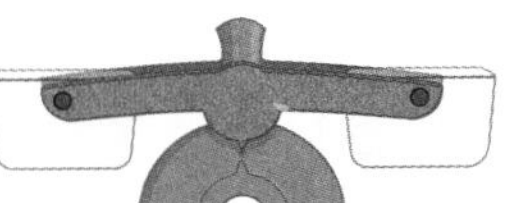
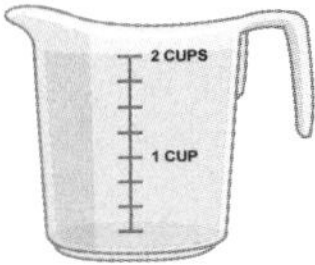

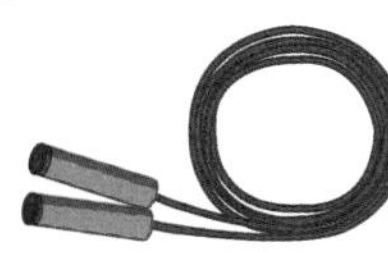
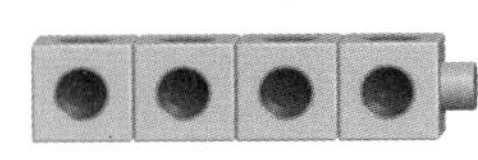
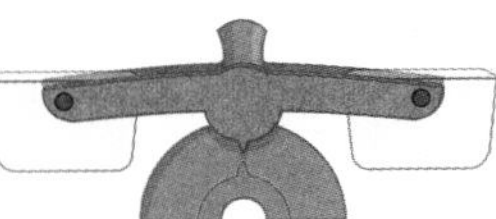
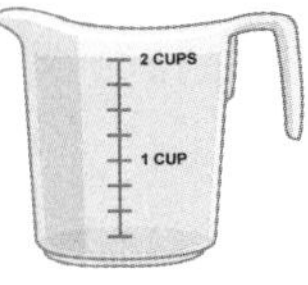

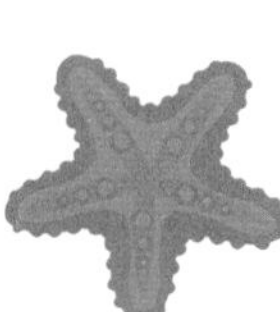
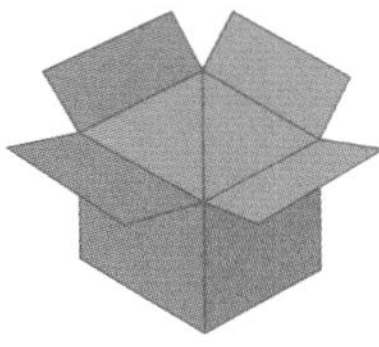

Directions: 1–4 Circle the measurable attributes of the object. 5 Circle the objects that have capacity as an attribute.

Think and Grow: Modeling Real Life

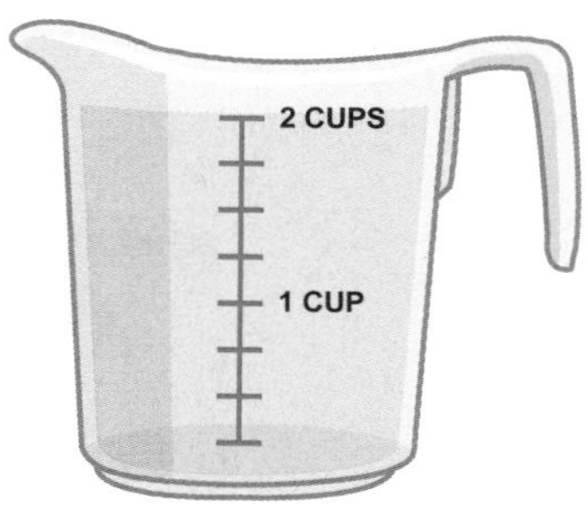

Directions:

- Draw an object that has capacity as an attribute.
- Draw an object that does *not* have capacity as an attribute.

Name ________________________________

Learning Target: Identify the measurable attributes of an object.

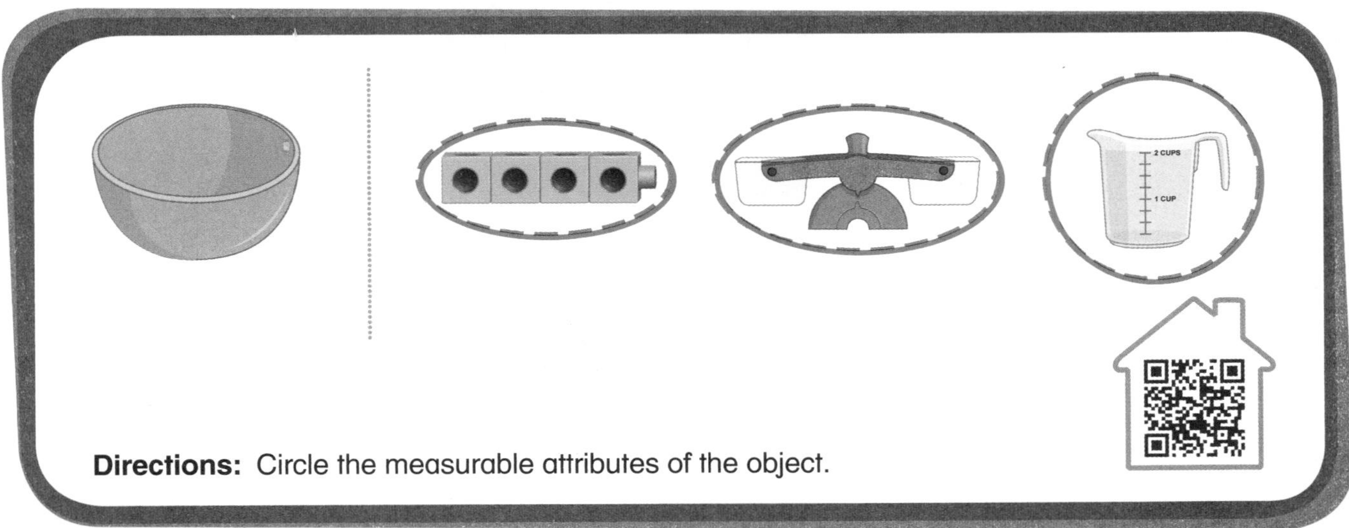

Directions: Circle the measurable attributes of the object.

1

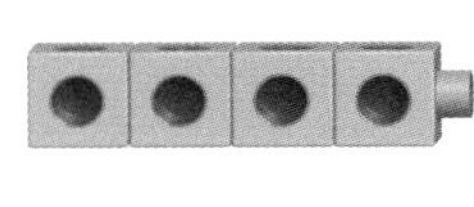
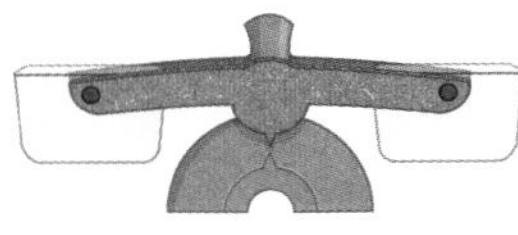
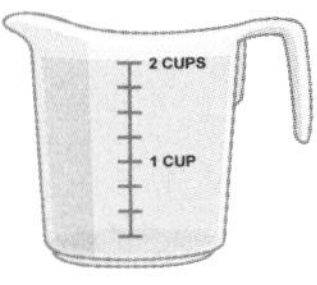

2

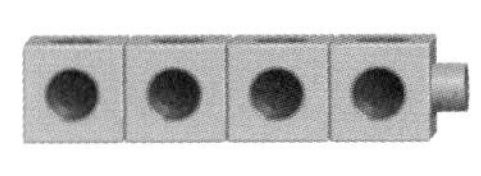
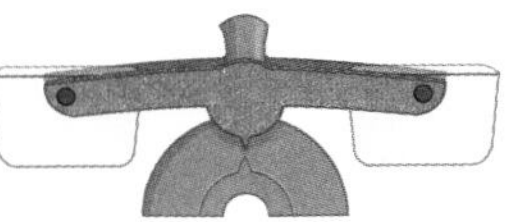
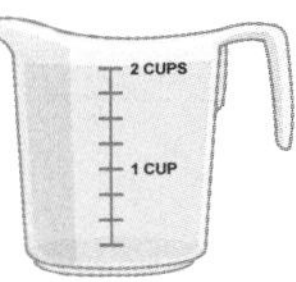

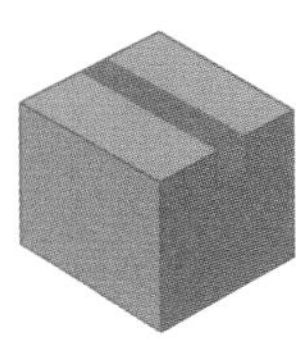
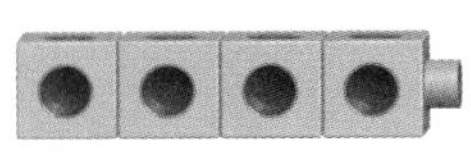
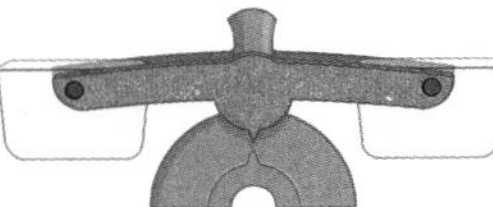
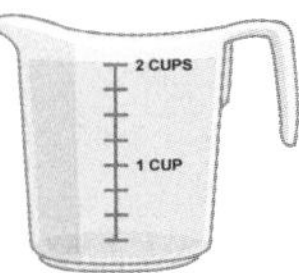

Directions: 1–3 Circle the measurable attributes of the object.

4

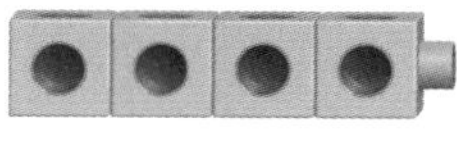

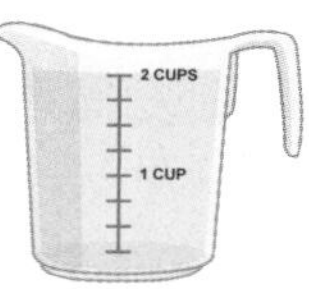

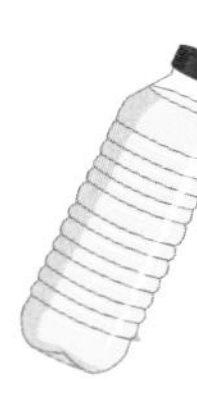

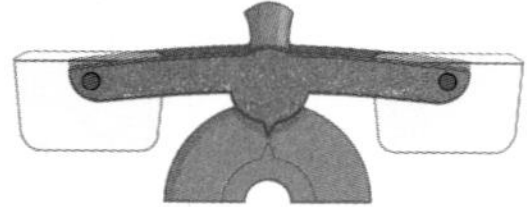

Directions: 4 Circle the measurable attributes of the broccoli. 5 Circle the objects that have length as an attribute. 6 Draw an object that has length as an attribute. 7 Draw an object that has weight as an attribute.

Name ______________________

Performance Task 13

1

2

3

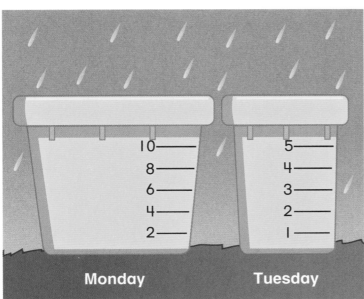

______ 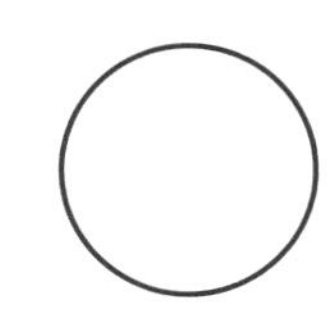 ______  ______

Directions: You use one bucket to collect rainwater on Monday and a different bucket to collect rainwater on Tuesday. On Monday, you collect 1 less than 7 fluid ounces of rainwater. On Tuesday, you collect 1 more than 3 fluid ounces of rainwater. 1 Circle the number on each bucket that shows the amount of rainwater you collect. Then circle the day that you collect more rainwater. 2 Draw a bucket for Wednesday that is taller and holds more water than Monday's bucket. 3 The amount of rainwater you collect on Wednesday is the same as the amount you collect in all on Monday and Tuesday. Write an addition sentence to tell how much rainwater you collect on Wednesday.

Measurement Boss

Player 1	Player 2

Directions: Each player flips a Measurement Boss Card and places it on the page. Compare the objects based on the attribute of the card. The player with the object that is longer, taller, heavier, or holds more takes both cards. Repeat until all cards have been used.

Name ____

Chapter Practice 13

13.1 Compare Heights

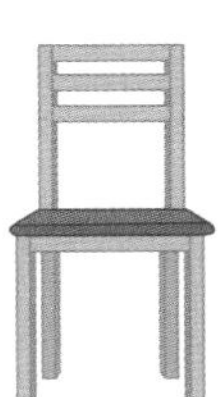

13.2 Compare Lengths

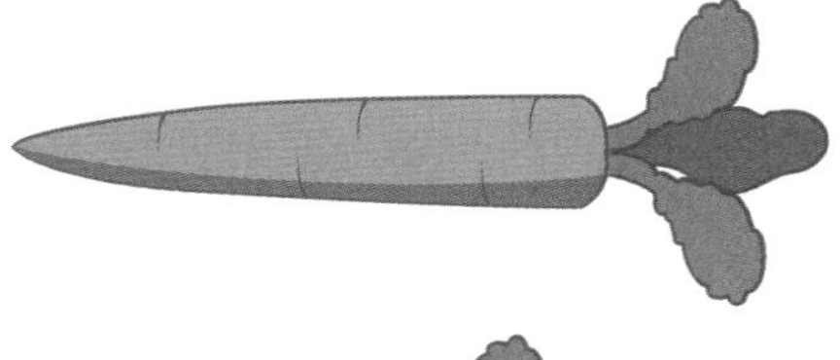

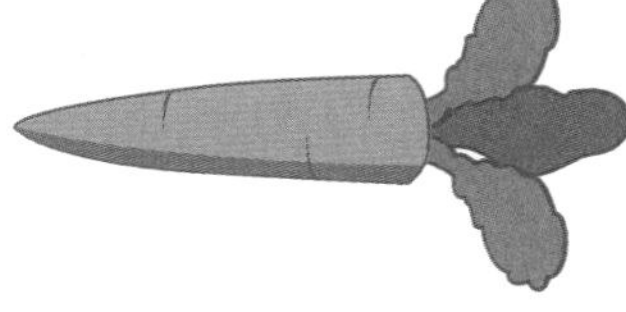

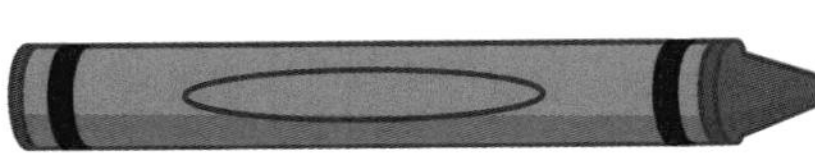

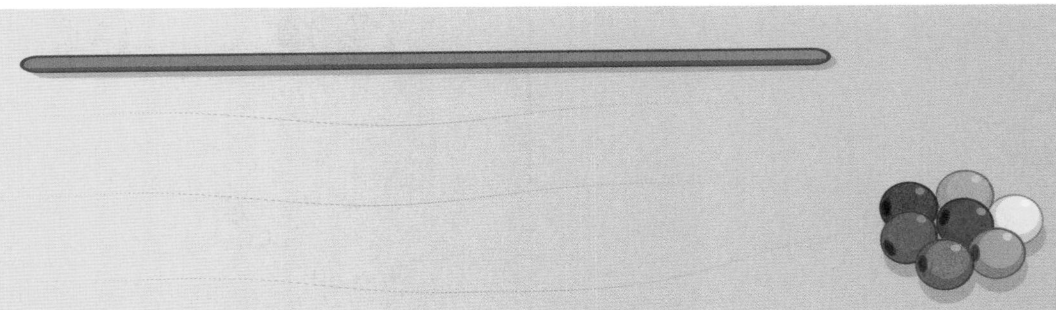

Directions: 1 and 2 Circle the taller object. 3 Draw a line through the shorter object. 4 Are the crayons the same length? Circle the thumbs up for *yes* or the thumbs down for *no*. 5 Draw a string that holds the same number of beads as the string shown. Tell how you know.

13.3 Use Numbers to Compare Lengths

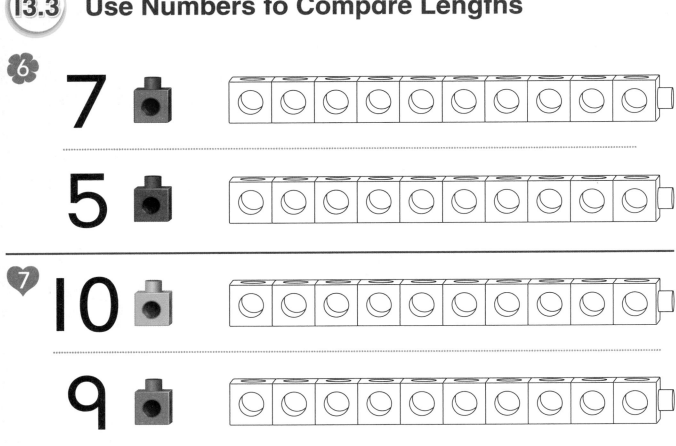

6

7

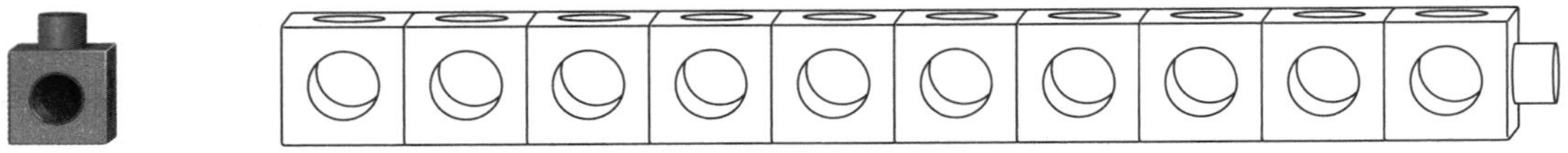

5

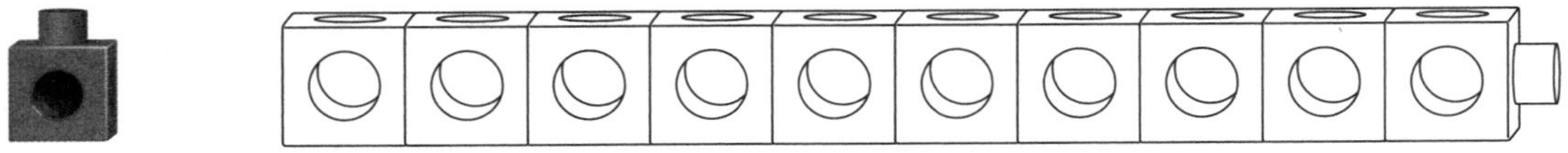

7

10

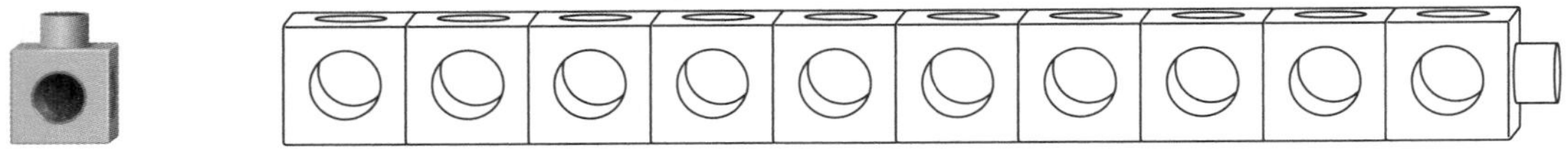

9

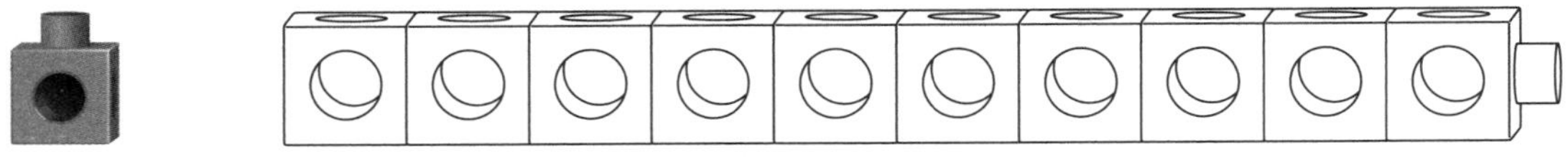

13.4 Compare Weights

8

9

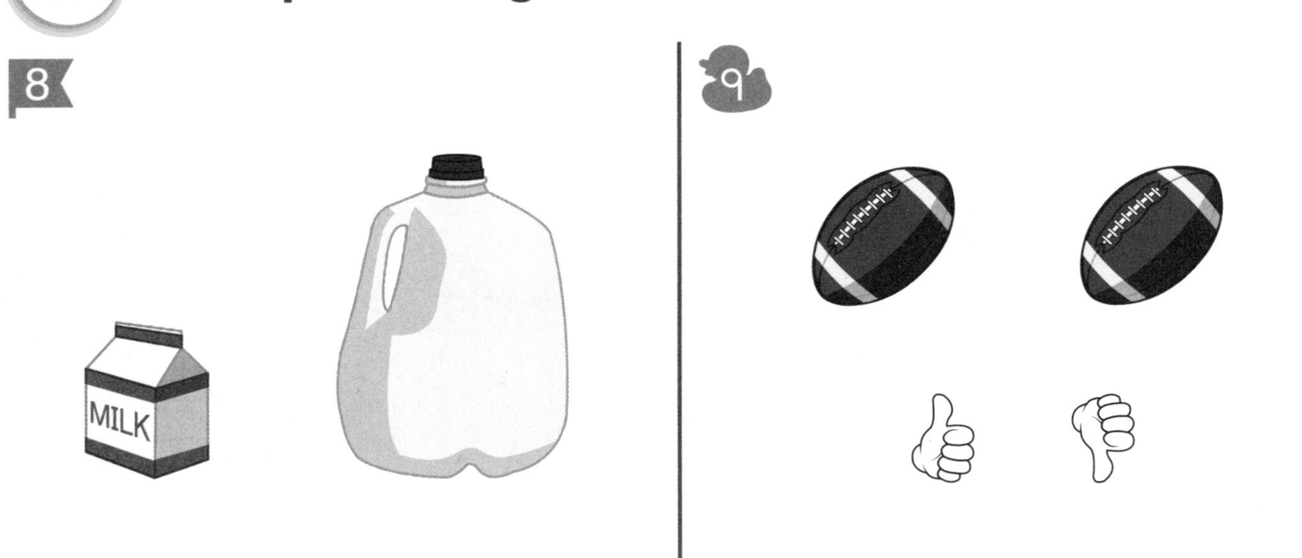

Directions: 6 and 7 Compare the lengths of the cube trains that have the given number of cubes. Circle the number of the train that is longer. Color to show how you know. 8 Draw a line through the lighter object. 9 Are the footballs the same weight? Circle the thumbs up for *yes* or the thumbs down for *no*.

13.5 Use Numbers to Compare Weights

2 4

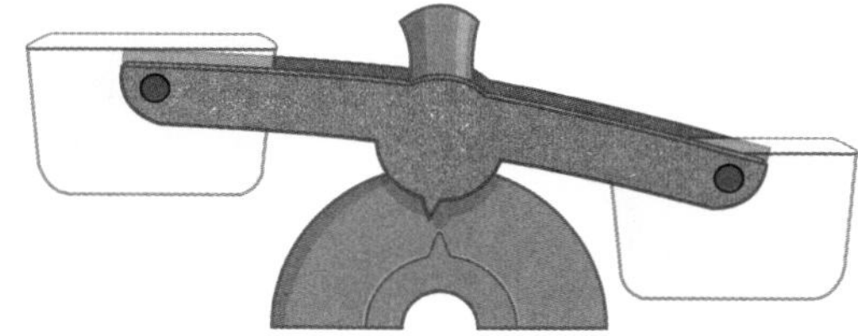

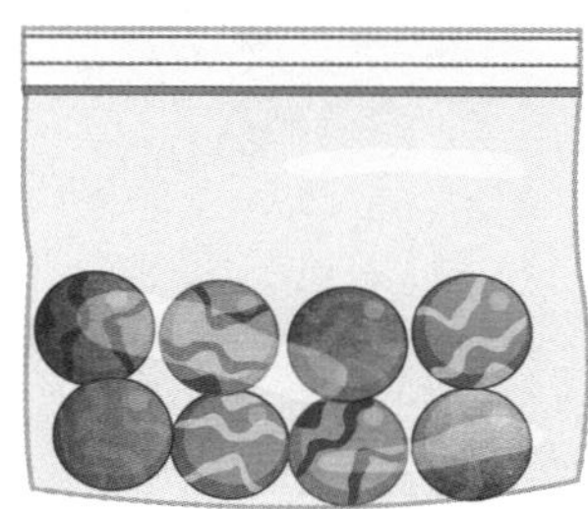

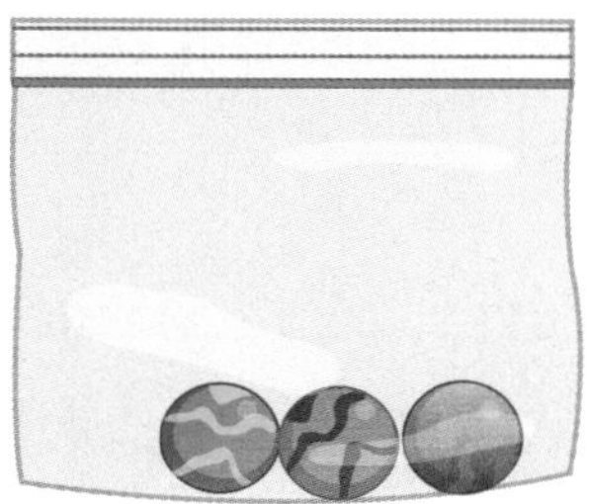

13.6 Compare Capacities

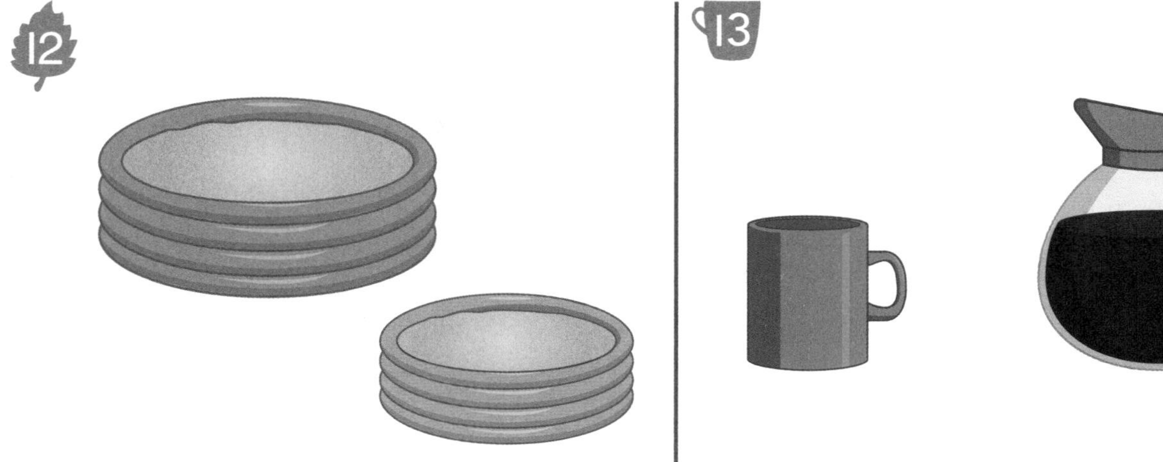

Directions: 10 Compare the weights of the groups of linking cubes. Match each group of linking cubes with the correct side of the balance scale. 11 Circle the bag that is lighter. Tell how you know. 12 and 13 Draw a line through the object that holds less.

13.7 Describe Objects by Attributes

15

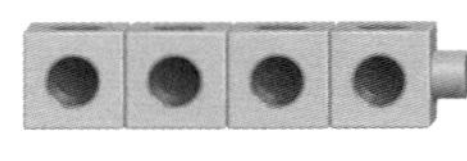

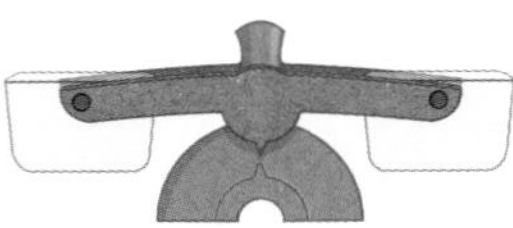

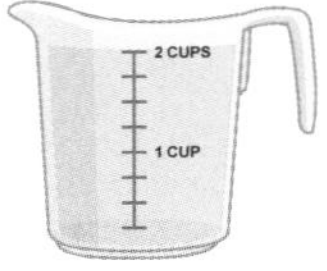

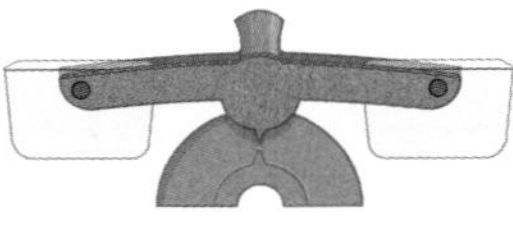

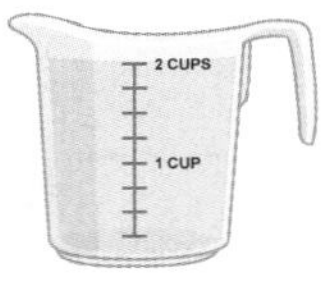

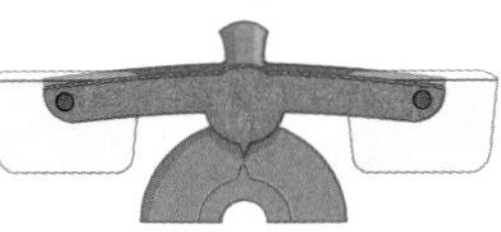

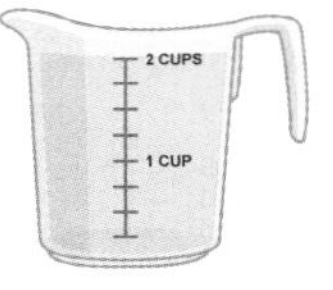

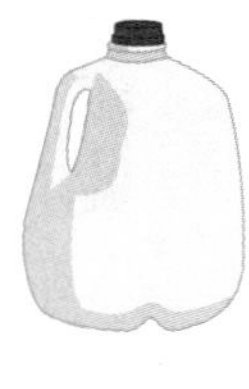

Directions: 14 Do the water bottles hold the same amount? Circle the thumbs up for *yes* or the thumbs down for *no*. 15–17 Circle the measurable attributes of the object. 18 Circle the objects that have capacity as an attribute.

Name ____________________

Cumulative Practice 1–13

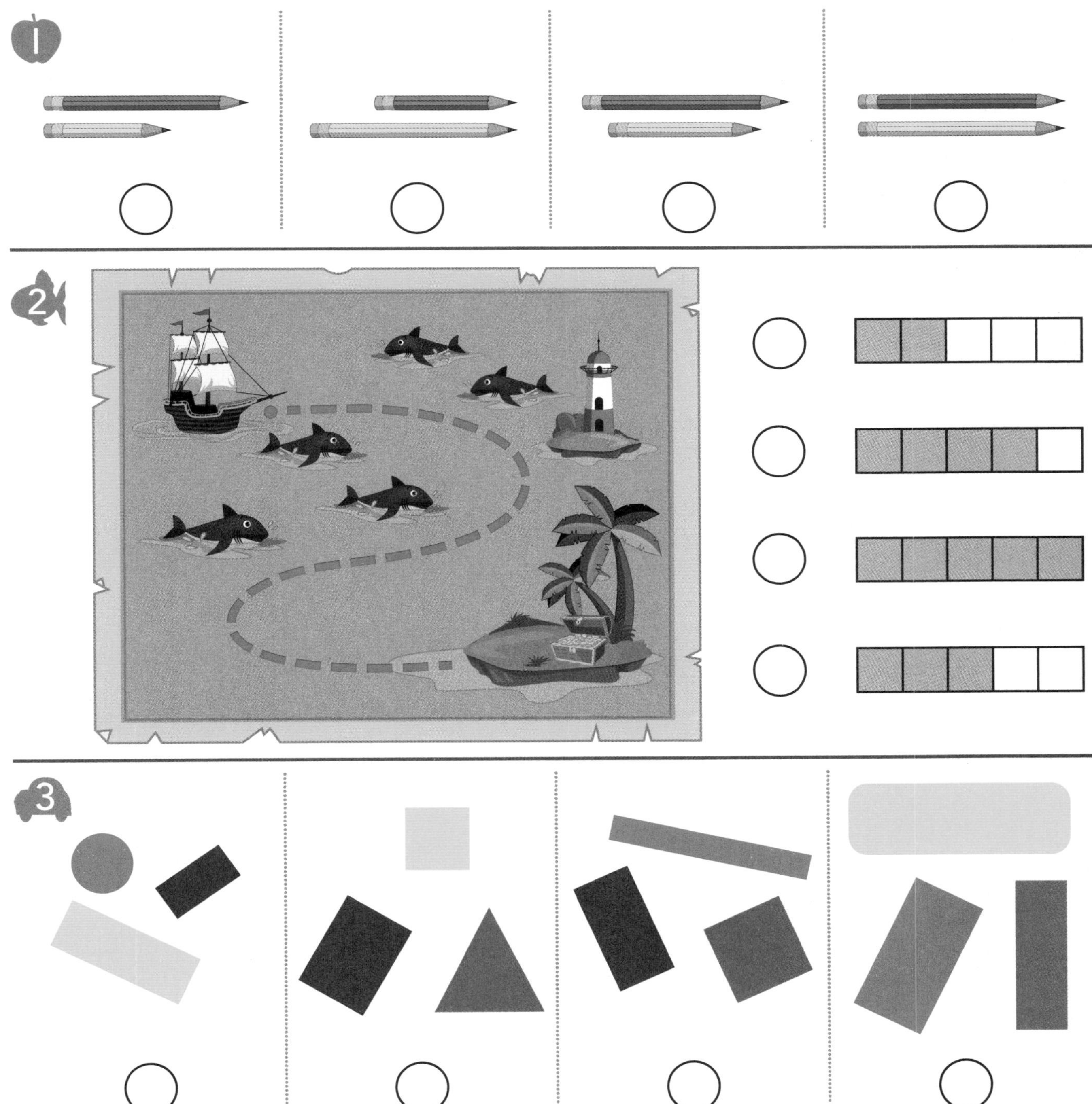

Directions: Shade the circle next to the answer. 1 Which group has a yellow pencil that is longer than the red pencil? 2 Which five frame shows how many sharks are in the picture? 3 Which group has all rectangles?

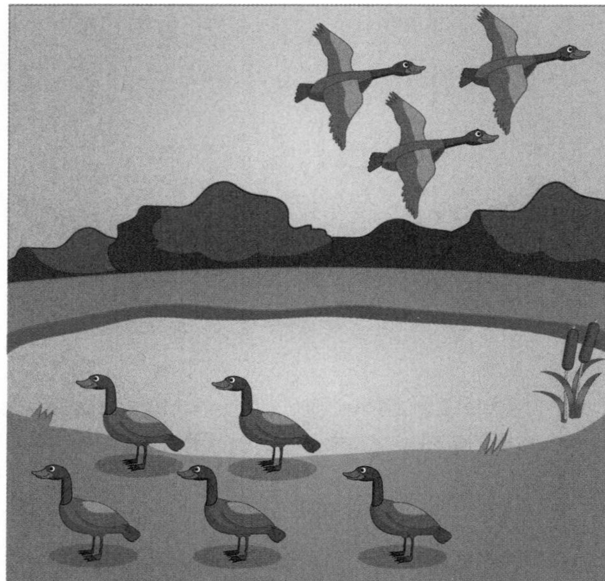

○ $8 - 3 = 5$

○ $4 - 3 = 1$

○ $5 - 3 = 2$

○ $6 - 3 = 3$

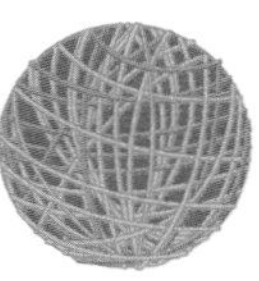  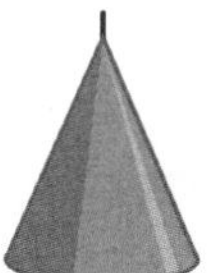 

  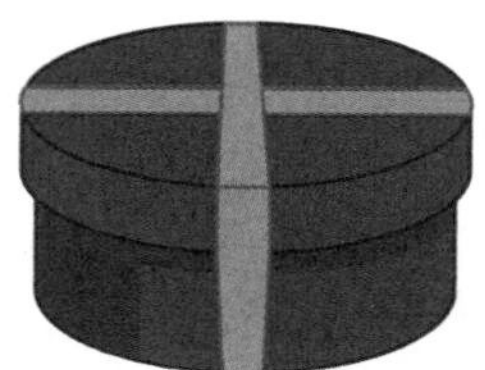 

   ○

Directions: Shade the circle next to the answer. 4 Which subtraction sentence tells how many geese are left? 5 Which shape is *not* a solid shape? 6 Which solid shape does *not* stack or slide?

7

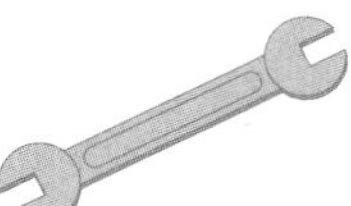

8

9

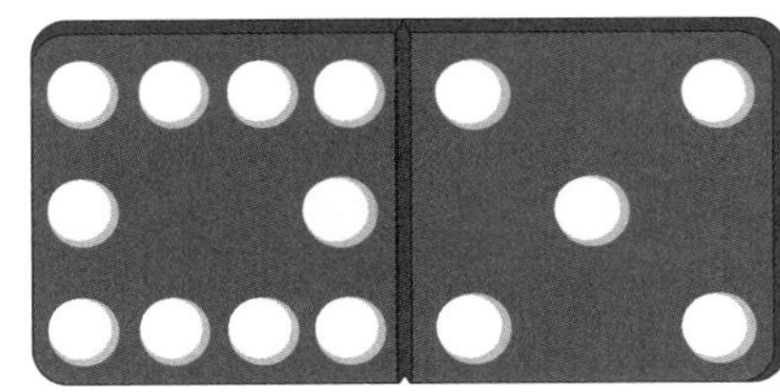
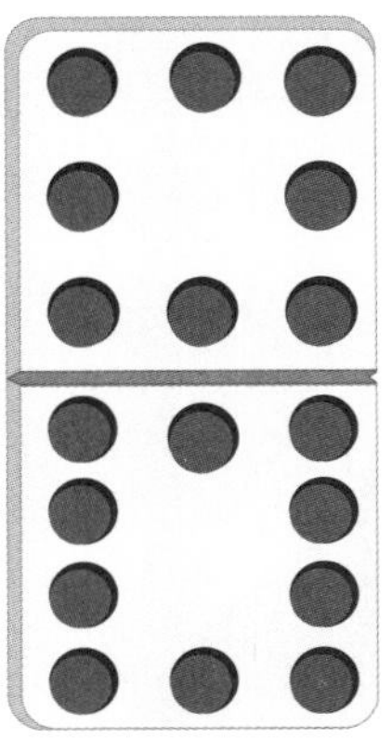

Directions: 7 Circle the objects that have capacity as an attribute. 8 Circle the object that looks like a cylinder that is *above* the ball. 9 Find the number of dots on each domino. Write each number. Draw a line through the number that is less than the other number.

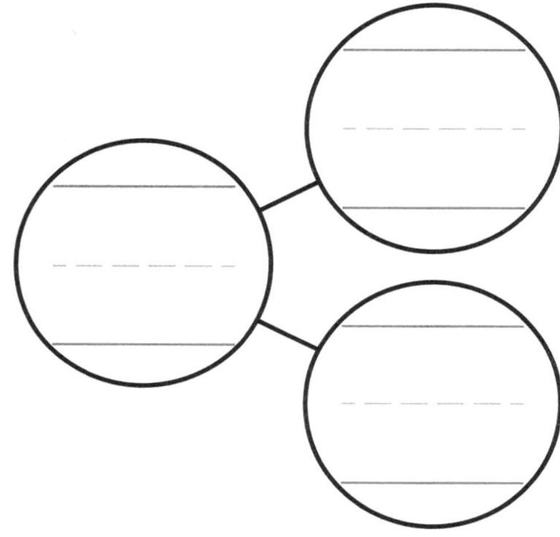

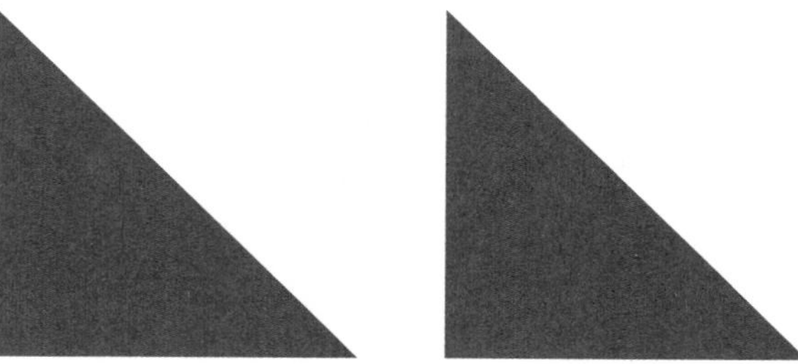

Directions: 10 Trace the shapes that are hexagons. Write the number of sides and the number of vertices of a hexagon. 11 You have 10 apples. Classify the apples into 2 categories. Circle the groups. Then complete the number bond to match your picture. 12 Draw a larger triangle that can be formed by the 2 triangles shown.

Glossary

above [arriba, encima]

add [sumar]

$$2 + 4 = 6$$

addition sentence
[enunciado suma]

$$2 + 3 = 5$$

balance scale [balanza]

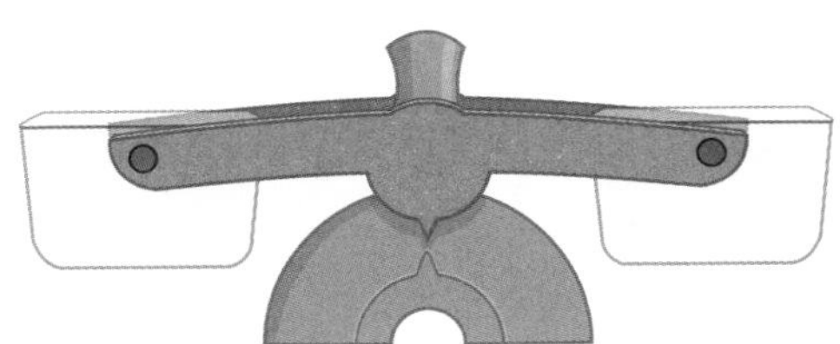

behind [detrás]

below [debajo]

beside [al lado]

capacity [capacidad]

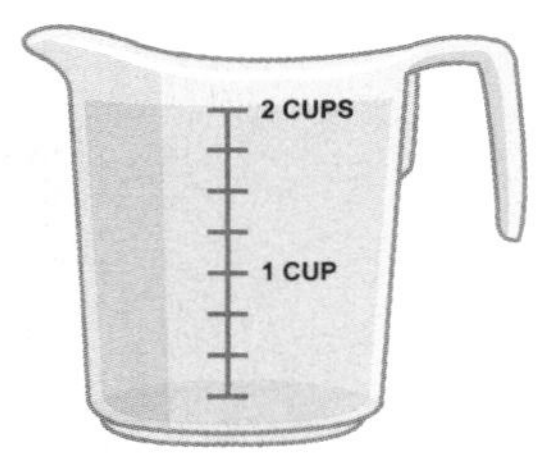

category [categoría]

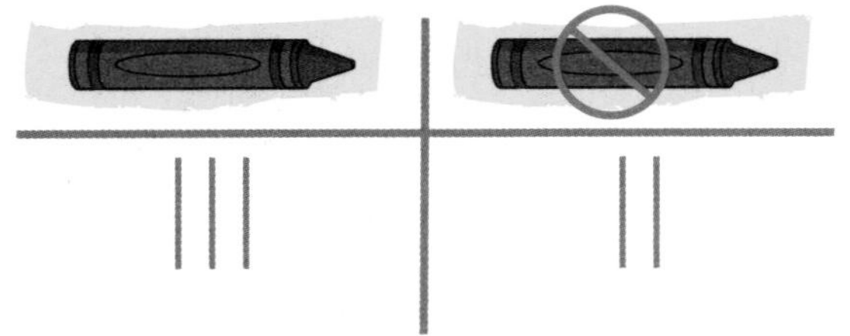

chart [gráfico]

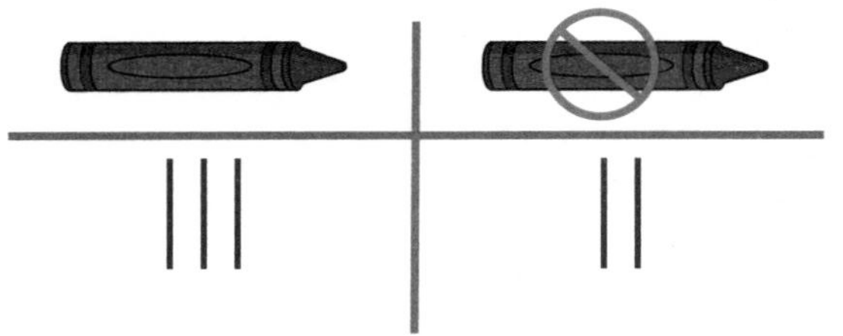

circle [círculo]

classify [clasificar]

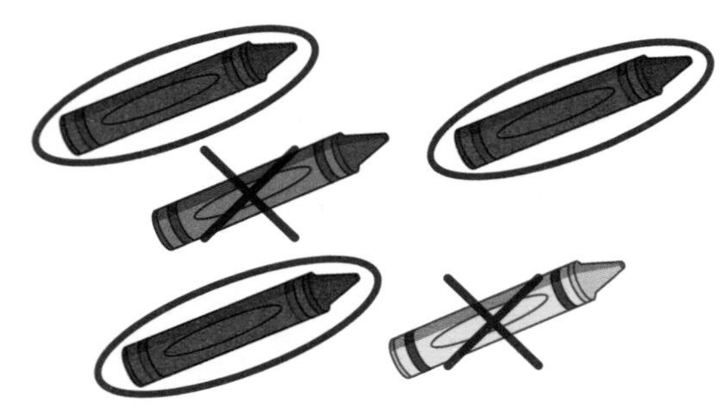

column [columna]

1	2	3	4	5	6	7	8	9	10
11	12	13	14	15	16	17	18	19	20
21	22	23	24	25	26	27	28	29	30
31	32	33	34	35	36	37	38	39	40
41	42	43	44	45	46	47	48	49	50
51	52	53	54	55	56	57	58	59	60
61	62	63	64	65	66	67	68	69	70
71	72	73	74	75	76	77	78	79	80
81	82	83	84	85	86	87	88	89	90
91	92	93	94	95	96	97	98	99	100

compare [comparar]

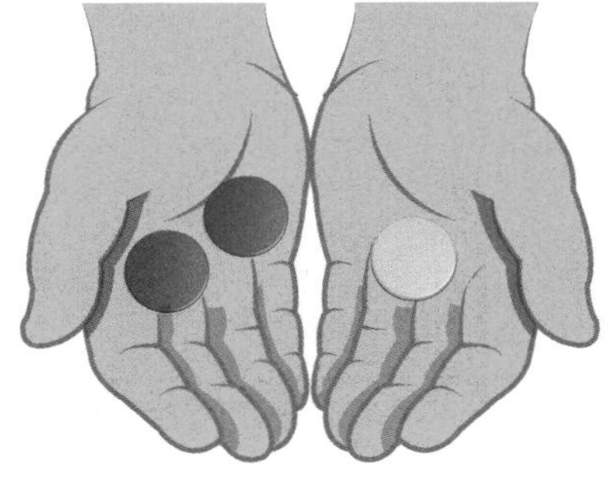

cone [cono]

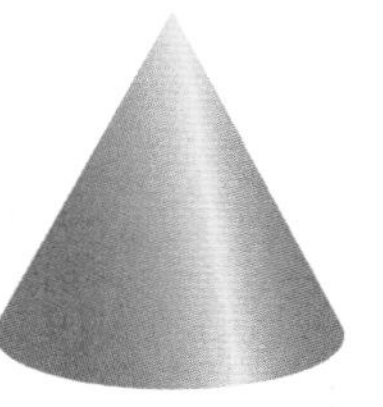

count [contar]

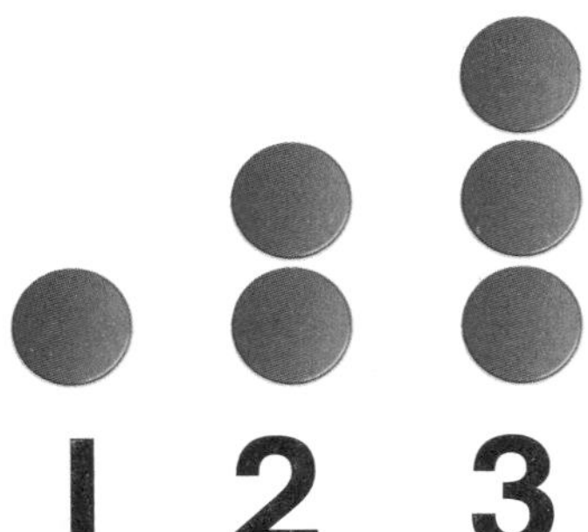

cube [cubo]

curve [curva]

curved surface [superficie curva]

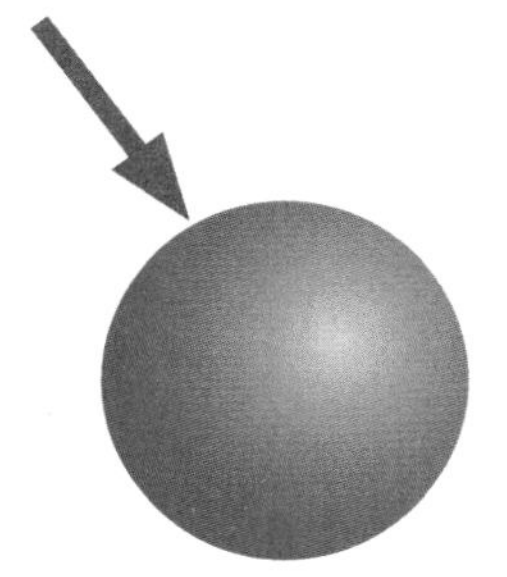

cylinder [cilindro]

D

decade number
[número de década]

1	2	3	4	5	6	7	8	9	10
11	12	13	14	15	16	17	18	19	20
21	22	23	24	25	26	27	28	29	30
31	32	33	34	35	36	37	38	39	40
41	42	43	44	45	46	47	48	49	50
51	52	53	54	55	56	57	58	59	60
61	62	63	64	65	66	67	68	69	70
71	72	73	74	75	76	77	78	79	80
81	82	83	84	85	86	87	88	89	90
91	92	93	94	95	96	97	98	99	100

E

eight [ocho]

8

eighteen [dieciocho]

18

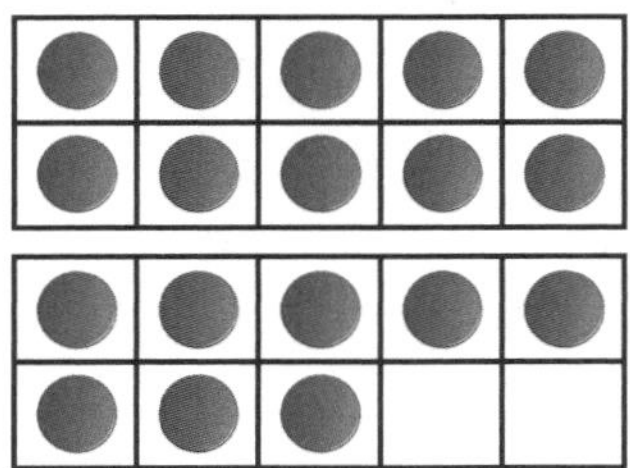

eleven [once]

11

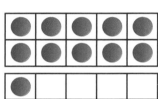

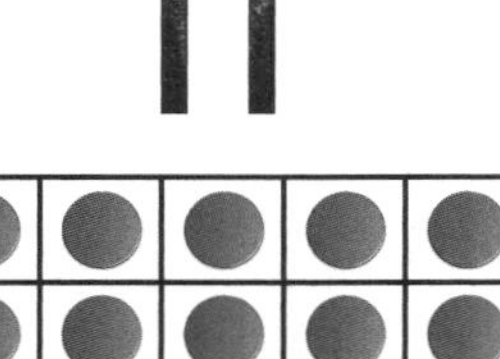

equal [igual]

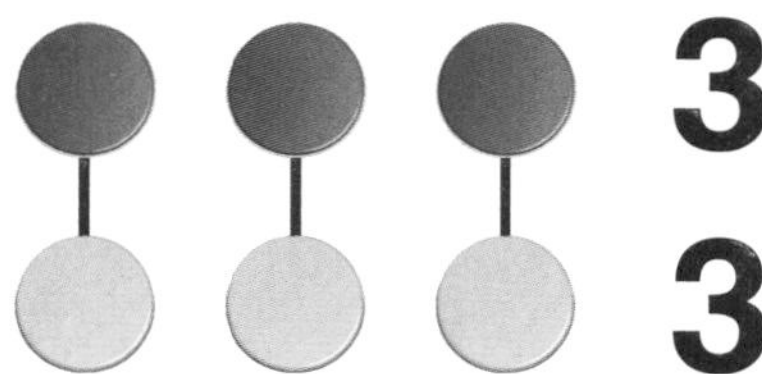

equal sign [signo igual]

$$3 + 4 = 7$$

fewer [menos]

fifteen [quince]

15

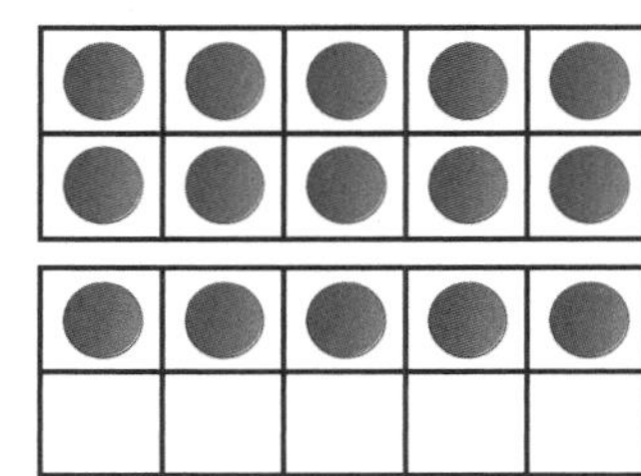

five [cinco]

5

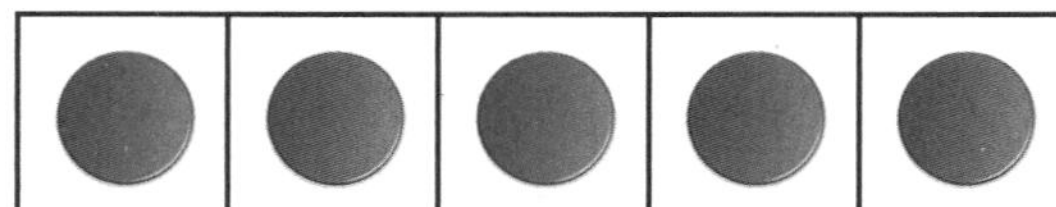

five frame [cinco marco]

flat surface [superficie plana]

four [cuatro]

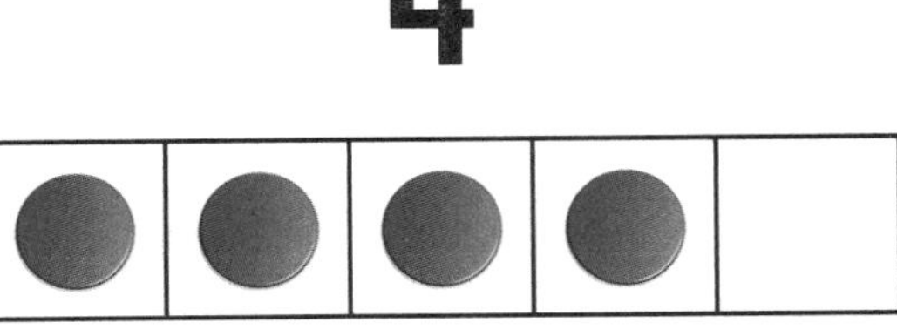

fourteen [catorce]

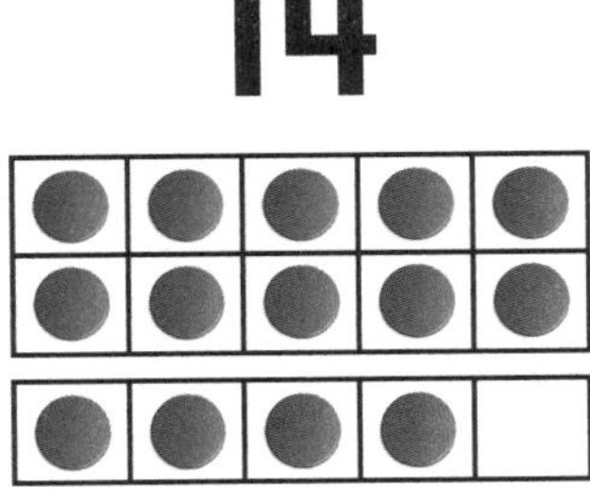

G

greater than [mas grande que]

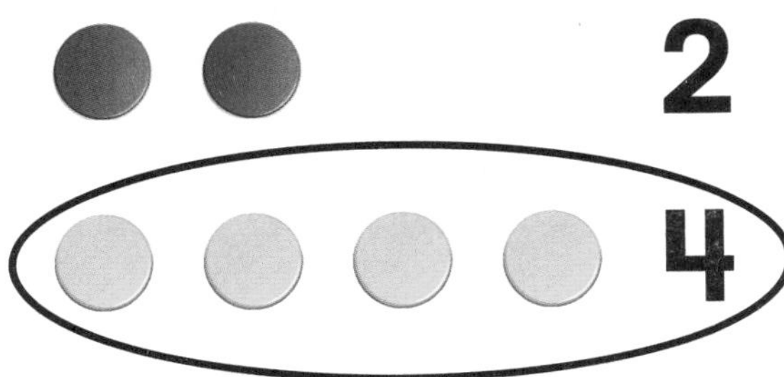

H

heavier [más pesado]

height [altura]

hexagon [hexágono]

hundred chart [cientos de cartas]

1	2	3	4	5	6	7	8	9	10
11	12	13	14	15	16	17	18	19	20
21	22	23	24	25	26	27	28	29	30
31	32	33	34	35	36	37	38	39	40
41	42	43	44	45	46	47	48	49	50
51	52	53	54	55	56	57	58	59	60
61	62	63	64	65	66	67	68	69	70
71	72	73	74	75	76	77	78	79	80
81	82	83	84	85	86	87	88	89	90
91	92	93	94	95	96	97	98	99	100

in all [en todo]

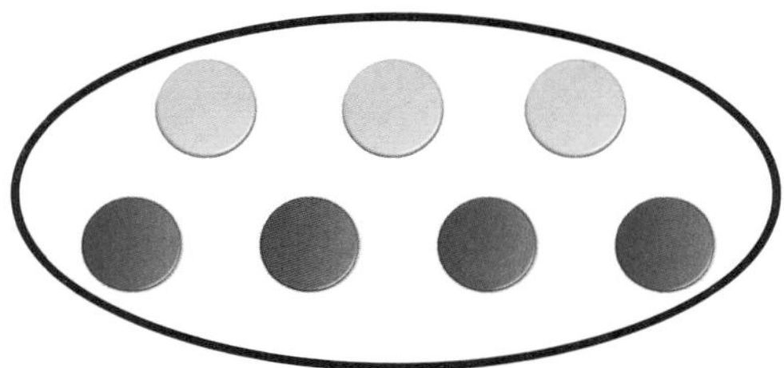

in front of [delante de]

join [unirse]

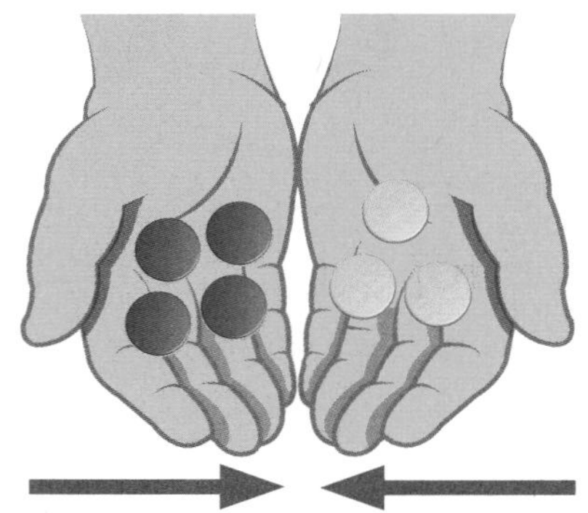

L

left [izquierda]

length [longitud]

less than [menos que]

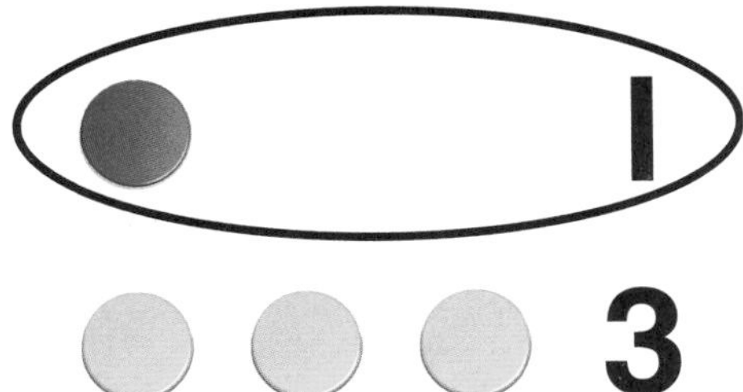

lighter [más liviano]

longer [más largo]

M

mark [marca]

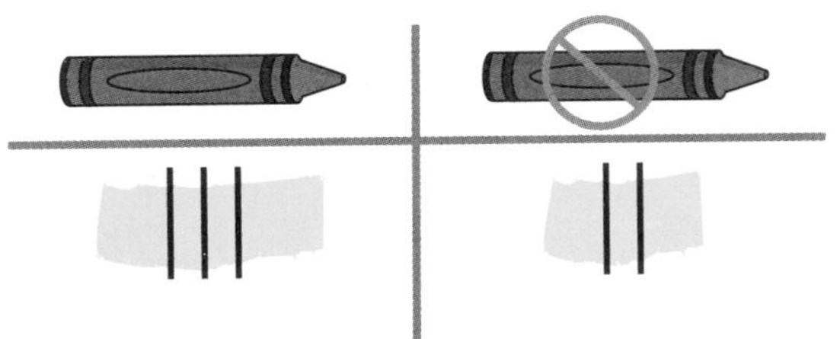

measurable attribute [atributo mensurable]

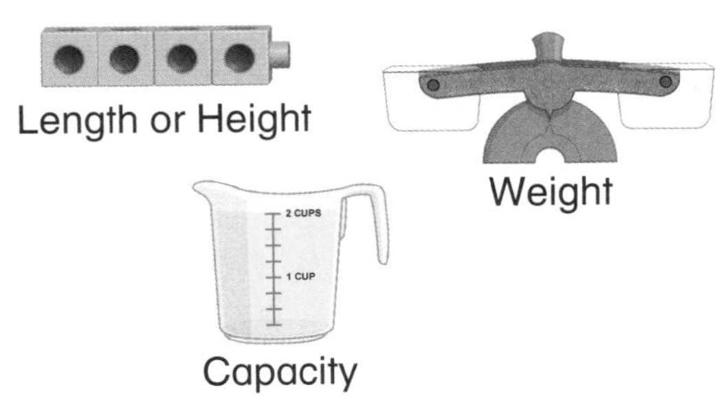

minus sign [signo menos]

$$3 - 2 = 1$$

more [más]

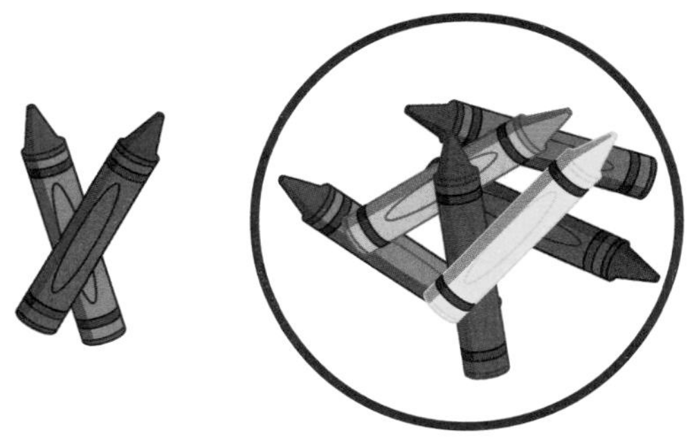

N

next to [al lado de]

nine [nueve]

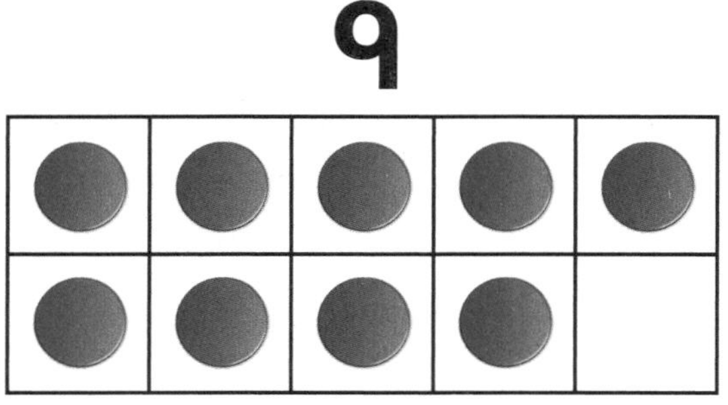

nineteen [diecinueve]

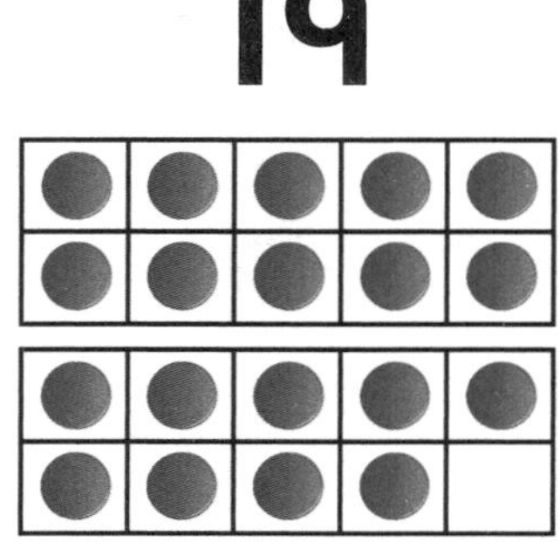

number [número]

number bond [número de bonos]

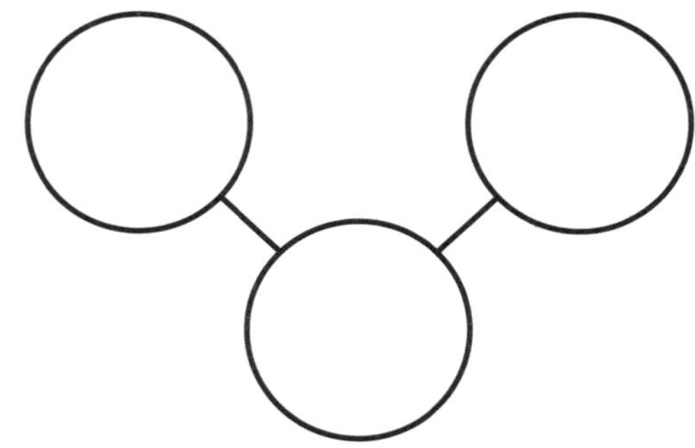

one [uno]

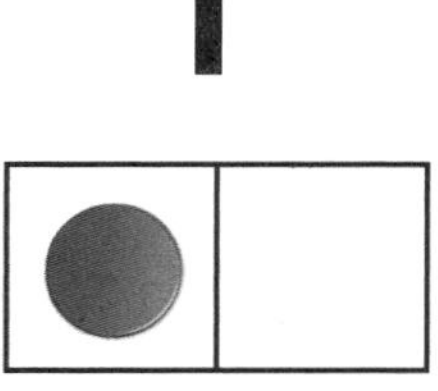

order [ordenar]

part [parte]

partner numbers
[números de socio]

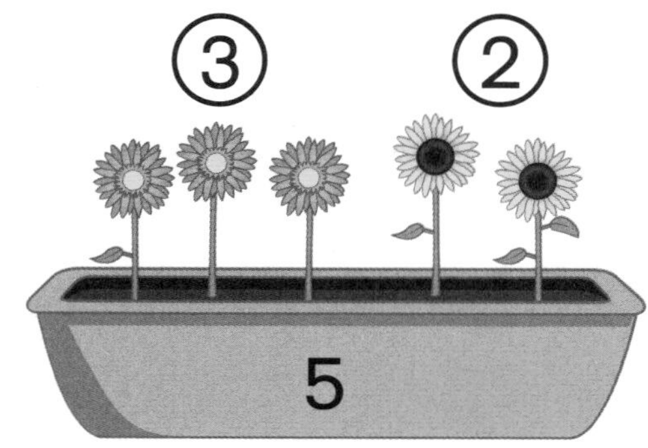

pattern [patrón]

$1 + 1 = 2$

$2 + 1 = 3$

$3 + 1 = 4$

plus sign [signo de más]

$2 + 1 = 3$

put together [juntar]

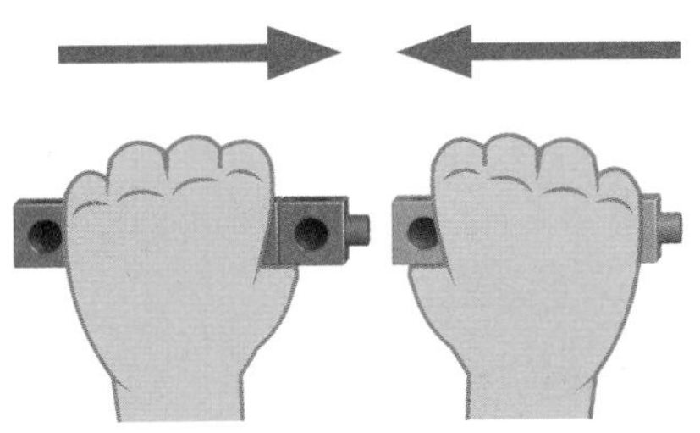

R

rectangle [rectángulo]

roll [rodar]

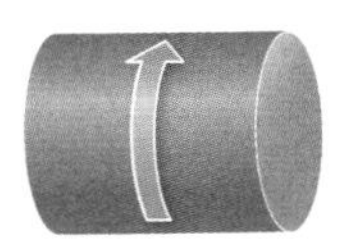

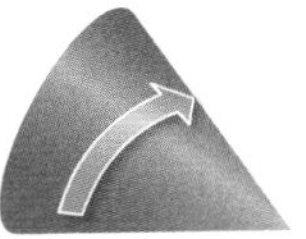

row [fila]

1	2	3	4	5	6	7	8	9	10
11	12	13	14	15	16	17	18	19	20
21	22	23	24	25	26	27	28	29	30
31	32	33	34	35	36	37	38	39	40
41	42	43	44	45	46	47	48	49	50
51	52	53	54	55	56	57	58	59	60
61	62	63	64	65	66	67	68	69	70
71	72	73	74	75	76	77	78	79	80
81	82	83	84	85	86	87	88	89	90
91	92	93	94	95	96	97	98	99	100

S

same as [igual que]

separate [separar]

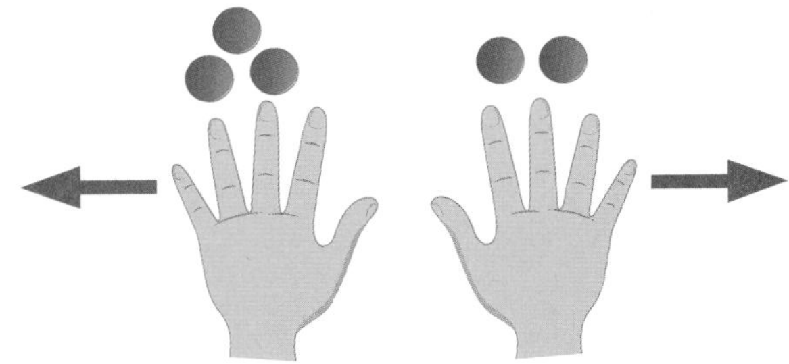

seven [siete]

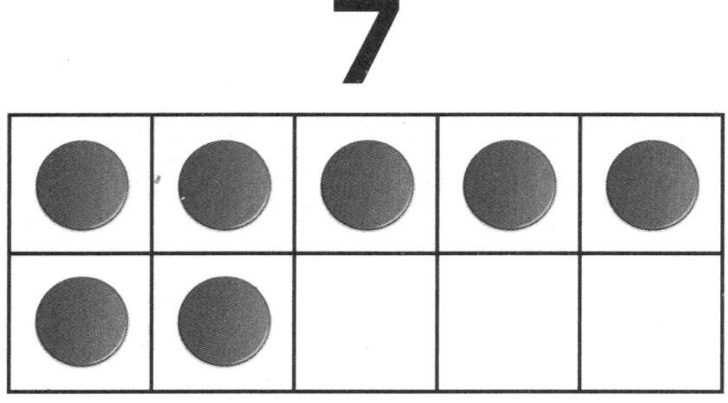

seventeen [diecisiete]

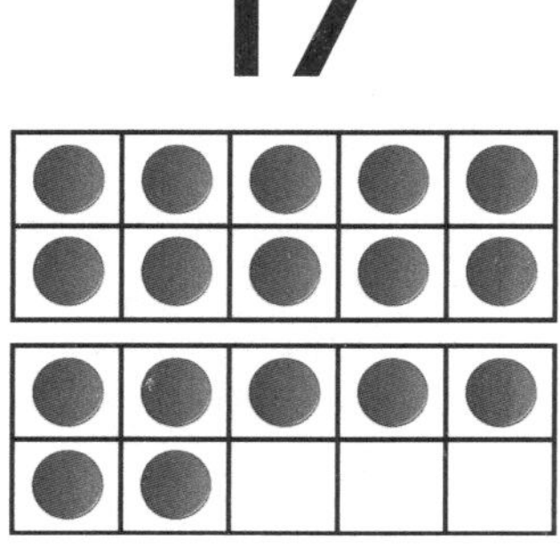

shorter [corta]

side [lado]

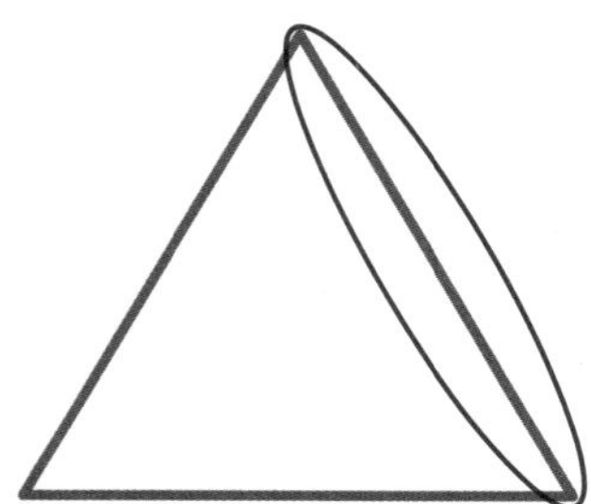

six [seis]

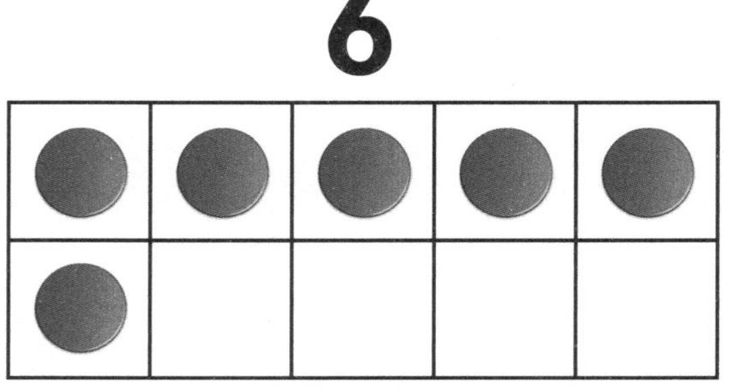

sixteen [dieciséis]

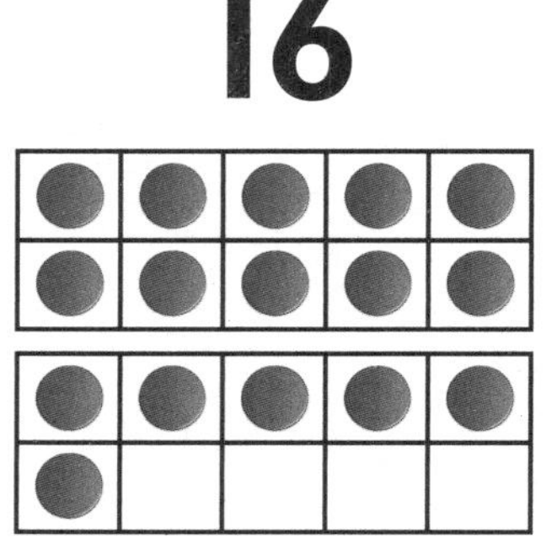

slide [deslizar]

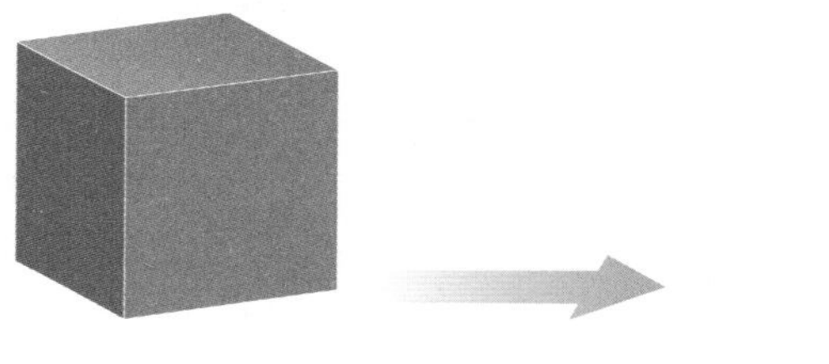

sort [ordenar]

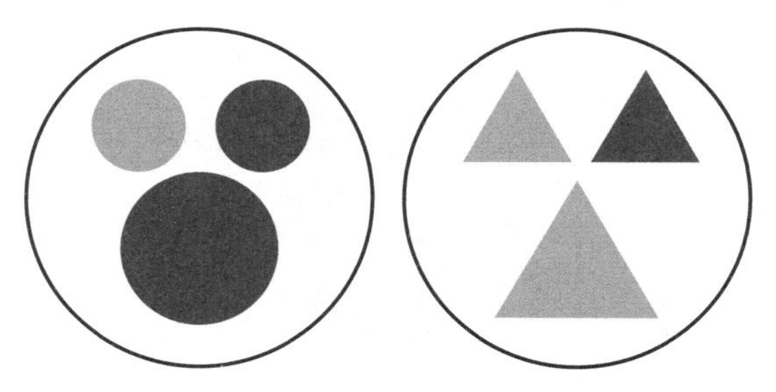

sphere [esfera]

square [cuadrado]

stack [apilar]

subtract [restar]

3 − 1 = 2

subtraction sentence [oración de resta]

4 − 1 = 3

T

take apart [desmontar]

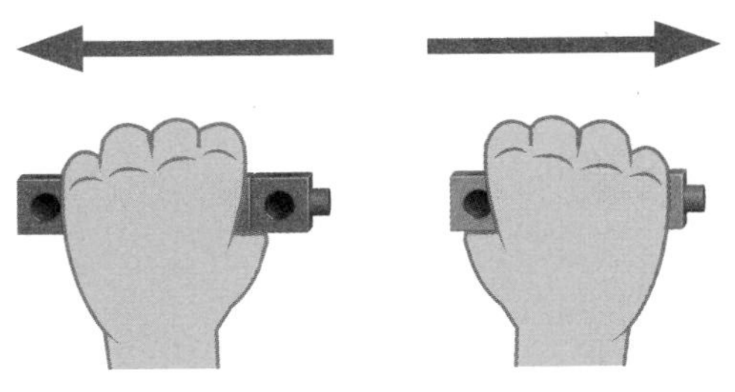

take away [quitar]

taller [más alto]

ten [diez]

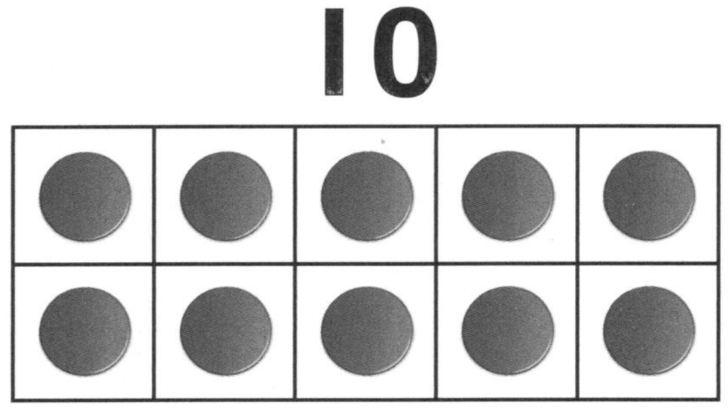

ten frame [diez marco]

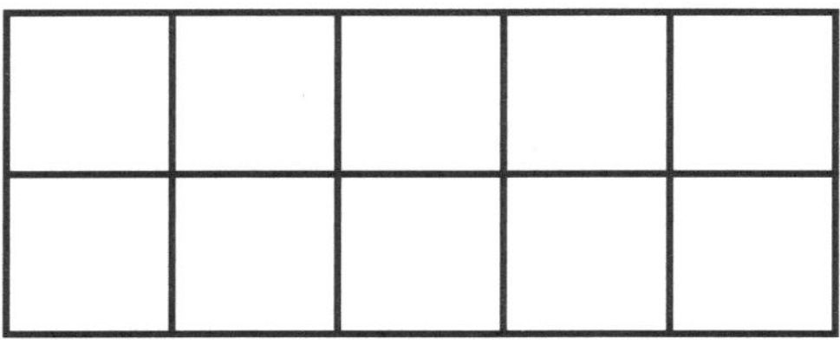

thirteen [trece]

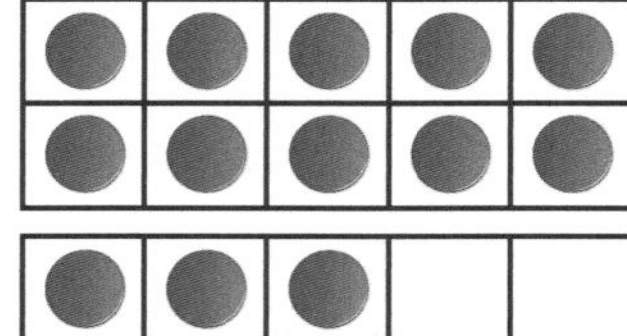

three [tres]

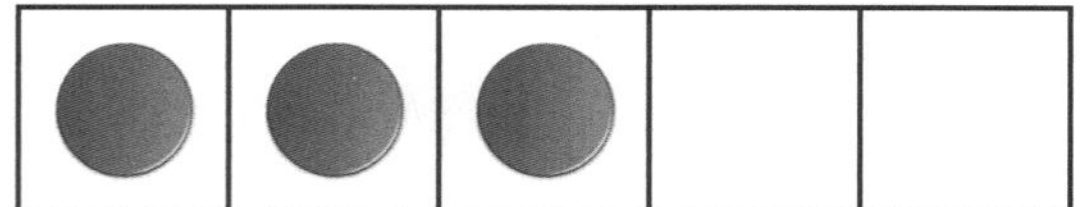

three-dimensional shape [forma tridimensional]

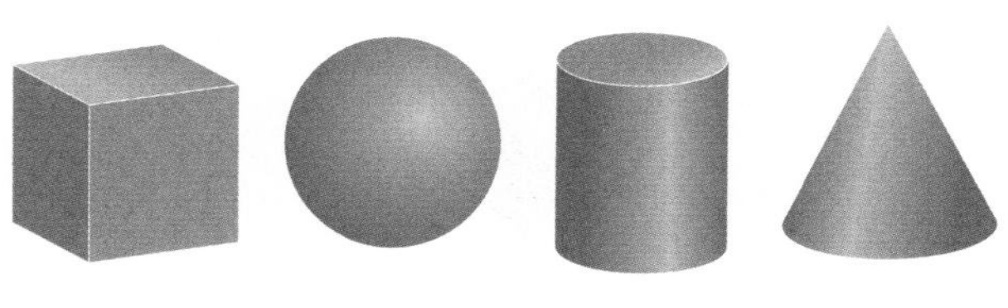

triangle [triángulo]

twelve [doce]

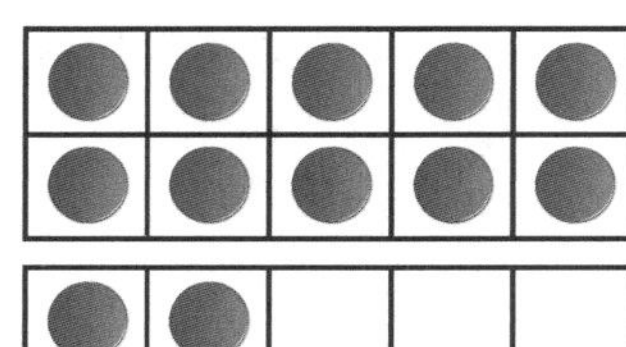

twenty [veinte]

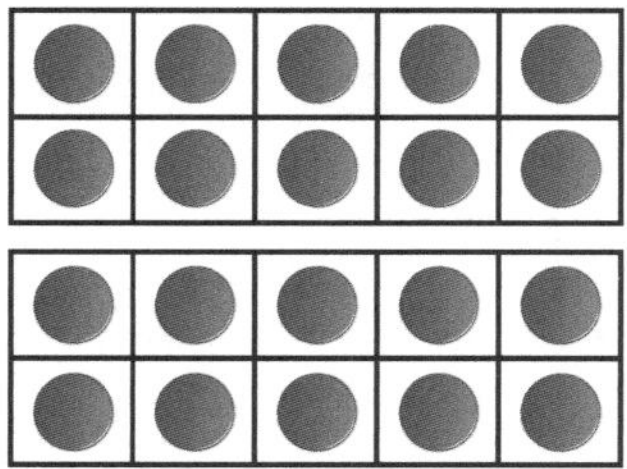

two [dos]

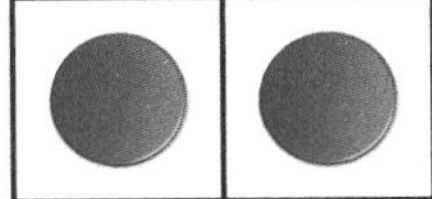

two-dimensional shape [forma bidimensional]

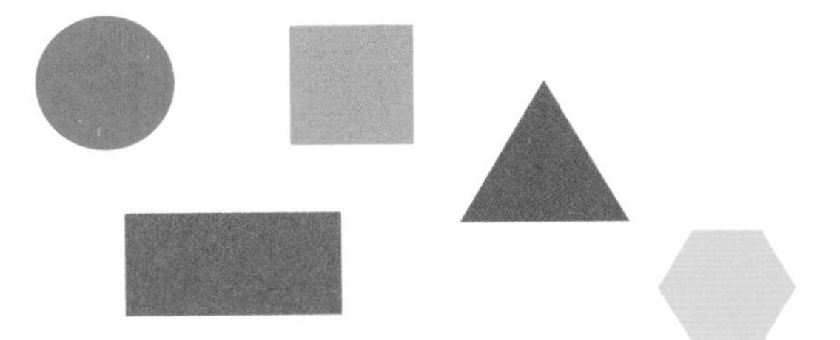

vertex [vértice]

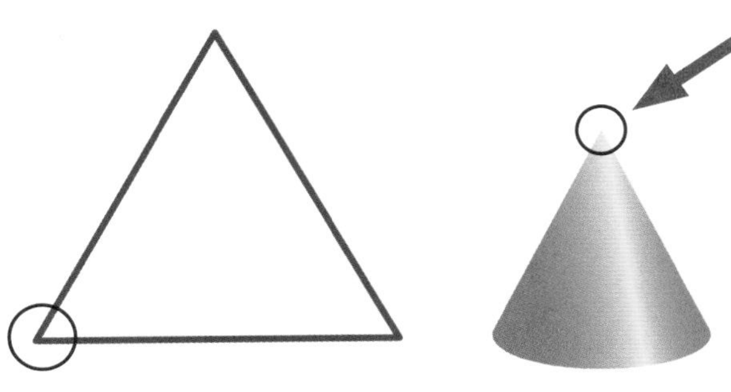

vertices [vértices]

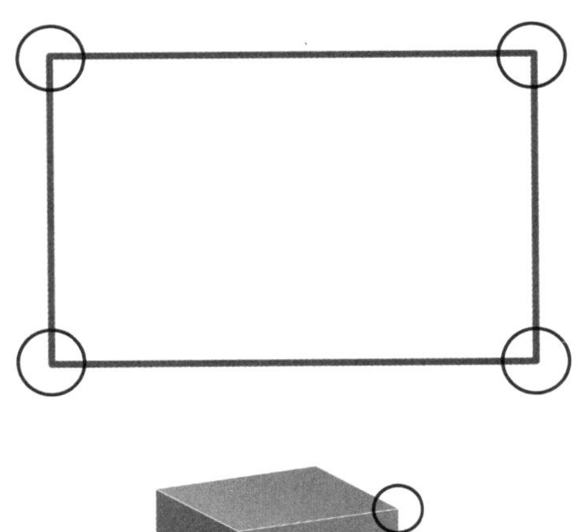

weight [peso]

whole [todo]

Glossary

zero [cero]

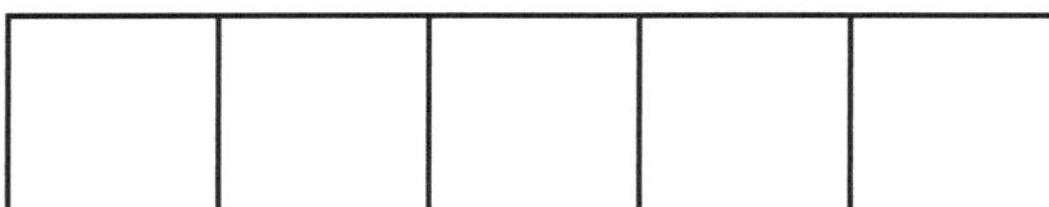

Index

A

B

C

D

E

F

G

H

I

J

L

M

N

O

P

R

S

T

Credits

Front matter
i enmyo/Shutterstock.com; **vii** Steve Debenport/E+/Getty Images

Chapter 1
1 BackyardProduction/iStock/Getty Images Plus, Liliya Drifan/iStock/Getty Images Plus, yotrak/iStock/Getty Images Plus, Tatomm/iStock/Getty Images Plus, kadmy/iStock/Getty Images Plus

Chapter 2
57 Mikael Dubois/iStock/Getty Images Plus

Chapter 3
95 PytyCzech/iStock/Getty Images Plus

Chapter 4
169 hugocorzo/iStock/getty Images Plus; **201** m_pavlov/iStock/Getty Images Plus

Chapter 5
211 borchee/iStock/Getty Images Plus; **262** billnoll/iStock/Getty Images Pus

Chapter 6
267 inusuke/iStock/Getty Images Plus, richcarey/iStock/Getty Images Plus, dwphotos/iStock/Getty Images Plus

Chapter 7
323 rustamank/iStock/Getty Images Plus

Chapter 8
377 wnjay_wootthisak/iStock/Getty Images Plus

Chapter 9
453 Big Ideas Learning

Chapter 10
497 Roman Pyshchyk /Shutterstock.com; **536** pixel_dreams/iStock/Getty Images Plus

Chapter 11
454 Paul Park/Moment Open/Getty Images

Chapter 12
595 Ian Lishman/Juice Images/Getty Images

Chapter 13
639 OlegDoroshin/Shutterstock.com

Cartoon Illustrations: MoreFrames Animation
Design Elements: oksanika/Shutterstock.com; icolourful/Shutterstock.com; Paul Lampard/123RF